THE SERVICE OF FAITH

THE SERVICE OF FAITH

An Ethnography of Mennonites and Development

PHILIP FOUNTAIN

McGill-Queen's University Press
Montreal & Kingston • London • Chicago

ISBN 978-0-2280-2248-0 (paper)
ISBN 978-0-2280-2249-7 (ePDF)
ISBN 978-0-2280-2250-3 (ePUB)

Legal deposit third quarter 2023
Bibliothèque nationale du Québec

Printed in Canada on acid-free paper that is 100% ancient forest free (100% post-consumer recycled), processed chlorine free

This book has been published with the help of a grant from Te Herenga Waka–Victoria University of Wellington.

McGill-Queen's University Press in Montreal is on land which long served as a site of meeting and exchange amongst Indigenous Peoples, including the Haudenosaunee and Anishinabeg nations. In Kingston it is situated on the territory of the Haudenosaunee and Anishinaabek. We acknowledge and thank the diverse Indigenous Peoples whose footsteps have marked these territories on which peoples of the world now gather.

Library and Archives Canada Cataloguing in Publication

Title: The service of faith : an ethnography of Mennonites and development / Philip Fountain.
Names: Fountain, Philip, author.
Description: Includes bibliographical references and index.
Identifiers: Canadiana (print) 20240332229 | Canadiana (ebook) 20240332318 | ISBN 9780228022480 (paper) | ISBN 9780228022497 (ePDF) | ISBN 9780228022503 (ePUB)
Subjects: LCSH: Mennonite Central Committee. | LCSH: Mennonites—Indonesia Relations. | LCSH: Mennonites—Missions—Indonesia. | LCSH: Economic development projects—Indonesia. | LCSH: Humanitarianism—Religious aspects Mennonites. | LCSH: Indonesia—Religious life and customs.
Classification: LCC BV2545.F68 2024 | DDC 266/.97598—dc23

This book was typeset in 10/13 Sabon Pro.

For Iris

Contents

Figures

Preface and Acknowledgments

During my fieldwork on the Mennonite Central Committee (MCC), I visited the head office of the organization in Akron, Pennsylvania. In between a busy schedule of interviews and hours spent at the microfiche on archival research, I was invited to deliver a brown-bag lunch presentation for MCC staff. These informal seminars were a regular feature of MCC life in Akron. My presentation was facetiously entitled "A Sheep among Wolves," and I used it as an opportunity to reflect on my experience of the previous eighteen months of ethnographic research exploring how MCC workers engaged in development, disaster relief, and peacebuilding in the context of Indonesia. I suggested that the practice of service is always a translation between multiple differing groupings that compose transnational aid chains, including North American Mennonite constituents and Indonesian communities. The paper was well received by most of the audience – consisting of volunteers, administrators, managers, and constituency-oriented field staff – although it is also fair to say that my light-hearted needling was not always appreciated.

About a month after I had arrived back in Indonesia, I met with the MCC Representatives – a wife-and-husband team whom I have given the pseudonyms Anna and Jake Friesen – to talk about the paper. I had sent around a copy to MCCers in Indonesia to spark conversations while the research was still ongoing. Opening the conversation, Anna announced that congratulations were in order: "We think we ought to be congratulated and thanked for letting you come and research MCC in Indonesia because of what a great service your presence here has been to MCC." To my great delight we proceeded to systematically work through their detailed notes on the paper. Corrections were suggested, further examples discussed, problems teased out, and my analysis was greatly enhanced and deepened. It was one of many profoundly energizing conversations that were littered across the entire length of my fieldwork. At the end of this discussion, which took well over an hour out of their perennially busy schedule, I had a renewed sense of how extraordinarily fortunate I was to have had the chance to research MCC. The development industry is notorious for its lack of transparency about its internal operations. In contrast, MCC leadership granted me an astonishing level of access to its organization. As an outsider to MCC I was given a generous mandate to interview personnel, dive into the archives, and peruse many other documents.

I wholeheartedly agree with Anna's suggestion of deserved thanks. Their willingness to entertain an anthropologist among their flock should be loudly applauded. While the tasks of anthropologists are not the same as development or humanitarian workers, I nevertheless also wanted to be of service. Of course, and MCC workers know this better than I, service comes in many different forms. Anthropological service may take the form of careful critique. I hasten to add that anthropologists have no critical monopoly; and indeed, I have met few NGO workers who are uncritical about development and humanitarian processes, including those of which they have been a part. This is perhaps especially so for MCCers who, in addition to being located somewhat on the margins of the development sector, are also able to draw on a contrarian theological tradition that has facilitated vociferous disagreements among Mennonites about their own ethics and practices. In the service of MCC, critique and passionate involvement are often bound together. I hope it is clear in what follows that something of this dynamic has rubbed off on me.

Yet it is important to note at the outset that when I embarked on this research over a decade ago I did not seek to pursue a project that would ferret out, negate, and expose the (no doubt many) problems and failures of "Christian development." A fault-seeking approach is a very limited form of scholarly engagement. My interest lies, and my primary act of service remains, in the task of descriptively narrating MCC's processes and practices. Although this narrative-centred approach resonates with some modes of contemporary anthropology, it is also an emphasis I have learned from Mennonites. Stories can vividly and compellingly illuminate an object of inquiry. They can also get under our skin in unnerving ways. The service I offer here is to narrate MCC in its particularity and complexity. It is this commitment to ethnographic "thickness" that is my version of an anthropological *leitourgia*.

This book would not have been possible without generous gifts from many. An acknowledgments section is a poor medium to communicate my deep gratitude, and it is a perilous task to list the names of those who have been of assistance, for even the most extensive inventory will fail to provide a full account. Still, some cannot but be thanked.

This book's first incarnation was as a dissertation supervised primarily by Patrick Guinness, and significant revisions to the manuscript were carried out while I was a researcher in the Asia Research Institute's Religion and Globalization Cluster led by Michael Feener. Both were masterful mentors and the influence of each is imprinted on every page. They read and commented on whole drafts and provided incisive feedback and critique. My debt of gratitude to both is more than I am ever going to repay. The book has also been greatly enriched by conversations with Robin Bush, Kersty Hobson, Christine Helliwell, Sin Wen Lau, Hannah Bulloch, Emily Welty, Vern Jantzi, Terry Jantzi, Elizabeth Phelps, Philip Quarles van Ufford, Maia Green, Jonathan Benthall, Matt Tomlinson, Johann Lindquist, Laura Meitzner Yoder, Royden Lowen, Tobias Tanton, Bram Büscher, Kamal Solhaimi Fadzil, Gillian Lê, Greg Vanderbilt, Cathy Day, Doug Hynd, Jesse Grayman, Andrew Shepherd, Geoff Troughton, Tim McKenzie, and Chris Joll.

At the Asia Research Institute, conversations with Michael Feener, Robin Bush, Catherine Scheer, Till Mostowlansky, Giuseppe Bolotta, Bernardo Brown, Josh Gedacht, Ronojoy Sen, Jeremy Kingsley, Zhong Yijiang, Keiko Tosa, Martin van Bruinessen, Anne Blackburn, Liang Yongjia, Jeffrey Samuels, Julius Bautista, Martin Saxer, Malini Sur, Eli Elinoff, May Ngo, Wu Keping, and Amelia Fauzia were always energizing and enjoyable. I am grateful for the space that ARI provided for expansive intellectual horizons and rich collaboration. The nearby Mr Prata twenty-four-hours restaurant was a godsend. My research benefited from support from the Henry R. Luce Initiative on Religion in International Affairs, Henry Luce Foundation, as part of a project on religion and NGOs in Asia. I am grateful especially to Toby Volkman.

The manuscript was completed during a sabbatical from my teaching in religious studies at Te Herenga Waka–Victoria University of Wellington. I am grateful to the university for allowing me time to bring my thoughts and writings together, and for financial support for publication. Thanks to colleagues in religious studies, both past and present, including Rick Weiss, Paul Morris, Eva Nisa, Michael Radich, Joe Bulbulia, Sara Rahmani, Lina Verchery, and especially Geoff Troughton. I am also grateful for the warm collegial space for scholarship provided by the School of Social and Cultural Studies. I have had the pleasure of supervising many fabulous PhD and MA students, and I am grateful for all they have taught me in the process. Undergraduate students in many different classes have indulged me by listening, often at great length, to tales from my fieldwork. I also want to thank Sara Kindon, Bronwyn Wood, Eli Elinoff, Chamsy el-Ojeili, Stephen Epstein, Māmari Stephens, and Lorena Gibson for their friendship and for many valuable conversations. James Urry has always supported my research, and I have learned much from his scholarship.

In Indonesia the MCC Reps invited and facilitated my research. I was consistently encouraged to think deeply and critically about the organization. I am profoundly grateful for their support. The rest of the MCC team in Indonesia were also hospitable and gracious. If this book begins to reflect something of the work of MCC, it is because of their willingness to narrate their experiences to me. Two consecutive MCC Asia Desk directors, Ed Martin and Joe Manickam, welcomed the research and enabled it to take place. Frank Peachey and Lori Wise were extremely helpful in guiding me around the MCC library and archives in Akron. The participants in the MCC July 2008 orientation at Akron were wonderful company. Among the many who were instrumental during my fieldwork in the United States and Canada, Luke Schrock-Hurst, Ken Sensenig, and Ron Mathies deserve particular mention for facilitating connections and enabling interviews. Terry Jantzi and Vern Janzti were both instrumental in encouraging me to research MCC through inspiring stories and their willingness to broker connections.

My fieldwork in Indonesia and in North America was made possible by grants from the Australian National University and the Religious Research Association's Constant H. Jacquet Award. My doctoral studies were made possible through an Australian Postgraduate Award. The Indonesian Institute of the Social Sciences (LIPI), and later also the State Ministry of Research and Technology (RISTEK), issued me with research permits. Pusat Pengkajian Islam dan Masyarakat (PPIM); Universitas Islam Negri Syarif Hidayatullah, Jakarta; and Universitas Kristen Duta Wacana (UKDW), Yogyakarta, willingly sponsored my research permit. At PPIM Ismatu Ropi and at UKDW Jeanny Dhewayani and Farsijana Adeney Risakotta were generous hosts. In Central Java I learned much from, and enjoyed the friendship of, Suwarto Adi, Pradjarta Dirdjosanjoto, Sung Min Kim, Singgih Nugroho, Putut Bayu Prakosa, and Saptono.

McGill-Queen's University Press has been wonderful to work with. Richard Ratzlaff believed in this project, and his support, patience, and sage advice have been invaluable. Thanks also to Kathleen Fraser, Alyssa Favreau, Chelsie Vaillancourt, Joanne Richardson, and the rest of the team at MQUP for their professionalism and efficiency throughout the publication process. It has been a real pleasure to work with you all. Two anonymous reviewers provided valuable suggestions for revisions, and I am thankful for their careful reading of the book manuscript.

I am grateful to the communities that sustained me at different points in the research and writing of this book, including Canberra Baptist Church, GKMI Salatiga, GKMI Siloam, St John's–St Margaret's Anglican Church, Porirua Gospel Chapel, St Michael's Anglican Church, and St Christopher's Anglican Church.

Over the many years of my research Ariadne and Dennis Fountain have been pillars of encouragement and enthusiasm. The extended Fountain, Fritschi, and Lee *whānau* have always been generous in their care and support. The chapters were revised in between playing games and creating mischief with Jeffrey and Samuel. The book is, of course, dedicated to Iris, to whom no words of thanks could ever be enough to express my gratitude.

PUBLISHED MATERIAL

I am grateful to the following publishers for allowing me to use (parts of) the following published papers, albeit in revised form, in this book:

Fountain, Philip. 2011. "Orienting Guesthood in the Mennonite Central Committee, Indonesia." In *Inside the Everyday Lives of Development Workers: The Challenges and Futures of Aidland*, ed. Anne-Meike Fechter and Heather Hindman, 83–106. Sterling, VA: Kumarian Press.

– 2012. "Blurring Mission and Development in the Mennonite Central Committee." In *Mission and Development: God's Work or Good Work*, ed. Matthew Clarke, 143–66. London, Continuum.

– 2014. "Development Things: A Case of Canned Meat." *SITES: A Journal of Social Anthropology and Cultural Studies* 11, no. 1: 39–73.

– 2016. "Mennonite Disaster Relief and the Interfaith Encounter in Aceh, Indonesia." *Asian Ethnology* 75, no. 1: 163–90.

– 2017. "Creedal Monologism and Theological Articulation in the Mennonite Central Committee." In *The Monologic Imagination*, ed. Matt Tomlinson and Julian Millie, 203–30. Oxford: Oxford University Press.

THE SERVICE OF FAITH

Introduction

Early in the morning we departed Salatiga. The road to Surakarta, commonly known as Solo, was already thick with traffic and the air was hazy with diesel fumes and dust. Trucks, buses, cars, and motorcycles competed for space alongside the occasional donkey cart and pedicab. Javanese roads are a volatile mix of the excessively fast and exaggeratedly slow. This combines with a laissez-faire approach to road rules by drivers who weave their vehicles across the full width of the road with little discernible attention to the grey smudges that might once have marked the centre lines. The bedlam of the roads tends to distract from the surrounding countryside. On a clear day the summit of Mount Merbabu could be glimpsed looming above. The combination of volcanic soils, tropical temperatures, and a dependable rainy season have produced a fertile landscape. Taking advantage of this, many of the hills of Central Java are layered in terraced rice paddy.

On this day there were four of us sitting in the Toyota Kijang. Adi Sutjipto sat behind the steering wheel.[1] *Pak* Adi was a long-time Javanese member of the Mennonite Central Committee's (MCC) small Indonesian staff team. In his role as a "partner advisor" he often accompanied such journeys. Anna Friesen was disconcertingly wide awake for this hour in the morning, and she took the lead in initiating conversation. Anna's husband, Jake, was feeling unwell and so had stayed home. Anna and Jake were Americans and "Swiss-German" Mennonites. Together they were the MCC Representatives in Indonesia, with overall responsibility for running the organization's programs in the country. Also in the car was Jacob Klassen. Jacob was a Canadian "Dutch-Russian" Mennonite and the epitome of a Mennonite elder statesman. He had served in senior leadership roles within MCC for many years and had only recently stepped back from full-time work in

Figure I.1 | Central Java

the organization. Jacob was visiting Indonesia as part of a study tour of MCC's peacebuilding programs across Asia. The purpose of our car journey was to meet with MCC's partners in Solo, a city with a reputation throughout Indonesia for hardline Islamist groups as well as being a major historical centre of Javanese culture.

I was the other passenger. It was mid-October 2006 and I had just arrived in Indonesia a week earlier for a pre-fieldwork trip to explore the possibility of researching MCC in Indonesia. During my visit I stayed as a guest in Anna and Jake's house, sat in on office meetings, talked with staff, and had my first taste of Indonesian cuisine. By happy coincidence my visit to Indonesia overlapped with Jacob's study tour and a generous invitation was extended to me to accompany the group as they visited partners and projects. It was the richest of introductions to both MCC and Indonesia. By the end of my visit I was well and truly hooked. I knew I wanted to spend the next two years conducting ethnographic research on MCC. With encouragement from Jacob, and with permission from MCC's Asia director located in the head office in Akron, Pennsylvania, Anna and Jake agreed to allow me to do so.

After the collapse of the authoritarian New Order regime in the late 1990s, civil society in Indonesia bolted off in all directions. The country witnessed a staggering proliferation of groups, organizations, and collectives. This new space for "non-state" actors enabled the rapid rise of all kinds of NGOs. It also saw the formation of groups of both militants and peacemakers. In Solo we met both kinds. MCC's key partner in Solo was a group of leaders from various officially recognized religions (In. *agama*). The Interfaith and Intergroup Forum for Peace (Forum Perdamaian Lintas Agama dan Golongan, FPLAG) was loosely knit and semi-formal. Lukas was a pivotal figure in FPLAG. A Chinese Indonesian pastor in an Indonesian Mennonite denomination, Lukas had formed a surprising relationship with members of Pasukan Islam, a Muslim paramilitary unit.[2] The meeting we had that day at Pasukan Islam's unsettlingly conspicuous Solo headquarters was a window into the quotidian meetings across difference that are typical of all of MCC's work in Indonesia. A Javanese militant Muslim, an Indonesian Chinese Mennonite pastor, a Javanese Mennonite Christian, a Swiss-German American Mennonite, and a Dutch-Russian Canadian Mennonite Brethren, accompanied by a Protestant Christian anthropologist from Aotearoa New Zealand, sat together on a worn plastic mat in an inner room in the militants' compound, sipping sweet tea and chatting about religion and peace.

The conversation primarily took place between Jacob and Rachmad, Pasukan Islam's unassuming and quietly spoken commander. But their discussion passed through *Pak* Adi, who continually translated between Jacob's English and Rachmad's Indonesian. Others chipped in occasionally, often also needing translation. Rachmad told us that soon after the fall of President Suharto in 1998 his militia participated in the bloody Muslim-Christian conflicts that had engulfed Ambon and Poso in Eastern Indonesia. Pasukan Islam had also carried out "sweepings" in Solo, shutting down activities it considered offensive to Islam and systematically searching through hotels for American visitors to "inquire" of their views about the recently launched American-led war in Iraq. Rachmad told us that a year ago FPLAG had initiated a peace training program for his militia. He viewed these trainings positively because he wanted to help inspire his group. Rachmad noted that initially many within Pasukan Islam were suspicious of the involvement of Christians in the training. Some in his group had speculated that the Christians were covertly proselytizing. However, over time, as relationships were formed and trust was established, these fears dissipated. Rachmad declared that as long as the peace trainings did not contradict Islam he had no problem with them.

At one point Rachmad quite abruptly stated that he liked MCC. This was greeted with warm smiles and words of appreciation. But his statement was immediately followed with a rather pointed question: "But why does MCC not try to influence politicians in the United States as it wages war in Iraq and Afghanistan?" It was obvious to Rachmad that, while Muslims seek peace wherever they can find it, and while they enact violence only as a last resort, this was patently not the case for the US government, which had proven itself to be persistently hostile and violent towards Muslims. He went on to say that, although he once thought that the United States was a Christian nation, he had come to the conclusion that it was not. Clearly, he said, the US was dominated by Jews who harboured deep anti-Muslim prejudice.[3] Rachmad concluded that MCC should stop working in Indonesia and focus its resources on the US, where peacebuilding was obviously needed most. Indonesians did not need MCC's involvement to get along peacefully, but the US required all the help it could get.

Rachmad's antisemitism made the MCCers uncomfortable, but Jacob's response was diplomatic. As a Canadian, he said, he didn't want to speak for Americans. He nevertheless reassured Rachmad that MCC was indeed active in both Washington, DC, and Ottawa in opposing war and lobbying for peace and justice. Mennonites have long affirmed a theology of peace, and this led them to oppose all forms of violence, including American military operations in Iraq and Afghanistan. Anna also joined in, arguing that it was for this reason that MCC does not have its own peace program in Indonesia but only works through local Indonesian partners. It was not MCC's place to dictate what happens in Indonesia, she reasoned, although MCC does want to work with others to help make peace wherever it can.

At the end of a long day, which included a series of other meetings in Solo, we piled back into the Toyota Kijang and returned to Salatiga. Such car rides were the ideal times to debrief the day, and we mused over the various conversations. Jacob told us that throughout his experiences of extensive travel around the world he was frequently told that MCC should focus its activities on challenging the US's destructive approach to global politics. During his time in senior management in MCC he had received letters every week from Mennonite supporters telling him to do the same thing: American and Canadian politics desperately needed a prophetic Christian voice for peace. Yet, at the same time, many Amish and Mennonites wanted MCC out of Ottawa and Washington as they perceived such political engagement as thoroughly unchristian. They thought that it was mistaken for Christians to get too entangled in the morally ambiguous realm of worldly politics. Somewhere in the precarious space located between these opposing requirements MCC carried out its work and tried to enact its mandate as an international service agency in the Mennonite tradition. Taking a somewhat different track Anna succinctly summarized her take on the day's conversations: "Faith colours everything."

The Service of Faith is an ethnography of the Mennonite Central Committee. MCC is a relief, development, and peacebuilding organization – commonly summarized by the term "service agency" – of Mennonite and Brethren in Christ Churches in Canada and the United States. My study focuses on its work in the context of Indonesia. While MCC first began its operations in Indonesia immediately after the Second World War, the organization remains decidedly North American. MCC is indelibly linked to the churches who support and staff it, and who provide it with its mandate: to faithfully carry out Christian service around the world. MCC's service in Indonesia, therefore, necessarily involves meetings across cultural difference. In this book I explore the relationships and the interactions that take place in these intercultural meetings. I examine the frictions, connectivities, and disjunctures that arise from attempts to bridge, or cross over, cultural gaps. The translation of Mennonite theologies of service involves complex and continual negotiation. It is these negotiations, along with those who do the negotiating, that are the subject of this study.

MCC works in over sixty countries around the world. It is a thoroughly transnational organization. In 2008 I visited MCC's international head office in tiny Akron, Pennsylvania. There I encountered a carefully composed Christian cosmopolitan space. Walls and glass cabinets were full to overflowing with art and artefacts from all over the globe, gifted to the organization as expressions of gratitude for its work. African carvings, Indian cloths, Latin American paintings, and Indonesian batik were displayed alongside ubiquitous Mennonite quilts throughout the office buildings and guest accommodation blocks. Among this multicultural display hung posters produced by the organization. One poster presented a mosaic of happy faces from around the world clustered beneath a quote from the Bible, a favourite among MCCers, calling for the practice of justice: "What does the Lord require of you but to do justice, to love mercy and to walk humbly with your God. Micah 6:8." Another poster advanced a "modest proposal for peace" ("Let the Christians of the world agree that they will not kill each other") superimposed on an image of warm embrace across racial difference. These aesthetics of globe-crossing internationalism and transcultural encounter were also reflected in other features of the Akron office's office space. Wandering between open-plan cubicles I caught snippets of phone conversations taking place in different languages. More difficult to observe, but vastly more voluminous, are the e-mails that flow instantaneously through cyberspace arranging programs, providing guidance, voicing critique, communicating reports, providing pastoral care and support, venting frustration, and, of course, complaining about the never-ending influx of e-mails. Senior MCC staff follow these digitally encoded messages, albeit at a much slower speed, on frequent international trips punctuated by windows of "office time."

The MCC office was located squarely in the middle of Lancaster County, itself in the heart of Pennsylvania Dutch country.[4] Akron's one traffic light – the butt of frequent MCCer jokes – situated this quiet town well beyond the borders of the American cosmopolis. Various Amish and conservative Mennonite groups live in the area, and horse-drawn wagons frequent the country roads that wind their way through the farmland.[5] Amish generally avoid travelling on planes themselves; Amish *Ordnung*, or rules, normally don't forbid it, but it also isn't encouraged. However, this doesn't inhibit many Amish communities from being generous donors to MCC's work around the world. Along its annual circuit across rural Mennonite heartlands the MCC mobile meat canner usually includes a stopover at nearby White Horse, PA, where volunteers converge for a period of some days to prepare and package turkey meat intended as emergency sustenance for communities facing hardship around the world. The Material Resources Center in nearby Ephrata is a major locus of voluntary activity, facilitating financial donations and gifts of material aid for programs in far-flung places like Afghanistan, Sudan, Colombia, and Indonesia.

For most of their history in North America, Mennonites have been a rural people. During and after the Second World War, however, Mennonites migrated to American and Canadian cities in growing numbers. In the process of establishing themselves as city-dwellers, those urban Mennonites discarded some of the visual trappings of their previous lives. While this geographical shift precipitated some broad-ranging theological transformations, Mennonites nevertheless also brought their churches with them. Philadelphia, less than two hours' drive from Akron, is home to a diverse range of Mennonite fellowships, including churches that reflect the city's ethnic diversity along with highly educated, professional, and urbane Mennonites, sometimes humorously dubbed "Muppies."[6] Many of these urban communities too are passionate and committed supporters of MCC's work. On top of their kitchen benches *A Common Place*, MCC's colourful magazine for supporters, frequently found a particular prominence. Their churches and high schools were often on the receiving end of storytelling tours from returned MCCers and other overseas partners. Many attended MCC trainings such as the Damascus Road anti-racism program or supported the lobbying efforts of the MCC offices in Ottawa and Washington, DC.

MCC's connections with both rural and urban Mennonite communities run very deep. Its active intermediation works between diverse Anabaptist groups across North America, while also serving to connect distant peoples around the globe. While participation in such global networks has, for the wealthy at least, become an ordinary feature of contemporary life, these links are nevertheless extraordinary in their complexity. MCC's work in Indonesia is incomprehensible without paying close attention to the specific tradition of North American Mennonite-Anabaptist Christianity out of which the organization originates and by which it continues to be sustained.[7] The vernacular theologies, values, ideologies, myths, narratives, practices, and representations that permeate MCC, as well as most of the finances it channels and many of the personnel that it sends to undertake fieldwork, are formed and shaped by what is known within MCC as "the constituency." It is from this constituency that the notion of service, a keyword in Mennonite discourse, is drawn. Ethical ideals of service animate giving to MCC's programs and profoundly shape Mennonite involvement in the organization. Yet what it means to serve remains contested among Mennonites, and also within MCC. This is because MCC's supporters are far from homogeneous. North American Mennonites are a deeply divided people, with pronounced historical tendencies for schism and division. They are fragmented along ecclesial, theological, and ethnic lines. MCC is one of the few locations in which members from the whole "patchwork quilt" of groups that make up the Mennonite "household of faith" are gathered together. It is simultaneously a remarkably durable and precarious collaboration.

An understanding of the Christian constituency that supports MCC is, however, only part of the story. MCC's service must be translated into the many different locations in which it carries out its work.[8] Linguistic translation is an everyday feature of MCC in Indonesia. Conversations that cross between English and Indonesian (In. *Bahasa Indonesia*), and between many other languages, dialects, idioms, slangs, and jargons, such as narrated in the vignette with which I begin this chapter, are absolutely necessary for MCC's work to take place. Linguistic translation, however, is only one part of a larger constellation of practices of movement and exchange whereby things, programs, people, relationships, and ideas are transported into new localities and in the process give birth to novel formations. MCC is more than just a conduit of such movements. It is itself perpetually in movement. Moreover, the process of translation involves both transference and transformation, carrying-over as well as rupture. Intermingled dynamics of continuity and disjuncture ensure that translation is imbued with what Michael Cronin calls a "recurrent ambiguity."[9] Theologies of peacebuilding that have been incubated within Mennonite communities in Canada and the US must be put to work in collaboration with actors formed in the context of Indonesia, where conceptions about the meanings of peace (or faith and service, etc.) have been shaped by distinctive histories, politics, theologies, and personalities. Among these differences, of course, is the fact that Indonesia is predominantly Muslim. This translational movement between North America and Indonesia is charged with potential for communicative ruptures, peculiar associations, unexpected innovation, and uncanny continuities.

The service of Mennonite faith is only ever enacted via practices of cultural translation. To say this, however, is not to offer an explanation but, rather, to pose a series of questions. Translation does not furnish ready-made answers that merely require application; instead, to study translation is to examine relationships and mediators. The question of how things are actually related is open-ended because it is never fully predictable in advance. Studies of cultural translation, therefore, require the tracing of interactions across time and space as well as investigations into the identities, practices, techniques, and communities that shape the translators. In the case examined in this book, it also requires attention to theology.

Christianity and practices of translation are entangled through long histories. Lamin Sanneh argues that translation is the "taproot" of Christianity such that Christianity is realized only through intercultural movements and exchange across difference.[10] Sanneh regards Christianity, from its very origins, as exhibiting a striking preference for articulation in the "vernacular," thereby necessitating processes of negotiation and interaction demanded by translation. The earliest

Christian communities were formed in the movement between Judaic and Hellenistic cultures. The symbolic birth of this community, as the author of Acts of the Apostles narrates it, was the polyvocal feast of Pentecost, self-consciously framed as a reversal and undoing of the linguistic incomprehensibility imposed at Babel. But the descent of "tongues of fire" on the faithful did not result in a single, common language. The ensuing cacophonous ruckus among the followers of Jesus was decidedly not the suppression of difference but, rather, its transcendence. The members of this emerging group gained the capacity to communicate across enduring difference. Despite concerted attempts to reign in the ambivalence of translation, all such articulations of Christian concepts and practices refract again this dialogic and carnivalesque excess.[11]

In focusing on the translation practices of MCC, this book undertakes an ethnographic analysis of one particular development organization. Surprisingly, despite a long history of anthropological engagement with development, our understanding of how development organizations actually work remains quite limited.[12] This is at least partially because, as Dorothea Hilhorst points out, anthropologists have tended not to bother studying them.[13] This ethnography joins wider efforts to peer inside the "black box" of development and probe its "inner workings."[14]

My approach to MCC takes up the descriptive task advocated by David Mosse, who proposes that anthropologists of development should ask not so much whether, "but rather *how* development works."[15] I focus on the practices of MCC and the ideas – especially the theological ideas of service and peace – that animate them. I am interested in the formative and transformative encounters and interactions that take place within and through the organization.[16] MCC is not just a site where different cultures meet – it is not merely a "contact zone" – but, rather, through these interactions differences become imaginable and enacted.[17] Translators are more than just conduits. They are active actors in recalibrating the very boundaries they claim to mediate.[18] New possibilities are created in such encounters as all involved undergo a shared transformation, even if this is not experienced equally. As Bruno Latour argues, to trace translations, mediations, and interactions is to attend to that which takes place "in the middle."[19]

SITUATING MCC INDONESIA

The field of international aid and development encompasses such a vast range of actors and processes that it defies easy categorization.[20] Governments, not-for-profit organizations, multinational corporations, security contractors, billionaire philanthropists, and activist collectives all claim to do development.[21] Clearly development is not a single coherent project but, rather, a series of projects that operate according to diverse logics.[22] Practices carried out in its name span a plethora of domains such that, in its many different forms, development encompasses us all in a late modern sacred canopy. This omnipresence is particularly acute when development is viewed not simply as a field of actors and projects but also as a key shaper of temporal and spatial imaginations; although, of course, even as a social imaginary development operates in complex and contradictory ways. If any study of development is to be of any use – if it is to be illuminating – then it must delve into particularities, textures, and details.

My research included fieldwork with many of MCC's partner organizations in Indonesia and with donor constituents and MCC administrators in North America. My focus, however, was on the experiences of MCC's staff team in Indonesia. This small grouping is located within much wider networks of affiliation and belonging. During my research with MCC Indonesia the number of staff working with the program fluctuated but generally hovered around thirty workers and volunteers. Each MCCer is assigned to a particular position within the organization, with each role fitting into a series of distinct categories. There are differing criteria for participation in these programs. The MCC Representatives (MCC Reps), Anna and Jake Friesen, oversaw all of MCC's operations in Indonesia. In this work they relied heavily on a local staff team of around five or six persons, including Adi Sutjipto mentioned above. Unlike expatriate workers, who as volunteers receive a small stipend on top of their living expenses for the duration of their fixed-term period of service, local staff members were salaried according to what was regarded in Indonesia as a respectable middle-class income. During my research MCC also had an office in Banda Aceh, supervised by a North American with another three to four Indonesian staff. This office was accountable to the MCC Reps in Salatiga. Various other MCC types were also part of the staff team, all of whom were expatriate visitors and who for the duration of their assignments were seconded to other organizations. Most of these secondees worked in the education sector.

MCC's work in Indonesia is not especially prominent within the organization, and its operations are not regarded as typical. However, MCC does have a long history in Indonesia, and its changing profile and programs offer insights into Mennonite practices of service. Moreover, a number of MCC's programs in Indonesia connect closely with broader organization-wide concerns prominent in the organization at that time.

One such concern was the disaster relief and reconstruction work that MCC has supported across the archipelago. Relief work was not the primary focus for the organization during my research, but large-scale disasters in Indonesia, including the devastating Indian Ocean Tsunami of December 2004 and the Yogyakarta Earthquake of May 2006, became prominent parts of MCC's operations.[23] This ascendency closely parallels broader humanitarian trajectories in the early twenty-first century. These changes, as Didier Fassin and Vincanne Adams have masterfully analyzed, are influenced by transformations in ethical sentiments and the growth of an affective economy that invests humanitarian responses to disasters with a weighty moral onus.[24]

Another key issue was MCC Indonesia's work in interfaith peacebuilding. As an organization associated with historically pacifist or non-resistant churches, MCC actively engages in peacebuilding initiatives around the world. Since the 9/11 attacks on the World Trade Center in 2001 in New York, and as an intentional alternative to American militarism in Iraq and Afghanistan, a significant focus of MCC's peace initiatives was with Muslims. MCC's partnership with the interfaith forum and its work with Pasukan Islam in Central Java, discussed above, was a new programmatic effort in this area. This partnership placed MCC Indonesia at the cutting edge of the organization's peace work.

The notion of partnership was a recent innovation in MCC. While MCC has long worked through partnerships of a wide variety of types, the shift to partnership as a moral imperative, rather than merely a pragmatic option among a repertoire of strategies, dates only to the early 2000s.[25] In the opening vignette of this chapter Anna's explanation to Rachmad as to why MCC does not run its own projects in Indonesia is a concise précis of the moral valences of partnership within the organization. MCC Indonesia only supported initiatives carried out by other organizations. It prioritized partnership in order both to avert imperialist impulses (and so intentionally contrasts with the international engagements of the American and Canadian governments) and to join with (different, diverse, local, legitimate) others to enact peace. The recent rise to prominence of this partnership model in MCC paralleled partnership's trajectory within the wider development sector. Yet, again as with the wider development sector, the morally compelling qualities of partnership are frequently clearer as abstract ideals than as actual practices. As a consequence, within MCC, partnership remained extensively debated and it was operationalized in a range of different ways.

Finally, MCC's extensive history of engagement with the Indonesian Mennonite churches connects with issues that were at the forefront of organizational priorities at the time. During my field research the possibility was broached in various quarters as to whether or how Mennonite churches from the "Global South" might become increasingly involved in MCC's management and ownership. MCC's work with Indonesian Mennonites over the decades has included warm rapport, frosty distance, and deep concern over possible negative ramifications due to close cooperation. These dynamics sometimes played out synchronously and overlapped in awkward ways. MCC has long played a central role in the networks, institutions, and discourses of global Anabaptism. This places MCC squarely in the midst of the fraught politics of global economic inequality, contested political influence, efforts at decolonization, and disparities in religious discursive and financial power.

In the context of the wider development industry MCC is best understood as a peripheral "out-of-the-way" organization.[26] MCCers frequently profess their belief that their organization definitively contrasts with development-as-usual. Prominent in this juxtaposition is that MCCers foreground interpersonal relationships against the technocratic inclinations of the wider industry. These claims have some truth, although the difference of MCC is frequently overemphasized, or at least represents a selective reading of the organization's characteristics. After all, MCC has channelled considerable funding from the (now defunct) Canadian International Development Agency (CIDA), it is enmeshed in North American legal frameworks for philanthropic tax deductibility, it has rolled out results-based management (RBM) procedures for monitoring and evaluation, staff members are sometimes required to compile logical framework analysis (Logframe) spreadsheets, and its changing priorities can and do overlap with shifting emphases within the wider development industry.[27] Nevertheless, if the Bretton Woods institutions, Washington Consensus policies, United Nations Development Program projects, and bureaucratic official development agencies are considered "core" to the development industry, as Richard Rottenburg argues, then MCC is indeed rather marginal.[28] Its awkward location in relation to the mainstream has resulted in contested engagements with development actors and practices. This is apparent, for example, in that CIDA funding and RBM were among the most hotly debated issues within MCC at the time of my fieldwork. Or, even more revealingly, the very term "development" was only rarely used as a description of MCC's work in Indonesia. Mirroring wider post-development critiques, development discourse tended to be seen as implying problematic power relations, including ideas of technocratic expertise.[29] Even when MCC deploys technocratic development practices, it retains resources for reconfiguring these in important ways. These resources stem directly from theology and ethics derived from the Mennonite-Anabaptist tradition.[30]

One thing that MCC does share in common with many other development actors, and this is a feature that is remarkably consistent across the field, is the claim it lays to doing good things.[31] Drawing on research among NGO workers in the Philippines, Dorothea Hilhorst argues that the term "NGO" should be seen as an attempt to situate an organization as "doing good for the development of others."[32] In their analysis of development language Andrea Cornwall and Karen Brock propose that industry buzzwords are designed to "connote warm and nice things, conferring on their users that goodness and rightness that development agencies need to assert the legitimacy to intervene in the lives of others."[33] In an uncanny parallel to these allusions, in Winnipeg I purchased a T-shirt produced by MCC Canada adorned with the tag line "MCC: Doing Good Things." The shirt was marketed to the broader community of supporters as part of an array of paraphernalia that materializes affiliation with, and support for, the organization.

The phrase "Doing Good Things" was used even though few MCCers I met could be accused of being naïve about the complexity, messiness, and ambiguities involved in attempts at doing good to others. Indeed, for some MCCers the attempt to do good was a moral minefield, beset with intransigent tensions, discomfort, paradox, and unintended consequences. Nevertheless, MCC's work is sacralized with a normative moral vision, and not just by those responsible for publicity or T-shirt design. MCC workers in Indonesia saw their activities as enacting a specifically Christian ethical praxis and hoped that their service would benefit the lives of others. They shared, therefore, as Tania Li argues, a developmentalist "will to improve"; although this was translated into a distinctively Christian idiom of service.[34] Their work in Christian service is carried out in the midst of the energies and ambiguities that are produced through this "moral ambition."[35]

It is sometimes suggested that the stated intention of doing good is a mere cynical ploy (barely) veiling insidious neo-imperialist projects.[36] Such a possibility should not be ruled out a priori and may well be ingrained within the practices of actors within the development sector. Development has certainly been used to smuggle in projects with all manner of intended effects. But it would be tragically sardonic to posit that all development actors lack any earnest desire for another's benefit. Such a broad brush is incapable of illuminating a sufficiently nuanced and textured picture. A more productive approach, and one that attempts to display the "respect" that Anna Tsing regards as the hallmark of ethnography, is to take statements of good intention as indicating exactly that: intentions to do good.[37] This was my starting point in this research, and, over the course of more than a decade of researching MCC, I have uncovered little that would make me question the validity of this conjecture. But even so, the fundamental question is not about whether MCC actually does good or otherwise. Instead, the crux concerns the moral logics of goodness that are at work, how these are enacted in practice, and the effects that they afford. In examining the moral practices in MCC I respond to Joel Robbins's invitation for an "anthropology of the good."[38] The goodness of MCC is intertwined with Mennonite understandings of faith, and in order to understand Mennonite moralities it is necessary to attend to theology.

FAITH'S COLOURS

Anna Friesen's conclusion that "faith colours everything" runs against the grain of much development scholarship over the past sixty years, which has often occluded religion from analysis.[39] Yet, since the early 2000s, this neglect has been squarely challenged, and religion has re-emerged as a key term in the analysis of development. Development scholars now extensively debate whether, how, where, and when religion and development combine, collide, and diverge.[40] The rapid rise of a literature around religion and development has significantly reconfigured our understanding of the history, politics, and cultures of development. Within this literature, diverse ethnographies have provided invaluable insight into their complex entanglements.[41] If in the past religion was seen as insignificant or irrelevant, it is now "no longer avoidable."[42]

Anna's chromatic sensibility, however, was not a response to the ebbs and flows of development scholarship. Rather, her appreciation of this faith-filled aesthetics – of a thoroughly *religioned* world – came from years of interacting with Muslims and Christians as part of her MCC service in Indonesia and, prior to that, on assignment in various African countries. It was also nurtured by her upbringing in the American Midwest by Mennonite parents who had previously served with MCC in Indonesia in the 1960s. It was inculcated through her attendance of Mennonite schools and colleges, by participating in Mennonite congregations, and by being a volunteer for MCC since she was a small child. Her passionate involvement in MCC service was conceived as a deeply Christian act of giving and receiving. Her "faith" is not a generic religiosity – the sort that is frequently presumed in development scholarship concerned with whether an abstracted religion can serve as a manageable partner for secular donors – or the kind that can be mapped onto charts that graph changes in global religious metrics.[43] That her Mennonite faith would be connected with her service in MCC (or that the same might be said for Muslims with whom she worked) was hardly a question that needed to be asked. This much was obvious. The issue, rather, was how faith is, or should be, enacted in the particular contexts in which she worked.

Discerning how faith colours the work of MCC is the preoccupation of this book. This task necessitates inquiring into the meanings of faith or religion. Following Talal Asad I argue that the attempt to propose universal definitions of religion hinders investigation.[44] Attempts to identify religion are always historically specific. Moreover, identifying essences detracts from the more important work of examining actual relationships and processes through which notions of religion are formed. With William Cavanaugh I argue that "there is no transhistorical and transcultural essence of religion."[45] What counts as religious or otherwise is not predetermined but must always be examined within specific, situated sites. The historicity of religion ensures that understandings of what is included in the category changes across time and space. "Religion" has a biography or, rather, various biographies. It follows that locating religion in any given context is never a simple task.

My approach to religion makes a critical intervention into contemporary debates about religion and development. Much current research in the field assumes that religion is always and everywhere an easily identifiable feature of human society, which, without much difficulty, may be clearly demarcated and circumscribed. In constructing the categories of "religious NGO" and "faith-based organization," development scholars have grouped a vast array of different organizations together, apparently assuming that they share something in common. Regardless of the exact assessment of the potential for religion to advance development outcomes, the attempt to situate a generic, abstracted "religious NGO" involves the construction of a myth that obscures more than it reveals.[46]

Rather than assessing religion in the abstract this study focuses on a particular tradition. This grounding of research in specific cultural formations is characteristic of an ethnographic approach, such as was adopted by Erica Bornstein in her seminal ethnography of two Christian NGOs in Zimbabwe. Through specific programs and particular interactions Bornstein traces an "enchanted development" imagined as a distinctly Christian practice.[47] Bornstein locates these Christian organizations as embedded within the distinct political, social, and Christian contexts of Zimbabwe in the 1990s. *The Service of Faith* is concerned with analyzing a similar dynamic in its focus on the ways Mennonite theology informs the practices of MCC. While the ethnographic research for this study primarily took place in Indonesia, the Indonesian context plays a rather different role to that of Bornstein's Zimbabwe. The context in which MCC operates is an intercalary one as it works between North America and Indonesia.[48] This book foregrounds transnational connections not as additional to MCC's work but as a vital and consequential location in which it is emplaced. This methodological geography reflects a growing interest among anthropologists in reconfiguring the spatialities of fieldwork, including via multi-sited ethnography.[49]

In keeping with my critical approach to the modern category of religion, my exploration of the workings of Christianity within MCC is not restricted to spaces of prayer, worship, and ritual. This follows a broadly shared sense among MCCers that service in all its forms is a faith-filled act. Because ethics and theology are closely intertwined within the Mennonite tradition, faith can permeate even the most mundane practices of manual and administrative labour. All manner of practices within MCC are animated, in significant part, by vernacular Mennonite theologies of service.

I explore Mennonite theologies as vernacular religious articulation. In his framing of vernacular theology Nicholas Watson describes the term as "a catchall, which in principle could include any kind of writing, sermon, or play that communicates theological information to an audience."[50] Watson argues that theology is not the sole domain of formal clerical or academic discourses but, instead, can be found in everyday expression. This approach shares much in common with Joyce Burkhalter Flueckiger's study of vernacular Islam in India, in which she examines "popular" forms of religiosity as they are "lived locally … on the ground."[51] This attentiveness to the quotidian is the gift and calling of ethnography, and ethnographically informed anthropology has reimagined the theological as inhering in the minutiae of normal life. Indeed, the anthropology of Christianity has powerfully illustrated the value and potential of paying careful attention to everyday theological dispositions, formations, and practices.[52]

By vernacular theology, therefore, I mean everyday expressions of theological ideas and practices.[53] It is often suggested that Mennonites in North America have downplayed attempts at constructing formal systematic theology.[54] Vernacular theology, however, is not so much systematic or scholarly as it is the quotidian circulation of theological discourse, and of these circulations North American Mennonites – as with Christians around the world – have been prodigious producers.[55]

While vernacular theologies may be informed by academic articulations, this is by no means necessarily the case, and vernacular theologies may differ substantially from official, published, and sanctioned renditions.[56] Vernacular theologies may be, and in MCC's case often are, contested. Such disagreements should not come as a surprise. Contestation is woven into community life as part of a dynamic social exchange. This dynamism is neatly encapsulated in Alasdair MacIntyre's framing of tradition as "an argument extended in time."[57] Vernacular Mennonite theologies participate in, and further extend, an ongoing theological and communal argument.

At the outset of a seminal contribution to the anthropology of Christianity, Fenella Cannell asks: "What difference does Christianity make?"[58] My argument is that the influence of Anabaptist-Mennonite Christianity on MCC is profound and far-reaching. The connection between MCC and North American Mennonites is theologically, financially, materially, and politically consequential. It is this relationship that furnishes MCC with its ideological repertoire for enacting self-conscious alternatives to the mainstream. Among the most important differences is a pronounced self-confidence in Mennonite distinctiveness. This belief in difference, even when overdrawn, creates fissures in which other possibilities are incubated. By locating themselves as decidedly different, MCCers open up space to rework the meanings and practices of development in important ways. While this potential is not always realized, while it always operates alongside powerful integrationist dynamics, and while the effects could be uncomfortable and ambiguous, this belief in difference was highly productive for actual differences: it was difference-enabling. The belief in difference always implicitly rests on the idea that Mennonite faith is only ever enacted in the midst of diverse other ideas and practices. Only through their interactions with others are Mennonite differences identified and inscribed.

THEOLOGICAL ANTHROPOLOGY

Cannell's question about the differences Christianity makes invites attention not only to the subjects of anthropological research but also to other domains and fields, including the theologies of anthropologists themselves. Joel Robbins characterizes the relationship between anthropology and theology as thoroughly "awkward," stemming from sharply contrasting commitments.[59] For Robbins this contrast is laden with an immense productive potentiality. In anthropological writings, however, the contrast is frequently more apparent than the potential. In Elmer Miller's memoir *Nurturing Doubt* a former Mennonite missionary turned anthropologist details his "pilgrimage" in departing from the Mennonite faith of his childhood and learning to embrace the secularity of anthropology.[60] Miller mourns the loss involved in this journey from faith to doubt, but he also clearly understands the situation as irreversible. A more aggressive dissonance is apparent in Susan Harding's encounters with fellow anthropologists in the 1980s, who expressed shock that she should be interested in "repugnant" conservative Christians.[61]

Recent scholarship in the anthropology of Christianity turns frequently to proselytizing encounters as sites characterized by dissonance. In introducing her ethnography of Christian NGOs in Zimbabwe, Erica Bornstein addresses her sense of "spiritual vulnerability" in relation to her field site.[62] She situates herself specifically as a "non-Christian" and "secular" academic. In an evocative and self-reflexive vignette, Bornstein vividly describes attempts by her Christian research participants to convert her to Pentecostal Christianity. She is resolute in her determination not to cross the line of conversion, at least in part out of an expression of disciplinary fidelity. For Bornstein, not having a Christian identity situated her as a bona fide anthropologist. Kevin O'Neill notes that he was repeatedly asked whether he had a Christian faith by both his Guatemalan neo-Pentecostal informants and by his anthropological colleagues.[63] While to his informants he answered in the affirmative, O'Neill notes for his readers that this was only in "a North American demographic sense." His answer does not appear to have been especially satisfying for his interlocutors as O'Neill goes on to describe how his informants "worked hard to convert me" and how he refused all offers for impromptu baptisms. Likewise, upon returning from his fieldwork in Tennessee, where he researched engaged evangelicals and megachurches, Omri Elisha records the questions of his friends: "Did they try to convert you?"[64] In answering this question Elisha locates himself as a "non-Christian" and as a "nonobservant secular Jew." But he also suggests he had his own missional agenda: "I do not think I had much of a role in changing the minds of any conservative evangelicals, but I must admit that on some level I probably looked forward to their possible conversions as eagerly as they hoped and prayed for mine."

In my research with MCCers I am not aware of any occasion when an MCCer actively sought to convert me. Part of this is undoubtedly related to the faith habitus of North American Mennonites, which, with only a few exceptions for my research participants in Indonesia, is far removed from Bornstein's encounters with the Prosperity Gospel of African Pentecostalism, O'Neill's neo-Pentecostal Guatemalans, and Elisha's engaged evangelical Americans.[65] But another reason, at least as important as the first, was that I was not seen as an eligible target. My ineligibility stems from the simple fact that, right from the outset, in my interaction with MCCers, I was happy to identify as Christian. I am confident that most MCCers saw me as occupying a shared space within the broad Christian household of faith. This was certainly my understanding and I engaged in my fieldwork accordingly.

Consequently, I willingly participated in communal worship, responded to invitations to pray for meals, was slotted into the prayer roster for the regular MCC Indonesia office prayer time (though my fulfilment of this duty was somewhat irregular), helped lead a morning devotion during my visit to the MCC binational head office in Akron, Pennsylvania, and discussed (or, more frequently, debated) theology. My involvement in Christian rituals was not merely participant observation; rather, it was thoroughgoing participation, even if I was also sometimes observing. Locating myself within the Christian tradition informed my interactions with MCCers and others in this research, and it shaped the kinds of conversations upon which this book is based. In its own way, this, too, involved everyday translations of theologies of embodied service.

At no point that I am aware of did my Christian position constitute what Matthew Engelke has called a "problem of belief."[66] But this is not to suggest that my position was unproblematic. I am not Mennonite in either ethnic or ecclesial senses.[67] The importance of this was not fully apparent to me at the outset of my research, but it became increasingly notable during my fieldwork. I have no doubt that my being non-Mennonite influenced interactions within MCC, although it is more difficult to ascertain whether this mark of difference inhibited or enhanced the quality of my research. Nevertheless, drawing on theological commitments that preceded my fieldwork, I am sympathetic to key emphases within Mennonite theology and ethics. My experience of researching Mennonites has also had a significant impact on how I understand my faith. During her fieldwork on Zimbabwean Pentecostal Christianity, discussed earlier, Erica Bornstein confesses to feelings of "claustrophobia," such that she desired to escape from the hyper-goodness of Christian rhetoric and practice around her to do "evil things." She also faced a profound sense of "intellectual disagreement" with her religious participants.[68] This was not at all like my experience in researching MCC; instead, perceptions of commonalities between our theologies worked in the opposite direction, opening new lines for discussion and stimulating an expansive shared horizon.

This acknowledgment of a theological position places me at odds with anthropological commitments to methodological agnosticism. Indeed, I regard methodological agnosticism as a flawed framework for ethnographic research. The bracketing of faith, as Joel Kahn rightly argues, is a secular incarceration that inhibits authentic and original research and that does a profound disservice to both anthropologists and their informants.[69] *The Service of Faith* is a modest experiment in an anthropological theology, and, this being the case, it draws on recent developments in the anthropology of Christianity and in Christian theology that have sought to redraw the relationship between the two disciplines.[70]

NARRATING MCC

My central concern in this book – to explore how MCC works in Indonesia – calls for a descriptive approach that involves narrating MCC's practices. Gregory Reck muses on the paradox that, while humans are "story-creating and story-telling animals" who "live by stories," narrative is oddly confined to the "fringes" of anthropological knowledge.[71] Through his study of the ethnographic monograph in the late nineteenth century Robert Thornton traces the historical reasons for this marginality.[72] Thornton argues that the monograph emerged from two distinct traditions: first, the analytical approach of the natural sciences, which aspired to universal explanation and, second, detailed stories as narrated in travelogues and missionary reports by those living in "the field." These two were not equally weighted. The making of anthropology as an academic discipline involved metropolitan scholars capturing narratives from the field and converting them into the analytical discourse of the classifying sciences.[73] In the process, stories, and the memory of the missionaries and travellers who wrote them, were suppressed or conveniently forgotten. This step was considered necessary for establishing the young discipline as a legitimate, secular academic field that pursued an objective and universal science. At the same time an "ironic" mode of discourse was established in anthropology such that "reality, among the primitives, was never what it appeared, and the outcome of events might not reflect the intentions of the actors themselves."[74] Native stories and native explanations were considered a distraction, if not irrelevant, for understanding native practices.

Thornton regards these narrative conversions as necessary for the ethnographic monograph to operate as a successful cultural "bridge" from so-called primitive society to the sophisticated modern scientifically trained readership of anthropological monographs.[75] This view is not shared by John Milbank. Milbank's landmark theological critique of secular social theory argues that it is this very feature of anthropological writing that makes the discipline untenable. Anthropological tendencies to reach towards universal explanations of human action and its essential structures is, for Milbank, premised on a false conceptualization of ahistorical absolutes that betrays a slavish commitment to scientific positivism. He calls into question the "founding suspicion" that aspires "to show that, universally, something 'questionable' is reducible to something else which is 'unquestionable.'"[76] Far from enabling more sophisticated theorization, Milbank regards universalizing impulses in anthropology and sociology as mechanisms for managing religion by delegitimizing theological rationales for praxis. Rather than a vain search for universal sociological laws, Milbank argues for a re-embrace of specificity through narrative: "human interaction in all its variety can only be narrated, and not explained/understood after the manner of social science."[77]

This critique perceptively diagnoses the dislocation of narrative within prominent versions of anthropology. But Milbank, Thornton, and Reck fail to adequately ascertain another strand – a minority report – which locates ethnography as precisely a textured, detailed narration. This failure is only partially explained by the dates upon which their critiques were published. For while the last two decades has witnessed what Michael Jackson calls a "return to narrative" within the discipline, this efflorescence took place on the back of a rich and extensive history.[78] At least since Clifford Geertz's influential examples of "thick description," a narrative approach has been an important mode of ethnographic writing.[79] While Geertz remained susceptible to universalizing analytical tendencies, his stories of cock fights and *slamatan* rituals were detailed, evocative, and widely read.[80] Marshalling this narrative legacy, recent ethnographies revisit an Aristotelian etymology for anthropology as those who tell stories (*logoi*) about other people (*anthrōpoi*).[81] For Anna Tsing an ethnographer is a "listener and teller of tales."[82] For David Graeber the purpose of ethnography is "essentially descriptive."[83]

In narrating MCC I have adopted what Sherry Ortner calls the "ethnographic stance," with its attention to "thickness" and a privileging of "richness, texture and detail."[84] The narratives I recount dwell on ambiguity and paradox. They seek to detail the complexity, passions, and challenges that are faced in the practice of service through MCC. My goal has not been to provide solutions or to furnish advice. My approach is "noninstrumental, nonnormative."[85] This stance does not derive from a dismissive approach to the management of development projects as somehow inferior to the task of anthropology. Those working in development or humanitarian activities occupy an important ethical space. Through their actions they help shape not only the material and economic possibilities of many others but also inform a much broader social imaginary of what is considered possible, desirable, and moral. Practices of administration influence the trajectories of development projects and therefore also guide resources towards certain ends and away from others. While such decisions are certainly morally fraught, if not perilous, it is not clear to me that contemporary academic practices – including, of course, those of anthropologists – are any less so.[86] But not all tasks should be attempted in any given piece of work, nor is any individual equally competent across all possible projects. As an attempt at textured description I hope to pry open space for further critical reflection and creative engagement.

My narrative approach is in significant part inspired by the prominence of storytelling practices among MCCers. Story is a privileged mode of discourse among North American Mennonites.[87] One vivid example of the preference for narrative, drawn from a plethora of similar cases, is provided by John Paul Lederach, a leading Mennonite sociologist and peace scholar. In *The Journey Toward Reconciliation*, Lederach recounts a time he was preparing a presentation on his work in international mediation and conflict transformation. Lederach wrestled over what to say and how to say it. As he tells the story, just before he was scheduled to deliver his presentation his daughter tells him "the most solid piece of advice I had received in some time." The advice was to "just tell stories and forget the rest!"[88]

MCC has long utilized story as a primary mechanism for communicating about its activities to constituents, and within and across the many different parts of the organization. This has included frequent use of narratives from the field in Mennonite magazines and church periodicals as well as delegating returned MCCers to conduct itinerant tours of Mennonite schools, churches, and institutions to tell stories about their experiences with MCC. Some MCCers have gained solid reputations of being master storytellers, and much of the literature produced about MCC is narrative, often in autobiographical style.[89] I frequently encountered storytelling events in MCC Indonesia, both informal and pre-arranged. The twice-yearly report form that service workers filled out about their activities, for example, included a section for the narration of stories. A similar requirement was made for MCC partner organizations that were asked to submit a narrative about their work to MCC as part of the regular reporting process.

The critique of the universal pretensions of positivist social science is premised on the attempt to proffer better, richer descriptions. But good description is no easy task.[90] The process of learning about something is always fragmentary and incomplete. Moreover, in the process of telling our tales anthropologists are (to use a Latourian distinction explored in more detail later in this book) translators rather than mere intermediaries. We are not just conduits of information but active shapers of what is communicated and what is left out. As authors, anthropologists deploy all the creativity and imagination we can muster to tell stories of our choosing. This ensures that anthropological description is also always already political. The choice of concepts, the selection of narrations, and the motivations undergirding the telling are all inflected with questions of power and authority.[91] By what right does the author speak? What voices are silenced? To what ends are the stories told? Such questions don't lend themselves to easy answers. The promise of neutrality has operated as a powerful anthropological ideal, but it hardly serves as an adequate descriptor of ethnographic practice. Stories are always told in contexts in which versions of events and their meanings are contested. Other stories could be narrated. Even the richest descriptions will not garner unanimous support. The inescapably partial accounts that are offered in the following pages are told from a particular perspective.

The narratives I relate were accumulated over the course of twenty-two months of ethnographic research between 2006 and 2008. For the majority of this time, about nineteen months in total, I was based in Indonesia. For the most part, the stories I narrate in *The Service of Faith* took place during this time span, although there is also extensive historical discussion and some more contemporary forays. Because, as I argue, context clearly matters for the kind of projects that MCCers carried out, being cognizant of the timing of my fieldwork is important. Of course, much has changed since then, both in MCC and in Indonesia. If I carried out fieldwork again today, I would necessarily explore different social, political, and theological dynamics. Although some readers may wish for a more contemporary account, the timing of my fieldwork is not an analytical deficiency. Anthropology is best understood not as a form of foreign correspondence, nor as a technocratic development report, nor as a guidebook for the interested traveller, all of which are preoccupied with the present and therefore privilege expeditious communication. Rather, as Paul Stoller puts it, "anthropology has the particular distinction of being a slow science in a fast world." For Stoller, this is one of anthropology's primary virtues: there is a "power to slowness" that facilitates a distinctive openness to the world and affords convivial possibilities.[92] The account I present in this book should be read as something akin to the practice of meditation – it has taken time to distill the stories that I have chosen to tell.

MCC Indonesia's head office is located in Salatiga, Central Java, a former colonial-era Dutch hill station perched in the foothills of Mount Merbabu.[93] Salatiga was as ideal a location as any from which to be based. Most expatriate MCCers are seconded to local organizations for the duration of their service, and they are therefore spread across the archipelago with clusters in Central Java, Aceh, and Papua. MCC's organizational partners are similarly distributed. The wide spatial spread in the organization contrasted with the limitations of my own physical presence. I was necessarily located in some place and not others. I was often disappointed at being unable to attend a meeting or event. My fieldwork was replete with gaps and absences.[94] This is an unavoidable feature of conducting ethnographic research on transnational actors. I also consoled myself with the knowledge that my focus was not on headline events but, rather, with "quotidian practices."[95] I am concerned with the ordinary humdrum of MCC service out of a conviction that everyday practices are an important site for analyzing development.

Although it is impossible to be everywhere all at once, it was nevertheless still my goal to get around as much as possible to understand how MCC works in different locations. I therefore adopted a "patchwork" approach to fieldwork.[96] The intention was not to achieve comprehensive coverage but, more modestly, to gain some perspective on particular parts of the organization and thereby come to trace, even if only in outline, the wider transnational network. This patchwork approach involved frequent travel around Central Java and to other parts of Indonesia, including a two-week visit to Aceh and three months in the US and Canada. During my time in North America I visited MCC offices and staff, supporting constituents, fundraising events, and various other Mennonite institutions. My multi-located fieldwork reflected MCC's multi-sited, dispersed cartography.

The kinds of research tools I used resembled Hugh Gusterson's "polymorphous engagement," involving an eclectic ensemble of methods drawing on "a disparate array of sources in many different ways."[97] I collected stories and fragments of stories wherever I could find them. The material I weave together in narrating MCC includes field notes jotted down during meetings, interview notes, e-mails, websites and blogs, and magazine and newspaper articles. In the MCC international head office in Akron, Pennsylvania, I was given unhindered access to the MCC Indonesia archives, which included documents dating to the 1940s as well as archived e-mail correspondence. A substantial published literature has built up on MCC over the course of its history.[98] Most of this was written by Mennonite authors and much of it was published by Mennonite publishers. The arguments advanced are often sophisticated and incisive. While largely by insiders (of various sorts), it is precisely this feature that makes these texts so ethnographically valuable. Many of the most illuminating conversations I had during my research took place simply as a consequence of being present; or in James Clifford's famous phrase, simply "hanging out."[99] Basketball games, casual chats over street-side hawker food, visiting MCCer homes and hosting MCCers in turn, sitting in the backseat of MCC's car as a "go-along" on frequent partner visits[100] – all of these were valuable sites of learning. By making liberal use of diverse sources, the restrictions commonly associated with ethnographies of formal organizations were, if not overcome, then at least partially circumvented.[101]

My ability to hang out with MCCers was due to the extraordinary access I was granted by the organization to conduct my research. Research access to development organizations is notoriously difficult.[102] Many development organizations are highly protective of their public image, and, while they commonly proclaim the virtues of transparency to local partners and governments, many are reluctant to relinquish the monopolization of information held by their own publicity departments. With funding streams and reputations at stake, the operation of development is frequently a clandestine affair. As a result, few anthropologists have been able to conduct research as researchers within development organizations. Instead, anthropologists have often carried out their research while employed as organizational insiders, or as "outsider-insiders."[103] But although I offered to join MCC and underwent the job application process (including filling in the application form and being interviewed for a position), this possibility was eventually declined. My formal identity in MCC was as an outsider researcher. The level of access to information that I was granted is, therefore, all the more remarkable because of this. The few MCCers that declined to participate in formal interviews and the occasional meeting in which it was suggested that it would be best for me not to join the conversation were rare exceptions to the rule of extraordinary openness to my research project.

My status as organizational outsider, however, was frequently blurred during the course of my fieldwork. After almost two years spent around MCCers – participating in staff meetings and team retreats, playing sports and watching movies, undertaking the occasional task, and extensively discussing MCC politics – the line between insider and outsider was considerably more ambiguous than it had at first seemed. This was candidly acknowledged in the wake of a conversation that had taken place during a car ride a few months into my research. I had joined in a small tour of MCC Indonesia's programs for two senior MCC administrators who were visiting from Akron. Also in the car were the MCC Reps and Lukas, the Indonesian Mennonite pastor mentioned in the opening vignette. I was feeling relaxed and offhandedly talked about my views on Christian Eucharistic ritual practice and the disadvantages of Indonesian Mennonite approaches to this (in short: not nearly frequent enough). It was jovial and light-hearted banter, of the sort that New Zealanders frequently deploy among new acquaintances as a technology of social lubrication. A few days later I met with the MCC Reps and was told: "You are almost an MCCer!" This was intended as a compliment. MCCers tended to hold voluntary service within the organization in high regard. The associative implications of the statement were therefore generous affirmations. But the "almost" indicated, of course, that I was *not* an MCCer. The comment was therefore also a gentle reprimand and served to remind me of my place in relation to the organization. My attempt at humour in the company of an Indonesian Mennonite pastor had been seen as inappropriate. I had behaved a little too much as if I was at home and their comment was intended to help reorient me as a guest. All ethnography involves the researcher being interpolated into relational networks and hierarchies in which ongoing negotiations of the researcher's identity are unavoidable. The conviction that drives ethnography is that such interactions can be rich provocations to reflect on issues that might have remained concealed had the researcher kept a more respectable distance.

What particularly muddied an insider-outsider distinction was that my wife, Iris, worked within MCC as a volunteer Service Worker.[104] Iris and I were interviewed for MCC at the same time, and her offer to volunteer for MCC during my field research was enthusiastically welcomed. Iris's work in MCC was unusual and necessitated the bending of standard MCC practices. In the case of a married couple both spouses are generally required to be MCCers. To join MCC as service workers is to join as a family unit. There are few exceptions to this. The MCC reps created a position for Iris in the MCC office in Salatiga. As a validated insider she participated in the daily life of the office and, through her work, learned much about the organization. As a result, Iris has been an invaluable partner with whom to ruminate about MCC. That my spouse worked in the organization I researched was hardly a situation of clear-cut boundaries and unambiguous identities.

The politics of friendship during my field research also extended in other directions. During my research many MCCers became close friends and respected academic colleagues, and this continued after my fieldwork was completed. These sorts of "tangled allegiances and loyalties" are widespread, even if anthropologists have been reticent to examine them.[105] Arguably the process of ethnographic research is productive, intellectually and personally, precisely because professional-personal distinctions are actively muddied during the course of research.[106] Ethnography is all about relationships, and thicker relationships facilitate thicker ethnography. My ability to tell stories about MCC is directly dependent on these relationships. Of course, the social topography of friendship is always uneven, and all friendships experience tension and miscommunication at some point. These, too, were part of my experience. But a number of friendships formed over the course of fieldwork have continued long afterwards with ongoing correspondence and visits from Mennonite friends while my wife and I lived in Australia, Singapore, and New Zealand. Various MCCers have also been careful and critical readers of my writings, correcting mistakes, suggesting alternative explanations, proffering advice, and sharing other stories. MCCers and Mennonites have always been one of the intended audiences for my writings. These friendships have an enduring effect on my writing, informing the stories I tell and the ways in which I tell them. I have never been able to presume a bifurcated anthropological life in which field relationships and academic work could be divorced.

Two further relational dynamics at work in my research deserve consideration. The first is that, throughout my research, I have had a persistent sense of "studying up."[107] Entering the field, I found myself researching people who were academically inclined, and indeed many were established scholars. Most MCC service workers in Indonesia were seconded to teach in Indonesian universities. Many had graduate degrees from Canadian or American universities. Of those who did not, after completing their terms of service in Indonesia, a significant number undertook further graduate study in North America. MCC workers in the US and Canada often move between academia and their work in the organization. On any given day of my field research, it was not at all peculiar to discuss the work of Clifford Geertz, Anna Tsing, Tania Li, Bob Hefner, or Mark Woodward. We dissected recent publications in development studies and debated the ideas of leading figures in contemporary continental philosophy. Since completing my fieldwork, I have collaborated with former MCCers in presenting research at conferences and in writing projects. Aptly summarizing the symbiosis between scholarship and service in MCC, one MCCer told me that "MCC is good to think with." I thoroughly agree. I frequently received informed, knowledgeable, and critical advice on methodological and theoretical matters from research participants. The most perceptive insights I gained into MCC came from MCCers themselves or from Mennonites who drew on long personal histories with the organization.

Another dimension of this same dynamic was my admiration for the adeptness with which MCCers worked across cultures. MCCers, especially those who had worked with the organization for some time, were "interface experts."[108] For example, MCC's Indonesian staff who worked as partner advisors had linguistic mastery of three or more languages, were astute interpreters of the inner workings of the partners they were assigned to liaise with, and were familiar with negotiating American and Canadian cultural habits. They moved constantly between cultures. Their ability to catch information and interpret nuances far outstripped my linguistic abilities. I often found myself asking questions to find out what was going on and relying on their interpretations to help make sense of events and conversations. This said, although MCCers were often acutely aware of what was happening in their areas of responsibility and with those actors immediately adjacent to them, they also often experienced frustration with incomplete information flows and communication gaps. MCC was plagued by what some MCCers described as an endemic "silo effect." As one MCCer evocatively put it, "mushrooming," that is, "sitting in the dark and being fed shit," was a constant challenge. Nevertheless, my ability to engage with the complexity of MCC processes was due in large part to the guidance that MCCers gave me as to how to understand what was going on.

Related to this is the striking parallel between expatriate MCCer and anthropological field experiences. In many ways MCC field practice was a kind of parallel or mirror ethnography, minus the obligation to write a book at the end of it. If it is field experience that makes a "real anthropologist," then the standard three-year term for service workers means that MCCers are often more anthropological than many anthropologists.[109] If ethnography is "putting oneself in the place of another" and "undertaking a journey, broadening one's horizons," then MCCers are ethnographers par excellence.[110] Expatriate MCCer attendance at wedding ceremonies, funerals, Christmas (In. *Hari Natal*) and Easter (In. *Hari Paskah*) celebrations, the Prophet's birthday (In. *Maulid Nabi*) and Islamic New Year (In. *Idul Fitri*) festivities, and their presence in workplaces, neighbourhoods, and social networks was such that MCCers often had remarkable insights into Indonesian cultural worlds. Their ethnographic understanding of the neighbourhoods in which they were embedded was nuanced and textured. Here, too, I had a definite sense of studying up. This positioning could certainly be awkward, but it was also productive, and it played a vital role in shaping this present study.

The book's chapters move back and forth between Indonesian and North American contexts. In chapter 1, "The Pilgrimage of a Peoplehood Movement," I explore the historical relationship between the Mennonite Central Committee and the Mennonite peoplehood in Canada and the United States. I trace how MCC was birthed by Mennonite communities and also how it reshaped those same communities by furnishing a vehicle through which Mennonites could assume a theological identity as a people of service. The second chapter, "Translating Service," focuses on MCC's disaster relief and reconstruction work in Aceh following the 2004 Indian Ocean Tsunami. This turn to Indonesia involves an exploration of concepts of cultural translation, which are pivotal for the remaining chapters. The next chapter, "The Missions of Development," examines key moments in MCC's history in Indonesia. I show that the organization has changed dramatically over time, illustrating the dynamic nature of cultural translation. The following three chapters – "Theology and Development," "Peace and Friction," and "Orienting Guesthood" – combine analysis of both North American and Indonesian contexts. Each chapter provides a different layer of understanding regarding the tensions and affordances of Mennonite theologies of peace and service. The final chapter, "Everyday Embodiments," focuses on expatriate MCCers themselves as they engage in service, are transformed by the experience, and then head back home to their Canadian and American Mennonite communities. The end of the story, therefore, loops back to the beginning to consider the impact of MCC on North American Mennonites. In the conclusion, I close with a meditation on the theology of service, both Mennonite and ethnographic.

I

The Pilgrimage of a Peoplehood Movement

If you head into unfamiliar woods, you had better find companions first; if you want to buck traffic, organize a convoy.

Doris Janzen Longacre[1]

The anthropology of development and humanitarian organizations has tended to presume, as I started out presuming, that development is about what happens *out there* in "developing" countries or the "Third World."[2] In this imaginative cartography, research on development parallels the anthropological fixation with "the field" as a site elsewhere in which *real* anthropology, or in this case *real* development, takes place.[3] The fieldwork that I draw upon for my narratives was initiated and concluded in Indonesia, "the field" for both the Mennonite Central Committee and myself. However, as my fieldwork progressed it became apparent that I also had to conduct research in North America. If I had been unable to come to this conclusion on the basis of my own observations, it would have been made perfectly apparent by the frequent repetition by which MCCers told me that this was unavoidable. Their organization, they said, could only properly be understood with reference to Mennonite communities in North America.

The reason this was so important was made clear to me when MCCers sought to correct what they saw as another misconception I had at the outset of my fieldwork. I chose MCC as the object of my study because of my interest in Christian development NGOs and faith-based organizations. However, soon after initiating my fieldwork MCCers informed me that MCC was not an NGO at all; rather, it was what they called a "peoplehood movement." To understand this claim it is necessary to trace a history of MCC that locates it within the North American Anabaptist-Mennonite tradition.[4] MCC originated within, and remains firmly entangled with, this denominational constituency.[5] It is this particular, if also deeply fragmented and heterogeneous, Christian tradition that infuses the ideas, moralities, practices, and logics of the organization. As a church agency, MCC is a broad-based collective endeavour. It is a Mennonite "convoy" in the sense suggested in the epigraph for this chapter, quoted from Doris Longacre's exceedingly popular (and MCC-commissioned) Mennonite recipe book *Living More with Less*. It is a collective journeying of North American Mennonites, the aggregate of which is much more than the sum of its parts. It is a communal pilgrimage that self-consciously and audaciously runs against the dominant flow of traffic in its pioneering into new territories and exploration of other worlds. This chapter outlines the beginnings, and retraces some of the contours, of MCC as a peoplehood movement. Understanding this religious context is crucial for exploring the impulses, dispositions, theologies, and imaginations that continue to influence the activities of the organization in Indonesia.

A PECULIAR PEOPLEHOOD

The historiography on North American Mennonites is voluminous, much of it written by Mennonites themselves.[6] The extraordinary flourishing of what Daphne Winland calls "native scholarship" among Mennonites in the past half century provides a rich historical and sociological resource for tracing the contours of Anabaptist-Mennonite identity.[7] The birth of the Mennonite movement in the sixteenth century in Europe has been recited so repetitively that it constitutes a Mennonite "creation myth of origins."[8] Located initially in western and northern Europe and emerging as part of the widespread socio-political ferment of the period, Mennonites frequently describe their forebears as the radical wing of the reformation.[9] Its founders articulated a powerful theological critique of the perceived excesses and abuses of the medieval Roman Catholic Church and also of emerging reformational Protestantism. Rather than a coherent movement, it is better understood as a series of loosely connected groupings that gained momentum in dispersed communities across the continent.[10]

Though initially largely urban in origins, drawing particularly on disaffected clergy and intellectuals, incipient Anabaptism soon underwent a series of far-reaching transformations.[11] These changes were fuelled by various concerns, two of which are particularly worthy of note. First, early Anabaptists faced severe persecution from religious and political authorities throughout Europe.[12] The memorialization of the martyrdom of many of its early members is recorded in disturbing detail and imagery in Tieleman van Braght's *Martyrs Mirror*, first published in Dutch in 1660; this weighty tome remains highly influential and widely read among Canadian and American Mennonites today.[13] Second, and clearly interconnected with this baptism of blood, was the coalescing conviction about the need to separate the community of believers from wider society. Mennonites increasingly came to see themselves as a distinct and separated community – a "people apart."[14] This sense of uniqueness is expressed perhaps most clearly in a pronounced "two kingdom" theology that came to characterize the movement. This "sharply dualistic" and "bifurcated" theology imagined social life to be characterized by a clear delineation between "the church" and "the world."[15] This theopolitical framing led directly into an enduring sense of the uniqueness of the community of believers. If, as anthropologist Fenella Cannell has argued, exceptionalism is a characteristic feature of Christianity in general, then Mennonites have tended to see themselves as exceptional exceptions.[16] Whether this exceptionalism is mythical or otherwise, the Mennonite belief in their own difference has been imagined and reinforced over the centuries through pervasive vernacular theologies and myriad daily practices.[17] Distinctive practices include, at various times and for different groups, plain clothing; the use of Plautdietsch, or Low German, with other Mennonites and High German in church services; and the establishment of geographically separated rural communities. Although the signs of distinctiveness have changed over time, the self-identification of Mennonites as "a peculiar people" remains pertinent, if not pervasive.[18] "By now, most Mennonites are visibly indistinguishable from other people in the street," writes Mennonite sociologist Fred Kniss, but "nonconformity remains central to their ethical discourse and practice."[19]

Spurred on by persecution and belief, early Anabaptists moved to the countryside. The now popular designation *Die Stillen im Lande* (Pl. The Quiet in the Land) became increasingly apt for this emerging sectarian and quietistic movement.[20] Many Mennonite communities remained resolutely rural up until the middle of the twentieth century. Paralleling the urban-rural transition, and for many of the same reasons, Mennonite communities embarked on a series of mass communal migrations. This included emigrating across the Atlantic, beginning in 1683 but peaking in the eighteenth and again in the twentieth centuries. These Mennonite migrants to the "New World" disembarked initially in Pennsylvania and became part of the burgeoning "Pennsylvania Dutch" community. From there, and with later migrations, Mennonites spread across the continent. Another large wave of immigrants settled in the Russian Empire after 1789 under special dispensation from Catherine the Great, which provided for land, freedom of religion, and exemption from military service. Further "Russian" Mennonite migrations to North America took place in three stages in the 1870s, 1920s, and 1950s.[21]

Over time Mennonite identity in North America began to coalesce under theologico-ethical emphases that have been remarkably durable. These included an ecclesiology that presumed a believers' church that could only be joined via baptism on confession of faith (i.e., adult baptism), differentiation between the community of believers and wider society, an associated strict demarcation between church and state, and a belief that the faithful would embody and enact ethical behaviour in everyday relationships. Mennonites have also tended to emphasize a literal interpretation of biblical injunctions for non-resistance and, as is written in the Gospel of Matthew, to "love your enemies." This theology of nonviolence has resulted in Mennonite self-identification as a Historic Peace Church.[22] However, interpretations of this peace position have changed over time, and Mennonites today hold to a range of understandings about the practice of nonviolence.[23] Another important enduring focus has been simplicity of lifestyle, involving a distaste for ostentatious displays of affluence and a rather Weberian-style Protestant ethic of conscientious industriousness.

Two further prominent theological emphases need to be noted. Both concern the nature of Mennonite politics and each is examined in Calvin Redekop's seminal sociological study of American Mennonite society.[24] First, the belief in the priesthood of all believers, premised on a powerfully egalitarian ethic, has been highly influential. This conviction, though, did not supplant a continuing practice of the ordination of (historically, mostly male) ministers and a hierarchical ordering of authority under the aegis of bishops (or "elders"), and therefore also an ongoing formalized and institutionalized leadership. Mennonites experience considerable tension between an ethos of radically democratic participation and powerful, if frequently also fragile, accumulations of authority in key leaders.[25] This form of bishopric democracy has always been fraught with contradiction, and this has led to what Redekop regards as an enduring "ambiguity of leadership" within many Mennonite communities.[26]

The second emphasis parallels the first. According to Redekop, the Mennonite ethic is based on a "congregational axiom" such that autonomous communities, the body of believers or *Gemeinde*, remain largely independent of wider structures of ecclesial or denominational authority.[27] Mennonite congregations have tended to be tightly knit communities with strong mutual aid structures providing for common assistance. But while congregationalism can be seen as a founding principle of

Mennonite sociality, this radically parochial ethos has been tempered by a penchant to associate, consult, and confer in wider conferences. Some of these groupings of affiliated congregations have consolidated considerable centralized authority. Although by no means unique to Mennonites, the relationship between central conference and peripheral congregation has also been a perennial source of internal tension.

Over time the Anabaptist-Mennonite movement formed what historian Perry Bush calls a distinct "ethno-religious tradition."[28] There is a strong sense of Mennonite "peoplehood," a term widely used by Mennonites and other commentators to describe a particular sense of Mennonite identity. Anthropologist James Urry provides this explanation:

> By "peoplehood" I mean the particular Mennonite sense of identity based on their faith and sense of being and belonging. Core features of what it means to be a people of faith are often expressed in their confessions of faith and include adult baptism, nonresistance, and remaining separated from "the world." There is, however, less agreement among Mennonites on other religious matters, including ritual and practice. But throughout history this core proved remarkably persistent. Belonging is centered on a strong sense of social community founded on the interconnections of people through descent, both from founding ancestors and the historical experiences of the people of faith and often also through the genealogical descent of the community's members. The popular concept of "ethnicity" does not quite capture this sense of being and belonging, which is informed by a culture of faith rather than faith in culture. The choice of the term "peoplehood" is intended to reflect this aspect of identity.[29]

The Mennonite peoplehood are often also described colloquially as "Germanic," "ethnic," "cradle," or "birthright" Mennonites. However, the meanings of "Mennonite" and "peoplehood" are heavily debated. These contested meanings are most apparent at those points at which they are blurred or brought into question.

Mennonite belief in difference is maintained in the face of their own chronic fragmentation. The plethora of groups, conferences, and factions that make up contemporary North American Anabaptism are bewildering, even for many Mennonite insiders. Mennonite scholars describe this diversity as a "rainbow," "mosaic," and "patchwork quilt" of many pieces.[30] Less positively, Mennonite sociologist Fred Kniss remarks about the "surprisingly conflict-ridden character of Mennonite history" as witnessed in frequent schisms, protracted disputes, and the proliferation of splinter groups.[31] These divisions include deep doctrinal disagreements that span the full breadth of the liberal-conservative continuum as well as variances over practices, rituals, authority, clothing, technology, ethics, gender, and sexuality. Another common demarcation highlighted by Mennonites themselves is the existence of "Dutch-Russian" and "Swiss-German" identities, stemming from place of origin, migration experiences, and cultural markers.[32] A further marked division within the North American Mennonite peoplehood concerns national identity. While Canadian and American Mennonites share extensive transnational kinship and denominational connections with each other (as well as with Mennonite communities in Russia, Europe, Mexico, Paraguay, Bolivia, Belize, and Brazil), nevertheless their national identities have become increasingly important over the past century. Discussing "Russian" Mennonites in Canada, James Urry notes how the twentieth century saw a growing sense of "being *Canadian* Mennonites," an identity that was strengthened "through an underlying opposition to the United States and to American-run Mennonite religious bodies."[33] Many American Mennonites have likewise increasingly embraced their American citizenship as an important component of their identity.[34] Affiliation to a broadly conceived Mennonite peoplehood has, therefore, contended with a plethora of intra-Mennonite rifts and divisions.

The ethno-religious Mennonite peoplehood, however, are not the only kind of Mennonites. Calvin Redekop proposes that Mennonite identity in North America is "bipolar," including not only the peoplehood discussed above but also another group that he describes as "converted and convinced nondescendents."[35] These Mennonites (often labelled "non-Germanic" or, more clumsily, "non-ethnic-Mennonite") regard themselves as adherents to a Mennonite faith without belonging to a "cradle" ancestry. This includes those who joined Mennonite churches as a result of Mennonite mission activity in North America and elsewhere. Although this group now constitutes the majority of Mennonites worldwide, Redekop acknowledges that many non-Germanic converts struggle with feeling outside the core "in group" such that:

> Unless one came from German parentage and was reared on the heritage of German preaching and Bible reading, enhanced by the sacred mythology of the martyrs ... one could never fully identify with the Anabaptist-Mennonite heritage ... The division between the Germanic and non-Germanic is so sharp that a knowledgeable Mennonite can tell immediately by a surname alone whether a Mennonite is a birthright or convinced member.[36]

The presumed ability to discern ethnic and/or religious heritage by noting distinctive surnames has resulted in a practice colloquially known as the Mennonite Name Game, which I observed frequently during my research.[37] This "game" functions as an introductory ritual when, upon first becoming acquainted, "Germanic" Mennonites seek to establish kinship and relational associations by tracing which particular lineage their surname belongs to and how that might connect with their conversation partner. It is a means of identifying genealogical and kinship relationality within a densely interconnected but geographically dispersed community.

Languages of birthright and genealogy point to racialized identities. Conrad Kanagy, an American Mennonite pastor and sociologist, classifies "convinced" Mennonites as including "racial-ethnic congregations," and he juxtaposes this group to "cradle" Mennonites, which he regards as constituting a "historically white denomination."[38] In his study of Mennonite diasporic identities Benjamin Goossen argues that the postwar growth in historical research among Mennonites was fuelled and supported by racialized ideologies associated with the National Socialist German state.[39] Whereas Kanagy laments a racialized demographic church profile, and descries the sense of displacement among racial-ethnic members of the Mennonite Church, Goossen frames the current picture as deriving from long embedded histories of racial identification.

A significant complicating factor here is the active involvement of North American Mennonites in international mission and evangelism since the late nineteenth century. With Mennonite missionaries embarking overseas on church-planting work, converts adopted the Mennonite faith and the boundaries of what it meant to be Mennonite were reconfigured. In these missional practices theologies of evangelism worked in complex relationship with ideologies of ethnicity and race. Given the emphasis on Mennonite distinctiveness and the grounding of the Mennonite peoplehood in "Germanic" subcultures noted above, the success of these missions produced new challenges to Mennonite identity. Indeed, for many North American Mennonites, "the need to missionize and the will to separate remained unresolved tensions."[40]

The Mennonite World Conference (MWC) is the global umbrella body of Anabaptists and includes church membership from virtually every continent and a wide range of ethnic groups, in part as a consequence of the mission efforts of North American and European Mennonite missionaries. In her analysis of ritual "pilgrimage" to the fourteen MWC assemblies held between 1925 and 2003, theologian Nancy Heisey describes the emergence of what she calls a "global peoplehood."[41] Heisey proposes that through these multi-national and multi-ethnic gatherings

Anabaptists from all over the world come to experience an emergent and shared ecclesial identity. But Heisey also notes that this weaving of new identities is accompanied by an enduring awareness of difference. This difference has often been exoticized and celebrated, though at other times it has been the cause of conflict in relation to theological, economic, political, and ethnic concerns. Within Heisey's analysis the Mennonite peoplehood emerges as fraught, squeezed between global religious affiliation and enduring parochial loyalties, including "ethnic" Mennonite affiliation in North America.

The boundaries of Mennonite identity have been challenged by those groups who occupy an ambiguous position vis-à-vis the "Germanic" peoplehood. During the course of the twentieth century several Mennonite denominations, influenced by evangelical theological currents, "intentionally jettisoned their Mennonite identity" in favour of expanding their membership to those beyond the ethnic Mennonite fold.[42] These denominations now have only weak associations with other Mennonites. A particularly important case of ambiguous membership is that of the Brethren in Christ (BIC), which is one of the church groups that "owns" MCC. Often colloquially called "River Brethren," the BIC denomination was a Pietist-informed splinter group that began distancing itself from other Anabaptist-Mennonite churches in Pennsylvania around 1780.[43] While BIC derives its roots from Anabaptism it also has long been considered distinct. As with other Mennonites, BIC churches include an emphasis on practices of non-resistance, but there are also theological differences.[44] The question of BIC membership in the Mennonite peoplehood has been equivocal and it has often "hovered on the edge" of the Mennonite mosaic.[45]

Another blurred boundary of Mennonite identity concerns the question over whether Mennonite is necessarily a religious or theological category. Rodney Sawatsky has mused over the possibility of "non-religious" or "secular" Mennonites. He points to the artist Patrick Friesen who declared himself to be Mennonite, and to operate out of a Mennonite "ethos," but who no longer identified as Christian. Sawatsky probes into whether such non-believers should be considered Mennonite and what, in either case, this would mean for how the term is understood. While he suggests that non-Christian Mennonites may be seen as occupying a creatively ambivalent space of "not quite in and not quite out," he also wonders whether "faith and ethnicity can be separated even if we might want them divided into discrete camps."[46]

While Sawatsky might not consider faith and ethnicity to be easily divisible, such divisions are regularly drawn by other Mennonites. The question of the relationship between Mennonite faith and ethnicity was put to me particularly pointedly at the Leamington Mennonite Community Festival, which I attended in June 2008. The festival is in part intended to raise money for MCC through a variety of fundraising initiatives. It is also a celebration of rural Ontarian Mennonite identity. Mennonite women baked zwieback (double yeast buns), boiled wareneki (dumplings), and stewed large pots of borscht (soup) for eager consumption by the nostalgic or curious. A youthful Latino band jammed away on worship songs sung in Spanish on an open-air stage. A well-attended quilt auction saw fierce competition for beautifully crafted patchwork quilts. In one corner of the hall the local MCC representative set up a display about the organization's work, and a bathtub collected "penny power" donations for MCC's work. Bonnet-wearing Old Order Mennonites, lads in jeans, kids in packs, and cowboy hat-wearing gentlemen mixed together in an intergenerational mélange. In the midst of the carnivalesque fray I had a passing conversation with one of the festival attendees, an older quietly spoken gentleman who philosophized with me over the meanings of "Mennonite sausage," which at the time was being served in large quantities for lunch. Without provocation, my companion asked me rhetorically what it meant to pronounce these greasy, encased tubes of ground meat to be Mennonite. "Are sausages truly Christian?" he asked. Pushing the issue further he framed the question differently: "Is the sausage *saved*?"

Mennonite identity is dynamic and contested.[47] While a sense of peoplehood has strong resonance among particular groups of Mennonites, and its meaning is frequently assumed in both casual conversations and academic publications as relating to a particular ethnic grouping, there remain enduring ambiguities over who belongs in this imagined community. Therefore, while Urry's definition of peoplehood, quoted above and relating exclusively to ethno-religious tradition, is analytically helpful, it is itself also caught up within the disputed politics of identification. The sense of belonging that peoplehood implies remains ill-defined. The inclusions and exclusions, and where the boundaries fall, as well as what is considered central or marginal characteristics, are all contested. "Mennonite" may be a religious, ethnic, or racial category, or it may be an amalgam of those features in myriad combinations and permutations. Nevertheless, Mennonite historiography both indicates and constructs a distinctive Mennonite tradition. This tradition is formed as much through the conflicts and ambiguities, the blurred and contested edges, as through any other mechanism. And it is this history that is invoked by Mennonites themselves in the stories they tell of MCC.

When MCCers describe their organization as a "peoplehood movement" it is these connotations – and these ambivalences – of peoplehood that are drawn upon and engaged. The meanings of MCC as a peoplehood movement are foregrounded in the next section in an examination of the history of MCC from its birth in 1920 until the late 1950s.

GENESIS, EXODUS, AND WAR

The 1917 Bolshevik Revolution marked a decisive turning point in Russian history, with the rise of a Communist regime that would profoundly reshape global geopolitics. For Mennonites living in Ukraine it spelled disaster.[48] Throughout the First World War the Plautdietsch-speaking Mennonites faced intense anti-German pressures, but the rise of the Soviet Union saw a further sharp deterioration in Mennonite fortunes. Mennonite communities were attacked, farm land was confiscated, and families dispossessed. The turmoil surrounding the socialist revolution resulted in widespread famine. This had devastating effects on forty-eight thousand Mennonites, though of course they were not alone. Between 1921 and 1922, there were around 9 million fatalities across the Soviet Union in one of the largest famines of the twentieth century.[49] Many Mennonites also found themselves caught in the midst of fierce fighting between Red and White Armies. In this context of multiple, overlapping crises Mennonite prosperity in the Russian colonies came to a grinding halt. Subjected to violence, starvation, and communal disintegration their situation was dire. In desperation, Mennonites in Ukraine sent a four-member *Studienkommission* (Pl. study commission) as emissaries to their co-religionists in North America with requests for urgent assistance.

The organizational capacity among Mennonites in North America at this time was limited. Numerous regional and denominational relief committees were in operation, which drew upon practices of mutual aid within rural Mennonite communities to include service to those beyond. But these were fragmented, and no overarching body was able to coordinate an international response of the magnitude that was clearly required. In July 1920, at the urging of the *Studienkommission*, a group of Mennonite church leaders and relief committee representatives gathered for a meeting at Prairie Street Mennonite Church in Elkhart, Indiana. Their task was to discuss what could be done.[50] The result was the creation of a "Mennonite Central Committee" as a temporary centralized mechanism to coordinate the diverse and disparate existing relief committees to proffer an efficient channel of assistance to the "household of faith."[51] Though well connected with Canadian Mennonites and the various Canadian Mennonite relief committees, and though strongly supported by many Canadian Mennonites, at its founding MCC was considered an American Mennonite organization.[52] MCC's links with Canadian Mennonites would be greatly strengthened during the Second World War, though it was only in the 1950s and 1960s that MCC formally become a binational agency and, therefore, also a Canadian organization.[53]

The birth of MCC for the Russian relief work provided the critical elements necessary for the establishment, in time, of a more durable central committee. Crucial was the circulation of a founding organizational myth that located MCC as the key mediator connecting diverse and distanced co-religionists and as an indispensable tool in delivering relief to desperate Mennonite kin. MCC's identity, established in frequent reiterations of this founding narrative, was as an "inter-Mennonite" organization.[54] It was a centralized meeting place, or a "conglomerate," which sought to bring the fragmented peoplehood together.[55] This celebration of what historian Lucille Marr calls "Mennonite ecumenicity" became the raison d'être of MCC in North America.[56]

This myth was given particular power through MCC's first martyrdom. Clayton Kratz was a twenty-four-year-old Mennonite volunteer from Bucks County, Pennsylvania, who was part of the initial three-person team sent by the newly formed MCC to assess and help assist in the relief effort to the Russian Mennonites. While serving in the Mennonite colonies in Russia, Kratz, as bluntly put in Unruh's sparse text, "lost his life."[57] The exact circumstances remain unclear, though members of the Red Army are widely regarded as being the likely perpetrators. The martyrdom of Kratz reverberated throughout Mennonite communities in North America for decades. Still today the Kratz story is narrated through written and oral storytelling, videos, pilgrimages, the naming of a residence hall at Goshen College (a Mennonite tertiary institution), and a memorial fund.[58] Many Mennonites, brought up steeped in the stories of the persecution of their ancestors, saw Kratz's martyrdom as a tangible affirmation of how MCC's work continued in the Anabaptist tradition of faithful, dedicated, sacrificial service. The bloody violence wreaked upon Kratz's youthful body was taken as irrefutable legitimation and an unparalleled stamp of authority for the organization.[59]

In one of the earliest accounts of MCC's history, John Unruh argues that the organization's early work in relief provision in Russia and the associated efforts to help Russian Mennonites immigrate to the Paraguayan Chaco ensured that a "channel had been cut deep enough so that it could be widened with confidence."[60] A significant part of the construction of this channel was the bringing together of a capable group of leaders who shared a talent for organizational entrepreneurialism. Harold S. Bender was a prominent and respected church leader and a professor of history at Goshen College, with degrees from Princeton and a doctorate from the University of Heidelberg. Bender held a variety of important leadership roles in the organization. Peter Hiebert, a prominent Mennonite Brethren pastor, evangelist, and educator who helped found Tabor College, served as MCC's chairperson for the first thirty-three years; an extraordinary period of service. Orie O. Miller was perhaps the key early organizational architect of MCC. He was one of Clayton Kratz's companions during the first MCC relief operation in Ukraine, and he remained intimately involved in the organization for decades, serving as its executive secretary from 1935 to 1958. Miller was widely known in Mennonite communities as "Mr MCC."[61] He was renowned for his dedication, hard work, and political acumen as well as his imperious approach to leadership. Through their creative innovations, accompanied by a keen ability to grasp the intricacies of denominational politics and a willingness to provide decisive leadership, these men were pivotal in the dramatic growth of MCC in its formative years.[62] Despite a hiatus in organizational activity in the mid-1920s, the opportunity for reopening the "channel" arose again with great urgency with the onset of the Second World War.

The First World War was a period of profound disruption for Mennonites. As a consequence of their ongoing use of Plautdietsch and other ethnic German markers that associated them with "the enemy," their long history of separation, and the refusal of many Mennonites to prove their patriotism through participation in the armed forces, many Mennonites were severely derided.[63] When war broke out again in Europe, Canada plunged into the conflict alongside the United Kingdom. While the United States delayed direct involvement, the Japanese attack on Pearl Harbor in 1941 abruptly brought its declared isolation and neutrality to an end. Both nations were immersed in war, and Mennonites, again, faced a decisive challenge.

In response, Mennonite leaders worked frantically with their governments to create opportunities for young Mennonite men to avoid conscription into the armed forces.[64] In the US these lobbying efforts resulted in the creation of Civilian Public Service (CPS), in which conscientious objectors (COs) carried out work of national importance instead of participating directly in the war. Over twelve thousand American Mennonites, Quakers, and Brethren in Christ members worked with

CPS during the war years. The administrative burden and organizational oversight for CPS was entrusted to MCC, and so, in taking up this critical function, the organization was reborn. CPS not only involved the young Mennonite men who faced conscription but also drew in entire Mennonite communities who supported the operations. The costs of the camps were carried by the historic peace churches. Although largely occluded by a male-dominated church leadership, Mennonite women volunteered alongside men on a range of tasks and were vital in the running of the camps. The pattern of intensive community established at this time has remained surprisingly durable in the way MCC engages with its constituency relationships.

Simultaneous to the domestic work of CPS and while still in the midst of the Second World War, MCC leadership initiated international relief operations to war-torn Europe. Volunteer workers were sent out and constituents were organized to donate money and material resources. When the war came to an end in 1945 the relief work to Europe quickly expanded.[65] This period produced another narrative that would become a defining myth for MCC for much of the rest of the century. Again, it involved Russian Mennonites. The battles fought between the Soviet Union and Germany swept right through Mennonite communities in Ukraine, resulting in enormous devastation. When Germany invaded the Soviet Union in 1941, Mennonites were awkwardly – and violently – caught between the "two poles."[66] Many Mennonites feared, with justification, that their "Germanic" ancestry would make them targets for reprisals and persecution. But some Mennonites also harboured sympathies for the National Socialist cause, and some fought alongside the Germans against the Red Army.[67] As the war came to a close, German troops were forced to retreat and around thirty-five thousand Mennonites fled with them. At the end of the war, therefore, thousands of Russian Mennonite refugees found themselves homeless and desperate in occupied Germany. The prominent role that MCC played in the mass Mennonite "exodus" from Berlin to Canada and Paraguay has been told repeatedly in Mennonite literature and oral storytelling.[68] One of the most compelling and widely read narratives is Barbara Smucker's children's book *Henry's Red Sea*, first published in 1955, which describes MCC as a "wonderful organization" and depicts key MCC leader Peter Dyck as a modern-day Moses.[69] For years afterwards many Russian Mennonites living in Canada and elsewhere felt a powerful sense of travel debt (Pl. *reiseschuld*), which was accrued in the process of emigration. A significant recipient of this enduring sense of indebtedness was MCC, a debt that many Canadian Russian Mennonites continued to pay through donations and service throughout their lives and that was also handed down to their children. [70]

After the war, and on the back of the extensive relief work in war-torn Europe, MCC leadership embarked on an aggressive expansion of MCC's mandate into other parts of the world also considered needy.[71] This expansion paralleled the explosive postwar growth of the modern NGO movement as well as a newly emerging American self-confidence in the ability of its "development" – a newly potent term that quickly became a pivotal keyword for global politics – to alleviate worldwide suffering through technological innovation and economic growth.[72] The radical reorientation of MCC during the birthing years of modernization witnessed a dramatic expansion of volunteers, both men and women from the US and Canada, who took up new positions in field programs and in fundraising initiatives. MCC benefited from ongoing US conscription, which eventually came to an end only in 1972, as this produced a continuous supply of CO recruits requiring service assignments.

Many COs joined MCC's Pax program, which sent over 1,150 young Canadian and American men to serve internationally with MCC.[73] The sending of international volunteers was further expanded with the launching of the Teachers Abroad Program (TAP) in 1962. Over the following decades MCC sent 2,380 Canadian and American teachers to countries in Africa and another 477 teachers to Bolivia and Jamaica.[74] The extensive participation by Canadians in these initiatives, in what had initially been an American organization, stems in large part from the proactive attempts of MCC leaders to expand the organization to Mennonite kin north of the border. The first organizational inroads into Canada were made in Ontario during the Second World War.[75] These initial forays melded with pre-existing local institutions with their own distinctive history. The institutional infrastructure of MCC Canada was established in 1963, which led to MCC officially becoming a "binational" entity.[76] The relationship between Canadian and American branches of MCC has long been characterized by tension, and the careful management of this relationship over the years has, according to one prominent organizational insider, "absorbed much MCC energy."[77]

As with CPS, women were active volunteers and significant figures in the emerging MCC, although much early historiography neglected women's important roles.[78] Lucille Marr's *The Transforming Power of a Century*, a rich and layered history of MCC Ontario, does significant work in correcting this situation. Marr pays close attention to women's involvement as a simple acknowledgment that "the MCC Ontario story is also theirs."[79] Indeed, a large part of the success of MCC, in Ontario and elsewhere in North America, was that almost all Mennonites were able to make MCC *theirs*. While until recently men tended to dominate leadership positions, women found diverse avenues of involvement. Significant new opportunities opened for Mennonite women following the Second World War. Internationally, women were among the relief workers sent to war-torn Europe and elsewhere.[80] Closer to home, women were actively involved in supporting MCC's work through sewing circles, canning fruit and vegetables to send overseas, supporting other family members as they engaged in distant service duties, in administration tasks within MCC offices, and by preparing relief kits to send as long-distance humanitarian care packages, among many other forms of service.

The postwar organizational development of MCC took place at a time of far-ranging social change in North American Mennonite society. The experience of being conscientious objectors thrust many young Mennonites out from small and isolated rural Mennonite communities into vastly expanded spatial, social, and cultural worlds. For these young Mennonites, their quietness was shattered and the cultivated separation from the world was unravelled. But the shattering was not mere negation: it was also a period of significant theological innovation, with new ideas being experimented with and new frameworks being proposed. Harold Bender's highly influential essay, "The Anabaptist Vision," set the theological-historical tone for increasing interaction of Mennonites with "the world." First published in 1944, Bender proposed that Mennonites should assume more activist forms of engagement with those around them on the basis of an ethic of peace and service.[81] According to historian Paul Toews, the Anabaptist Vision became "the identifying incantation" for American Mennonites and "legitimated an outward missional activism."[82] When Mennonite religion scholar Keith Graber Miller summarizes Anabaptist ethics as being concerned with "pacifism, humility and service," he builds on an understanding directly indebted to Bender's articulation of the Anabaptist Vision.[83] MCC was profoundly animated by the new ideological consensus Bender forged, such that, for both American and Canadian Mennonites, MCC became the "epitome" of the Anabaptist Vision.[84] The concepts of service and peace, so powerfully and normatively articulated by Bender, have become key words in North American Mennonite society in the sense that they articulate core, or sacred, values.[85] Peace and service are also dominant animating ideas for the work of MCC. I address each briefly in turn.

MCC was a decisive avenue through which Mennonite service was enacted. MCC was also a primary vehicle through which a reformulated notion of service was imagined and disseminated.[86] MCC helped enshrine service as an ideal and established it as an intimate part of the faith habitus of the Mennonite peoplehood. Sociologist Donald Kraybill evocatively charts these transitions:

> MCC has helped to define, reinforce and transform the identity of North American Mennonites. For others, the programs and projects of MCC have sharpened an image of what Mennonites and Brethren in Christ are all about: *They* are the people who care about the impoverished, the destitute, the refugee. Participating in MCC programs through giving, serving and volunteering has also reinforced the meaning of Mennonite identity for Mennonites themselves: We are the people who send material aid to the needy and facilitate development projects for the disenfranchised around the world.[87]

But MCC was also birthed and shaped to meet the needs of the North American Mennonite peoplehood. It existed to *serve* Mennonites, and they were a primary beneficiary. Indeed, for Marr: "for most of its history, MCC had meant service, a theology that implied blessing as much for the giver as for the receiver."[88] The services of MCC have always been dual. The needs of the Mennonite peoplehood from 1920 to the 1950s were to help their suffering Russian co-religionists, to gain access to exemptions from the draft, to funnel Mennonite compassion, and to embody vernacular theologies. Their needs also included the desire to form an organization that could bring the fragmented peoplehood together in a common, uniting, and identity-creating endeavour. Even so, as Alain Epp Weaver notes, MCC service "has never been static, has often been contested, and has always been under construction."[89]

The practice of international volunteering in MCC arose out of a desire for conscientious objectors and the wider communities that supported them to corporeally enact their belief in *peace* and non-resistance, a tangible theological embodiment. Notions of peace had long been pivotal to Mennonite self-identity. In CPS and also in the programs that followed, and especially after the growing momentum generated by the publication of the Anabaptist Vision, volunteering in MCC was conceptualized as a direct, positive parallel to participation in war. Just as other young citizens were conscripted to fight for their nation, so Mennonite young men and women would practise an alternative to war. Their service was envisaged as being the "moral equivalent for war."[90] However, ironically, although MCC was born out of pacifist Mennonite commitments and later articulated an explicit peacebuilding mandate, it was also very much what historian James Juhnke describes as "the product of 20th century total war."[91] War created needs that MCC was formed to help meet, and during the war persuasive nationalist propaganda in the US and Canada, which called for sacrifice and determination, provided a compelling impetus that stirred Mennonites into action.

In the decades after the Second World War, Mennonites gave generously to fund the rapidly expanding MCC. Their generosity was a necessary precondition for MCC's work. Among the reasons for this was that MCC was undoubtedly perceived as carrying out a mission that meshed with widely shared vernacular Mennonite theologies and prominent Anabaptist visions. But there were also other powerful pressing needs: COs needed opportunities to work other than in the military, the "household of faith" in Ukraine and Germany desperately required assistance, and fragmented Mennonite groups were open to finding practical ways to work more closely together. Fred Kniss also perceives a certain "philanthropic guilt."[92] Mennonite farmers benefited greatly from wartime agricultural prices but did not contribute their young men to the war effort in the same way as had their neighbours. American Mennonite involvement in MCC and other associated avenues of service is also partially explained, according to historian Perry Bush, by a desire to remain "a separate and identifiable people."[93] As previous markers of Mennonite uniqueness dissolved with the war and accompanying social changes, Mennonites preserved their identity as different through their peculiar generosity and by engaging in activities that "fueled their growing self-definition as a people of service."[94] But their exuberant philanthropy also indicated Mennonite "aspirations to citizenship," and active service became an alternative route to proving that Mennonites were both good Christians and good citizens.[95]

The historical sketch given here is necessarily brief and does not address the ongoing evolution of MCC after the 1960s. However, I hope this truncated window into the birth and early decades of the organization demonstrates the intimate historical links between MCC and the North American Mennonite peoplehood. MCC's origins and growth are intertwined with its constituency. Attending to its early decades begins the work of uncovering what David Lewis has called the "hidden histories" of development organizations, which are frequently ignored within popular formulaic periodizations of the NGO movement.[96]

THE MENNONITE UNITED NATIONS

MCC continues to have extensive reach among North American Mennonites. Financially, MCC is largely dependent on Mennonite constituent funding, including private, church, and community-fundraising initiatives.[97] I was told by a former senior MCC administrator that the organization has actively de-emphasized endowments in order to intentionally cultivate this dependency. As a peoplehood movement MCC remains at the whim of those who propel it. If they choose to withdraw that support, then the organization ceases to function. The major exception to this constituent dependency has been the willingness of MCC Canada to channel significant funding from the Canadian government.[98] This exception was thoroughly contested within MCC and its broader constituency. But attention to finances alone is insufficient. Actual cash donations are by no means the most significant intervention MCC makes in the lives of constituents. Through MCC, the Mennonite peoplehood cooperate together in embodied communal action.[99]

A crucial component of this embodied activity, and one that is a central focus of analysis in the following chapters, is the sending out of North American international fieldworkers throughout the world, many on three-year service assignments. The number of MCC service workers serving internationally peaked in the 1980s, with 498 workers serving overseas in over fifty countries. By 2008 this number had dropped by almost half to 245, a still not insignificant number.[100] By the mid-1990s, over fifteen thousand alumni had served with MCC in a formal capacity.[101] Most of these returned from their place of service to their home countries, bringing with them their stories, experiences, and broadened horizons. These numbers pale in comparison to those directly involved each year in MCC fundraising and service work in North America. In the mid-1990s over fifty thousand volunteers connected with MCC programs each year.[102] The numbers of volunteers are substantially higher today. There are multiple avenues into volunteering for and donating to MCC, including short-term international study tours; sewing circles; lobbying and advocacy programs at MCC offices in Ottawa, Washington, and New York; and the mobile meat canning unit. With over one hundred stores across the US and Canada, the extensive Thrift Shop network draws on a large pool of voluntary labour to sort and re-sell secondhand clothing and other items to raise money for MCC. The multiple Material Resource Centers likewise see thousands of volunteers every year directly participate in sorting and packing school kits, relief kits, comforters, and other items destined for shipment overseas.

The relief sale phenomenon, introduced earlier in the anecdote from the Leamington Mennonite Community Festival, is another such avenue for volunteer involvement.[103] Relief sales emerged spontaneously in the wake of the Second World War without MCC oversight and support.[104] In 2010 there were forty-three relief sales scattered throughout the US and Canada, and collectively they raised over US$6.6 million.[105] Most of this was donated to MCC.[106] Each relief sale is an autonomous, volunteer-run annual event. They are festive occasions as well as fundraisers for international relief. Through numerous independently operated stalls a diverse cross-section of Mennonite tastes and aesthetics are made available for consumption. Prominent among these are large quantities of "ethnic" Mennonite foods, leading theologian Malinda Berry to wryly point out the contradiction of "stuffing ourselves to feed others."[107]

An iconic part of many relief sale events is the "Penny Power" fundraising campaign.[108] The campaign is aimed at encouraging children to collect coins throughout the year, which they bring along and donate at the relief sale in large, prominently located containers. The accumulated coin donations – amounting to $462,665 in 2010 – are then handed on to MCC.[109] The Penny Power song and jingle (see below) reinforce a particular ethics of gifting in which donations, even in seemingly small and insignificant quantities, can accumulate and combine to world-changing effect. The multiplication logic of this vernacular theology is facilitated through enumerating solutions to poverty and conflict ("Fifty pennies feeds a family for a day") and, by implication, placing the power of providing solutions into the hands of the donors ("we can do something 'bout that"). The power of pennies is the giver's puissance. These acts of giving are sacralized through both positive affirmation ("You'll be a blessing to someone") and by locating such acts as aligned with theological imperatives ("We're doin' what Jesus commanded us to do").

Penny Power Song
Chorus:
Penny power, penny power.
Here is something where a little means a lot.
Penny power, penny power.
We can make a difference in the world.

Verse 1:
Sometimes people are hungry,
Sometimes people are thirsty,

sometimes people just need to get along,
well, we can do something about that.

Verse 2:
Fifty pennies feeds a family for a day,
five hundred pennies builds peace a better way,
five thousand pennies brings water to a town,
now we can do something 'bout that.

Verse 3:
We can collect our pennies in a jar,
find someone to match them right where we are,
and when we take them to the collection bin
maybe they will double again …

By Les Gustafson-Zook (2007)

Penny Power Jingle
Look high, look low; we're collecting coins,
We're searching to and fro.
We'll use nickels, dimes, quarters, dollars, too;
Won't you help us, we challenge you.
Be a part of penny power; let's gather coins;
Penny power, we'll work together.
Penny power, let's get rollin'.
You'll be a blessing to someone today.
We'll use penny power to help those in need,
Around the world, they'll add up to a good deed.
Let's pull together give help and comfort too,
We're doin' what Jesus commanded us to do;
We'll use our penny power, let's gather coins;
Penny power we'll work together.
Penny power, let's get rollin'.
You'll be a blessing to someone today.
You'll be a blessing to someone today.

By Lori Yoder (n.d.)

In Virginia I interviewed a fundraising consultant who worked with MCC on relief sales. He told me that MCC's fundraising was unlike any other model he had encountered. The classic "donor relation cycle" involves a series of carefully orchestrated steps: *identifying* with potential donors; *listening* to them and learning their passions; *aligning* and sharing the case for support; *involving* potential donors in the life of the organization; *appealing* to them to invest in their ideals through the organization; *thanking* in seven different ways; *reporting* on the outcomes of the donation; and *reassessing* what the next step could be for that donor. However, when he suggested these concepts to MCC he was rebuffed. MCC did not have (or want) a strategic eight-point approach to facilitating donations, nor did it chase up donors with seven different kinds of thank you. Instead, if MCC put out a general appeal for donations, say in response to a natural disaster, it almost always got a "huge response." This was because, the consultant proposed, MCC does involvement and participation uniquely well. Specifically, in terms of the relief sales, he found a remarkably "passionate ownership" over them by locally organized committees. The annual Virginia Mennonite Relief Sale, for example, involves over one thousand volunteers and is attended by over ten thousand visitors. It is much more than just a fundraising campaign; rather, it is understood by eager participants as an opportunity to "share our story" on a public stage. Over the course of the weekend all the volunteers at the Virginia relief sale diligently do their own little thing such that it all works like "a machine." Such a powerful sense of ownership, he confessed, made his job of initiating change a complex task. The approach that he found worked the best was not to offer suggestions or advice but, rather, to merely tell stories of how things were being done elsewhere. In this way the local committees would themselves own the changes and their ownership would remain unequivocal. Many donors at relief sales, and many of the volunteers who run them, have little concept of where donations go. All they know is that the money goes to a "good cause" and that the relief sale itself is a "community experience." In this sense, each relief sale is a "world in and of itself."

The observation that relief sales occupy discrete systems is ethnographically astute, but it should not be taken to indicate a lack of attention to constituent-directed information flows on the part of MCC. Narrative is the primary means through which MCC communicates with its constituents. First-hand narrative is a particularly privileged mode of discourse. Constituents are frequently given opportunities to engage with itinerant MCC storytellers and returned MCCers who visit Mennonite churches and educational institutions. The preference for stories is also reflected in the remarkably prolific publications about the organization.[110] These find an engaged readership among MCC's supporters. Of even greater importance for its constituency relationships is the publicity MCC receives in popular Mennonite media. Over the course of my field research I diligently read the *Mennonite Weekly Review*, a widely distributed "inter-Mennonite" newspaper,[111] and on only one occasion could I find no article directly discussing MCC. Often, MCC was given front-page coverage and was addressed in multiple articles in the same publication. In this literature, MCCers frequently played the role of Mennonite "foreign correspondent" by providing on-the-ground insights into far-away places and events. MCC leadership has over the years ensured that there was a continuous flow of reading material that helped MCC remain in the forefront of Mennonite imaginations.[112]

MCC is an organization with many different levels. In a research paper on MCC's structure published in 2005, MCC was described as a "federation."[113] During the period of my research MCC was made up of twelve legally distinct entities. These twelve entities included MCC "binational," which had primary responsibility for MCC's international programs, two national MCCs (MCC Canada, founded 1963, and MCC US, founded 1979), five Canadian provincial MCCs (MCC Alberta, MCC British Columbia, MCC Saskatchewan, MCC Manitoba, MCC Ontario), and four US-based regional MCCs (MCC Central States, MCC East Coast, MCC Great Lakes, and West Coast MCC). Each entity was overseen by separate boards made up of representatives from constituent Mennonite churches. This organizational structure was infamously convoluted. Former executive secretary John A. Lapp is said to have commented that, "with its complex and nebulous structure and its incredible complex and diverse constituency, MCC really should not work."[114] Likewise, at the MCC US Board Meeting I attended in June 2008, the gathered audience was told that every consultant who has ever worked on the structure of MCC eventually scratched their head in confusion and admitted: "This is the most complex organization I've ever seen. It shouldn't work!" MCCers are fond of describing the unworkable structure of their organization with the rhetorical question: "How does a bumblebee fly?" Just as the physics of the bumblebee's flight astounds science, so too MCC's organizational structure is inscrutable, and its operations defy social gravity. But perhaps more important than *how* it works is that its structure is tailor-made to facilitate participation. Throughout North America, Mennonite communities and churches are within fairly close proximity to an MCC entity. This closeness facilitates participation.

MCC has also spun-off numerous organizations. Mennonite Disaster Service (MDS), a disaster relief agency that sends voluntary teams on building reconstruction projects, was formed initially as an MCC department but has since become a separate organization.[115] MTS Travel began as the travel department of MCC in 1947, becoming a separate legal entity in 1955.[116] Most famously, Ten Thousand Villages, a fair-trade pioneer, also began its existence within MCC.[117] In 1946, Edna Ruth Byler, the wife of an MCC administrator, started importing handicrafts from Puerto Rico and Jordan and sold them from the trunk of her car. It remained Byler's personal project until the 1960s when it became a formal MCC project and began working in close cooperation with the Thrift Shop network. Sales expanded quickly, and a series of separate stores was established. In 1996 Ten Thousand Villages was established, and a few years later it was incorporated as a non-profit charitable organization wholly owned by MCC. [118] MCC's influence extends well beyond its direct progeny into virtually every corner of the institutional infrastructure of North American Mennonite life.

As MCC is the only overarching organization that brings the entire North American Mennonite mosaic together, it has become the default location where the peoplehood negotiate their politics. It is, as James Urry aptly notes, the Mennonite "United Nations."[119] Contentious issues over the politics of peace and conscientious objection, particularly during attempts to revise nonresistance into a more activist stance during the 1960s and 1970s, were debated and processed in the MCC Peace Section (1942–86).[120] Women's Concerns, reflecting wider gender politics of the 1960–80s, was also situated within MCC and served as a catalyst for feminist discussion and debate. Likewise, racial and Indigenous politics – particularly fraught issues in many "Germanic" Mennonite communities – were given forums in MCC programs and initiatives such as the Damascus Road antiracism training in MCC US and efforts to address social justice issues with Canadian Aboriginal Peoples.[121] MCC was also pivotal in engaging with national politics and has operated as something of a Mennonite embassy, at certain times representing Mennonite concerns to government authorities, though issues of lobbying and advocacy have always been deeply contested.[122]

Some of the programs discussed above have been explicitly aimed at transforming constituent identities and theology. MCC's anti-racism work is one example that has taken a proactive approach to challenging racism among Mennonite communities.[123] Other programs also sought to provide a service to Mennonites, including Mennonite Conciliation Services, which offers to mediate among church groups experiencing conflict.[124] Various MCCers have explicitly understood their work as involving the attempt to rework Mennonite theology. For example, some MCCers have seen themselves as a kind of "peace evangelist" to

North American Mennonites and have actively sought to evangelize the church.[125] For Ron Kreider, returning MCC workers were "a kind of lay missioner" with "his [*sic*] inevitable collection of color slides… [which are shown] to Sunday School classes, relatives, schools, and civic groups."[126]

The extensive, multifaceted, and multi-tentacled engagements between MCC and its constituency had transformative effects as narrated by Lucille Marr in her history of MCC Ontario. In Marr's telling, MCC's Mennonite "ecumenicity" profoundly reshaped Mennonite self-understandings with a reinforced sense of belonging to a common peoplehood.[127] Through its transnational connections, MCC extended and broadened Mennonite horizons. MCC also educated its constituency by organizing speaking tours for eyewitnesses of international conflicts, distributing letters from MCC workers overseas, providing a peace library for use by churches and making available other literature, and organizing workshops and forums. MCC's influence was extraordinarily far-reaching.[128] While my survey in this section examined a broad range of entanglements between MCC and its supporting constituency, in the following and final section in this chapter I focus on one particular program to provide more texture regarding what being a peoplehood movement means in practice.

CANNED MEAT

Early during my field research, the MCC Representatives in Indonesia – Anna and Jake – introduced me to stories of MCC's canned meat.[129] Anna and Jake traced the canned meat phenomenon to the very origins of MCC, when, in the early 1920s, famine-stricken Mennonites in Ukraine pleaded for aid from Mennonites in North America. After organizing a central committee to coordinate efforts, Mennonites initiated a transnational humanitarian operation. These initial efforts involved shipping material goods, including tractors, foodstuffs, and the like. Canned meat was not among these shipments, but, Anna and Jake told me, participation in MCC through "physical things" was cemented at this time as an important dimension of MCC's work. Canned meat fits into this long and venerable tradition of the materiality of the gift in MCC.

Anna and Jake explained that MCC operates a mobile meat canner that undertakes an annual pilgrimage around rural Mennonite communities in the US and Canada. At each stop volunteers help with the canning process. The end result – literally tons of the stuff – is then stored in MCC warehouses before being shipped off around the world. As this story of canned meat was narrated to me while we sat in an office in Central Java

I couldn't help but conclude that this canned meat was utterly out of this world. Not only did the idea of canned meat shipments seem completely disconnected from everyday Javanese life, but the whole thing seemed extraordinarily anachronistic. It surely was a return to the hand-out models of charity so scorned in contemporary development literature. I had pursued the possibility of researching MCC partly because a friend familiar with Christian NGOs in Latin America had suggested that MCC was among the most progressive and innovative of all the organizations he knew. Whatever canned meat was, it seemed clear to me that avant-garde it was not.

Throughout my fieldwork in Indonesia, I never once came across an actual can of MCC meat. I only eventually managed to hold one of these iconic cans at the Ephrata Material Resource Center in Lancaster County, Pennsylvania. I also did not have an opportunity to accompany the mobile meat canner on its route. Nevertheless, canned meat was a recurring topic of conversation with MCCers, and my fascination with it grew as I came to learn more. Canned meat is an iconic object in Mennonite newspaper articles, blogs, and published texts.[130] I eagerly learned all I could about canned meat.

MCC began canning meat for relief in 1946. The date is not insignificant as it was in the 1940s that MCC underwent its "second birth" and was established as an enduring relief organization.[131] This was the period during which Mennonite altruism became an indispensable aspect of Mennonite society, spurred on by Bender's Anabaptist Vision, philanthropic guilt, insecure citizenship, and the growing affluence of rural Mennonite farmers. MCC's meat canning began at a particular historical juncture during which MCC became the dominant channel for transnational connections among North American Mennonites. Canned meat was to accompany young Mennonites then being sent out on their overseas assignments.

But canned meat was not designed by MCC administrators as a means to cement its importance among constituent churches. In fact, it was not *designed* by MCCers at all. MCC was, rather, the location in which the canned meat project came to be housed. The idea of a mobile meat canner was a creative response to rural Mennonite resources and new opportunities. Mennonite families had long bottled – "canned" in popular expression – vegetables, fruits, and meat to preserve supplies for winter. When Mennonite communities were called upon to provide foodstuffs for those serving as COs in the CPS camps, they found that fragile glass jars used for traditional canning transported poorly. The fragility of glass was emphasized when they sought to ship supplies to Europe for Mennonite refugees and others suffering from the war. Industrialized metal canning came to be seen as a viable alternative. It equalled the temporal longevity provided by bottling but greatly expanded the geographic horizons for travel through a much hardier container. While traditional glass jar canning could be done in any Mennonite kitchen, metal canning required machinery that was not so readily available. The solution was a mobile meat canner that could be transported wherever it was needed. Working independently of each other, a Mennonite business in Virginia's Shenandoah Valley and a group of Mennonites in Hesston, Kansas, built and operated portable canners to facilitate the processing of food for overseas relief. After some initial experimentation, the Hesston canner was handed over to MCC so as to be accessible to the wider Mennonite community.

Donate Money[132]
Funds are welcome to cover the costs of this operation.
$3.00 covers the expense to can one can of meat (28 oz./794 grams).
$72.00 will cover cost for one complete carton of meat (24 cans).
$0.25 is the average cost of shipping a can of meat to a hungry family.
$6.00 is the cost to ship one carton of meat.
⇨ Donate now

MCC canned meat is still produced through a mobile meat canner. The current machinery is mounted on a flat-bed trailer. Each year, from October to May, the truck-canner travels around rural communities to can meat for relief, making over thirty stopovers in thirteen US States and two Canadian provinces. A canner team of four young men accompanies the truck and manages the canning process, but the work also relies upon local communities donating money or meat, arranging facilities, and organizing volunteers. This requires dedicated commitment from the local committees that organize the work. While there is some MCC coordination, these committees are essentially autonomous. In effect, they own the canned meat operations in their respective communities. Previously the meat used to be taken from donated cattle, but after mad cow disease (bovine spongiform encephalopathy or BSE) became an acknowledged threat in the US and Canada in the early 2000s the main meat source has largely shifted from beef to turkey.[133] Some beef and pork is also canned using the same equipment, causing potential problems for international distribution to Muslim communities as this is likely to be seen as not meeting halal standards.[134] In 2009, MCC shipped 563,648 cans of meat to fifteen countries.[135]

Wanda Yoder's *Together We Can* provides a detailed description of her seven-month journey with her husband as they accompanied the canner.[136] Initially posted online as blog entries, the revised and published text maintains an informality and immediacy reminiscent of a personal diary. From Yoder's descriptions of the locations visited by the canner it is clear that this is a cartographic roll call of Mennonite heartlands. The volunteers were almost entirely rural, largely from more conservative Anabaptist groups, with Holdeman Mennonites, Old Order Mennonites, the Apostolic Christian Church, Amish, and Hutterites all receiving mention. The list of new acquaintances Yoder made during her travels includes prominent Mennonite family names such as Friesen, Brenneman, Redekop, Swartzendruber, Dyck, Stolzfus, Burkholder, Showalter, and Epp. Yoder (itself a well-known Mennonite surname) celebrates the "shared bond" among Mennonites and declares that they are part of "a very small world with so many connections."[137]

Canning Recipe[138]
Ingredients
– 300 pounds of meat (136.4 kgs)
– 1½ pounds of salt (.68 kgs)
– 140 – 28 oz. cans
– labels and glue

Procedure
Trim the fat from 300 pounds of meat. Cut meat into 2 pound slabs. (Do not be tempted to remove tenderloins for your dinner.) Reduce meat to ¾ inch chunks by running it through a grinder. Dump meat into cooking vat and add 1½ pounds of salt. Cook and stir until meat reaches 160 degrees.

Scoop out as much juice as possible and save in the broth vat (to be canned later). Scoop meat into 28 oz. cans; press meat tightly into the can. Seal the cans with a sealing unit. Cook for 2 hours in a retort steam cooker at 242 degrees. Cool cans in water bath for 30 minutes. Remove from water bath, wash grease from can, and apply label with glue.

Makes 140 cans.

Yoder's experience is movingly narrated as "overwhelming, wonderful."[139] Particular attention is given to matters of generosity, care, and hospitality, both that which is shown to her by host communities and their enacting of kindness in volunteering and donating to make the canning operation work: "These are such great people who volunteer their effort to benefit others who are mostly unknown strangers."[140] She summarizes the canning process as giving people "a tangible opportunity to share their time and money to benefit other people who need assistance."[141] A clear distinction is thereby drawn between generous giver and needy recipient, one that permeates the narrative.[142] Yoder's own experience of the "romance of service" was seen as a great "privilege," even though the hard work, cold weather (the canning takes place during winter months), and absence from home were challenging.[143] At the stopover in Leamington, Ontario, Yoder conversed with Uncle Jack, who told her his life story. Uncle Jack was a child in Ukraine in the early 1920s when many Mennonites died of starvation. He survived because of MCC's aid. Uncle Jack remarks to Yoder: "You can understand why I do all I possibly can for the work of MCC!"[144] Yoder's rich descriptions of the canning journey offer a window into the production of canned meat among rural Mennonites who bond together through acts of selfless giving to distant and unknown, but desperately needy, strangers.

Insights into the canning itself can be gleaned by viewing a promotional DVD entitled *Manna from Heaven*, the first of a two-part series called Taming Hunger.[145] The story focuses on the production of canned meat in Winkler, Manitoba. It is clearly a visceral and sensorial process. Canning involves active, sometimes vigorous, work that transforms raw meat into a packaged commodity ready for global travel. Men wearing white butcher jackets, hardhats, and earmuffs trundle around cramped spaces with trolleys of caged cans; carcasses of meat hang by metal hooks awaiting deboning and grounding; and other men with hair and beard nets stir meat chunks with large clubs while the broth stews in super-sized vats. Always there is hissing, the source of which is eventually revealed as white columns of steam escape from giant pressure cookers. The background is austere, clinical: stainless steel shelves, white walls, and industrial-sized machinery. After the meat is canned and then cooled, women (wearing the same white butcher jackets and hair nets or head coverings) clean the cans in large tubs of soapy water and then send them on to be labelled and glued. Finally, the cans are packed neatly away in boxes.

The camera repeatedly focuses on the image of the can itself, which, in simple black and white, portrays MCC's logo with the words "FOOD for RELIEF" and "*In the name of Christ.*" At one point Don Peters, then the executive director of MCC Canada, tells viewers that, through the canning, "MCC is sending a message, 'service in the name of Christ,' MCC is sending the message to people wherever they are going to receive these cans that people in Canada and the United States care about them." The male narrator reinforces the theme: "Hungry people all over the world now know the love of Christ thanks to the dedication of hard-working volunteers, the generosity of the people and organizations donating meat and money, the committees who work tirelessly day and night to pull it all together."

The documentary closes with images from four different countries – North Korea, Guatemala, Iraq, and Bosnia. People are shown happily consuming the canned meat during a family meal. Others are reaching out for it so that they can add it to their bags of emergency provisions. Ken Reddig, an MCC Canada staff member, narrates this transnational ambit with a story from an unnamed foreign country:

> And it was an orphanage in which they were giving, I think, one can of meat to about fifteen young kids and the woman who was the head of the orphanage said to one of the MCC people, "Don't you ever think about not doing this because this is about the only protein these kids get."

This comment constructs a moral imperative to continue meat canning because of the benefits it has brought in the past and in response to petitions from those who rely on it. As in Wanda Yoder's descriptions, canned meat is situated as a tangible service to help others facing desperate need.

However, canned meat has its fair share of critics within the Mennonite constituency. Vegetarian Mennonites tend to find the practice of canning meat thoroughly distasteful. Many "Muppies" (Mennonite Urban Professionals) consider it antiquated. Some professional development workers familiar with "participation" and "empowerment" discourses consider the approach to material aid as dependency-inducing and, therefore, counter-productive. Former MCCer Will Braun, writing in the "New Order Voice" column of *Canadian Mennonite* magazine, offers some of the most forthright and public criticisms.[146] Braun examines what he calls "buckets and blankets," a shorthand for MCC's work in material resources of which canned meat is a part. He argues that MCC fails to engage constituents in the politics of globalization and instead is "bogged down in an us-helping-them framework." Rather than addressing underlying socio-economic inequalities, MCC serves to placate Mennonite consciences through encouraging participation in feel-good relief efforts. Braun rejects merely offering "help" and instead calls for work that aspires to "redeem broken economic relationships." He calls on MCC to facilitate these transformations among North American Mennonites by engaging in proactive political conscientization.

While familiar, and sometimes sympathetic, with such critiques, MCC administrators are unlikely to dump canned meat any time soon. A senior administrator in MCC's Akron office told me that canning meat was an important part of "being MCC." It helped facilitate a "deep and broad sense of ownership" of MCC by its constituents, which was important to maintain. Moreover, and to my surprise, rather than being seen as anachronistic, canning was presented as a form of radical, anti-capitalist politics:

> The day and age of capitalism and raw economics is on the way out. MCC practices *progressive* development because it is more than just about money ... There are other ways into the organization. While meat canning might not have been progressive thirty years ago, it has come back in.

Also welcomed were the opportunities for community-building that take place during the canning. These feed into a powerful sense of participation and belonging. Implicit in this suggestion is the dual service of canned meat: both volunteers and consumers are envisaged as "recipients."

In rendering these dual services through canned meat MCC is located in an interstitial space, negotiating and mediating between different communities. While their respective needs sometimes mesh, there are also plenty of opportunities for misconnections and disjunctures. An example of such divergence is the label controversy, which continued throughout my field research. The phrase "In the name of Christ," displayed prominently on the can label, resonates strongly with North American Mennonite Christian discourse. The phrase has been used by MCC for decades to evoke the specifically Christian nature of its work.[147] The phrase endows the cans with powerful sacralized significance. This is reinforced by a ritual "blessing of the cans" during the production process.[148] Indeed, comments quoted from the *Taming Hunger* documentary illustrate that the cans were intended to convey a specific theological message, encapsulated by the phrase imprinted on the label. But while the phrase conjured associations of Christian generosity, love, and compassion among Mennonites, it could be read quite differently by others. For example, in predominantly Muslim communities the dissemination of the cans and labels could be taken to be a subversive act of Christian proselytisation.[149] I was told by

Figure 1.1 | Canned meat label

an MCC administrator that such a situation was encountered by MCC workers in Iraq when, after the Second Iraq War, MCC shipped large quantities of canned meat there. When these were transferred over to a local partner organization for distribution, they were stripped of their potentially inflammatory labels. The can and the meat were considered beneficial in the postwar context of food shortages and so the distribution elicited willing support from the Iraqi partner, but the label was not seen in the same light.[150]

Stemming from experiences such as this, MCC initiated a review of the label with the intention of floating possible alternatives. It was hoped that a different phrasing would prove to be less problematic for ease of distribution. Various possibilities were explored, including a change to the more innocuous phrase: "A Christian Resource for Meeting Human Need." This was also drawn from the repertoire of MCC catchphrases used over the years. But modifying the label did not prove to be straightforward. This proposal was met with stern opposition from many volunteer canners. At the Hinton Relief Center in Virginia I was introduced to one of the organizers of the canning work in the region. I asked him what he thought about the possibility of changing the label, and his reply, intended at least as much for the MCCer who accompanied me as it was for me, was conspicuously direct: "If MCC changes the label, I stop canning tomorrow; the whole of Virginia stops canning tomorrow." "In the name of Christ" was not up for negotiation. "That pile of meat is a small drop, but that's *our* drop," he told me. The response is revealing of the sense of ownership over the meat-canning process held by volunteers. MCC may have found the label awkward, but it had to proceed very cautiously if it wanted to attempt to arrange an alternative. In this negotiation there is a sense that MCC retains responsibility for organizing the mobile canner only insofar as it continues to meet constituent needs and expectations. The threat of withdrawal ensures that constituent participation cannot be taken lightly. And yet the Iraq example, in which the practice of tearing off the label operates as a vivid metaphor of disconnection, highlights the ways in which MCC can be awkwardly located between the inalterable and the impossible.

The canned meat phenomenon, therefore, illustrates what it means for MCC to operate as a peoplehood movement. The idea for the canner arose out of "Germanic" Mennonite communities in North America, it belongs to the volunteers that make it happen, and its future depends on their ongoing participation, which takes place significantly on their own terms. Though not without critique, which can itself be a form of participation and an expression of belonging, canned meat attracts support from MCC administrators who perceive benefits for both producers and consumers. Whether or not canned meat is viewed as anachronistic, progressive, or simply burdensome, a key reason MCC continues to coordinate a mobile meat canner and ship canned meat around the world today has to do with a historically embedded relationship with a particular constituency – the Mennonite peoplehood. This concern with cultivating and maintaining its constituency is a crucial part of figuring out how MCC works in practice. Clearly, for MCC administrators and staff workers, the field is only one part of the transnational operations of the organization.

CONCLUSION

The framing of MCC as a peoplehood movement takes place within this context of multiple entanglements with its constituency. These connections run so deep that MCC should be regarded as an integral part of the cultural fabric of many North American Mennonite communities. MCC's mandate for service derives from its constituency, and it continues to operate with remarkable, though not unchallenged, levels of support.[151] Mennonites actively participate in MCC and many feel a deep sense of ownership over it. It is not that every Mennonite community is active within the whole organization but, rather, that they own *their* part of the whole. Belonging is grounded in active involvement in a particular part. Vernacular Mennonite theological ideas also animate MCC's practices, with discourses on service, peace, and generosity helping shape the organization. The groundswell of moral ambitions for communal acts of giving and voluntarism is premised upon, and enacts, the theological imperatives that circulate widely around Mennonite communities. This theology of service supports and legitimizes MCC's extensive operations around the world.

But MCC does not just emanate from the peoplehood: it is itself constitutive of that peoplehood. MCC has played a pivotal role enabling the kind of interactions that produce this imagined community. However, Mennonite identity remains contested and in-process. Contrasting understandings of the peoplehood articulated among Mennonites and MCC are, necessarily, caught in the midst of these identity conflicts. This is because, at least since the Second World War, it has been one of the primary locations for the negotiation of Mennonite politics. Ambiguities of who exactly the peoplehood are (and are not), what influence they should have on MCC's practices, and what it means to represent the peoplehood to others are interwoven into MCC's everyday practices, including those in Indonesia.

While MCC can be framed as a peoplehood movement, this is not the only possible conceptualization. In her ethnography of NGOs in the

Philippines, Dorothea Hilhorst argues that "there is no single answer to the question of what an NGO is, what it wants and what it does."[152] Instead, she proposes:

> NGOs are many things at the same time. An NGO may adopt a certain structure, but in practice where are its boundaries? NGOs present different faces to different stakeholders, for instance in relating to donor representatives, clients or colleagues. Which is the real face, or, in case they are all real, what does that mean for our understanding of NGOs? There are always different ideas of what the NGO should be, among and within staff, management and stakeholders. How do these notions compete, and what role do they play in shaping the practice of the organization?

Accordingly, the framing of MCC as a peoplehood movement should be understood as just one of the ways in which MCC is conceptualized and performed, even if it is an especially prominent framing within MCC circles. The realization that NGOs present multiple faces, for Hilhorst, means that the most important question for her is not what an NGO is but, rather, how "NGO-ing" is done.[153] This involves a shift from understanding NGOs as "things" to conceptualizing them as ongoing open-ended processes in continual flux. Accordingly, while I start this chapter with the question "What is MCC?," and although I continue to pay attention to the different faces MCC presents in Indonesia, in what follows I am primarily interested in exploring how "MCC-ing" is done.

2

Translating Service

> MCC is a patchwork quilt. The workers of MCC come in different colors, patterns and textures. Some of us are old and worn, some of us are new and torn … We love the MCC quilt and take pride in its beauty and use. We cherish the history of the MCC quilt … Individually we are rags. Shaped, cut and sewn together we are a functional, beautiful "us."
>
> Bill Loewen[1]

PROBLEMS WITH LABELS

In the previous chapter I discuss the movement of MCC canned meat between an intractable constituency, who viewed the label as inalterable ("If MCC changes the label, I stop canning tomorrow"), and MCC's partner in Iraq, who viewed the same label as impossible. The Iraqi partner tearing off the label before distributing the cans operates as a vivid metaphor of cultural disjuncture. Between production and consumption, the object of canned meat wound its way across vast spatial and cultural distances and, in so doing, became entangled in new meanings and subjected to the effects of different moralities. As it moved into new terrains the social life of this development thing was contested and reworked.[2]

A similar story of the circulation of MCC's canned meat derives from its travels to Indonesia. In early 2007 an MCC staff member in Akron, Pennsylvania, initiated plans to ship cans to the Indonesian province of Nanggroe Aceh Darussalam (referred to hereafter simply as Aceh), which had been devastated by the massive December 2004 Indian Ocean earthquake and tsunami. His task was to locate destinations for shipments. The production of the cans takes place on an annual cycle, propelled by dynamics that are largely divorced from the needs of any specific recipient community. The MCC staff member's task was to dissolve a generic "needy" other and to replace it with specific consumers in actual places. To do this, the canned meat had to navigate its way through the convoluted politics of access. Given that it was over two years after the tsunami had devastated the coastlines of Sumatra, MCC staff in Indonesia were dubious about whether the distribution of canned meat was really an appropriate intervention at that time. The emergency phase of disaster relief was well and truly over, and so distributing food supplies was no longer seen as a high priority. Some thought that long-term initiatives, such as offering training in sustainable agriculture, would better facilitate durable food security than would dispersing large quantities of chunked turkey. But the Akron-based MCCer was persistent, and so Indonesia-based MCCers sought meetings with the appropriate Indonesian government officials to try to arrange a shipment. These discussions met a proverbial brick wall. The label's explicit Christianity – not least the boldly adorned proclamation that it was "In the name of Christ" – was a significant part of the officials' disinterest, if not distaste. The Aceh population is almost entirely Muslim, and it has a reputation of being especially pious, a fact that is acknowledged in the common slogan that Aceh is the "Veranda of Mecca." Indeed, following the tsunami disaster, Aceh experienced a significant growth in the movement to implement Islamic law in the province, reflecting new political, ethical, and legal ambitions to make the province increasingly Muslim.[3] Government officials and community leaders were consequently very sensitive to charges of Christian evangelism (In. *kristenisasi*), and anxieties were widespread that Christian missionaries would use the disaster as an opening to make incursions. The unambiguously Christian label was, unsurprisingly, considered inflammatory. Faced with a direct rebuff, MCC Indonesia staff called off the attempt to get the canned meat to Indonesia.

But the story did not end there. The Akron-based administrator was unconvinced that all avenues had been pursued. He doggedly continued to try to fulfil his mandate of getting the canned meat sent out. Bureaucratic concerns and collegial indifference were obstacles to be traversed. He consequently bypassed MCC staff in Indonesia and located another organization that agreed to seek to arrange shipment and distribution of the cans. This partner organization was called Tsunami Earthquake American Relief Services (TEARS). It was formed in January 2005 by the Lake Jackson Church of Christ, Texas, in response to the tsunami. Its work was mostly conducted in South Nias and consisted at first largely of short-term medical missions, in which American medical personnel would spend some weeks in Indonesia carrying out voluntary healthcare. A group of islands off the coast of Sumatra, Nias was also affected by the Indian Ocean earthquake and tsunami as well as another significant earthquake in March 2005. These disasters presented significant humanitarian challenges, but they were not on the same scale as the disasters faced by coastal Aceh. Unlike Aceh, however, the population of Nias is predominantly Protestant Christian. TEARS somehow arranged to have the cans pass through Indonesian customs. This was allowed on the basis that the cans would only be distributed in Nias. The cans got through, in this instance, with the labels still on.

This chapter initiates an analysis of *how* MCC – its objects, people, programs, and ideas – travels across cultural gaps. To do so I focus on translation practices and intermediaries.[4] The concepts of translation, brokerage, and mediation are key analytical terms in what David Mosse calls the "new ethnography of development."[5] This approach, rather than a formalized school, seeks to reinvigorate anthropological research into development by weaving between dominant trends of "interventionist developmentalism," characteristic of the development industry and burdened with concerns for policy prescriptions and expectations of instrumental applications, and the over-determinism of "post-development" critiques, which have tended to treat all actors as mere tools of imperial structures and thereby constructed images of an unassailable and monochrome development landscape.[6] Both tendencies displaced ethnographic imperatives, which emphasizes instead the value of textured, detailed description.[7] The new ethnography of development furnishes theoretically rich and detailed ethnography with interstitial brokers and translators positioned as pivotal agents. In examining practices of translation this chapter focuses on the workings of ambivalence, agency, and relationality.

Homi Bhabha notes the etymology of translation derives from the idea of "carrying over."[8] This implies a sense of transference and therefore of ongoing association. But as the tearing of the canned meat label vividly illustrates, travel also involves transformation and therefore a sense of departure and rupture. This is the intrinsic paradox of translation: it operates between connection and disconnection, continuity and disjuncture, bridges and borders.[9] This paradox is the source of an irresolvable yet productive ambivalence.

The sketch "A New MCC Project" (see figure 2.1), published in the MCC internal newsletter *Intercom* in 1979, offers a comical meditation on this paradox.[10] This chapter is essentially an elucidation of this graphic with illustrations drawn from MCC's work in Indonesia. As the sketch so aptly illustrates, development projects are collaborations between multiple actors who hold divergent visions. In the interactions between these actors, development projects are transformed from initial

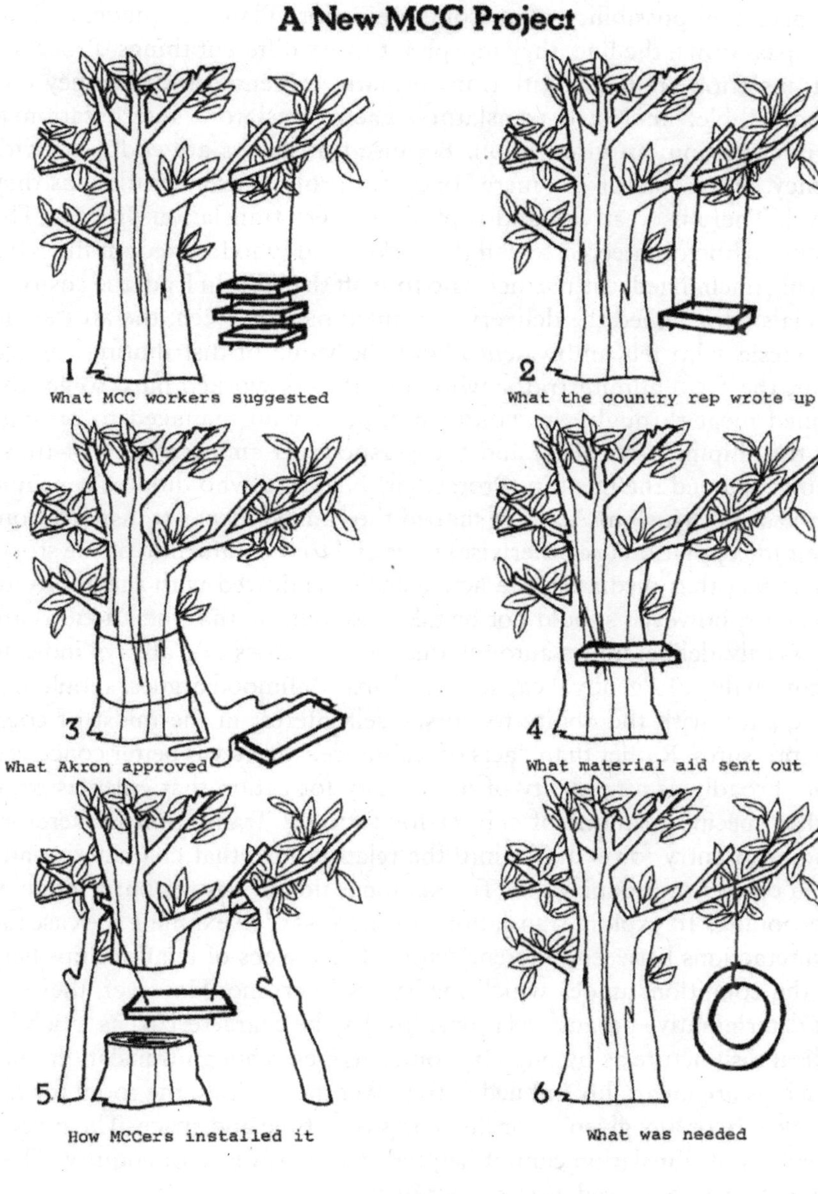

Figure 2.1 | A new MCC project, artist unknown

imaginings to actual implementation. Embedded in these exchanges is the perennial possibility of miscommunication. Plans are made, and, as they pass down the line, they morph into very different things. Processes of translation are laden with transformative potential because they rely upon fallible, interested translators. Each translator's interpolation is an intervention, an interjection. Because translators are endowed with agency, no translator is a mere conduit.[11] Projects are reworked as they travel. There is creativity and rupture in every translation process. The donors who volunteered to can the turkey and who insisted on the label staying unchanged, the partner who tore off the label in Iraq, the customs officials who denied the delivery of canned meat in Aceh, the MCCers in Indonesia who felt ambivalent about the value of distributing canned meat, the MCC administrator who nevertheless worked hard to get the canned meat through, the TEARS personnel who managed to arrange for the shipment to Nias, and the perspectives and practices of those who consumed the meat in (Protestant) Nias and who did not consume the meat in (Muslim) Aceh all shaped the canned meat's transportation. Their interpolation (or otherwise) is crucial to the unfurling of the story.

The fact that mediators are active agents endowed with the ability to intervene, however, should not be taken to indicate that their actions are necessarily deliberate or autonomous. Agency does not always indicate intentionality.[12] Agentival capacity, as Saba Mahmood argues, should not be equated with the ability to pursue self-interest in the midst of coercive pressures. Rather than "acts of resistance," agency is better conceived more broadly as a modality of or capacity for action that emerges from within specific relations of subject formation.[13] Translation is therefore a point of entry for enquires into the relationships that characterize any given project or organization. Translation is not an answer but a mode of questioning. To explore translation, it is necessary to examine the cascade of interactions between different actors. These webs of relationships help set the conditions under which mediators intervene. However, they are not determinative because relationships may be characterized as much by radical disjuncture as by ongoing connectivities. Though translation relationships are invariably imbued with power inequalities, the room for the manoeuvre of any given actor fluctuates over time and space. The precise dynamics of translation cannot be predicted in advance of enquiry. They can, however, be traced after the act of translation.

In the study of the unequal, disjunctive, and complex transnational flows, development scholars have sometimes used the metaphor of an "aid chain."[14] During my field research I used the idea of an aid chain on a number of occasions to try to frame how MCC worked in practice.[15]

Towards the end of my fieldwork, however, I was taken to task over this conceptualization. Anna Friesen suggested that it was an inappropriate metaphor for the dynamics that informed MCC's work. For Anna, "aid chain" conveyed connotations of linearity, apparent also in the comical sketch "A New MCC Project." Its metallic imagery also implied inflexibility and rigidity. Anna suggested that it be replaced with the metaphor of a "patchwork quilt," a Mennonite-friendly image that intimated a diffuse and softer relationality across multimodal networks. Bill Lowen's epigraph (also from *Intercom*) at the start of this chapter illustrates that the image of MCC as a patchwork quilt has a long history within the organization. The particular aesthetics of quilting – evoking rural traditionalism, functionality, beauty, simplicity, piety, and a (gendered) labour of love – resonates powerfully among many ethnic Mennonites. Of course, in celebrating the constitution of an "us" from disparate, disjointed "rags," Loewen's patchwork quilt immediately raises questions about the boundaries of this "us." This chapter probes the practices within, and the constitution of, the MCC patchwork quilt. The first two sections centre on MCC's post-tsunami response in Aceh, and the final examines the practices of partnership in the delivery of education scholarships in Central Java.

INTERPOLATING MEDIATORS IN POST-TSUNAMI ACEH

The Indian Ocean earthquake and tsunami of 24 December 2004 left a swathe of destruction in its wake. In Indonesia alone 170,000 died and over 500,000 were displaced.[16] But such figures are inadequate to describe the swathe of destruction along coastal Aceh and Nias. All humanitarian actors responding to the disaster had to grapple with the sheer scale of what had happened. Humanitarian projects after major disasters are extraordinarily complex. A series of complicating factors in northern Sumatra exacerbated these considerably. Most important was that Aceh had been embroiled in a protracted thirty-year guerrilla war between the Movement to Liberate Aceh (Gerakan Aceh Merdeka, GAM) and the Indonesian military.[17] This pervasive conflict meant that humanitarians were responding to a dual disaster, the effects of which were multiplied by their proximity. One effect of the conflict was that very few NGOs were operating in Aceh at the time of the tsunami. While associational networks through mosques and Islamic organizations were strong, there were few civil society organizations operating in the early 2000s with links to international humanitarian networks. The lack of established local humanitarian actors helped contribute to a particularly chaotic disaster relief process during the early months, which was rife with "confusion and distrust."[18]

A further complication was the sheer volume of aid that came in the wake of the tsunami. Throughout the 1990s there was an exponential growth of NGOs in Indonesia.[19] Gaining momentum during the *reformasi* (In. political reform movement) period, the collapse of Suharto's New Order in 1998 saw politics shoot off in multiple directions. In early 2005 the tsunami of relief finances crashed into these fledgling organizations with requirements of unprecedented expansions in size, volume, and sophistication of their projects. This was "the most rapidly and generously funded disaster response in history."[20] The sheer volume of funds led to competition between donor agencies as they sought partners to assist in meeting the requirements of aid conditionality, including the demand to expend budgets in tight time frames. This aid "wave" crashed into the Acehnese social and political landscapes, with lingering downstream effects throughout the Indonesian NGO sector.

At the time of the tsunami, MCC Indonesia had a disaster response plan in place, prepared in the early 2000s by Anna and Jake Friesen, the MCC Reps. This plan not only responded to the apparent susceptibility of the archipelago to natural hazard events but also acknowledged the limitations of MCC as a small organization. The plan outlined how MCC would only engage in disaster relief work in areas where it already had active partnerships. In 2004, this effectively limited MCC's disaster response work to Central Java and parts of Papua. In the early days after the tsunami, in accordance with the disaster response plan, MCC Indonesia made preparations to channel whatever donations were given to MCC through to other organizations that were establishing operations in the disaster area. It soon became clear that this was untenable. The scale of donor response was unprecedented, and MCC was inundated with funds. MCC administrators in North America instructed MCC Indonesia to initiate its own program. The designated tsunami funds eventually added over US$10 million to MCC Indonesia's budget, which at that time was only around US$700,000 per annum.[21] These funds were to be spent over just three years. As with many organizations involved in the relief process, MCC's work was a case of supply-driven relief.[22]

In its first few months the new MCC Aceh program sought to ground its relief programs by hiring staff and forming new partnerships. I discuss each in turn. The initial staffing of MCC's Banda Aceh office was by North American short-term volunteers. These volunteers were all MCC alumni and, like other expatriate MCCers, most were ethnic Mennonites.

Some had previous experience of working in development projects, but none were trained specialists in disaster management. Over the first nine months the office had five different coordinators. North American teams of volunteers were also brought in to undertake relief work. Only a few of these short-term workers had previous experience in Indonesia, and they therefore lacked both language and other cultural capabilities. MCC's high staff turnover at this time meant that the program was slow to gain traction and focus. Each new coordinator brought new expectations and had to establish new relationships with staff and partners, creating a disjointed and transitory effect. Over time, this unstable and precarious situation was eased through two mechanisms.

Initially, Anna and Jake Friesen, as part of their country-wide mandate to lead MCC in Indonesia, had overall responsibility for MCC's work in Aceh. However, as they were based in Central Java and were still tasked with overseeing the rest of MCC's programs in Indonesia, they were not in a position to deal with the extra administrative load required for daily management of the disaster response in Aceh. A program coordinator was clearly needed who would play a hands-on management role over the Aceh programs. Willis Bender, an American Mennonite, was appointed to this role. He arrived in Aceh in mid-November 2005. Willis coordinated MCC's response in Aceh for the remainder of the tsunami relief and reconstruction program, which formally concluded in June 2008. Willis was competent in Bahasa Indonesia as he had previously been an MCC service worker in the province of Papua. He had also previously worked with other NGOs, including in post-independence East Timor and, briefly, in Aceh in the immediate aftermath of the disaster. He therefore was familiar with the idioms and practices of "Aidland" – the transnational culture of humanitarianism[23] – as well as those specific to MCC and Indonesia. This "rhetorical competence" in a range of intersecting domains was a major strength.[24] Willis could be regarded as an archetypal "interface expert."[25]

However, Willis's role in Aceh was ambiguous in the structure of MCC. Reflecting the ambiguities of North American Mennonite politics, MCC fieldwork is located in the midst of tensions between centralized hierarchy and decentralized egalitarianism. These tensions are constantly in flux, but a long-standing tradition has privileged a "field-driven" approach as normative in the organization. This arrangement can be traced back to the "concern movement" in the 1950s, which challenged the centralized decision-making practices then characterizing MCC and other Mennonite organizations. The concern movement was composed of an informal group of young American Mennonite men based in postwar Europe. Most were relief workers, but the group also included Mennonite graduate students and missionaries. They held a series of meetings and produced pamphlets for wider circulation that critiqued the Mennonite church in Europe and in the US based on historical and social analysis and a revisionist Anabaptist theology.[26] As part of this project they challenged the leadership style of Akron-based MCC management, which had a reputation for domineering and unilateral leadership, and argued for greater devolution of authority as being a better fit with historical Anabaptist ethics and theology. The pattern of MCC as a field-driven organization emerged as a direct consequence of the concern movement's incisive critique.

In practice, the field-driven model meant that the MCC Reps, as the highest level of in-country leadership, accrued considerable authority in MCC's organizational structure and were endowed with wide-ranging powers to develop and manage programs as they saw fit.[27] This system shares remarkable continuities with North American Mennonite bishopric church politics. In the case of Willis's appointment to head up MCC's work in Aceh it had to be determined where in MCC's structural hierarchy he would be located. Of importance were questions of whether he would operate as a "Country Representative" himself (and therefore locate Aceh as a separate unit within MCC's structure) or work under the leadership of Anna and Jake in Central Java.[28] The former would provide the Aceh coordinator with significantly more room for manoeuvre. The negotiation of these political relationships was, for a period of months prior to Willis's arrival, a locus of heated debate. The eventual resolution was to preserve the status quo in which Aceh programs fell under Indonesian MCC leadership. Anna and Jake maintained overall responsibility, and Willis was accountable to their leadership. As a consequence, the normal route of communication from Willis's office in Banda Aceh to North American offices was via the MCC country office in Central Java. While this solution resolved the ambiguities of leadership, it inserted an additional node of intermediation into MCC's informational flows, which remained a point of contention throughout the duration of the tsunami response. These ongoing tensions about where authority was best located, and circumvented, neatly illustrate the negotiations involved in implementing organizational innovation to deliver MCC's tsunami response program.

The other mechanism of stabilizing MCC's response in Aceh was to recruit Indonesian staff members to work on tsunami relief projects. The MCC Reps asked their Indonesian office staff to contact International

Volunteer Exchange Program (IVEP) alumni to invite them to work with MCC in Aceh. Just as with its North American staff, MCC therefore sourced its Indonesian staff from among its existing relationships. IVEP sends young people to the US and Canada on an eleven-month youth exchange. Many of these young people come from countries in which MCC has active development, relief, and peacebuilding programs. The three Javanese staff members that eventually made up the core of the Indonesian staff team in Aceh were all ex-IVEPers. They were all also members of Indonesian Mennonite churches, and two were children of Indonesian Mennonite pastors.[29] Their association with Indonesian Mennonite churches was part of an intentional effort to include Indonesian Mennonites in the tsunami response work.

None of the Indonesian staff had previous experience in development or humanitarian work. Their primary competencies, as sought by MCC, appear to have been translation capacity, with the ability to speak fluent English and Indonesian, and their familiarity with MCC and North American Mennonites, as a consequence of their experience in IVEP. The Indonesian staff members were tasked with logistics, translation, and other support roles. Although initially on a voluntary basis the roles later became salaried. None of these Indonesian staff had previously lived in Aceh, and they did not have language skills in Acehnese, which is widely used throughout Aceh and is unintelligible to speakers of Indonesian. Each found that they were perceived by at least some Acehnese as being foreigners, or even intruders. They too, therefore, had to work hard to translate and connect with Acehnese. During my field research MCC had only one staff member, the office driver, who was Acehnese and Muslim. I was told by MCCers in Aceh that despite his somewhat ambiguous status – he was on the MCC payroll but was not considered part of the MCC Indonesia "team" – he played a particularly pivotal role in translating and interpreting between Acehnese partners and MCC workers.[30] The workload in MCC Indonesia's main office in Central Java was also burgeoning with tsunami-related work, and so new Indonesian staff members were hired at this time to help ease additional administrative requirements.

The second initiative for grounding MCC in Aceh was to form organizational partnerships. MCC Indonesia has worked with partner organizations since its earliest days in the country. However, the practice of partnership and its place within MCC's overall operations in Indonesia has changed considerably over time. With Anna and Jake Friesen's arrival in Indonesia in 2001, partnerships were elevated into the primary mechanism through which MCC's work was conducted.[31]

The implementation of the new partnership model at this time resulted in the closure of many of MCC's programs running at that time, which now no longer fit the preferred model. The motivation for implementing a partnership-only mechanism for programs was ethical: for Anna and Jake all MCC's work should be carried out through partners in order to support local organizations and Indonesian action for change. The intent was therefore decolonial. Rather than disseminating North American organizational forms and priorities, partnership enabled MCC to assist in the emergence of independent, endogenous organizations that, because they were local, could operate appropriately and have greater longevity than a foreign organization.

The ideal of partnerships in MCC Indonesia was less a technical matter than a relational one. The purpose was not expertise transfer but, rather, relational rapport and an imperative to work alongside. The partnership process was shaped by moralities of mutuality, which were seen as the only viable way through which external and local agencies could work productively and responsibly together. As such it relied on a marked sense of difference between MCC as a "foreign" entity and the "local" partners. While MCC Indonesia's shift to a partnership model reflects trends in the wider development industry, in which, since the late 1990s, the term became a key "buzzword" in development discourse, MCC's partnership discourse also reflected the logics of a Christian ideal of non-coercive interaction, itself cultivated in Mennonite theologies of peacefulness.[32]

The relative lack of a formal NGO relief sector in Aceh was problematic for MCC but not debilitating. Anna and Jake maintained their openness to engaging with organizations that lacked formal status as either an institute (In. *lembaga*) or a foundation (In. *yayasan*) with the Indonesian government.[33] MCC worked with similarly informal organizational structures in both Central Java and Papua. However, the lack of pre-existing partnerships in Aceh was a significant challenge. The absence of established relationships coupled with entering into a decidedly unfamiliar context led to significant debate within different parts of MCC as to whether the partnership model was the most appropriate mechanism for delivering efficient and effective relief. The most prominent alternative to working solely through local partners was to revert to the prior model of MCC directly managing its own operational projects. This would have necessitated a substantially larger staff team and also required a shift in the moral logics of MCC Indonesia's approach to service. Discussion of this issue was often tense. The final decision was to continue with the partnership model for MCC's relief and reconstruction work in Aceh. Consequently, MCC's staff team would remain small, but it also had to quickly locate viable partners. All of MCC's disaster response partnerships were new.

At first the forging of these partnerships was a frantic scramble. MCCers attended snap meetings in Jakarta and elsewhere with environmental organizations (including the Wahana Lingkungan Hidup Indonesia/Indonesian Forum for Environment, WALHI), Christian NGO networks (including Jaringan Kerja Lembaga Pelayanan Kristen/Network of Christian Service Organizations, JKLPK), and with sundry other potential partners. MCC eventually arranged to work with twenty-four different partner organizations, with partnerships varying between one-off short-term engagements to others that lasted for almost the full three years of its operations in Aceh. Partnerships involved Muslim, Christian, and interfaith organizations. MCCers were particularly proactive in seeking partnerships with organizations affiliated with the Indonesian Mennonite Churches, all of which were based in Central Java and none of which had any previous presence in the affected areas.

Some of MCC's partnerships in Aceh were fraught with tension. Formed in the cauldron of a highly pressured relief context involving large financial expenditure, tight timeframes, and unfamiliar relationships, it is unsurprising that some partnerships faced turbulent encounters and a few ended in disappointment. In one case some money – 60 million Indonesian rupiah (around US$6,000) – was apparently siphoned off by the staff members of a partner organization. In another case involving a partner affiliated with Indonesian Mennonite churches, finances were not adequately accounted for within MCC's financial system. In this case, the discrepancy was thought to be due to mismanagement rather than corruption. The lack of formal status for some of MCC's partners was accompanied by highly flexible structures, loose membership, and informal leadership. On several occasions MCCers in Aceh wondered whether some of the partnerships were *organizational* at all, or whether they were merely with key individuals with a shadow of an organizational structure in place simply as a public performance of legitimation. Such situations raised accountability concerns. Many partnerships went through rocky periods as the respective spokespersons learned to interact with each other and to respond to the fast-changing conditions in which they were working. A sense of shared expectations and interpersonal rapport – so critical for the practice of partnership but often ignored in technocratic development discourse – had little time to develop during this frantic start-up period. The actual work of initiating and running partnerships was slow, convoluted, and laborious. Only in the latter half of MCC's three-year stint in Aceh did its programs begin to stabilize.

The projects that MCC supported in Aceh were remarkably diverse, almost appearing to be haphazard. Many of them represented a significant departure from "normal" practice elsewhere in MCC Indonesia at that time. In the kinds of work it supported MCC looked and behaved a lot like other humanitarian NGOs. Its identity as a "peoplehood movement" was muted and backgrounded, although not completely effaced, as the example of canned meat illustrates. Initially, MCC focused a significant number of its programs on education organizations, including a medical school, an agriculture faculty, an Aceh-based Islamic university, and various groups associated with Christian and state universities in Central Java. While some of these groups had expertise in areas that they could draw upon in disaster relief work, many of their activities fell beyond their professional mandates and represented an active entrepreneurialism in the context of Aceh's organizational vacuum. MCC pursued these initial educational partnerships because MCC's legal status in Indonesia was, at the time, based on an "in process" (i.e., submitted but unsigned) Memorandum of Understanding with the Ministry of Education. The goal was to remain as much as possible within the education sector so as to help buttress MCC's (notably ambiguous) status with the Indonesian government. These education partnerships, however, were not restricted to educational activities. Over time the gamut of activities expanded along with increasing access for foreign NGO personnel due to changes to government regulation of disaster relief and reconstruction processes.

In the immediate aftermath of the tsunami, MCC supported various clean-up tasks, medical assistance, and the distribution of relief supplies. It also carried out work in trauma healing, agriculture, and education. However, the most significant area of expenditure was infrastructure, with two-thirds of its budget going towards construction projects.[34] This emphasis on later phases in the disaster management cycle reflected a widespread view among MCCers that they were better placed to be involved in reconstruction work than in more immediate emergency response initiatives. It also drew on Mennonite peace theology and ethics. Peter Redfield argues that the methods and practices of the crisis-focused humanitarian agency Doctors Without Borders derived from military strategies first deployed during conflict situations.[35] Clear lines of command, medical "kits," quantitative assessments for triage, the prioritization of efficiency and technical expertise, and a focus on "saving life" (rather than promoting the good for which life is saved), all recall militaristic origins. In contrast, MCC's grounding in the experience of Mennonite peace theology meant it was less inclined towards practices of emergency response. The emphasis on forming warm relationships, the insistence on involving volunteers rather than professionals, the choice of the partnership model for delivery of services, a relatively weak capacity to implement a speedy response, and the stress on reconstruction all draw upon the peace theology that infused the organization.[36] An additional attraction of construction projects was that they are able to absorb significant finances through single partnerships, thereby allowing for high-expenditure interventions. The largest projects that MCC supported included major relief housing (In. *rumah bantuan*) projects and a school complex.

One prominent issue within reconstruction partnerships concerned how MCC, as a Mennonite Christian organization, would engage with Acehnese Muslims.[37] Here there was considerable ambiguity. While MCC actively sought out partnerships with Muslim organizations (and given that Aceh was overwhelmingly Muslim, it would have been very difficult to completely avoid them), some MCCers expressed wariness about the kinds of projects that were enacted. On one occasion, Anna Friesen noted her relief that MCC did not have to build a mosque attached to the school complex with which MCC was involved. However, Willis Bender told me that if another Muslim organization had not already offered to build the mosque, MCC would have happily done so. At one point the MCC staff in Aceh initiated a partnership with an Islamic university, but this was cancelled from higher up in the organization, with the reason being that (as an MCCer in Aceh told me): "We are not supporting the spread of Muslim teaching." These sorts of disagreements also took place within the MCC Aceh staff team over the construction of *meunasah*. One Indonesian staff member argued against supporting the construction of these buildings within their housing construction projects. The objection concerned questions as to whether *meunasah* were prayer rooms or community meeting places. While they are not mosques, *meunasah* are used throughout Aceh as spaces of Islamic prayer and for learning to recite the Quran. However, *meunasah* are also the de facto location for many community meetings and can also serve as dormitories for adolescent men.[38] While at first MCC avoided building *meunasah*, they eventually did provide funds for a partner to construct them. However, in written reports to be sent back to MCC head offices in North America *meunasah* was translated as "community meeting place." This explanation was supplemented with a further note indicating its potential use for learning the Quran and prayer.[39]

In placing personnel and forming partnerships during the first few months of its work in Aceh, MCC sought to commission the necessary "go-betweens" needed to become a humanitarian NGO able to operate in that context.[40] Without these Aceh-based intermediaries who could broker relationships between different actors, initiating projects was impossible. However, effective intermediation is never straightforward. Some of the partnerships failed. Others were worked through only with great and persistent effort. It was also difficult to locate staff willing to go to Aceh and work in a high-stress environment. When a staff team was put in place, the members experienced considerable tension in their interpersonal relationships within the transnationally dispersed MCC as well as with partners. These mediators were caught in the midst of the differences emerging from their intercalary positions. Such differences included cultural and linguistic practices as well as expectations and goals. The disagreements within MCC over construction of *meunasah* and the school mosque – with some encouraging construction, some resisting, and others opposing MCC's support – illustrates that a range of positions were taken on particular issues. The fault lines, and what they meant, were not predictable in advance. While the sketch at the start of this chapter correctly emphasizes differences of perspectives on MCC projects, it doesn't adequately illustrate the relationships between these differences. As the various visions of MCC's operations interacted, these differences were negotiated and contested. The next section builds upon this discussion by exploring a specific set of relationships around a particular object-in-translation.

TRANSLATING AN EIA

Among MCCers the most universally praised partner organization in Aceh was undoubtedly GenAssist. The partnership between MCC and GenAssist was formed eighteen months after MCC began work in Aceh, after the initial turmoil of initiating programs. The partnership was worked out in a less stressful time, when extended conversations could be had and relationships formed without the demand of immediate activities. The story I address in this section focuses on the collaboration between MCC and GenAssist in a *rumah bantuan* construction project. However, the translations I trace extend well beyond the Aceh context and incorporate multiple organizations and networks. Central to this narrative is that, while GenAssist received MCC funds, MCC received substantial funding from the Canadian International Development Agency (CIDA), the now defunct Canadian official government development agency. These funds were provided via a matching grant that CIDA made available to Canadian NGOs. The object that was translated, in this case in quite literal as well as more metaphorical senses, was an environmental impact assessment (EIA) report. The EIA was a conditionality of CIDA funding. Both the involvement of CIDA funds (which MCC Indonesia has tended not to channel) and the EIA (the only example of such a requirement that took place during my fieldwork) make this example unusual for MCC in Indonesia. Nevertheless, it throws into sharp relief issues of translation within, through, and by MCC. Rather than focusing on the content of the EIA, I am interested in processes, communication practices, and relationships.

The first time I heard about this EIA was in a coffee shop (In. *kedai kopi*) in Banda Aceh during a conversation with Jed, an American MCC service worker in his twenties. We had started our evening over a dinner of root beer floats and curly fries at A&W, a recently opened American fast food chain in Banda Aceh catering to humanitarian workers from Jakarta and overseas. Jed patronized it occasionally as something of a guilty pleasure, knowing that its conspicuous foreignness ran against the grain of an MCC ethic to "go local." It was midnight and we had already visited three other coffee shops. Fixed-up on caffeine and clothes reeking of clove cigarettes (In. *kretek*) we spent the evening chatting about MCC and Jed's experience of expatriate life in Aceh. It was in his role as an MCC liaison with GenAssist that Jed came to know about the EIA story he told me that night. Following from this initial conversation I sought to follow the transnational flows by later interviewing others who were also involved at different places and times.[41] This is my retelling of these collated narratives.

In his first assignment for MCC Indonesia Jed was seconded to an Indonesian NGO based in rural Aceh. Secondment is the primary mechanism by which expatriate MCCers work in Indonesia, and Jed's assignment was in keeping with the main contours of the general model. At the time of my interview with Jed this secondment had fallen apart. This was the partner, mentioned earlier, who had siphoned money into private pockets. Numerous MCCers told me how this partner was rife with corruption, managerial coerciveness, collegial vindictiveness, and a remarkable level of inactivity. The incidents that led up to the eventual closure of this partnership were perhaps the most bitter in MCC's experience in Aceh, and the slow devolution of this partnership had personally been a painful experience for Jed. With the collapse of this partnership, Jed had been reassigned to work with GenAssist, but this time, and unusually, not as a secondee but as a "partner advisor" based within MCC. The role of partner advisors was usually only held by Indonesian staff. Jed was the only expatriate service worker during my field research that was involved in this role.

As noted above, the logic of partnership pursued in MCC Indonesia was that, as a foreign entity, MCC would partner with local Indonesian NGOs that were seen, as a consequence of their localness, as legitimate transformative agents in Indonesian politics and society. However, in this case GenAssist was not a *local* organization; or at least it was "local" only in some senses and not others. While it was registered as a local NGO with the Indonesian government and was led by an Indonesian manager, organizationally it was indivisible from another North American-based Christian NGO, the Christian Reformed World Relief Committee (CRWRC). GenAssist was directly accountable to North American leadership and was seen, by CRWRC staff, as entirely coterminous with their organization. It is therefore ironic that MCC formed a strong and ongoing partnership with GenAssist given its own refusal to become operational in Aceh due to a self-identified extraneous identity. As is often the case, this mistranslation was crucial to propelling the collaboration.[42] This irony was clearly noted among MCCers themselves. It is apparent in the initial reluctance among MCCers to partner with GenAssist – a hesitation that eventually gave way on account of the pressing need to spend the allocated budget as quickly as possible.[43]

Some MCCers suggested to me that a key reason they experienced such a strong rapport with GenAssist was because it exhibited North American cultural norms and expectations that made for a better, easier "fit." This included such mundane matters as the ability to provide reports on time and to a desired standard of clarity. Particularly important in this regard was the American Country Team leader who, though not based in Aceh, was extensively involved in helping organize the relief work. GenAssist conformed to the professional requirements of CRWRC, and this ensured a mutual sharing of expectations. Moreover, MCC and CRWRC had an extensive history of working together on various projects, including collaborating in founding the Canadian Food Grains Bank (CFGB) in 1983. Contrasting this view, other MCCers suggested to me that the close rapport existed because GenAssist had a talented Indonesian field manager and professional, diligent, and skilled Acehnese staff. These local GenAssist staff members were adroit in navigating the complex worlds of Acehnese society, religion, and politics.

This view held that it was because GenAssist was thoroughly Indonesian that it was such a proficient and effective partner. I regard the apparent contradiction between these two assessments as illusory. In fact, the two suggestions are equally plausible, and the differing assessments merely highlight the inherent ambivalence stemming from GenAssist's intercalary position.

Before forming their own partnership, MCCers had a chance to assess GenAssist's previous involvement in constructing 550 *rumah bantuan*, partly with CIDA funds, in the Blang Mee area in North Aceh. This project was greatly admired. It was on the back of this initial success that MCC sought out GenAssist to undertake further reconstruction projects. In June 2006 the partnership was officially formed and GenAssist staff started searching for a suitable site for the new project. Eventually, Meunasah Lhok (also in North Aceh) was selected in negotiation with the Government Coordination Agency for Rehabilitation and Reconstruction (Badan Rehabilitasi dan Rekonstruksi, BRR). MCC then began the process of submitting an application for CIDA funds to assist in the construction. CIDA had expressed its interest in supporting housing reconstruction projects, and this was a significant area of CIDA funding.[44] The Meunasah Lhok project was small-scale in comparison to some others, with only two hundred houses designated in the project design. *Rumah bantuan* were permanent concrete constructions that replaced the militaristic-sounding "barracks camps," temporary shelters, in which displaced persons were housed in the first few months after the disaster.[45]

In the 1980s the Canadian government sought to situate itself as a "progressive" actor in emerging environment and development debates. This included the introduction in 1986 of environmental screening and assessments for CIDA projects. The impetus for this new emphasis was a mix of political imperatives under both Liberal and Conservative governments, including ongoing disputes with the Reagan administration over acid rain, the popularizing force of the Brundtland Commission (convened between 1983 and 1987), and the highly publicized Bhopal (1984) and Chernobyl (1986) disasters, which generated considerable outrage and concern among the Canadian public.[46] The shift to prioritizing "the environment" in the 1980s, and then "sustainability" in the 1990s, was part of a broader process of "chasing fashions."[47] CIDA's apparent new environmental consciousness saw the rolling out of environment-related procedures, which gained in momentum in the lead-up to the 1992 Rio Earth Summit. The EIA – a "rendering technical" of this policy focus[48] – became mandatory for CIDA-funded projects with the passing into law of the Canadian Environmental Assessment Act, also in 1992. Consequently, when MCC sought funding from CIDA in 2006 it was required to carry out an EIA.

The EIA for the Meunasah Lhok project was conducted by an Indonesian environmental consultant hired by MCC in Aceh. The report was written in Bahasa Indonesia, the bureaucratic and technical language of Indonesian business, science, and consultancy. It was then submitted to GenAssist and MCC offices in Banda Aceh. CIDA required that reports written in Bahasa Indonesia be translated into English or French to be comprehensible to program staff in Ottawa. The EIA was then sent to MCC staff in Salatiga who sought translation assistance from a Javanese Indonesian language teacher in Central Java.[49] The translated report was then sent from MCC Indonesia to the CIDA liaison team, which was in the Winnipeg office of Mennonite Central Committee Canada (MCCC). MCCC was a part of the federation of MCC entities in North America and was legally distinct from MCC, which has its headquarters in Akron, Pennsylvania, which was called "MCC binational" or, more often, simply "Akron" by organizational insiders. At the time of this research, MCC binational was predominantly tasked with administering MCC's international program, which was sometimes described as the "North Star," a navigational allusion pointing both to its priority as well as to the fact that the horizon is cluttered with numerous other potential interests. But MCC binational was not the only entity responsible for international work. Among the exceptions to this general rule was the fact that CIDA funds were channelled through MCCC as a Canadian NGO. While these funds were then distributed through field programs administered by MCC binational, MCCC maintained some involvement in administration and project management. Accordingly, the usual organizational and informational hierarchy that flowed from Banda Aceh through the MCC Reps in Salatiga and on to Akron was reworked in this case such that MCCC was also an active transnational participant.

The long-distance communication of and about the EIA largely took place through the medium of e-mail. Since the late 1990s e-mail has become a ubiquitous part of NGO business-as-usual and is now virtually obligatory for performing even the most mundane tasks. The widespread adoption of e-mail during the 1990s substantially reshaped NGO activities and politics. The possibility of instantaneous global communication via e-mail and other information technologies restructured decision-making processes and facilitated new patterns of authority. For MCC, e-mail contributed to an erosion of the "field-driven" philosophy, which was institutionalized in the 1970s and 1980s, by enabling a recentralization of authority and by reducing the relative independence of in-country decision making. Whereas earlier reliance on slow and unreliable postage systems promoted autonomy and flexibility for field-based leadership, by the turn of the millennium even relatively minor decisions could be made quickly and with little cost by managers located thousands of kilometres away. These technologically driven innovations, however, remained permeated with ambiguity. This is partially because widespread e-mail usage resulted in vastly increased informational traffic, which has been at least as debilitating as empowering. Willis Bender, for example, produced regular detailed reports of MCC's work in Aceh and e-mailed them to his supervisors in Salatiga and Akron. But he was told by a senior MCC administrator in Akron that these regular and comprehensive reports were practically never read due to the large volume of e-mails already occupying the administrator's in-box. The ability of distant managers, including the MCC Reps, to intervene in decision making was enhanced through the medium of e-mail, but the capacity to process the information flows was not. The entire EIA translation process I narrate here would have played out very differently if the medium of communication had been the postal system.

It is important to note that CIDA government funding has long been controversial within MCC. MCC has refused to channel finances from the parallel American government development agency, the United States Agency for International Development (USAID), on the grounds that to do so would associate the organization with American imperialism and compromise its goal of presenting a distinctly Christian (and peaceable, non-imperial) alternative. USAID funding would have been inconceivable to most MCCers in Indonesia. Associated with the rejection of partnership with USAID is a residue of Mennonite two-kingdom theology, with its sharp demarcation between church and state and a belief in the value of embodying a separate Anabaptist Christian presence. However, MCCC actively sought CIDA grants since 1968, only five years after the Canadian organization was founded and in the very same year in which CIDA itself was created by Pierre Trudeau's Liberal government.[50] During my research Canadian Mennonites and MCCers expressed to me a sense of considerable pride that MCC had earned the respect of their government so that they were trusted to channel funding through the organization. This situation reflected a marked difference in approach to the politics of nationalism and citizenship compared to many American MCCers. Unsurprisingly, some American MCCers remained deeply suspicious of CIDA funding, and there was significant antipathy towards CIDA funding among MCC's field staff. A CIDA liaison team member in Winnipeg suggested to me that the primary reason for this field resentment of CIDA was the added administrative burden placed on field staff. The additional bureaucratic requirements were undoubtedly a factor. However, in Ontario I interviewed Elizabeth Detweiler, another Canadian MCCer, who suggested that tensions existed over a perceived lack of appreciation by CIDA staff for MCC's emphasis on "relationship building." I was told that CIDA "want statistics and 'we have a good relationship' just doesn't cut it." There was also a sense of wariness among some MCCers about the threat of "secularization" as a consequence of CIDA's reluctance to sponsor "mission" activities.[51] Despite these tensions, CIDA grants made up a not insignificant portion of MCC's overall finances. This flow of funds was disrupted in 2011 when CIDA rejected a large MCC funding request.[52] Then the partnership folded in March 2013 when the Canadian government dissolved CIDA as a separate entity, and its work was brought into a renamed Department of Foreign Affairs, Trade and Development.

To return to MCC's preparation of the EIA, the general pattern of communication for this report within the various parts of MCC was established early in the process at the insistence of Robert Fast. Robert was an MCCC staff member in Winnipeg who was both Mennonite and a former CIDA employee and therefore, as he put it, ideally situated as a "facilitator" between the organizations. Robert urged that communication over the EIA should be direct between himself and Willis Bender in Banda Aceh. This was necessary, Robert told me, so as to avoid "transmission-with-qualifiers" and lackadaisical flows of information. He saw the normal informational cascades through multiple other MCC intermediaries as unnecessarily cumbersome. As noted above, this arrangement was unusual in MCC Indonesia, where communication with North American offices took place primarily via Anna and Jake, the MCC Reps. When the EIA arrived on Robert's desk in Winnipeg, however, he considered the translated text to be incomprehensible; it was a "bastardized translation" he told me. It had to be substantially reworked into passable English before it was sent on to Ottawa.

CIDA was a major official development bureaucratic organization, but it was neither static nor mechanical. As they exchanged e-mails and phone calls, Robert and the other MCCC staff in Winnipeg interacted with people, not machines. They learned that they had to tailor their communications differently with each of the three CIDA country "desks" (Sri Lanka, India, and Indonesia) connected with tsunami funding as different personnel had different preferences and approaches.

They experienced particular frustration with the Indonesia desk. While a project officer in CIDA was generally assigned to a particular desk on a three-year rotation and could during that time provide some sense of continuity and communicate clear expectations, in this case the personnel in charge of the Indonesia desk changed three times in six months. These changes caused substantial delays and renegotiations. One MCCer described it as an example of "basic bureaucratic incompetence and sloppiness." Normal CIDA communication flows included a geographically dispersed set of actors, including CIDA staff in the country office in Jakarta and personnel in Aceh as well as those at the (high turnover) Ottawa desk. This communication chain covered much of the same geography as MCC's but through entirely distinct channels.

When CIDA received the (retranslated) report and a project officer had processed it, the report was then sent on to a Canadian consultancy for review. The consultancy hired an environmental technical expert to review the report. Unfortunately, the consultant was on vacation at this time and so the review process took considerably longer than had been anticipated. Robert told me that, because the consultant "had to" find something to criticize, a few minor issues were raised in the review. These questions were sent to the project officer in Ottawa who sent them on to Winnipeg who sent them to Willis Bender in Aceh. Only, at the time, Willis was away on home leave in North America. He was, however, still accessing his e-mails and was therefore able to forward the e-mail to Jed in Banda Aceh, who was tasked with finding the answers to the questions that the Canadian consultant had raised. Jed, a university graduate who has since completed graduate school, told me that when he read the report he found it altogether incomprehensible. The language and style of the review meant it was an entirely foreign genre. Purportedly in English, the review assumed a specialized technical lexicon that Jed, unused to the parlance of environmental and development consultants, found impossible to decipher. So, Jed sent the report back to Willis (who was still on home leave) asking for a translation into everyday vernacular English. As a trained engineer with extensive NGO and development experience, Willis was fluent in the language of consultants. The translation (between English "dialects") was duly provided.

With a version of the clarifications in hand, Jed visited the GenAssist office in Banda Aceh and met with Stella, GenAssist's Indonesian program manager. The conversation took place in Bahasa Indonesia, in which Jed was fluent as a consequence of everyday learning and practice over his two years of living in rural Aceh. Jed systematically went through each of the questions that the consultant had raised and that

Willis had translated. The questions addressed issues of endangered species, water, and sanitation. Jed recounted to me (in English) how this conversation went:

> JED: First question, are there any endangered species located in the planned construction site – either plants or animals?
> STELLA: What?! No! There are no endangered species. You can go there and look, but you will not find any tigers or elephants!
> JED: There could be a rare plant or something?
> STELLA: No! There are no endangered species at the site.
> JED: Ok. Next question ...

Jed felt embarrassed asking questions of Stella because they were clearly thought to be absurd, inappropriate, and entirely disconnected from Aceh realities. Stella's responses to Jed reflected this incredulity. Whatever the consultant in Canada was useful for, Jed did not think that the content of the questions was at all relevant or informative. There is reason to suspect that CIDA staff members were also not especially interested in the content of the answers. Whether the EIA is an adequate tool for ensuring that "environmental" issues are addressed in development programs or otherwise is perhaps secondary to the usefulness of the EIA in providing organizations such as CIDA with plausible deniability. That is, such reports facilitate the devolving and subcontracting of responsibility. They also afford the possibility of agencies being able to present themselves as ecologically conscious. These outcomes did not require detailed answers as much as they demanded the appearance of interrogative questioning and rigorous analysis. This was certainly the understanding of many of the individuals I interviewed who were involved in this EIA, and it helped inform the way they engaged with CIDA bureaucracy.

On the few points that required further clarification, Stella asked GenAssist's Acehnese staff (in Indonesian) who discussed the issues (in Acehnese),[53] undertook further investigations (also largely in Acehnese), and then provided their answers to Stella (in Indonesian). Having received oral answers (in Indonesian) for each of the consultant's questions, Jed then returned to the MCC Banda Aceh office and wrote an e-mail (in English), which he sent to Willis, who was still in the US on home leave. Jed knew he "couldn't write in CIDA's language," but Willis took his vernacular English and reworked it into the technical dialect appropriate for environmental assessment reports. These answers were then sent to MCCC staff in Winnipeg who forwarded them on to the CIDA Indonesia desk in Ottawa. It is worth further noting that the numerous conversations about the EIA in and between MCC offices in Banda Aceh, Central Java, Akron, and Winnipeg all took place in terminology shaped by the cultural and linguistic particularities of MCC, which I call here "MCC Talk." MCC Talk has its own specialist terminology, nuances of meaning, (profuse) acronyms, and colloquialisms. Just like Consultant Speak (or any other language), MCC Talk also had to be learned, and only through extensive practice was it possible to achieve fluency.

Bogged down by personnel changes and laborious translations, communications over the EIA had taken months. While the process dragged on the situation in Aceh had changed. The most consequential change was that, as part of ongoing negotiations with the different Aceh-based actors involved, the housing project had been relocated. The Meunasah Lhok site described in the EIA report was now no longer the project site; instead, the planned construction was now going to take place in Ulee Tuy on the outskirts of Banda Aceh.[54] Consequently, an entirely new EIA was solicited and the whole process began again.

Remarkably, given this extraordinarily convoluted process, the translations actually *worked.* This is apparent in the construction of 212 *rumah bantuan* in Aceh, although of course in Ulee Tuy rather than in Meunasah Lhok.[55] I walked around the almost-finished houses with Jed in mid-2008 when I visited Aceh and was struck by the scale of the project. We passed by rows and rows of brand new concrete houses. Most were still vacant, but a few residents had just begun moving in and were embarking on the process of making themselves at home. Later that year the Canadian ambassador to Indonesia attended the hand-over ceremony and declared the project "impressive."[56]

An analysis of the translation of the EIA enables consideration of the relationships that make up the MCC patchwork quilt. It is clear that translating a mundane EIA report is a profoundly complex process. It involved at least three languages (Indonesian, Acehnese, and English) and various dialects, including Consultant Speak and MCC Talk. The translations spanned at least six organizations (CIDA, MCC binational, MCC Canada, GenAssist-CRWRC, the Aceh EIA consultant, and the Canadian reviewer) and extended across three countries (Indonesia, Canada, and the US). On any given day the medium of communications switched from e-mail, to paper, to text message, to phone call, to verbal communication in face-to-face meetings, and back again. While the involvement of CIDA and the requirement of an EIA was unusual for MCC Indonesia, the level of complexity was not. The multiple

Figure 2.2 | Recently constructed *rumah bantuan* at Ulee Tuy, Aceh

intralingual, interlingual, and intersemiotic translations just described are entirely business-as-usual.[57]

This narrative also foregrounds the textured nature of the MCC patchwork quilt. The translations relied on particular translators endowed with specific linguistic, cultural, technical, and organizational "competencies."[58] Heather Hindman and Anne-Meike Fechter critique the development literature for leaving development workers "out of the story" and for treating them as "mere tools" rather than as active and creative agents.[59] The translators are the makers and performers of translation. If Jed had not been a part of the EIA translation, the process may have turned out quite differently. The same applies to Willis Bender, MCC's Indonesian staff, Robert Fast, Anna and Jake Friesen, Stella, the consultants, and the CIDA staff who likewise shaped the way the process unfurled. These mediators didn't "simply play roles or execute norms" but, rather, were active participants in the process.[60] The patchwork quilt is constituted through the interpersonal interactions between these active participants.

A final feature I want to reiterate is that differences were both transcended and reinforced in the translation process. Actors related to each other through connections and disconnections, translations and mistranslations. At times the gaps that permeate the "patchwork quilt" were traversed, but at other times they were reinscribed. By imagining GenAssist as a "local" NGO, MCC maintained its philosophy of facilitating Indonesian ownership of development processes. By not communicating their shock at the farcical nature of the questions posed by the Canadian environmental consultant, Jed and Stella kept the required relationships functionally intact. By requiring an EIA, but by devolving responsibility for (1) how it was carried out, (2) the review process, and (3) cross-checking the required clarifications, CIDA ensured that it could claim to have gathered all the necessary information while remaining essentially ignorant of realities on the ground in Aceh.[61] These paradoxical dynamics point towards the fundamental ambivalence in translation relationships.

BROKERING IN CENTRAL JAVA

In a seminal article Clifford Geertz analyzes the role of Javanese *kyai* (Jv. Muslim teachers) as mediators between key divisions in Indonesian society: rigid Islam and syncretistic-minded villagers, nationalist intelligentsia and rural peasantry, and "traditional" and "modern" cultural patterns.[62] Geertz argues that these religious leaders were crucially located to play pivotal roles in processes of culture change and development. His sharp dichotomization of Javanese society has since been critiqued as simplistic.[63] But his attention to "cultural brokers" has continued to generate considerable interest, with historical and contemporary research examining diverse brokers across different tasks.[64] This attention to brokers reflects everyday Indonesian with its profuse nomenclature for such roles, including *makelar*, *calo*, *broker*, *perantara*, *cengkau*, *pialang*, *penengah*, and *pelantar*. This fulsome language and the diverse roles ascribed to brokers point to a lack of determinacy of the functions and activities of cultural brokers. This indeterminacy is, I suggest, a direct consequence of the nature of brokers, whose very lack of clear delineation is constitutive of the position itself. A go-between is inherently ambiguously placed. Brokers are "Janus-like," simultaneously facing in many different directions.[65]

Maarten Kuitenbrouwer discusses the specialized roles that Indigenous elites and ethnic minorities – including Eurasians, Ambonese, Minahasa, Arabs, and Chinese – played in collaboration with Dutch colonial rule in Indonesia.[66] He argues that, while their connecting roles were crucial, they also operated as a "buffer" between colonial rulers and Indigenous populations. They functioned as much as obstacles as they did as connectors.[67] Paradoxically, this separating function is vital for ensuring ongoing association. This is because the disjunctures between divergent perspectives can be so severe that, in the absence of mediation, the gaps become too apparent, potentially leading to a complete breakdown of relationship.[68] A buffering role is necessary for disconnecting development partnerships, which is often a precondition for making them work.

The changing positioning of the Mennonite Scholarship Commission (Komisi Beasiswa Menonit, KBM), a long-standing MCC partner in Central Java, illustrates the ambivalence of buffering and connecting involved in brokerage and mediation. Throughout my field research MCC's relationship with KBM was an ongoing saga resembling the notoriously convoluted plotlines of *sinetron*, Indonesian TV soap operas. When I visited Indonesia for the first time in October 2006 I joined in on a partner visit that included meeting with KBM staff and board members in their office in Pati, Central Java. My field notes recorded the conversations with MCCers in the car on the way home. KBM was the cause of much agitation. When I left Indonesia in December 2008 the partnership with KBM was still stirring animated discussion and concern. The eventual outcome, which began to emerge just as I concluded my fieldwork, was the demise of this remarkable partnership.

In the 1950s MCC helped establish several private (non-government funded) primary and secondary schools (Sekolah Dasar, SD; Sekolah Menengah Pertama, SMP; and Sekolah Menengah Atas, SMA) by providing funds for construction and development. These schools were owned and operated by the two largest Indonesian Mennonite churches, Gereja Injili di Tanah Jawa (GITJ) and Gereja Kristen Muria Indonesia (GKMI). After construction, MCC settled into a pattern of providing these schools with regular ongoing finances. In order to help channel this funding, and also the financial support from the European Mennonite Evangelism Committee (Europäisches Mennonitisches Evangelisationskomitee; EMEK),[69] a scholarship commission was created. In Winnipeg I interviewed David Epp, a Canadian who had worked with MCC in Indonesia in the late 1960s. As part of our conversation, we discussed the evolution of this scholarship commission. David wasn't sure exactly when the scholarship commission began, but he knew that it was already operating before he arrived in Indonesia. During his period of service in Indonesia it acquired the name Komisi Beasiswa Menonit. At this time MCC in-country leadership was finding it problematic to adjudicate between competing demands for school funds. David told me that KBM was designed "to get us out of direct institutional support" of the various schools by creating a buffer between the MCC's provision of finances and the many needs of the different schools.

KBM provided scholarships to students to attend the church schools to make them more accessible. The scholarships themselves were donated by individuals in North America who, in parallel to broader "child sponsorship" practices, received letters from the sponsored child on a regular basis with an update on their progress.[70] The flow of finances was paralleled by a reverse flow of information. But David told me that the plan didn't work out as intended. Throughout the 1960s KBM staff found that each scholarship, intended initially for just one student, was more than adequate to support three students. Although only one student wrote the obligatory thank you letter to their sponsor, another two students "piggy-backed" on the same funds. David thought that MCC staff in Akron were aware of this, but he never found out if the donors themselves were informed.

Fifty years is an extraordinarily long period of time for any organizational partnership across the development sector. Yet nearly five decades later KBM was still supported by MCC. It was one of the longest-standing MCC partnerships anywhere in the world. For the first few decades KBM was led by Karto, a Javanese man who had formerly worked directly with MCC as a local member of staff. He was well connected with, and respected by, the Mennonite school principals, Indonesian Mennonite leaders, and expatriate MCC staff. Karto provided KBM with continuity and proven reliability. He was the only staff member employed by KBM, although he was responsible to a board of representatives of the Indonesian Mennonite churches and, for a time, MCC. During Karto's tenure KBM was housed within the same building that used to be MCC's head office in Indonesia.[71] The proximity between MCC and KBM meant it became a taken-for-granted part of MCC's work in Indonesia. By the early 2000s, however, virtually everything had changed. The cumulative effect of these changes led directly to the crisis that embroiled KBM during my research.

Education at all levels was considered a pressing need in early post-independence Indonesia. It was identified as a priority for the purposes both of economic advancement and political unification. When the Mennonite schools were first established they quickly attracted strong support, including from Indonesian Mennonite families who wanted their children to receive quality education. Over the ensuing decades since independence, the Indonesian government rolled out a comprehensive system of public-funded schooling. Although quality remained variable, state schools became increasingly numerous and accessible.[72] By the time of the collapse of the New Order regime in 1998, state schools had established a widespread reputation as being among the most prestigious and competitive in the Muria region of Central Java. This growth of government-funded education placed increasing pressure on private schools such that some of the Mennonite schools MCC supported through KBM were regarded as struggling. Significant questions were being asked about their quality and viability.

Leadership roles had also undergone major transformations. When after many decades Karto finally retired from his role as the head of KBM he was replaced, at the behest of the Indonesian Mennonite synods, by a younger pastor. Sugeng had no background with MCC and no experience of working in an administrative position. This change in personnel was to prove decisive when combined with a number of other leadership transitions, including within the synods of GKMI and GITJ and, particularly, in the leadership of MCC in Indonesia. As noted earlier, MCC Reps are decisive mediators in MCC's field programs. So significant is their role that changes in the in-country leadership greatly increase the potential for disjuncture in MCC's programs. Historically, these points of leadership transition tend to produce the most dramatic and far-reaching reorientations of MCC's work in any given country context. Changes are not guaranteed at these points of transition, but the potential for reconfiguration is greatly increased. In KBM's case it managed to see through at least eleven such leadership changes, which is as astonishing as it is unique. When Anna and Jake Friesen arrived in Indonesia as the MCC Reps in 2001 a new partnership model was instituted and a number of MCC's programs underwent rapid changes. Because they didn't fit the new expectations, some partnerships were dissolved. However, no immediate changes were implemented in relation to KBM. Part of the reason for this is that Anna and Jake understood that they had been tasked at the time of their appointment specifically to resume close cooperation with the Indonesian Mennonite churches. The partnership with KBM was one of the ways in which they could do so.

Six years into their work in Indonesia, however, the MCC Reps began initiating changes with KBM. A series of conversations and meetings was held to address perceived problems. Three primary issues were identified. The first was that the programs run by KBM were regarded as outmoded, weak, and failing. Many of the schools that received student scholarships were delivering what was widely regarded in the Muria region as substandard education. On a quality basis alone, the partnership was not delivering desired results. Though the KBM programs had initially suited MCC's goals, they were now seen as inadequate. The second issue closely relates to the first. After nearly fifty years of partnership the Mennonite schools and KBM itself seemed more reliant on MCC funding than ever. This appeared to be a clear-cut example of dependency-inducing development, which was far from the ideal of encouraging endogenous, independent, and sustainable initiatives.

The third concern, expressed repeatedly by both Indonesian and expatriate MCCers, was their felt inability to work productively with the new head of KBM. Administratively, Sugeng failed to communicate in a way that MCCers felt was reasonable. He also rarely kept to agreed timing. MCCers responded by adopting a flexible approach with KBM deadlines, including making provisions for extensions and working around delays. But these allowances were frustrating and involved an increased administrative burden. There were numerous discussions in the MCC Indonesia office about possible financial irregularities, inconsistencies in budgeting, and uncertainty over the allocation of scholarships. MCCers also heard unsubstantiated stories that implicated Sugeng in using his position to gain benefits from the parents of scholarship recipients. Again, MCCers tended to give Sugeng the benefit of the doubt. But the persistent nature of these stories over a period of years was troubling. Personally, his demeanour was regarded as awkward, and MCCers found it difficult to feel that they could establish rapport and trust with him. Wisnu Suparman, an Indonesian MCC staff member, who along with Adi Sutjipto worked as partnership liaisons with KBM, told me that Sugeng had a reputation of behaving like a "master" (In. *penguasa*) who was often "harsh" (In. *kasar sekali*) in his interactions with others. This final issue was, I think, the most critical. All development partnerships are built on interpersonal relationships between individuals. The primary and irresolvable problem between MCC and KBM was the imagined impossibility of forming a good working relationship with Sugeng.

The cumulative impact of these concerns was that KBM was frequently regarded as among the most difficult partnerships that MCCers had to navigate. This was expressed directly in staff meetings and also through frequent jokes made in casual conversation. Consequently, questions were asked in the MCC Indonesia office as to whether KBM should be dropped altogether as a partner. This option was not viewed positively by all members of the staff team. Some MCCers felt a strong sense of loyalty to KBM. Wisnu and Adi, both of whom were Javanese, had each been recipients of KBM scholarships when they attended school, as had many of their friends. They knew that their current work in MCC, and their ability to access professional jobs more generally and therefore also to achieve a middle-class standard of living, was facilitated on the back of those scholarships. Wisnu and Adi were both reluctant to see KBM scholarships get dropped altogether.

For Anna and Jake questions of loyalty were also important. They were tasked with working with the Indonesian Mennonite churches, and KBM was a long-standing means of doing so. Connected with this, Indonesian Mennonite leaders had commented that, despite their geographical proximity and a shared Mennonite affiliation, there were few actual mechanisms for GITJ and GKMI to work together other than from KBM. Partnership between these Indonesian Mennonite churches was something Anna and Jake were eager to encourage. But perhaps their key concern was related to their theology of service. MCC's partnership model in Indonesia, as discussed earlier, celebrated an ideal that involved the meeting of equals in shared and responsive relationships. The mutuality of this model was asserted, implicitly, against the backdrop of major players in the development industry that were perceived as being heavy-handed and domineering in dictating terms and conditions – an approach reminiscent of colonial authorities and imbued with radically asymmetrical power imbalances. Their vision for equitable partnership was couched within a wider discourse of relationality.

In her ethnography of development in Indonesia, Tania Li introduces the concept of "rendering technical" – the way in which development actors construct a domain so as to make it amenable to certain forms of technical intervention. Li argues that development actors routinely screen out information that works against their preferred approaches, such that the "political-economic causes of poverty and injustice" are reposed "in terms amenable to a technical solution."[73] Development practitioners reimagine the world by bracketing out disruptive information so that what is imagined as being needed is precisely what development organizations are willing and able to provide. A world that can be "remedied by technique" is one in which development interventions are seen as legitimate, benevolent, and necessary.[74]

In contrast, I suggest that MCCers tended to engage in a practice of "rendering relational" – that is, complex political-economic concerns were perceived as being most adequately addressed through interpersonal interventions. In MCC Indonesia the technical – scientific expertise, quantifiable data, technology transfer, esteemed qualifications, etc. – was intentionally displaced for an emphasis on the value and priority of relationships. Relationships, as Anna Friesen once told me, were the "coal face" of expatriate service – a dynamic space in which the real, meaningful, and important work of MCC was enacted. This was because, for many MCCers, interpersonal connections were infused with transformative divine activity. God was able to take sincere and genuine interpersonal relationships and transform them into initiatives for change. Through relationships a Mennonite ethic of service could be enacted. That this emphasis on relationality was distinctively Mennonite was made especially apparent to me one day when, while reflecting on her MCC experience, Anna suggested that Mennonites (by which she meant Germanic or ethnic Mennonites) were more adept than non-Mennonite MCCers at building relationships. This appears to suggest that the prioritization of interpersonal relationality in MCC derives from a specifically Mennonite heritage. Regardless, this Mennonite ethics of relationality was clearly located at the centre of MCC's work.

Rendering relational was not unchallenged within MCC. As the example of the EIA testifies, the prioritization of relationships operated simultaneously with other logics and practices within the organization that emphasized technocratic imperatives instead. Nevertheless, when Elizabeth Detweiler, quoted above, discussed tensions with CIDA she attested to how widespread rendering relational is within MCC by pointing to the clash between CIDA's fixation with "statistics" and MCC's attention to "relationship building." Indeed, in my research I found relational discourses to be thoroughly widespread across many different parts of the organization. The partnership model that Anna and Jake held to in MCC Indonesia drew upon these widely circulating discourses.

However, in the case of KBM, this ethical framing led to a double bind. The status quo seemed inadequate and in need of change. This was clearly a defective partnership. But to institute changes unilaterally would be to replicate the sorts of neocolonialism that were regarded as core reasons for the dependency problem in the first place and would betray the ideals of partnership and mutuality. The challenge, therefore, was how to implement change without relying on a paternalistic and coercive imbalance between "donor" and "recipient." Because this was a question of financial control, it was fraught with awkward questions about power inequalities. Given that MCCers felt that KBM, under Sugeng's leadership, was unable to facilitate the necessary changes to rejuvenate the program, other possible strategies were explored. One option was that internal reform within KBM could be enabled by hiring a consultant to work with Sugeng to redesign its work. This strategy would involve the insertion of a proxy agent into KBM whose ability to leverage change would derive from being non-MCC (and therefore able to shepherd through new initiatives) yet also simultaneously representing MCC's interests (as is apparent in that MCC would appoint the individual in the first place). Various individuals were approached to take on this role. However, the most desired candidates were unavailable, and other possibilities were discounted because of their socially inferior position vis-à-vis Sugeng, which ensured that they would lack the necessary authority to leverage change. This strategy was therefore abandoned.

Another strategy was to displace the onus for change from the MCC Indonesia office to Akron. This involved MCC Indonesia downplaying its authority and locating itself as a mere intermediary for wider organizational imperatives. The problem with this strategy was that the MCC section responsible for education in the Akron head office, Global Family, was during this period quite unclear what its policy direction was on account of undergoing a rather prolonged leadership transition. During this changeover some of the guidance from Global Family directly contradicted earlier advice. For example, at one point the MCC Reps in Indonesia were told by Global Family personnel that MCC did not work with schools but, rather, preferred working directly with individual students. This was communicated to KBM. However, later Anna and Jake were informed that, in other countries, MCC did work directly with schools and that institution building could be considered an appropriate expenditure of Global Family funds. With some embarrassment this information too was handed on to KBM. The cumulative effect of these shifting articulations of policy was that Global Family was incapable of providing the sorts of leverage that MCC Indonesia staff desired.

A further strategy was to insert yet another broker between MCC and KBM who could help push through changes. The key proposal for enacting this strategy was that MCC should work only with the church synods in its partnerships with church actors. Those sub-synod partnerships, such as with KBM, therefore would be closed. The implication was that the church synods had the authority vis-à-vis KBM to facilitate change. MCC was contrasted to North American Mennonite mission boards that, it was thought, tended to bypass synod leadership to focus their support on evangelistic or mission organizations. However, while it did have a long history of working with the synods, MCC Indonesia was not consistent with this approach. For example, Mennonite Diaconal Services (Menonit Diakonia Servis, MDS), a GKMI humanitarian and peacebuilding organization, was funded directly by MCC. The appropriate synod was bypassed altogether in this funding relationship. Aside from inconsistency, a key problem with this strategy was that, up to this point, both church synods were uninterested in making substantial changes to the existing arrangement. MCC's money kept various struggling church schools afloat, which was considered by many church leaders to be a good and useful outcome. This funding was largely taken for granted by church leaders. Because the impetus for change came from MCC, if MCC wanted to pursue this strategy it would first have to convince the church leadership that it was worthwhile. Over the period of my research this was the primary approach that was pursued, with MCC distancing itself from KBM and encouraging synod leaders to assume greater synod authority over KBM programs.

Just before I left Indonesia this synod-centred plan of action was called into question and then dropped altogether. During a meeting between MCC and church leaders, a senior synod leader proposed a radical reworking of the scholarship process. In its place, a new, innovative, and informal education program would be implemented, possibly to be headed by the primary proposer of this new initiative. This proposal for alternative education, which he thought would appeal to MCC and its need for exciting stories to feed back to donors in North America, would completely displace the Indonesian Mennonite schools, leaving them without any of MCC's funding and therefore, for some at least, facing financial dire straits. The plan was met with a resounding MCC silence. It was not the content of this proposal as such that caused concern among MCC staff; rather, the radical nature of the plan suggested that the synod leader was acting on his own individual entrepreneurial impulse rather than according to the wishes and intentions of the constituency that, it was thought, he should have represented. Questions were asked regarding whether this synod leader was adequately connecting MCC and the Indonesian Mennonite churches or whether his interpolation into these relationships was merely obstructive.

Because of the perceived delegitimization of the synod leader, the strategy shifted again. In the last few weeks of my field research, Wisnu told me that MCC was planning to "cut off" (In. *akan melepaskan*) KBM and bypass the Indonesian Mennonite synods. The new plan was to work directly with the schools themselves. In three years' time, Wisnu told me, the financial flows from MCC to KBM would come to an "end" (In. *habis*). KBM would progressively phase out MCC-funded scholarships to allow students who had already entered the program to complete their education. No new students, however, would be added. This left KBM's future in doubt. Ironically, this solution returned MCC to the situation it faced in the late 1950s and which KBM had been created to avoid: MCC itself would now interact directly with the various Mennonite schools and adjudicate between their competing needs.

The inherent ambivalence of translation is apparent in the restive nomadism of KBM's brokerage as it moved from being perceived by MCCers as a buffer and connector, through to being a barrier, and finally to getting bypassed altogether. This final option had previously been rejected but was eventually embraced as a last resort; lacking other (appealing) mechanisms to leverage change, MCC Indonesia resorted to a unilateral rechannelling of its financial flows. This was considered something of a betrayal of ideals of partnership and mutual relationships, and it helps explain why it took so long for MCCers to come to this eventual conclusion and why numerous alternatives were explored first. Nevertheless, in the face of seemingly intractable concerns, MCC staff members enacted the changes they thought were necessary.

Describing his role in the negotiations, Wisnu told me that being a partner advisor was not easy. He held his hands parallel to each other, palms down, with one vertically above the other. Partner advisors were located in the middle. He then slapped his upper hand down on the lower hand. Those in the middle, he explained, are either crushed or forced into taking sides with one or the other. To be a good partner advisor meant preserving that space in the middle. But this task was very difficult to achieve. Olivier de Sardan similarly suggests that development mediators undertake a "mission impossible" as they work to fulfil contradictory aims, including defending their own interests, working with and for the interests of donor institutions, and promoting the interests of local beneficiaries.[75] These multiple competing priorities ensure that collaborations are always fragile and contingent. Given this precarious reality, the remarkable thing about the KBM-MCC partnership is that it lasted for as long as it did. Nevertheless, in the end, MCC Indonesia maintained control over the distribution of finances and was ultimately able to terminate the partnership unilaterally. The discourse of mutual and equal relationships in MCC Indonesia, while intending to counter power asymmetries typical of the development industry as a whole, was unable to entirely rework these dynamics.[76] As a funding agency, albeit one that did not recognize itself as such, MCC Indonesia rechannelled its finances along paths of its choosing.[77]

CONCLUSION

The MCC patchwork quilt is stitched together with a delicate thread, which I refer to in this chapter as translation practices. An assemblage of very different patches, MCC's work is contingent upon the translators who are interpolated into key sites within this multi-coloured mélange.

Far from mechanical processes, MCC's programs are reshaped in the midst of relational dynamics and through interpersonal idiosyncrasies. Accordingly, the description of MCC in North America as a Mennonite "peoplehood movement," discussed in the previous chapter, should not be imagined as determinative for what takes place through its programs in Indonesia. Donor intentions or head office imperatives, as the humorous sketch at the start of this chapter illustrates, are not conveyed on mere "transmission belts" but, rather, are actively reworked in encounters across difference.[78] The practices that are translated through and across the MCC patchwork quilt include a motley collection of EIA technical reports, canned meat shipments, scholarship provisions, *meunasah* constructions, and church synod meetings. This diversity suggests that MCC should be understood as a fluid and malleable form, which has the potential to be many different things at the same time. Accordingly, MCC can also be described (at different times and places) as both a "humanitarian NGO" and a "funding agency." The following chapter explores some of the other forms MCC has taken in Indonesia.

It is apparent that to be a mediator in the MCC patchwork quilt is not always comfortable or pleasant. Squished between contrasting imperatives and immersed in complicated organizational politics, MCC's brokers faced the difficult task of balancing demands and guarding their decision-making space from encroachment by other brokers, both adjacent and further afield. This political wrangling is not unique to MCC, but its particular form in this organizational structure emerged out of historical tensions between field operations and a head office that have remained under constant negotiation throughout its postwar history, and that closely resemble tensions inherent within the ecclesial politics of North American Mennonite bishopric democracies.

The ideals of partnership and relationality are key dynamics shaping MCC practices. The operating partnership model in MCC Indonesia is formed within an ethics of mutuality and non-coercive service between MCC, as a foreign organization, and its local partners. MCCers tended to "render relational" by privileging interpersonal relationships as a primary domain of meaningful, transformative engagement. Both of these logics are infused with vernacular Mennonite theologies of peace and service. Their implementation, however, is fraught. This is not only because attaining these ideals often proved difficult, particularly given inequalities of access to finances, but also because they are only ever articulated in the midst of competing imperatives. However, rather than negating the prioritization of rendering relational and partnership-as-mutuality within MCC, such disagreements and tensions highlight just how widespread and prominent these ideals are. While the question as to what exactly transfers over in any given instance of translation must remain inconclusive (at least at the level of abstract consideration), what is clear from the narratives given in this chapter is that MCC Indonesia is not only defined by its role – a mediator in a broad patchwork quilt – but also by the value-laden, culturally and theologically formed approaches that MCCers take in negotiating their relationships with those other sections of the quilt.

3

The Missions of Development

MISSIONARIES UNDER COVER

The front cover of *Time* magazine (US edition) on 30 June 2003 was emblazoned with a clenched white hand gripping a shimmering, golden cross. The headline queried: "Should Christians Convert Muslims?" Inside, the cover story – which was part exposé and part investigative report – discussed American Christian "Missionaries Under Cover" among Muslims in the Middle East.[1] Published almost two years after the 9/11 attacks and four months after the American-led invasion of Iraq and, therefore, in the midst of the mushrooming propaganda surrounding the global "War on Terror," the report was clearly designed to stir debate. In this critical appraisal of contemporary Christian evangelism, the author condemns the "clandestine" activities of missionaries, some of whom are said to combine "religious arrogance with political ignorance." Aggressive evangelists, however, are described as only one type of missionary, differentiated from others in their goals, motivations, and methods.[2] The key fault lines in the missionary world are dichotomized between social and spiritual, liberal and evangelical. There is a clear bias towards those missionaries of liberal persuasion who emphasize social work, development, or relief activities while also downplaying, or actively avoiding, proselytization.

In the midst of this article a box insert entitled "Keeping the Faith without Preaching It" focuses attention on Edward Miller, an MCC worker in Iraq.[3] Miller is shown in a positive light, embodying the virtuous missionary who is honest about his faith but refuses to engage in direct evangelism: "One thing is not on his to-do list: evangelizing. Mennonite representatives delivering aid in Muslim countries do not preach the Gospel." The article states that "more liberal" Christians focus on the parts of their Scriptures that emphasize material assistance. It quotes the executive director of MCC, Ron Mathies, as saying, "our stance is one of humility and respect." The final paragraph of this insert drives this message home:

> Back in Baghdad, Mennonite Committee [*sic*] employee Miller feels no impulse at all to share his faith with his clients. Miller is a devout Mennonite; he was raised in various locations in Africa where his parents did the committee's humanitarian work. While he was growing up in his church's "peace and justice" tradition, he says, "there was always discussion about the injustices and inequalities around the world and what we should do about it." But he does not think that Christ's word needs further elucidation in the region. Referring to indigenous churches that Evangelicals tend to ignore or scorn as compromised, he says, "You have to realize that Christianity has been part of the Middle East for 2,000 years. People here know all about my religion and don't need me to explain it. I don't feel I have anything more to teach the Muslims than they have to teach me."

As a very public representation of MCC's theological identity the article and insert were read and discussed widely throughout MCC's North American constituency. The general portrayal of MCC, and in particular Miller's quote about his relationship vis-à-vis Iraqi Muslims, sparked a firestorm of debate.[4] E-mail correspondence within MCC and between MCC leaders and the wider constituency was vigorous.[5] Questions were asked as to whether Miller had actually made the quoted statements, and much of the correspondence expressed annoyance at the author's simplifications and theological illiteracy.[6] But the most arresting feature of these e-mails is the stark differences in views proffered. One e-mail argued that Miller's quote "contradicts MCC's mission." Another suggested that the comments would be very damaging to MCC's reputation: "There are a lot of people who have been strong supporters and defenders of us [MCC], but many may stop defending us over the comments made in this article." Another stated that Miller "does not adequately represent MCC" and that this meant that MCC leadership had "serious damage control work to do."

In contrast to those expressing dismay at Miller's views, other correspondents were positively excited at their organization's portrayal. Correctly ascertaining that MCC was located firmly on the "good" side of *Time*'s characterization of international Christian mission activity, one e-mailer wrote that he was "proud to see ... MCC mentioned in a very positive light." He encouraged MCC staff to "keep up the good work." An equally exuberant supporter invoked divine providence: "I bless God for giving [Miller] the words to say when interviewed by TIME ... and I can accept and identify with what he (apparently) said." For another correspondent, reading the article buttressed his faith in the organization: "MCC has now my full 100% support for their approach and work." Apparently, for this writer, *Time*'s approval was more profound and reliable than MCC's own rather extensive publicity. One comment written by an MCC leader to colleagues captures the ambivalence that many others felt: "The firestorm will be hottest in our own Mennonite and MCC circles ... [And yet] the article was so close to getting it right." Miller's comments both deeply offended many in MCC's constituency and strongly resonated with others. Clearly the status of "mission" in MCC is deeply contested among the organization's constituents.

MCC leadership responded to the *Time* magazine affair by seeking to clarify its position through various outlets in the Mennonite media. However, one article posted on the website *Third Way Café* written by Paul Schrag, the editor of the *Mennonite Weekly Review*, illustrates the difficulty they faced in dispelling the air of ambiguity.[7] In response to the question "Do you preach?" Schrag proposes two answers: "yes and no." MCC's mandate "is not to win converts or plant churches." But "this does not mean that MCC is 'non-evangelical' or 'forbids preaching.'" Instead, Schrag suggests that MCCers believe "food for the body is also food for the soul. They believe meeting people's physical needs is a vital part of the gospel." Schrag outlines how MCC "presents the gospel in different ways in different places" but that "explicit evangelism" would be counterproductive in Iraq and would associate Christianity with imperialistic US military action. Instead, MCC's stance is "one of humility and respect, not arrogance and denigration; of invitation and gift, not crusade or coercion." Ron Mathies is quoted as saying: "With the coming of the troops, to people in Iraq that is the face of Christianity ... We want to offer a different face that has integrity of what the gospel is all about." The article concludes by noting that MCC plans to send more workers to Iraq and asks: "Will they play a role in sharing the gospel? MCC would say yes, and we agree."

The "yes-and-no" answer to the question of preaching the gospel points to a deep and widespread ambiguity within MCC over issues of mission. During my fieldwork in Ontario, I interviewed Elizabeth Detweiler, a staff member in the MCC Ontario office. While introducing the organization she pointed to Christian Scripture, specifically Matthew 25, which she glossed as "being Christ to other people" by seeking to "feed the hungry, give water to the thirsty, and welcome the stranger." Elizabeth told me that this is what MCC sought to do. MCC did not seek to hide its Christianity, but it was also "not there to convert." Its fulfilling of a Christian commission was disassociated from evangelistic intent. Similarly, at an orientation for new international volunteers at MCC's head office in July 2008 at Akron, Pennsylvania, those heading to Latin America were told that, while the term "missionary" was often used on their visas, they should avoid using that label in their everyday work. Instead, they should identify themselves as "development workers" with their colleagues, friends, and neighbours – a term that was felt to have more positive connotations. An interview I had in Winnipeg with an MCC staff member put the issue more explicitly. He narrated a story concerning when he had been involved in negotiations with Chinese officials over setting up programs in China. During these discussions a question was raised regarding whether MCC would seek to engage in evangelistic activities. The MCCer told me that his response was direct and clear: "MCC has been working in Bangladesh for forty years and there has never been a single convert as a result of its work there. We want communities to advance themselves and if they do so within their own faith tradition, then that is fine with us."

In attempting to introduce the organization to new audiences, Alain Epp Weaver highlights ambiguities about the status of mission: "MCC speaks much of the same language as the rest of the world of humanitarian non-governmental organizations (NGOs), be they religious like World Vision or secular like Mercy Corps, but in other ways MCC bears striking similarities to the world of mission agencies."[8] Clearly, MCC's missional identity does not conform to a rigid separation between "mission" and "development"; instead, within MCC, the demarcation between these terms is a matter of negotiation, contestation, and ongoing questioning. The controversy within MCC over "Missionaries Under Cover" illustrates how MCC occupies an awkward and ambivalent space between these two keywords.

This chapter analyzes the "yes-and-no" ambiguity as practised within MCC Indonesia. MCC has had a continuous presence in Indonesia since its personnel first arrived in 1948. Rather than providing a comprehensive historical account the chapter focuses on a few specific phases. These cases illustrate the remarkable differences in the kind of programs that MCC initiated or supported. I argue that MCC's work in Indonesia has taken contrasting forms. The changes over time and space provoke questions about how and why MCC could assume such disparate forms as well as about what these serial metamorphoses mean for the analysis of the relationships between religion and development.

Following on from the previous chapter, in which I examine the paradox inherent in translating service as MCC's programs worked between transference and transformation, "carrying over" and disjuncture, this chapter examines the history of MCC in Indonesia through the lens of "room for manoeuvre." Following Dorothea Hilhorst, this room for manoeuvre is understood as the "social space actors have, or lack, to enable their ideas and projects" to be actualized.[9] The heart of my argument is that, while MCC was a North American agency during its time in Indonesia, it was enmeshed in local ecologies of development. MCC's programs in Indonesia were carried out within shifting constellations of opportunities and constraints. Some, but not all, of these opportunities and constraints rested in the hands of MCCers. Importantly, while I pay attention to high-level political changes, as these clearly had an impact on MCC's room for manoeuvre, these structures were mediated by particular actors working within wider networks and coalitions. MCC's programs at any given time were shaped by these negotiated interactions.

NOT REALLY A MISSION BOARD (1948–75)

During my field research I was frequently told that MCC Indonesia had a durably unique identity within the wider organization. Over time I came to see the issue somewhat differently. In the fifty or so countries in which MCC carries out its relief, development, and peacebuilding work, exceptions are the rule. Because of the field-driven approach to MCC programming adopted after the Second World War, there has tended to be little uniformity in MCC operations across different countries, either in terms of ideological framing or in terms of its actual practices. In parallel to North American Mennonite ecclesial politics, characterized by local congregational ownership nestled within wider conference structures (each with varying accumulations of centralized authority and a concomitant fragmentation resulting in considerable diversity), MCC's country programs differ considerably from each other. MCC Indonesia's uniqueness is, therefore, quite typical. Working in Indonesia infused a distinctive tone into MCC's activities. One of the most important features of this was the long-standing organizational and interpersonal relationships with the Indonesian Mennonite churches. While even this has proved to be a malleable commitment, a point I return to below, these denominational relationships have been influential. Most of this section focuses on the early history of MCC in Indonesia as it interacted with the two oldest Indonesian Mennonite churches.[10] To understand the reason MCC began working in Indonesia in 1948 it is necessary to also understand the origins of these Indonesian Mennonite churches. I begin, therefore, with brief historical sketches of Indonesian Mennonites.

Gereja Injili di Tanah Jawa (Evangelical Church of Java, GITJ) traces its origins back to the encounter between European Mennonite missionaries and Javanese during the colonial era. The Dutch Mennonite Mission Agency (Doopsgezinde Zendingsvereeniging, DZV) was established in 1847 in the Netherlands specifically to send missionaries to the Dutch East Indies.[11] It was the first Mennonite mission society, and its missionary work in Indonesia was the first Mennonite mission field outside of Europe and North America. Pieter Jansz, the pioneering Mennonite missionary, was sent to Java in 1851.[12] His mission work was located on the northern coast of Central Java where he was joined by other Mennonite missionaries from the Netherlands, Germany, Switzerland, and Russia. Mennonite missionaries were also active in Sumatra (1871–1930s) and Papua (1950s), but these Mennonite congregations merged into wider Protestant denominations.[13] It was only in Java that the Mennonite missionaries planted an enduring church, although this endeavour was not met with immediate success. The new mission, according to Lawrence Yoder, was beset by translational and cultural challenges, such that "progress was slow and setbacks frequent."[14] Jansz also played an important role translating the Bible into Javanese.

Simultaneous to the work of Dutch missionaries, Kyai Ibrahim Tunggul Wulung (1800?–1885), a Javanese Christian convert who was a member of the royal family of Surakarta, undertook evangelistic work in the same region. He met with considerably greater success, and, in response to the growing number of converts, Tunggul Wulung formed new Christian villages.[15] In part influenced by Tunggul Wulung's success, the Mennonite mission also adopted the model of Christian agricultural villages, where converts would live separated from wider Javanese Muslim society.[16] When Tunggul Wulung died in the mid-1880s, the communities he had established were drawn under the authority of the Mennonite missionaries. This incorporation of an Indigenous Christian movement led to a significant expansion of the mission churches.

It wasn't until 1940, under the threat of Japanese invasion of the Dutch East Indies and German invasion of the Netherlands, that the Javanese Mennonite Church was formally established as an independent church. The war years were devastating for the young church. European missionary leadership was eliminated, and the Javanese congregations were decimated. It was in this context that Soehadiweko Djojodihardjo (1918–1988) succeeded his father as both a pastor and church leader.[17]

A capable and energetic leader, Djojodihardjo became synod chair in 1949 and went on to become an enormously influential leader in GITJ over the following four decades.

GITJ retains an ethnic Javanese character. Its leadership and most members are Javanese, and Javanese is often used in worship services. GITJ began in the Muria region of Central Java, and the vast majority of its congregations remain in that region. GKMI has quite a different ethnic character. Although originating in the same geographic region, it began as a Chinese Indonesian church. Persatuan Gereja-Gereja Kristen Muria Indonesia (Union of Muria Christian Churches of Indonesia, GKMI) traces its origins to the conversion of Tee Siem Tat (1872–1940), a Chinese businessman in Kudus, Central Java, in 1918. The impetus for his conversion had been Tee's experience of sickness and miraculous healing, attributed to the Christian God.[18] Tee and his wife, Sie Djoen Nio (1875–1962), received religious instruction from an Ambonese Salvation Army officer, and they also connected with the Seventh-day Adventist church and the German Neukirchener Mission, an evangelical organization active in nearby Salatiga. Tee eventually settled on the Mennonite Mission, at least in part because comity agreements between the mission agencies designated Kudus as within the Mennonite sphere of influence, although Tee also agreed with certain theological emphases.[19] In December 1920 a group of twenty-five Chinese converts was baptized by Russian Mennonite missionary Nicolai Thiessen.

The autonomous formation of this group, combined with disinterest and suspicion from the Mennonite missionaries who remained focused primarily on their Javanese congregations, meant that the Tees' incipient church developed largely independent of missionary involvement. In 1927 Tee was granted permission from the Dutch colonial government to form an independent church, registered as the Chineesche Doopsgezinde Christengemeente (Chinese Mennonite Congregation). In 1928 the community had raised sufficient funds to build its first church in Kudus.[20] Despite enduring significant challenges during the Second World War and during the struggle for Indonesian independence, the movement continued to expand across the Muria region.[21] It became increasingly multi-ethnic, including attracting Javanese membership. In 1958 it formally changed its name to the current Persatuan Gereja-Gereja Kristen Muria Indonesia.

The first MCC workers to visit Indonesia arrived in 1947. By early 1948 they initiated a relief and medical program in Sumatra.[22] Paul Erb suggests that MCC was "the first foreign agency in Indonesia" after the Second World War.[23] This claim is certainly plausible. The Sumatran relief program lasted only a few months before MCC shifted its regional focus to the Muria region of Central Java. The reason for this change was that MCC sought to provide support to the Indonesian Mennonite churches. This was in response to an invitation from Dutch Mennonite churches. Crippled by the devastation of war in Europe and unable to immediately return to active mission work in Indonesia, Dutch Mennonite leaders asked the American MCC to work with the Indonesian Mennonite churches.[24] Working in the Muria region was impossible when MCCers first arrived due to ongoing disruptions from the national revolution and Dutch-led "police actions." But by 1949 the situation was settled enough for MCCers to shift the focus of their operations to Central Java.[25]

According to Orie O. Miller, MCC's formidable executive secretary from 1935 to 1958, the types of assistance desired by the Indonesian Mennonite churches "more properly fall into the area of possible Mission Board concern and service than MCC relief service."[26] Before discussing what types of "service" MCC carried out at this time, it is important to understand where MCC fits within the wider institutional architecture of North American Mennonite society, particularly vis-à-vis the Mennonite "mission boards" mentioned by Miller. Part of what it means for MCC to be located within the Mennonite peoplehood is that the organization has a place within a wider ecology of organizations. Mission boards are institutions established to enact Christian mission, church planting, and evangelism. Between the mission boards and MCC two immediate differences can be distinguished. First, there is no equivalent umbrella mission organization that parallels the way in which the entire spectrum of the Mennonite peoplehood is brought together within MCC. Mission boards are established by specific conferences to carry out the tasks entrusted to them by their church group. Mission boards therefore tend to be aligned with conference structures.

One of the key reasons for this relates to the second distinguishing mark: different Mennonite church groupings in North America do not agree on a theology of mission and church membership. The meaning and practice of the rituals of baptism, communion, corporate worship, appropriate dress, and so on are all points of (sometimes considerable) contention among different Mennonite conferences. Mennonite groups disagree over appropriate forms of ecclesial authority, and they have assumed a wide spectrum of theological positions – including various "liberal," "evangelical," "fundamentalist," and "progressive" stances – within Christian discourses in North America. Mennonite mission boards therefore carry out "mission" as interpreted by their specific constituencies. In contrast, it is often suggested that the mandate given to

MCC by its constituency, as alluded to by Schrag above, is not to establish churches because this would necessitate alignment to a particular theological framework on how these should be formed, maintained, and affiliated.[27] Instead, MCC's mandate is to carry out a diaconal mission of service and peace.

But the question of mandates is not as clear cut as is sometimes imagined. In the absence of North American mission board activity in Indonesia, which though increasing over the course of the twentieth century nevertheless remained limited and sporadic, MCC has tended, sometimes awkwardly, to fill the gap. In his history of GKMI, Lawrence Yoder hints at these tensions: "MCC was not really a mission board, but a service agency whose general goals did not include evangelism and the planting of new churches. It would give primary attention to education, health, and development, and occasionally church building projects."[28] Here, again, an ambiguous "yes-and-no" answer to questions of mission is apparent; "not really" leaves considerable room for manoeuvre.[29] An interview I conducted in Winnipeg with David Epp reinforced this ambiguity. David had worked with MCC in Central Java in the 1960s. During that time MCC was, for David, very much an "ill-defined medium" for connecting with Indonesian Mennonites. On the one hand, MCC identified itself as a *badan sosial* (In. social organization, NGO) and sought to limit its range of activities to fulfil this gambit; on the other hand, David also thought it played the de facto role of a "mission board" and extensively supported the institutional Mennonite churches.

MCC's programs with the Indonesian Mennonite churches included the provision of relief supplies, funding and staffing medical and education programs, and financing agricultural development work. MCC also supported a range of other activities.[30] The Literature Project, launched in the late 1950s, printed Indonesian-language translations of European and North American Mennonite texts on "Mennonite history and principles (including war, peace and baptism); doctrinal and general problems; [and] tracts."[31] MCC also facilitated visits to Indonesia by North American Mennonite theologians. In the 1960s MCC helped finance the Wiyata Wacana Christian Academy (Akademi Kristen Wiyata Wacana, AKWW), a Mennonite seminary in Pati, Central Java. MCCers also assisted in writing its curriculum. MCC further facilitated opportunities for Indonesian Mennonites to attend North American Mennonite seminaries for theological training.

Through these sorts of activities MCC developed a particularly close partnership with GITJ. This was noted in the MCC Indonesia report to the organization's 1961 Annual Meeting in North America:

> In Indonesia ... MCC is continually seeking to integrate its program of service and outreach into the work of the local congregations. It [*sic*] objective is "to work alongside of" in a genuine partnership program. A former MCC worker made it explicit in 1958: "Today it can be said that MCC does not have a program in the Muria area, for our efforts are now entirely integrated into the churches' program."[32]

Another MCCer who visited Indonesia in 1960 made similar observations:

> MCC, as the only North American Mennonite agency serving in Indonesia, is relating to the Mennonite church in a variety of programs. Many of them are considered in the traditional sense as mission activity. The church is growing. Endless opportunities and responsibilities for evangelism and Christian nurture are open to the church.[33]

MCC Indonesia actively supported a wide range of ministries carried out by the Indonesian Mennonite churches, not all of which fall neatly under either "mission" or "development" categories. While MCCers worked closely with other church denominations around the Indonesian archipelago, the Mennonite churches were the mainstay of MCC's program through to the late 1970s.

Among the clearest indications of MCC's impact upon both GITJ and GKMI was that both continued to regard themselves as Mennonite.[34] The Japanese occupation of Indonesia (1942–45) initiated a period of dramatic change within the Indonesian Mennonite churches. Church members faced coercion and threats of violence.[35] The Dutch missionary leaders were removed from positions of authority in GITJ, necessitating new roles for Javanese leaders. Although continuing to identify as Protestant churches, their sense of having a distinctive Mennonite identity during this period was weak.[36] Further challenges lay just ahead.

Soon after the end of the Second World War widespread ecclesial currents encouraged a pronounced ecumenism. Dovetailing the rise of Indonesian nationalist sentiment, the Protestant ecumenical movement emphasized the creation of new structures and identities that could embody the spirit of national independence and unity. This ecumenism was institutionalized with the creation of the Indonesian Council of Churches (Dewan Gereja-Gereja Indonesia, DGI) in 1950, with the purpose of "creating one Christian Church in Indonesia" (In. *pembentukan Gereja Kristen yang Esa di Indonesia*).[37] The DGI sought to amalgamate all Protestant churches within a single ecclesial structure, and some previously separate denominations merged as a direct consequence of this drive for a national church. Both GKMI and GITJ were members of the DGI, and their leadership was influenced by this ecumenism.[38] However, the arrival of MCCers in the Muria region in 1949 provided a decisive sense of connection with Mennonite churches.[39] A Mennonite ecclesial identity became valuable. The work of MCC in helping GITJ and GKMI maintain a postwar Indonesian Mennonite identity was not evangelism as such, but it played a vital role in making a Mennonite identity appear valuable in a context in which there were considerable pressures working against this. MCC's presence afforded for Indonesian Mennonites a sense that they belonged to an imagined global Mennonite community.[40] MCC helped facilitate an imagined community by enabling flows of people, finances, and information between churches in North America and Indonesia.

The relationship between MCC and the Indonesian Mennonite churches was never static. The formative first three decades saw MCC focus its work in the Muria region to maintain maximum proximity to the Indonesian Mennonite churches.[41] But in the mid-1970s MCCers undertook two quite different initiatives, both of which substantially reshaped these fraternal church relationships. The first was to establish new development projects among transmigrants that saw MCCers engaged as technical experts in close cooperation with the Indonesia state. The second was to initiate new programs in West Kalimantan in partnership with GKMI. This work involved both community development goals alongside church planting and evangelism. These new trajectories involved significant breaks from past patterns. These contrasting initiatives illustrate how MCC in Indonesia operated in very different ways as opportunities and constraints shifted.

MCC NO LONGER WORKS FOR THE CHURCH (1976–91)

From the mid-1970s and for the next fifteen years MCC's work with transmigrants became the backbone of its operations in Indonesia. Working in partnership with the Department of Transmigration, these *transmigrasi* operations saw MCCers work as expert technical advisors for the government of Indonesia. MCCers were deployed as field scientists, agricultural extension workers, and project managers. To understand this partnership with the authoritarian New Order government it is necessary to consider the limitations of political space available to the organization during these years.

As a system of governance transmigration was initially deployed by Dutch colonial authorities, but it found its most zealous supporters among New Order technocrats.[42] In the late 1960s the Department of Transmigration, with financial support from the World Bank and other major donors, initiated a major resettlement program aimed at encouraging the migration of residents of densely populated Java and Bali to "underpopulated" areas in other islands in the archipelago.[43] The approach was imagined as both a mechanism to alleviate population pressure and as a way to promote economic growth for both the transmigrants and the communities in which they settled. The multi-million-dollar Indonesian transmigration programs were always controversial and were widely attacked by NGOs and other activists as an example of "destructive development."[44] The migrants themselves were often poor and vulnerable. Many were given little information about where they were going and the conditions they would face. Disease and crop failure in the new locations were common, resulting in sickness and death. Many Indigenous communities were resentful and hostile to the new migrants as they intruded into an existing community's social life and occupied ancestral land.[45] The Indonesian government's transmigration programs responded to political and security considerations. Transmigration was a strategy of pacification and was viewed as a mechanism for accelerating national integration.[46] One commentator describes the program as "development fraud," an attempt by a predatory military state to pacify and "Javanize" unruly provinces, leaving in its wake a legacy of "environmental destruction and social conflict."[47]

In 1975 MCC began working with a transmigration project in North Lampung, Sumatra. This shift to working with the Department of Transmigration took place at a particular historical juncture.[48] Throughout the 1970s MCC Indonesia, dependent as it was on North American expatriate volunteers, came under increasing pressure from changes over access to visas. Prior to this, expatriate staff had tended to apply for church-related visas, sponsored largely by the GITJ synod. But this type of visa became much more difficult to obtain as the state tightened its control over immigration. Some new expatriate MCCers had their visas declined at this time and were forced to change their assignments to different countries, where visas were more accessible.

The visa squeeze ran parallel to other strategies deployed by the military-dominated "draconian" New Order (1965–98) to rein in potential critics of President Suharto's authoritarian rule.[49] The regime emphasized the importance of national integration and increasingly promoted the Pancasila state ideology as a means by which national unity would be maintained.[50] In 1978 the government rolled out "Guidelines for Understanding and Enacting Pancasila" (Pedoman Penghayatan dan Pengalaman Pancasila, P4), which mandated a two-week indoctrination course for all members of the civil service and military, and at different levels of the education system. Attempts to monitor and control the NGO sector came to a peak in 1982 when Suharto's government infamously declared that all social and political organizations would be required to declare Pancasila as their "sole foundation" (In. *asas tunggal*).[51] In 1985 this was enacted into law. The New Order's approach to Pancasila indoctrination was combined with other mechanisms of surveillance and control, including intimidation and repression by members of the military and tight media controls.[52]

The New Order's active attempts to discipline the NGO sector did not mean it was opposed to NGO activity per se. Part of the reason for this was that, as Robert Hefner argues, the New Order was always an "unsteady coalition" composed of many different competing factions.[53] This internal fragmentation created significant room for manoeuvre for some NGOs, which actively sought patronage from those factions more sympathetic to their work than others. More importantly, development (In. *pembangunan*) was celebrated and fetishized by New Order technocrats. The regime understood development as a means of economic "catch-up" through industrialization, capitalist expansion, top-down social engineering, and technical programs of improvement.[54] The drive for development became the core ideological basis for the regime. This was potently symbolized in President Suharto declaring himself the "father of development" (In. *bapak pembangunan*). Insofar as NGOs were understood as helping achieve state goals of modernization, economic growth, and national integration, they could find the regime thoroughly supportive of their work.

MCC operated under the same pressures, constraints, and opportunities faced by other NGOs in Indonesia. As the New Order tightened its control over civil society, so too did MCC experience a reduction of political space available for its operations. Because MCC's expatriate service workers required visas to work in the country, the organization was particularly vulnerable to changes in government policy. MCC's collaboration with the state in *transmigrasi* programs runs directly parallel to the arrangements many Indonesian organizations formed with the state to continue their operations under the New Order.

An additional factor specific to MCC was also decisive in creating the conditions for a radical programmatic transformation during this time. Simultaneous to the increasing pressure from the Indonesian bureaucracy, MCC faced a crisis in its long-standing work with the Indonesian Mennonite churches. Various prominent projects and collaborations collapsed in the early 1970s in apparent failure. An anonymous summary report written by an MCCer in the mid-1980s provides a revealingly bleak assessment in which the author specifically notes the "depressing low points" and "real disappointments" in MCC's work with the Indonesian Mennonite churches.[55] The report goes on to link the breakdown of ecclesial relationships with a willingness to embrace new openings:

> By 1978 MCC's central Java program involvement appeared to be rapidly declining with the difficulty of obtaining work visas and a changing perception of the role of MCC workers in church programs. When in 1978 it appeared that the new MCC country representative could not obtain a visa, it was decided to terminate the position. This was also consistent with the church's desire to relate directly to Akron [MCC binational] rather than through a mediary in the form of a country director ... The changing vision of the Mennonite synods and the failure of placing MCC workers in Indonesia brought an era of MCC work to a close. This meant that the relationship between MCC and the church was to take new forms and MCC's desire to continue serving in Indonesia was to take new forms ... While the central Java program was declining, a new involvement in the government's transmigration program was emerging. This was due in part to the expectation that whereas church sponsored visas were exceedingly difficult to get, the only avenue for getting workers' visas in the future would be through signing an agreement with another government department.

Alongside changes in visa access, shifts in relationships with the Mennonite synods, and new models of MCC work, this report notes that MCC Indonesia had a change in leadership. The changeover in leadership was, I argue, crucial. In MCC Indonesia's history, moments of significant programmatic change have tended to coincide with transitions in the organization's leadership. New country directors brought with them fresh ideas and practices. They sought to implement alternative models of how development should be enacted in practice. Changes in leadership frequently shook up existing relationships. Long-standing friendships could be discarded and new associations formed. This general pattern was in keeping with MCC's field-driven philosophy, which entrusted daily management of programs to the hands of in-country leadership.[56]

MCC's first involvement in the Indonesian transmigration programs began in 1975 in Way Abung, Southern Sumatra. The initial impetus for this work was that GITJ leaders asked MCC to get involved. The church was concerned for several hundred members of its denomination who had joined the government-facilitated program. The new technical model of development therefore opened up within the terms established by the old model of ecclesial relationships. The Way Abung program served as a bridging initiative that led to a series of other *transmigrasi* projects in South Sumatra, West Kalimantan, and Central Sulawesi.[57] These latter projects were not linked to the Indonesian Mennonite churches.

An MCC report written three years into the Way Abung project provides insights into the discursive politics of MCC's work.[58] The report was written for an external audience rather than an MCC readership. It introduces MCC as "an international development organization" and describes in detail the sorts of "agricultural development" work that MCCers carried out in Way Abung, including introducing 160 draft oxen and an associated revolving credit program, forming a farmers' association for the management of the oxen program, encouraging farmer "self-reliance," undertaking "experimental research" with hot-weather tomatoes, introducing millet and "intermediary technology," establishing an education fund, and supporting family planning through increased access to contraception.

Further reports produced by MCCers throughout this period similarly and consistently emphasize the technical and scientific nature of MCC's development work.[59] Through these reports MCCers portrayed themselves as agricultural specialists and extension workers seeking to improve agricultural yields, modernize farming systems, and educate local populations in innovative technology. As with the EIA discussed in the previous chapter, these reports are also examples of MCCers "rendering technical."[60] The reports starkly contrast with discourses I encountered during my fieldwork of MCCers prioritizing relationships (also discussed in the previous chapter). The oscillation between technical and relational discourses is, I argue, an enduring tension within MCC's operations in Indonesia. At different times, and sometimes also with different audiences, MCC's work could be located at quite different points along this spectrum. Clearly, the approach of these reports resonated especially with a technical orientation, that is to say, with the notion that MCC's service should be primarily in the form of technical agricultural interventions built on widely circulating ideas within the broader development discourse – ideas that had considerable purchase in MCC teams around the world.[61] They also resonated with other New Order initiatives then being implemented, including the Bimas "mass guidance" (In. *bimbingan massal*) program launched in 1969, which aimed at modernizing Indonesia's agricultural production.[62] Given this congruence it was unsurprising that Indonesian state officials considered the model of technical assistance employed by MCC in Way Abung an unmitigated success. The Department of Transmigration consequently actively sought to partner with MCC in other initiatives. A working agreement was signed with the government of Indonesia on 22 January 1980, and soon after the Department of Transmigration became MCC's primary partner in Indonesia. Visas, access, and allocation of project sites were facilitated by and through this department until the early 1990s.

The background section of the 1980 Working Agreement clearly indicates that MCC's official stance on the *transmigrasi* projects was one of emphatic support.[63] Within internal documents support was also bestowed on the partnership, with one letter asserting that "MCC workers can be effective witnesses to God's love by being a Christian presence in transmigration areas."[64] This is not merely a strategy of discursive enrolment; rather, this statement should be read as a theological affirmation of active participation with New Order development projects. Clearly, MCC's transmigration programs were imagined as fulfilling a specifically Christian mission of "witness" and "presence."

However, this collaboration with a military dictatorship also raised concerns within MCC. Aware of the criticism other NGOs had levelled against *transmigrasi*, some MCCers felt anxious about whether the assistance they offered offset the political implications of the whole scheme. In part because of this concern in the mid-1980s, MCCers sought to revise their contract with the Department of Transmigration. This revision opened opportunities for MCC to extend its work beyond the transmigrants so that it could also design and implement programs for the Indigenous communities in project areas. Some MCCers were concerned about whether their work on *transmigrasi* programs might compromise MCC's Christian identity and mission. Writing in his Quarterly Report, an internal document, only six months after the 1980 Working Agreement was signed, an MCCer articulated these concerns:

> With all due respect for the many long weeks of labor spent bringing the agreement into existence, I must say that we still have reservations and apprehensions about it. Just how far we as individuals and MCC as a Christian organization can go in compromising our principles to accommodate the government of Indonesia is truly something we must search out carefully and prayerfully … One Transmigration official expressed what is perhaps the government's intent by saying, "MCC no longer works for the Church. You are now working for the government."[65]

The official's comments were interpreted as cutting because they highlighted how far MCC had become an ancillary arm of the Indonesian state. This intimate association called into question both MCC's Christian mission and its "non-governmental" status. In mid-1981 the same MCCer wrote a letter to the general secretary of the Department of Transmigration and, in concise language, terminated his work in Indonesia and indicated he was seeking reassignment: "My reason for leaving the project is twofold: (1) I feel that my calling is to work with the Church on issues of community/economic development, and (2) I prefer to work in a low-key, less formal manner with the local people."[66] Tensions over whether MCC was *too* close to the state continued to haunt MCC's work in *transmigrasi* through to the 1990s.

These unresolved concerns informed repeated attempts to articulate MCC's philosophy of development and to clarify its status as a development actor. For example, in a document written primarily for Indonesian government officials in 1979, MCC is situated as an "international community development agency," with the following explanation: "Community development is a process of developing, building, and improving the character of the people themselves. The goal of community development is to help people become more self-reliant in problem solving, to help them become better and more productive citizens."[67] The author explains that MCC chooses to "de-emphasize" material aid and highlight instead the possibility of a "dynamic partnership in mutual respect between technician and villager." The document includes guidelines on how community development practitioners should come alongside local communities in "participant observer"-type roles to gain an emic perspective.[68] This expression of MCC's philosophy and approach avoided mentioning its Christian identity. The reports from this period that did situate MCC as a Christian organization tended to do so only by acknowledging an association with North American Mennonite churches. But even in these reports a Christian identity is noted only in passing and is not dwelt upon at any length.[69]

There were good political reasons to downplay MCC's Christian mission at this time and to situate the organization as an agency that provided technical expertise in close collaboration with the state. As Mujiburrahman notes, during the early decades of the New Order some prominent Muslim leaders issued sharp criticisms of attempts at Christian evangelism, describing it as a new form of "foreign intervention" and a "new style of crusade."[70] The threat of Christian evangelism (In. *kristenisasi*) was portrayed as an affront to Muslims throughout the archipelago. They therefore demanded that the government "control foreign aid and restrict religious missions only to people who had no religion." The response of the government was, Mujiburrahman argues, "ambiguous." The New Order promoted a pluralist Pancasila ideology, and it used this as a buffer to dampen the legitimacy of Muslim criticism and lobbying efforts. But it was also deeply invested in maintaining socio-political stability and, therefore, remained very responsive to potential inter-religious tensions. In 1978, just a few years before the "sole foundation" regulations reshaped the NGO landscape, the Indonesian government issued significant new restrictions on foreign aid to religious institutions and on visa access by foreign church workers.[71] As the next section outlines, these restrictions were part of the background that facilitated the second programmatic evolution in Indonesia at this time – one that was explicitly evangelistic.

SPIRITUAL BEING FIRST AND FOREMOST (1975–84)

The *transmigrasi* programs, although initiated under the auspices of GITJ, culminated in a major reorientation of MCC's work in Indonesia. This trajectory did not involve a rejection of Christian mission but, rather, its incorporation into a mission of development. Nevertheless, it included a marked transition from MCC's earlier focus on church partnerships. But even during the first few decades of its work in Indonesia, when MCC was focused largely on working with the Indonesian Mennonite churches, MCCers were reluctant to engage directly in evangelistic or church-planting projects. MCC's identity as "not really" a mission board saw various checks and limitations on its programmatic repertoire. It is therefore interesting to note that, at the same time as its partnership with the Department of Transmigration was gaining momentum, MCC embarked on a new initiative that included planting churches in the Kapuas Hulu area of West Kalimantan among 'Kantu (Indigenous Dayak) communities. I call this MCC Indonesia's "evangelistic turn." I was initially alerted to this initiative through a series of conversations with Howard Miller, who was the MCC Indonesia Country Representative during the 1970s.[72] I later researched this initiative in the MCC archives and then, in collaboration with Laura Meitzner Yoder, conducted further research and interviews in West Kalimantan and Pennsylvania.[73]

MCC's evangelistic turn in West Kalimantan took place due to a convergence of factors. Within MCC, the in-country leadership expanded MCC's programmatic space to include the possibility of church planting. Expatriate MCCers were recruited who were amenable to embracing a "holistic" model, which combined development and church planting. Beyond MCC, actors within the New Order state facilitated MCC's access in a concerted bureaucratic attempt to incorporate "interior" peoples into the state's project of nation building and development. Further, the 'Kantu communities themselves saw value, and perhaps divine imperative, in engaging with Christian missionaries and adopting a new religion. The approach adopted by each of these actors afforded new evangelistic possibilities for MCC. I address each of these factors in turn.

A review of three consecutive MCC Indonesia Annual Reports gives a picture of how MCC leadership created space for this evangelistic turn. In the 1975 Annual Report, Howard Miller wrote that, in the past, MCC had sought to clearly articulate to the Indonesian Mennonite churches that its work was distinct from that of the mission boards. Howard raises questions, however, regarding whether MCC should remain "only interested in social services and not in the churches' evangelical witness." He goes on to note that specific efforts were being made by MCCers in Indonesia "to identify more closely with the churches in their total witness to Indonesian society."

The implications of this identification are spelled out more clearly in the following year's Annual Report in which, in addition to ongoing medical, relief, and agricultural development work, MCC's objectives for the year included the expressed goal "to support, encourage and facilitate the expansion of the witness and ministries of the Mennonite-related churches of Indonesia." A handwritten note on the otherwise typewritten report elaborates that one of the Indonesian Mennonite churches, GKMI, was in the early stages of planning "mission work" in West Kalimantan "encompassing evangelization as well as community development including attention to health, education and agriculture." GKMI had invited MCC to support the program, "especially in the community development aspect."

At the time the 1977 Annual Report was written, expatriate and Indonesian workers were being recruited to staff the proposed project. But the overall plan had by then been fleshed out. The lead partner in the project was the GKMI mission board, the Foundation for Service and Evangelism (Yayasan Pekabaran Injil dan Pelayanan Kasih, PIPKA). Founded in 1965 and modelled after North American mission boards, the Annual Report notes that PIPKA had already sent an evangelist to West Kalimantan. The area of evangelism is identified as the Kapuas Hulu region near Putussibau. This area was chosen because no other "missions" were located in the area. The Annual Report further outlines:

> The Dayak people in our focus area are still quite primitive compared to other areas, for this reason the nature of our ministry in this area is very different from our ministry in Java and Sumatra. It is comprehensive. The aspects of ministry which we want to carry on together are spiritual, educational, agricultural, health and others with spiritual being first and foremost.

These consecutive reports highlight a gradual shift in framing MCC's planned involvement in West Kalimantan. Prior to committing to a specific project there was an explicit attempt to create space, both discursive and practical, for associating with the "total witness" of the Indonesian churches (1975). This moved into formulating a concrete plan for MCC to provide support "especially in community development" (1976). A year later MCC actively engaged with an Indonesian mission organization to undertake "spiritual [ministry] first and foremost" (1977). MCC partnered with an organization to engage in evangelism and church planting.

Later in 1977 two expatriate families were seconded to MCC from the Eastern Mennonite Board of Missions and Charities (EMBMC), the mission board of the Lancaster Mennonite Conference in Pennsylvania. The EMBMC connection is important for this resolved MCC's lack of theological and ecclesial mandate for evangelism and church planting. EMBMC's conference affiliation provided the necessary credentials. These American MCCers worked alongside Indonesian PIPKA staff carrying out a range of tasks, including Bible teaching, agricultural extension, literacy training, and infant health care. This was framed as a "holistic" and "comprehensive" mission. An MCC News Service report at the time announced: "It is an adventure in overcoming past divisions and pulling together evangelism and service."[74] However, this holism was undermined by separating the tasks and workloads among the missionary team into distinct areas of responsibility, in which "religious-spiritual" matters was one component alongside "socio-economic," "health," and "educational" needs. Different members of the missionary team assumed quite different roles within this array of tasks.

In 1984 the expatriate MCC staff members completed their assignments and left the country, although Indonesian PIPKA staff continued working in the area.[75] Towards the end of the 1980s, American Mennonite missionary Stanley Shenk reported that there were thirteen Mennonite congregations established in West Kalimantan as a result of PIPKA and MCC's work.[76] When I visited the area in 2015 it was clear that the number of GKMI churches in the area had expanded considerably.

While this evangelistic turn can be regarded as an anomaly in MCC's praxis, it was not a unique or unprecedented deviation. Paul Toews notes that the work of MCC and North American Mennonite mission boards "often converged."[77] Toews argues: "Mission programs brought in MCC programs, and MCC's relief work brought Mennonite missionaries. In Taiwan, Ethiopia, India, Vietnam, Japan, Hong Kong, Uruguay, Puerto Rico, and Belize, MCC relief and development efforts preceded the establishment of Mennonite congregations." The possibility of crossing a mission-development line was clearly available to MCCers in other country contexts. Supporting evangelistic work could be part of the MCC discursive repertoire, and in-country leadership could organize such work at certain times and in certain places.

The successive Annual Reports discussed above illustrate the progressive construction of imaginative space in MCC Indonesia to support and engage church planting projects. Howard Miller, as the Country Representative during this time, played a pivotal role in reformulating MCC's work in Indonesia to enable the new programmatic direction. But Howard did not act alone. His reports were sent up the MCC hierarchy to administrators in Akron, Pennsylvania, and their approval of the new direction is apparent in the decision to recruit expatriate MCCers affiliated with EMBMC to participate in the work in Kalimantan. This could not have happened without the active involvement of North American leadership. At other times church-planting possibilities have been curtailed or negated; but, at this juncture, key actors within the broader MCC organization supported Howard's proposal. Further, PIPKA and wider GKMI church leaders were also supportive – indeed, enthusiastic – about the collaboration with MCC in this mission work. PIPKA provided the majority of the staff team in West Kalimantan as well as the team leader.

But the question of how MCC came to plant churches in West Kalimantan is not adequately addressed by attending only to dynamics internal to MCC or GKMI, as important as these are. Just as with MCC's partnership with the Department of Transmigration, analyzing the operations of MCC in this case also requires attention to the political environment operating around and on MCC. Crucially, actors within the New Order state were willing to facilitate church planting in the Kalimantan interior. While the role of the Indonesian state is largely absent from MCC documentation, attention to its interests is critical for understanding MCC's evangelistic turn.

In 1965 General Suharto's coup inaugurated the New Order regime and precipitated far-reaching political, social, and economic change throughout the Indonesian archipelago. The new regime quickly went about eliminating its primary opposition, the Indonesian Communist Party (Partai Komunis Indonesia, PKI), which was blamed for the assassination of senior military figures.[78] Communism was demonized in official public discourse and communists portrayed as vile threats to the nation. Estimates vary on the number of deaths resulting from the ensuing pogroms. Leaving plenty of room for uncertainty and a wide margin for error, Robert Cribb suggests that the figure is between 200,000 and 800,000 casualties.[79] The killings were carried out primarily by military and vigilante groups. Alongside state-sanctioned and extrajudicial mass murder, the New Order also detained thousands of suspected communists and others opposed to the new regime.

As part of its suppression of communism the New Order reworked the concept of "religion" (In. *agama*). In 1966 Suharto's government reinforced an earlier declaration that all Indonesians should profess one of only five officially recognized religions: Islam, Hinduism, Buddhism, Roman Catholicism, or Protestantism. This "truncated pluralism" amounts to what Jeremy Menchik calls a mode of "godly nationalism," in that the state demanded that citizens believe in God and belong to a religion, but it also remained ambivalent as to which religion they followed.[80] The expressed intent of enforcing a limited range of religions was to marginalize "atheist" communists. The requirement of religious adherence left those who did not belong to one of the officially recognized *agama* in a perilous position as they were open to accusations of being communist. Unsurprisingly, hundreds of thousands of alleged communists and awkwardly aligned groups sought refuge by adopting a formal religion, particularly Christianity. Observing these changes, Jennifer Connolly argues that Suharto's government rejected "a secularist separation of the state and religion" and became "actively involved in religious affairs." This took place to such an extent that the state took "control of the religious marketplace."[81]

The New Order suppression of non-religion and the active promotion of theism amounted to a comprehensive religionization of Indonesian society. This process took place at the same time as the roll out of government-directed economic development plans and an enhanced project of nationalist unification, both of which were socially transformative. I argue that the interweaving of these three processes should be understood as a godly developmentalism in which the state sought to achieve its developmental and unification goals through the imposition of a religious techno-politics.[82]

By the late 1970s, having cemented its hold on state power, the New Order further tightened its control over religious affairs. Especially important was a series of decrees issued by the minister of religion to limit missionary activity.[83] A 1978 decree disallowed religious propagation to people who held another recognized religion, and it also restricted some forms of proselytization. In 1979 a joint decree from the minister of religion and the minister of home affairs reinforced the earlier proclamation and provided further teeth for its implementation. These measures parallelled the tighter controls, discussed above, that the New Order exerted over all NGO activity. These policy changes had a significant impact on MCC, including the tightening of visa access. It was also at this time that MCC embarked on its evangelistic turn. If religion in general, and religious propagation in particular, was increasingly tightly disciplined by the state in late 1970s, how then did MCC carry out explicitly evangelistic work in West Kalimantan at this time? Three issues are particularly important.

First, not all decrees were implemented rigidly or comprehensively.[84] In the case of the laws on missionary activity, the practice of governmental discipline was sometimes lax or even contrary to stated policy. The Indonesian state was not a coherent or singular unit, and technocrat ambitions never lived up to the rhetoric of efficiency and orderliness. There were plenty of cracks through which alternative projects could emerge and flourish.

Second, while government decrees attempted to restrict "evangelistic" activities, the government also sought to promote an increasingly fetishized development, and this development was imagined as embedded within, and as enhancing, religion. Inherent to the godly developmentalism of the New Order, therefore, was a blurring of distinctions between mission and development. It is notable that the 1970s also saw the rise of what Michael Feener calls a new "*da'wa* paradigm," which brought together "mutually-reinforcing currents of Islamic reform, Indonesian nationalism, and economic developmentalism" in projects of Islamic revival and propagation, including through state-sponsored projects.[85]

Third, although evangelism of adherents of other official *agama* was restricted, the decrees did not limit proselytizing among Indigenous communities that were unaffiliated with the recognized five religions.[86] This crucial distinction meant that evangelism among most Indigenous groups was not foreclosed. In fact, the New Order state took active steps to encourage and enable Christian missionary activity during the 1970s and 1980s to those that it deemed "did not have a religion" (In. *tidak ada agama*). While Christian mission activity could be forbidden in some contexts, the Indonesian state actively supported missionary work in others. Just as MCC was shaped through an evangelistic ambivalence, so too the New Order provided yes/no answers to its deployment of Christian mission.

A focus on Indigenous Dayak and other "interior" peoples helps ground these wider dynamics. In West Kalimantan many Dayak communities found themselves in the unfortunate position of having no recognized *agama*. Many ethnic Chinese in West Kalimantan were suspected communist sympathizers, and state-sanctioned violence against them was rife in the fervently anti-communist atmosphere of Indonesia's early New Order period. There was therefore intense pressure for non-affiliated groups to identify with a religion that had official standing in the new political environment. The New Order was intent on encouraging precisely such a move and, as a consequence, actively facilitated Christian evangelism such that the "army and the local government supported the spread of Christianity in the remote regions."[87]

Lorraine Aragon's study of Salvation Army Protestant Christianity in the highlands of Central Sulawesi provides a textured comparison.[88] According to Aragon, Suharto's New Order viewed Indigenous minority populations as "isolated or estranged groups" (In. *suku terasing*) and backwards (In. *terbelakang*). They were regarded as problematic because of their marginal incorporation into the Indonesian nation-state and a perceived lagging behind in the drive towards development. For these groups the state initiated an aggressive campaign of "human engineering" promoted through "godly means" by making use of Indonesian churches and foreign missionaries.[89] This strategy made churches into "proxies" for the Indonesian state such that "the church … [was] the government of the interior highlands, or at least the most familiar branch of it."[90] Aragon suggests that government officials "recognize[d] that foreign Christian missions [were] still one of the most promising and cost-effective methods to extract knowledge, cooperation, and products from remote interior areas" and therefore facilitated their access through the provision of visas and tacit permission.[91] Such access was often tentative to ensure an ongoing vulnerability and dependence among missionaries on state largesse. It could be quickly revoked when state goals were accomplished, and missionaries could be redirected to other areas of "underdevelopment." Christian mission to interior peoples was an important tool in the governance apparatus of the New Order, with conversion to Christianity perceived as involving a triple transformation. In joining a "modern" religion, interior peoples were integrated into the Pancasila nationalism of the Indonesian state, which Aragon regards as the New Order's "civil religion," and were also initiated into national devotion to development.[92]

Aragon's analysis of Christian evangelism in Sulawesi suggests why the New Order state was willing to facilitate access for MCC's evangelistic work among 'Kantu communities in West Kalimantan. As conspicuous American foreigners, the expatriate MCCers required state approval for their presence in the Kapuas Hulu area. It is possible to read MCC's evangelistic turn as one in which MCCers became missionaries of the state.[93] The "religious" mission imbued in this evangelistic turn was intimately entwined with political and economic dynamics. MCC's "holistic" use of evangelism and agricultural development in West Kalimantan was enmeshed, even encapsulated, in wider imperatives for governance, development, and national integration. Aragon's concluding assessment over Christian mission in Sulawesi is pertinent to MCC's work in Kalimantan: "religious devotion and economic development have become quietly indexed to one another."[94] MCC's evangelistic turn, therefore, involved an annexing by the New Order state that directly parallels the politics of MCC's work on transmigration projects in this same period.

AN INDISSOLUBLE AMBIGUITY

It is tempting to contrast the two paths MCC's programs took in the 1970s as a collapse of the earlier mission-development nexus that had previously characterized MCC's work in Indonesia. The evangelistic turn in Kalimantan saw MCC transform into a church-planting organization; the partnership with the Department of Transmigration saw MCC discard its ecclesial affiliations for an embrace of technocratic state-led development. A simple dichotomy, however, is inadequate.

The case of the transmigration programs offers intriguing parallels with what Matthew Engelke describes as "strategic secularism."[95] In Engelke's study of an advocacy campaign by the Bible Society in England, he suggests that the approach adopted was to dissociate the Christian Scriptures from any "religious" association to render it acceptable and more appealing to a general contemporary English secular public. In this instance, the Bible society engaged in a kind of strategic secularism that was put to work for decidedly religious agendas. Documentary reports that rendered MCC as an organization endowed with professional technical and scientific expertise and that downplayed, or muted altogether, its association with Christianity can be seen as a similar kind of strategic deployment.[96] Although, in this case, given that the New Order state disavowed secularism (because of its apparent associations with "atheist" communism and the possible offence this could cause among Muslim leaders), it would be better to think of MCC's stance as a strategic Pancasilaism. MCCers relocated their work to be more amenable to the New Order's fetishization of technical and scientific paradigms of modernization, its ambitions for social engineering (including far-reaching interventions in defining, restricting, and disciplining religion), and its concern for incorporating "underdeveloped" "interior" peoples. The New Order's pursuit of a godly developmentalism did not require a strategic de-regionalization of MCC's programs, but it did discipline the religious framings that could be performed in different locations. This strategic Pancasilaism was a means by which MCCers communicated with, and enrolled, Indonesian government officials into supporting their work.

But strategic rhetoric does not equate to abandoning Mennonite theologies of practical, embodied, "quietist" service. Discourse should not be conflated with practice.[97] A rhetorical de-emphasis of MCC's Christian identity did not necessarily dictate the work MCCers actually carried out on transmigration projects. Nor did it necessarily equate with the representations of their work that were provided to other stakeholders, including other MCCers and donor constituents back home. In conversations I had with Stefanus, a former Indonesian MCC worker who was extensively involved in MCC's transmigration programs and who had helped negotiate its partnership with the Department of Transmigration, I learned that at least some of MCC's work on transmigration projects was deeply imbued with a missionary impulse. Stefanus used the opportunity of travelling to far-flung *transmigrasi* sites to minister in Protestant churches. While he was not an ordained minister, he nevertheless frequently preached the Christian gospel in church services and actively sought opportunities to support local Christians in the transmigration areas. It is worth noting here too that, after completing his work with MCC, Stefanus went on to work with PIPKA, the same organization that took the lead in church planting in West Kalimantan. Recall also that the initial impulse for the *transmigrasi* work was to assist Indonesian Mennonite church transmigrants to Sumatra. Moreover, Stefanus told me that it was as a direct result of a senior government officer in the Department of Transmigration that MCC was given the extensive access that it received; this Christian technocrat sought to facilitate Christian penetration into Indonesia through his position as a bureaucrat located within the New Order state.

Similarly, while MCCers worked as evangelists in Kalimantan, they were also engaged in a "holistic" enterprise that saw some MCCers play familiar roles as agricultural extension workers, rural health advisors, and technical experts. Their conversionary efforts involved planting churches as well as helping to incorporate 'Kantu communities into state ambitions for development and Pancasila nationalism. Their Christian preaching proceeded alongside the technical development work celebrated by the Indonesian state. If development can be mission, then mission can also be development.

The line separating development and mission is, as Inge Hovland argues, much easier to draw in theory than in practice.[98] Over the history of MCC Indonesia a division between "mission" and "development" has been asserted but also frequently contested and repeatedly blurred in the organization's practices. This is also an inevitable corollary stemming from an ambiguity, prevalent throughout the organization, regarding the relationship between the two: the ambiguous "yes-and-no" answer to the question of mission, as articulated in response to the "Missionaries Under Cover" saga, is pertinent for the analysis of MCC's field practices in Indonesia. While, for theological reasons, MCC was not given a mandate to engage in evangelism and plant churches by its sponsoring churches, it has nevertheless been endowed with a specifically Christian mission. The resulting ambiguity has created considerable room for manoeuvre for those who manage MCC's programs. But whether MCCers were working intimately with Indonesian Mennonite churches, planting churches in West Kalimantan, or partnering with the Department of Transmigration, the often uneasy and frequently contested development-mission nexus has proved remarkably durable.

MCC's leadership was crucial in enabling the imaginative and practical conditions for programmatic transformations. But it did not operate in a vacuum. MCC worked within an Indonesian political ecology of development and state building, which was also constantly evolving. While MCC staff had considerable flexibility to carry out a range of activities during the earliest period in Indonesia (1948–70s), as the New Order state consolidated its authority (1970s–90), the room for manoeuvre available to MCC was restricted. This saw state agencies deploy a variety of specific mechanisms of discipline and control, among the most important of which for MCC was visa access for expatriate staff. As a consequence of this reduction in available social space, MCCers shifted their organization into collaborations with agents of the New Order state. Although seemingly contradictory, the evangelistic turn in West Kalimantan and the partnership with the Department of Transmigration both saw MCC become, in effect, a branch of the New Order state. MCC was granted ongoing access to carry out its programs only insofar as it was seen as fulfilling state-directed goals of nation building and development. Given the traditionally strict split between church and state in much Mennonite theology, and MCC's long-standing hesitancy to collaborate with USAID on the grounds of its imperialist intentions (as outlined in earlier chapters), these collaborations with the military-dominated New Order regime are striking. The dramatic transformations of MCC's programs during the course of its history in Indonesia illustrate the flexibility with which MCCers adapted to changing political conditions and the impact of its field-driven approach to operations.

4

Theology and Development

> Throughout its history MCC often understood itself as bringing Mennonites together without the burden of extensive theologizing.
>
> Steven Nolt[1]

ENROLMENT PRACTICES

The previous two chapters trace MCC's translation practices into Indonesia in contemporary and historical formations. Translation involved transference and transformation, conveyance and disjuncture. These tensions resulted in considerable innovation in the ways MCC worked across time and space. This chapter returns to the North American context of MCC's work to address the ways MCC is framed and positioned to its donor constituency and among its own staff. The indissoluble "yes-and-no" missional ambiguity is not only found in MCC's practices in the field but also permeates the theological articulations of the organization at home. This chapter is therefore concerned with the interplay of policy and politics in theological articulation.

A focus on theology-as-policy involves a shift in my use of "translation." Bruno Latour argues that translation is synonymous with *enrolling* new actors into particular projects.[2] Translation is therefore the process of seducing divergent perspectives into participating together in common projects. This coming together is not unification but, rather, the formation of a still-heterogeneous assemblage. Translation is productive collaboration in which disparate interests intersect. Drawing on Latour, David Mosse and David Lewis also frame translation as the process by which development projects "become real through the work of generating and translating interests, creating context by tying in supporters and so sustaining interpretations."[3]

Policy articulations are a key mechanism through which development organizations enrol or recruit a constituency.[4] In this chapter

I investigate how MCC has been situated theologically. By treating theological articulation as policy, I explore not what theology should be normatively articulated within the organization but, rather, how theological articulations, and disarticulations, work in practice. While MCC is permeated by theological discourses and practices a particular episode of theological *dis*articulation in the early 1990s serves as a useful entry point into examining strategies of ambiguity, opacity, and vagueness that have been deployed by MCC to enrol its pre-constituted theologically diverse constituency. A disarticulated theology works effectively in enrolling the North American Mennonite peoplehood into supporting the organization. This lack of specificity in normative theological expression also affords significant diversity in MCC's field programs.

THEOLOGICAL (DIS)ARTICULATIONS

MCC is shaped by North American Mennonite Christianity in both tacit and perspicuous ways. Throughout my fieldwork I frequently encountered practices, representations, and narratives saturated in Mennonite Christian discourse and symbolism. Many MCCers perceived their organization as endowed with sacred significance. MCC's logo (see figure 4.1), in MCC slang fondly called "the pregnant pigeon," combines images of cross and dove, both richly endowed with Christian symbolism. Official MCC publicity material frequently references biblical texts and keywords such "service," "love," "peace," and "non-resistance" that are prominent within the vernacular theologies of historically pacifist Mennonites. Moreover, MCC representations draw heavily on Christian moral discourses of altruism, charity, justice, self-sacrifice, faithfulness, and generosity. Donors are appealed to in explicitly religious terms, with donations being represented as "bringing hope and caring in the name of Christ."

Echoing this pervasiveness, MCC's carefully crafted mission statement is explicit about MCC's Christian identity. The 1999 version of the mission statement (see below), prominent in what is colloquially known among MCCers as the "rusty nail" document on account of a vertical band of reddish-brown adorning the front cover of the brochure, locates MCC squarely within the Christian tradition, carrying out a specifically Christian vocation.[5] The statement opens by framing MCC's work as a demonstration of "God's love" and closes by affirming that MCC is committed to "sharing … faith in Jesus Christ."

Figure 4.1 | The "pregnant pigeon" logo

The "Rusty Nail" Mission Statement
MCC **seeks to demonstrate God's love** by working among people suffering from poverty, conflict, oppression and natural disaster;
MCC **serves as a channel of interchange** by building relationships that are mutually transformative;
MCC **strives for peace, justice and dignity of all people** by sharing our experiences, resources, and faith in Jesus Christ.

Christian ritual, too, permeated the organization. At a two-week orientation for new MCCers that I attended in mid-2008 in Akron, Pennsylvania, we began each morning with "devotions" and participated in communal sung worship. A month earlier I attended MCC's (binational) annual general meeting (AGM) in Waterloo, Ontario, during which prayers were offered for MCC's work around the world. An opening speech at the AGM described the organization as an "outpost of the church." The summary of international programs provided by senior staff explicitly referenced biblical texts. For example, Matthew 10:42, which refers to provision of a "cup of cold water," was used to validate sending material aid, including canned meat, as a form of relief work. We also heartily sang Christian hymns in four-part a cappella. Congregational singing is a prominent ritual practice among some groups of ethnic Mennonites.[6] According to Mennonite academic and poet Julia Kasdorf, in such singing practices a Mennonite congregation "simultaneously produces and consumes an aesthetic whole."[7] She continues: "Maybe in this, the quintessential communal activity, Mennonites most keenly feel what it is to *be* the Body of Christ."[8] The practice of singing together in harmony – orchestrating the intertwining of difference in such a way so as to produce aesthetic coherence – evokes and enacts an idealized ecclesial corporeality and instantiates a particular mode of religious community.

Visible expressions of Christian religiosity were common in the gatherings I attended of the twenty- to thirty-person MCC team in Indonesia. Team meetings and team retreats, both annual events, included time for communal prayer, theological reflection, communion, ritual foot washing, and worship singing – including singing hymns in four-part harmony. These rituals took place alongside discussions about strategic plans, emerging development projects, and reports about activities. In the MCC Indonesia country office the small group of expatriate and Indonesian staff often concluded staff meetings with prayer. This took place on a rotating basis among the office staff, and prayers were spoken in English or Indonesian, depending on the preference of the assigned person. As a regular face in the office, I was sometimes slotted in among the roster of those invited to pray. An example of such prayer took place in an especially full office meeting in January 2008, which was expanded by the presence of a number of expatriate service workers usually located on assignment elsewhere around the archipelago. While the rest of us sat silently with heads bowed, Jake Friesen, the MCC Representative, concluded this prayer time with these words:

> Lord, once again we pause and take time to recognize you as our God and ultimately in control of our lives. That we make all these plans and activities, reports, and yet it all comes down to remembering that you are in control. Help us, Lord, to remember that you are the reason we do what we do. Help us turn our attention

> towards you before making our plans; that, Lord, the things we do be according to your leading and be pleasing to you. Thank you for the opportunity to serve you. And for many of us far away from home, some of us not as far away, but sometimes it feels like it, and yet everyone here to serve you, as we are being led to. Amen.

MCC Indonesia's communal space is permeated by Christian language and ritual practice. The religiosity of the communal space is largely taken for granted as part and parcel of serving with a Christian organization. It is an unsurprising and expected feature of the organization. It was generally assumed that all members of the MCC Indonesia team, whether expatriate or Indonesian, shared a common faith, even if there were different understandings about what this was and how it was to be enacted. The shared Christianity of MCCers in Indonesia was one of the outcomes of the vetting process through which prospective MCCers joined the organization. Expatriate service workers with MCC, regardless of where they serve, are required to meet three "screens" to work with the organization: "exhibit a commitment to Christian faith, be active members of a Christian church and be committed to nonviolent biblical peacemaking."[9] Although this wasn't the case in all of MCC's field programs, in MCC Indonesia the same screens were also used in hiring local staff.[10] This kind of boundary policing allowed for a presumption of shared Christian identity.

Given these sorts of encounters, when I posed the question "What is MCC's theology of service?" to MCCers in Indonesia, I anticipated a straightforward answer. My expectation was entirely misplaced. In their responses to my question various MCCers confessed to not knowing what "the answer" was or should be. Others divulged that, although they once thought they knew what MCC's theology of service was, now that they were actually on assignment they were much less sure. Still others informed me that MCC had never actually articulated a theology of service. An interview with Anna Friesen, one of the MCC Reps, was particularly illuminating. During our frank conversation, Anna patiently walked me through MCC's theological complexities. I mentioned the peculiar conundrum that whenever I asked MCCers about their theology of service I got widely divergent answers. She was unsurprised. Anna told me that this was because MCC had avoided articulating an explicit theology. The crux of the matter was the challenge of keeping MCC's theologically diverse constituency working together on the common project of MCC. To articulate a theology of service in such a context would be to ensure that, at minimum, some supporting churches would find it off-putting, if not offensive. MCC's solution was that, instead of attempting to get constituents to agree on *why* MCC does its work, Mennonites were instead invited to *act together* through MCC. Except as "personal projects" undertaken on a private basis, MCC had not publicized a theology of development. Anna assured me that the MCC board would not adopt any statement that clearly indicated "this is our theology" or publish documents explicitly articulating a clear organizational theological paradigm. This lack of explicit articulation was part of what Anna regarded as "the fuzziness and ambiguity of MCC." While she continued to believe that MCC did good work and "moves toward God's kingdom," nevertheless, the theology is "not just laid out there."

To illustrate this, Anna referred to the "rusty nail" document mentioned above. What was important was not only what it said but also what it did not say. Rather than an explicit theology, there were only intimations towards selected biblical texts that could be consulted for guidance.[11] Anna's analysis was astute. While unambiguously Christian and clearly intended to consecrate the organization as attuned with dominant Mennonite languages of faith, the "rusty nail" document was also decidedly vague and allusive. The mission statement did not constrain the organization into certain practices but, through spiritual innuendo, appealed to broad ideas that could be read in multiple ways. This was not a systematically framed, formal, and prescriptive theology for MCC.

Another example is the three "screens" for prospective MCC service workers, discussed above, which imply a generic Christian identity without specifying what that identity means or how it should be practised. As basic requirements, the screens are just as important for what they do not require as for what they do. The level of commitment of MCCers is not measured, they are not required to affirm any formal doctrinal or credal statement, and no particular ritual practice is made prerequisite. Instead of clearly outlining a theological position, statements like these merely vaguely allude to a sacralized mission and identity. The following example expands on these insights with a narrative drawn from archival research.[12]

A MISSIOLOGY FOR MCC

In the early 1990s Ray Brubacher, at the time the director of MCC's Overseas Services, published a short article in the internal MCC newsletter *Intercom* calling on the organization to develop a formal missiology.[13] Brubacher's article, entitled "A Missiology for MCC," was fairly typical for the newsletter. Rather than a formal expression of official policy or a polished declaration of normative intent, Brubacher's tone, content, and style were conversational. The article sought to evoke discussion, and the substantial quantity of files lodged in the archives in response to Brubacher's article attests to a vibrant and vigorous response.[14]

In his article Brubacher states that, as a "personal interest," he had intended for a while to examine MCC's missiology and, after receiving encouragement from other MCCers, he began considering the possibility of an "institutional exercise" in the matter. Brubacher did not question whether MCC had a Christian identity as such. This had been clearly established in the recently approved "Mission Statement" and "Growing Edges" documents.[15] Rather, he was concerned with whether MCC's identity was grounded in a systematic, thorough, and coherent theology. "I sense sometimes," wrote Brubacher, "that we draw up plans using social science theories and then paste a Bible verse at the end to make it feel religious ... I fear we sometimes run the risk of proof-texting." Corresponding with his position in the Overseas Department, Brubacher was primarily concerned with field programs. He therefore believes that a key advantage of clearly articulating an organizational theology is the provision of "adequate guidance" to fieldworkers in carrying out their work for a "church agency that does not plant churches."[16] However, Brubacher assumed that, in addition to emerging from the contexts "in which we live and work," the planned missiology would also draw from an "understanding of who we are" and the distinguishing features of the Mennonite tradition of biblical reflection.

With the publication of this article the process of constructing a missiology for MCC began. A missiology file was initiated to house the accumulating documents and correspondence that arose in the wake of Brubacher's *Intercom* reflections. Fieldworkers, church leaders, and MCC administrators were invited to contribute their opinions, and many did so with enthusiasm. Discussions were held and meetings were called. Prominent Mennonite missiologist Wilbert Shenk was invited to Akron to present a one-day seminar to MCC staff on Mennonite missiology and mission praxis. The results of a survey of MCC workers' values and perspectives, conducted by graduate students in development studies at Eastern University in Philadelphia, were added to the mix.[17]

The actual task of drafting the missiological statement was delegated to Nancy Heisey. Heisey was particularly well situated to guide the process, given her many years of work with MCC, her familiarity with Anabaptist-Mennonite theology stemming from ongoing graduate studies at Eastern Mennonite Seminary, and her previous work on a major two-year "listening project" seeking to learn from the voices of those on the receiving end of MCC and Mennonite mission board programs.[18]

Heisey wrote four drafts and each was reviewed and critiqued. These are remarkable pieces of theological writing: engaged, concise, and insightful. They provide an analytical, rather than merely prescriptive, approach to the key missiological tensions within MCC's work. While parts of the text conform to genre norms characteristic of dispassionate bureaucracy, other sections employ the first-person pronoun and assume a personal, even intimate, tone. Accordingly, in a letter to Brubacher towards the end of the drafting process, Heisey wrote that much of the text could simply be filed as "my end-of-term report."[19] Heisey's approach neatly encapsulates a dynamic that I repeatedly encountered in conversations and interviews with North American MCCers: an engaging marriage of vigorous critique and passionate commitment.[20]

The final draft was titled "MCC Missiological Statement: Draft 4," which appears to indicate a formal organization-wide document.[21] However, Heisey quickly dispels any such expectations by writing that the draft is only "an in-house missiological working document." Written for an internal audience, devoid of formal status, and lacking clear organizational standing, the missiological statement had become a more modest project than Brubacher's initial *Intercom* article had sought. The purpose of this draft was to "codify… who MCC is and why we do what we do."

In her draft Heisey addresses two long-standing MCC mottos: "In the Name of Christ" and "A Christian resource for meeting human needs." Both were indicative of how MCC is endowed with a clear Christian identity, and its work is premised on a tacit Trinitarian theology. As an "inter-Mennonite" organization MCC had played an important role in bringing together diverse Anabaptist groups. Still, despite this Christian identity, Heisey suggests that MCC's work has historically been based in "action rather than theological reflection." Heisey proceeds to address a diverse set of concerns: the relevance of the theological concept of *missio dei*; the question of truth in other religions; a displacement of the priority of concrete results for the centrality of process and relationality;[22] and the recognition of fallibility within MCC itself, which necessitates ongoing repentance and openness to renewal within the institution. For each of these issues Heisey charts a delicate route between the liberal-evangelical division that dominated missiological debate in post-Second World War North American theology. This is perhaps most clearly articulated in Heisey's rejection of the false choice between "the destructiveness of fundamentalist systems" in their mistaken sense of certainty and the "secularist understandings" that rest on radical relativism and pronounced individualism.

Despite being reworked multiple times, and despite a careful and sophisticated examination of theological concerns within MCC, Heisey's statement went no further than this fourth draft; it was never published, and it did not garner a wide readership. None of the MCCers I talked with during my field research in Indonesia, and only a very few in North America, had ever heard of the stalled project. After all the effort to produce the text of Heisey's carefully crafted statement, the process fizzled to a standstill. The conversations dried up, the missiology file was closed, and the correspondence archived. The project of constructing a missiological statement was abandoned amid fading enthusiasm among all involved. Rather than articulating a theological identity, this is an instance of a disarticulation of a theology of service. It was a proactive avoidance of the production of a clear public statement about MCC's theological identity.

The documents in the file on the missiology of service hint at the reasons the project was abandoned. As the process went on, frequent doubts were posed about its worth and viability. In a letter to Brubacher and other MCC administrators just before submitting her final draft, Heisey notes her own wavering support:

> I do want to underline what I said to Ray [Brubacher]... That is, I am less and less convinced that a missiology statement is what MCC needs. More in-house conversation, absolutely yes. In some formal process, good! But an effort at definition that goes beyond the documents we have already hashed through seems to contradict what has been the genius of MCC's service vocation.[23]

A similar tone is expressed in a letter from Brubacher to two senior MCC administrators.[24] This was also one of the last pieces of correspondence to be entered into the archived missiology file. The letter outlines how Brubacher thinks Heisey's fourth draft of the missiology statement should be read:

> Attached is a missiological statement written by Nancy Heisey. Although it is titled "MCC Missiological Statement" neither Nancy nor I claim this to be MCC's definitive statement. In fact, there are some who say MCC should not have one at all. Two reasons are given: 1) MCC is a flexible and adaptive entity and should not be tied to something fixed. 2) MCC should not do a definitive statement without extensive consultation with "the field" and its network of partnerships. I agree with number two, but have questions about

> number one. I feel that it is appropriate to work at a missiological statement even at an "in house" level. We do too little of that. Nancy's paper, for the time being, is an in house document for purposes of discussion and discernment by MCC persons, whatever their context (leadership or primary assignment).

Brubacher and Heisey's eventual reluctance to pursue a formal theological articulation is revealing. MCC's "genius," in Heisey's account, is to *fail* to produce a comprehensive definition of its own theological identity and instead to focus on practices and active service. Brubacher's two reasons for not having a formal missiology are the need for flexibility in the field and the difficulty of adequately consulting all appropriate stakeholders.

Research in the anthropology of development policy furnishes valuable insights into Brubacher's and Heisey's reflections. According to David Mosse, the purpose of development policy – defined broadly to include "all kinds of development models, project designs and strategies" – is not primarily to direct or guide development practice.[25] Instead, policy is oriented in the opposite direction. Development policy has the social task of "legitimation, persuasion, and enrolment" of a supporting constituency.[26] That is, policy is a kind of implicit apologetics – it seeks to persuade and recruit a committed community. Policy is therefore a public transcript that operates, for Mosse, as "a bid for political support."[27] Policy articulations may therefore differ substantially from the hidden transcripts of development practice.[28] But constituencies are rarely stable or homogenous; effective policy must therefore attempt to address inherently fluctuating amalgamations of diverse and contradictory interests. One of the primary ways in which policy achieves this is via ambiguity:

> It is precisely the ability to achieve a high degree of convergence of disparate interests, contained in the official language of a single validating model, that characterises successful policy and project ideas. To achieve this the policy process requires ambiguous concepts like "participation" which mediate or translate between divergent interests.[29]

Vagueness is not, therefore, an unfortunate outcome of development vocabulary that can be countered through ever more precise and refined definitions. It is, rather, a requisite and inherent feature of development discourse.[30] Successful policy "generates mobilising metaphors … whose vagueness, ambiguity and lack of conceptual precision is *required* to conceal ideological differences so as to allow compromise and the enrolment of different interests."[31] Development policy fails if it is too specific and prescriptive to the point at which it excludes key constituents.

The attempt to articulate a missiological statement in MCC in the early 1990s should be read as an act of policy construction. A publicly available and officially sanctioned theological articulation functions in the same way as do project proposals, annual reports, strategy documents, and vision statements. As a policy statement the attempt at constructing a missiological statement failed on several fronts. It failed first by providing too much clarity. Heisey's Draft 4 was too specific and detailed. It lacked those features that Mosse regards as essential to making policy work in practice – ambiguity, opacity, vagueness. The problem was not that Heisey sought to chart a course between liberal and conservative theologies as such; rather, it was that a course was charted at all, for this opened the possibility that some MCC supporters would be unwilling or unable to be enrolled – *translated*, in Latour's sense – into the document. A substanceless missiology could have been practicable, but Brubacher had not asked for a vacuous statement. At least initially, he had sought a document that would *guide* MCC workers through the ethical and theological challenges they faced while engaging in field programs around the world. The desire for guidance and the need for ambiguity were incompatible.

The essential problem was that MCC already had a defined constituency in the Mennonite and Brethren in Christ churches in the US and Canada. This constituency is marked with theological heterogeneity. Pervasive processes of fragmentation and congregational ownership ensure that theological diversity is prevalent and immutable. Despite powerful coalescing processes, no attempts at theological clarity have succeeded in enrolling this entire disparate group. A clarified theological policy ran the risk of failing to adjudicate between their very different dispositions. Religious candour was antithetical to achieving "a high degree of convergence" among the disparate interests of this constituency.

For Mosse policy is *only* directed towards enrolling political support.[32] While this is generally accurate in the case of MCC, I argue for a somewhat modified account. Among the crucial components of any development organization's constituency are those that work directly within the institution. Expatriate MCCers serve in the field with the organization without financial remuneration. These volunteers are also "donors" and constituents in multiple senses. For example, they participate in a charitable economy through giving their time, they often face discomfort in the course of their work, and they forgo the possibility of earning a higher income elsewhere. Indeed, MCC service is often associated with a sense of sacrifice. Service workers and other international volunteers are somatic donors in that they "gift" their bodies for service to others and to MCC for the duration of their work. While MCC service workers are beneficiaries of donations to MCC, enabling international travel and modest financial support, they are also active givers within this moral economy. As a consequence, they blur or even erase distinctions between donors and recipients. The category "constituency" should therefore be broadened to include participants within as well as beyond MCC's organizational boundaries; and, in any case, in MCC these distinctions are extremely porous. MCC policy articulations must also enrol organizational colleagues into ongoing involvement and commitment to "sacrificial," generous, and committed participation. While policy may not *direct* practice, that does not mean that practitioners are dispassionate observers when it comes to its formulation. The willingness of MCCers to participate in international service takes place for a range of reasons. Among these is the belief that they are carrying out a moral and theological project that is closely aligned with their own values, commitments, and faith. MCC workers, therefore, have a stake in the theological articulation of organizational policy.

But here too MCC faced a nearly impossible task. MCC workers are primarily drawn from the wider Mennonite constituency, and they tend to reflect this diversity. This was neatly expressed in a letter sent to Brubacher and that was filed in the missiology archive. Discussing meetings among his MCC colleagues in Europe, Joseph Liechty writes:

> I was impressed with how often disagreements in the Europe Steering Committee were ultimately disagreements about the nature of MCC's missiology. Tim Reimer believes MCC is really a relief (and maybe a service) agency; John Wiens believes MCC is primarily for short term volunteers; Hugo believes MCC is really an agency to serve the southern hemisphere, and he is so consistent with his "guest" logic that he doesn't think MCC can invite people to a meeting because he wouldn't invite people into my house if he were a guest there; and I disagree with all of them. When these disagreements became explicit, we each argued our understanding of MCC's *implicit* missiology, but an explicit one might have been quite helpful at points.[33]

While Liechty believed that an explicit missiology might have eased their contentious team discussions, it appears that MCC administrators arrived at the opposite conclusion. Or, at least, that they perceived the easing of internal tensions as subordinate to the more fundamental role that MCC played as an "inter-Mennonite" organization that brought together the whole diverse and disparate peoplehood. Regardless, to have articulated a clear theological preference for one model of MCC praxis over another would have excluded some MCCers and constituents.

A related problem to internal theological diversity is the question of service workers' flexibility in the field. MCC is active in over fifty countries around the world in programs that span a wide range of activities. A clear, single statement would necessarily struggle to provide adequate, or even proximate, guidance in each of these contexts and for each of MCC's projects. The question of flexibility was one of the key qualms raised by Brubacher about the missiological project, but it was one that he ultimately dismissed. This is at heart an issue of translation. In their correspondence over the proposed missiology several other MCCers raised the same issue. In a letter to Brubacher, Harold Miller suggests that a missiological statement should be written for two purposes: "1.) to check whether we are more or less meeting expectations articulated or unspoken by our constituencies and 2.) to check whether we are absorbing and informed by learnings from recent and current experience around the world."[34] Miller rightly notes that there will be "some tension between these two" and that therefore the missiology statement should seek a "middle ground" between constituency and field needs. However, the letter does not attempt to map how, or even whether, this might be accomplished.

The failure to publish and distribute Heisey's missiological statement should therefore be viewed as a successful policy disarticulation. As a strategy employed to enrol diverse perspectives into participating in a common enterprise, this disarticulation of theological policy worked. It worked not by demanding theological congruence or coherence but, rather, hrough a dual approach of encouraging participation in practices, the meaning of which remains indeterminate, while also providing vague allusions to a sacralized mission via a plethora of opaque associations, polyvocality, proof texting, and spiritual insinuation. This was a successful strategy, if we take success to mean the ability of MCC to continue to operate over many decades as an "inter-Mennonite" organization of the Anabaptist-Mennonite peoplehood while both maintaining a resemblance of unity and providing for maximum flexibility for field operations in the many contexts around the world to which its service workers were assigned.

The pattern of disarticulating theology was candidly acknowledged within MCC by the mantra: "faith divides, service unites." The saying, which I encountered at various points in my fieldwork, operated as a justification for the absence of having to ensure theological coherence within their organization. The whole gamut of Mennonite types participated in MCC on the basis of an imagined shared praxis. Their perceived "unity amidst diversity" was facilitated through an emphasis on what they could share in common – such as ideas of "peace" and "service" – and a de-emphasis on doctrinal difference, the raising of which could result in long and intractable debate.[35] Commenting on this issue, Mennonite sociologist Donald Kraybill writes:

> Mennonites have had their own share of disagreements over doctrinal issues and social practices, and surely the old adage "doctrine divides; service unites," holds true today. Perhaps we should say, "Doctrine divides: but history, singing, auctions, and service unite." In any event MCC, for the most part, unites. Despite doctrinal differences, the call to service and peacemaking embodied by MCC has mobilized Mennonites of many stripes.[36]

The power of broad involvement by Mennonites is a vital animating impulse for MCC. North American MCCers often described to me how thrilled they felt to attend MCC board meetings – any one of the twelve boards in Canada and the United States – and witness, gathered around a common table and with the shared task of facilitating service, representatives from disparate parts of the Mennonite peoplehood. It is not that MCC lacked dissenters within the Mennonite world but that, within MCC, a broad and wide coalition of the household of faith was brought together to participate in shared action. MCC provided a "table of sharing" for Mennonites – a metaphor that evokes not only board meetings but also hospitality, generosity, family, and eucharistic ritual.[37]

MCCers frequently shared with me their deep affection for how MCC draws Mennonites together under a common canopy. For example, Joyce Wiebe, an MCC service worker who taught religious studies for her assignment in an Indonesian university, talked with great enthusiasm about the annual MCC relief sale in Kidron, Ohio. Relief sales are community-owned fundraising events for MCC. For Joyce, relief sales were an admixture, being part cultural festival, part donation drive, and part celebration of "Mennonite pride" in being "good people." In her words, Joyce held that the Kidron relief sale was the "only activity that all the Mennonites in the region – and there were hundreds of types – worked together on." With evident pleasure, she reminisced how "conservative" Amish and "liberal" gay Mennonites could be seen directing traffic

Figure 4.2 | The Gap Relief Auction

together year after year – a combination that she thought would rarely take place elsewhere. Despite sharp differences in theology and outlook, diverse Mennonites nevertheless came together to support MCC. Joyce told me that "nothing else brings Mennonites of all stripes together."

My experience at the two Mennonite relief sales I attended during my fieldwork – the Gap Relief Auction in Pennsylvania and the Leamington Community Festival in Ontario – thoroughly confirmed Joyce's portrayal.[38] Both were "folk festivals" celebrating Mennonite identity.[39] Mennonite artefacts, such as quilts and carvings, were prominently situated for sale. There were plentiful quantities of Mennonite cuisine: zwieback and "Mennonite sausage" among the Dutch-Russian Mennonites of Leamington, and "whoopee pies" for Swiss-German Mennonites in Pennsylvania. For each relief sale a wide range of Mennonites participated in many ways. A Latin American Mennonite youth group band jammed out some songs in Spanish during the Leamington lunch hour while Old Order women with their ankle-length skirts wandered past. The Gap Relief Auction was largely run by Amish communities. Bearded men and bonnet-wearing women made up a significant proportion of those selling items and auctioneering. Horses and buggies were parked outside the main hall next to pick-up trucks and station wagons. All "stripes" of Anabaptists came together for these events. They did so because MCC disarticulated its theology of service, thereby enabling widely divergent groups to be enrolled into supporting the work of the organization. This, indeed, is the "genius" of MCC.

I argue that a definite, structured missiology that has both substance and normative potential is untenable for MCC. The key reason for this is that the organizational imperative to enrol a diverse and predetermined North American Mennonite constituency into ongoing support and participation militated against theological clarity. Instead, MCC relies on vague allusion to a sacralized Christian mission. The next section analyzes three cases that probe the edges of this argument: the rapid growth of Christian Aid Ministries as a theologically explicit Anabaptist aid agency, the theological advocacy of MCC's Peace Section, and the adoption by MCC of a credal statement called Shared Convictions in 2009.

CHRISTIAN AID MINISTRIES

The work of theological disarticulation in MCC is helpfully illuminated when compared with the approach of Christian Aid Ministries (CAM), another North American Anabaptist aid agency. CAM was founded in 1981 as a channel of relief aid for Beachy Amish, Old Order Amish, and conservative Mennonites. Beginning its work in Romania, CAM quickly expanded to other parts of Eastern Europe and then also to Latin America, Africa, the Middle East, and Asia. In 2022 CAM worked in 133 "countries and territories" around the world.[40] It is a direct competitor with MCC for the conservative sections in MCC's constituency.

CAM's "Statement of Faith and Practice" is a list of twenty-three separate affirmations in a credal formation following the pattern of Amish and Old Order Mennonite *Ordnung*. Each statement in the list follows a "We believe..." formula that expresses a particular doctrinal commitment. The first four affirmations concern the Trinitarian nature of divinity and the centrality of the Scriptures, which are understood to be the "divinely inspired Word of God." These are followed by declarations on humanity (created by God but depraved by sin), salvation ("by grace through faith in Christ"), and the church (consisting of those who have been "born again" with the task to "evangelize the world ... and minister to the needs of all people"). Next are ten ritual practices and prescriptions for behaviour, including baptism, the Lord's Supper, feet-washing, the "holy kiss," "the woman's head is to be veiled, and her hair uncut," anointing with oil, marriage, modest personal appearance, a "nonresistant" lifestyle, separation of church and state, and grounds for excommunication. The final section outlines a doctrine of the "Second Coming" of Christ and the promise of "eternal bliss in heaven" for believers, and "eternal damnation in hell" for the unrighteous. The tone and content of the statement resonate with adherents of a particular mix of traditional Anabaptist concerns, American fundamentalism, and religious practices distinctive of conservative Mennonite and Amish sects.

Here, therefore, is an example of a forthright articulation of a systematic theological statement by an Anabaptist NGO. Yet the statement is striking for how little of the content directly relates to the practices of delivering CAM's relief aid. Its lack of specificity in this area is such that it could easily be transferred without modification to an entirely different organizational sector or organization. Indeed, the statement is substantively the same as one previously published in the Beachy Amish publication *Calvary Messenger*.[41] Because of this, CAM's statement should not be regarded as a "theology of service." It pays practically no attention to issues of relief, development, or service. Clearly, this too is an example of theology-as-policy, with the goal of articulation being to enrol a constituency rather than to dictate field practice. Whereas MCC's ambiguous theological stance helped to recruit a constituency across the widest possible spectrum of Mennonites, CAM's Statement of Faith and Practice operates in the opposite way. It is sharply sectarian and conspicuously conservative. Because CAM's constituency occupies a narrower niche, the work of enrolment through policy can afford to be much more specific. Those on the conservative end of the spectrum of MCC's supporters – perhaps frustrated with MCC's theological ambiguity and seeking a clearer statement of theological affinity – could be drawn to CAM's approach of unambiguous theological articulation.

The starkly contrasting approach of theological articulation of CAM vis-à-vis MCC illustrates the ways in which different enrolment strategies are deployed by different organizations. The sheer diversity of MCC's constituency required certain kinds of engagement that would facilitate ongoing involvement. CAM, as the more recent arrival, competed not for the whole Mennonite peoplehood but, rather, for only a specific cross-section of MCC's supporters. It did so through systematic and forthright articulation. This contrast noted, it remains important to also point out that, while CAM occupies a narrower niche in the Anabaptist spectrum, it too is an assemblage of different groups. In his historical study of Christian Aid Ministries, Steven Nolt suggests that the "genius" of CAM is the way it manages its own diverse constituency.[42] In much the same way that MCC provides myriad avenues of service for its constituents, so too CAM has proliferated different mechanisms for participation: "Its promotional literature repeatedly emphasizes that donors can choose the type of projects they wish to support – in effect, implying that CAM does not determine a particular agenda so much as makes available an array of possibilities from which donors can choose." The Statement of Faith and Practice enrols conservative and traditionalist Amish and Mennonites but does little to shape the actual forms of relief work carried out around the world.

PEACE SECTION

Another test case arises from the apparent contradiction that, while MCC actively disavows a specific organizational theology, it has simultaneously been an extremely active producer of theological articulation since the Second World War, and, moreover, these theologies have had far-reaching effects among North American Mennonites. Peace Section, although now defunct, was among the most important and active MCC units in this prolific production of theology.[43] "MCC's interMennonite Peace Section," according to Leo Driedger and Donald Kraybill, was "undoubtedly the most important institutional vehicle for change" for American Mennonite theology during the second half of the twentieth century.[44] Peace Section operated as a "clearinghouse, facilitator, and initiator of a vast array of peace concerns" and played a crucial role in legitimizing a widespread theological shift among American and Canadian Mennonites from "quietism" to peace "activism." This committee publicly addressed controversial issues, including "draft resistance, nonregistration, war tax resistance, and women's concerns," and it did this through explicit theological discourse.[45]

Attention to the institutional location of Peace Section within MCC is necessary to understand this proactive theologizing. Peace Section was able to take clear positions on hotly contested issues and to articulate clear theological responses to them because it was accountable to a governing board that ran parallel to, rather than being subsumed within, MCC binational. According to Driedger and Kraybill, Peace Section was regarded as part of MCC, but not without some ambiguity.[46] It maintained a semi-autonomous status, and this independence enabled Peace Section personnel to "say things that needed to be said and do things that needed to be done, all the while maintaining distance from MCC and denominational programs." Moreover, its radical "prophetic" theological work "would likely have been silenced had it been directly harnessed to a denomination or the MCC board itself." While Driedger and Kraybill focus largely on the advantages obtained by Peace Section through its independence, the same could be argued for benefits accrued by MCC. Because Peace Section's theo-political engagements were not official MCC views, donor constituents who might ardently disagree with them could continue to support the wider organization and regard the work of this "rambunctious institutional child" of MCC as merely an unsanctioned outlier.[47]

Other theological articulations by MCCers suggest a similar analysis. Heisey and Brubacher's missiological project was neither the first nor the last attempt to formulate a theology for MCC. But just as their project was progressively demoted from the organizational to the merely personal, these other publicly articulated theologies have been undertaken on a quasi-official or purely private basis. For example, Peter and Elfrieda Dyck's iconic narrative of the Russian Mennonite "exodus" during the Second World War has an extended discussion of a theology of service in the final two chapters.[48] But there is no reason to think this was an institutionally sanctioned theology. Various contributions to the MCC Occasional Paper series are relevant, including a report by Norman Kraus entitled *A Theological Basis for Intervention Ministries* and Susan Classen's *A Spirituality of Service*, but the entire series includes the disclaimer: "The papers do not necessarily reflect official MCC policy."[49] A similar disclaimer is made for the development monograph written for MCC by Tim Lind entitled *Biblical Obedience and Development*.[50] A variety of unpublished documents have also been produced seeking to examine MCC's theology of service.[51] These repeated attempts to address theological concerns show the enthusiasm many MCCers have felt for the issue. It is not the case that MCCers failed to theologize their work or to seek to communicate these theologies; rather, the organization did not own these as official policies.

Interestingly, while there have been numerous attempts to theologize MCC's service, there are also theological justifications for not doing so. Two of Gerald Schlabach's attempts to address the issue offer important insights. Schlabach's short and accessible *To Bless All Peoples: Serving with Abraham and Jesus*, published in 1991, is a meditation on the idea of service through interwoven biblical exegesis and personal narrative drawn from his experience of working with MCC in Latin America in the 1980s.[52] Schlabach argues that "God's way of working for change" is through "communities of service to others," and he promotes service as a sacred duty involving working alongside others in non-hierarchical relationships of mutual learning and transformation.[53] A decade later

Schlabach published an elegant "confession of sorts" in the Canadian Mennonite publication *Conrad Grebel Review*, which repudiates his earlier book.[54] In this second work Schlabach argues that "the act of writing about service may serve as rationalization for failing to serve."[55] One of the reasons Mennonites have been so successful at doing service is that the "Mennonite theology of service has been part of a tapestry" woven into other concerns and practices rather than separated out as a "discrete" field. To explicitly articulate it, and therefore to make it distinct, would be to run the risk of dissolving that fertile tapestry. For theological reasons Schlabach concludes that a disarticulated theology of service better serves MCC, Mennonites more generally, those suffering injustice around the world, and perhaps even God.[56]

A conversation over a basketball game in Central Java furnished a somewhat different theological argument. Albert Regehr and I were shooting hoops in a school playground in Salatiga. Albert was a Canadian MCCer who had recently arrived in Indonesia and was still going through language training. With his family he later shifted to Yogyakarta, where he worked as a philosophy lecturer in an Islamic university. As we played we got talking about MCC and I scribbled down notes of the conversation after the game. Albert told me that, while churches that supported and owned MCC had theologies of service, MCC did not and, further, that it should not. The reason for this was that MCC was not "the church": it was only a service arm of the church. As a service agency MCC should not do all the things that churches are properly concerned with doing, such as baptizing people. In response I wondered what would happen if Albert's colleague, a Mennonite pastor by training and vocation who had just begun his MCC assignment teaching in a Christian seminary in Papua, were to be invited to baptize Indonesians. Albert was unequivocal: "I would hope that he would decline." That was not the role of MCCers but only of the church. To have a clear organizational theology apart from its supporting churches would indicate that MCC had lost track of its identity and vocation. For Albert, any attempt by MCC to articulate an independent theology was an ecclesiological – and theological – mistake.

SHARED CONVICTIONS

A final test case is New Wines/New Wineskins, an extensive organization-wide consultation process using the appreciative inquiry method of analysis. The stated goal of this consultation was to reconfigure MCC for the twenty-first century.[57] As one of the outcomes of this process in mid-2009, for the first time in its history, MCC introduced a statement of Shared Convictions as an officially sanctioned, publicly accessible theological articulation. These convictions, along with other reformulated statements of identity, were affirmed by all twelve MCCs in North America by the end of the year.[58] This was clearly a departure from earlier policy statements. It raises questions as to whether MCC had, at last, articulated a theology of service and thereby shown my analysis of MCC's disarticulated theology to be erroneous. Of course, organizations are never static. They are processes formed out of webs of shifting relationalities and they are reworked across time and space. At times their evolutions follow expected paths and at others they assume unanticipated trajectories. This said, I argue that, in this case, the adoption of Shared Convictions was not a radical disjuncture from previous practices. Three key issues are at stake.

First, the Shared Convictions statement was another example of the masterful use of ambiguous language. It was not the kind of statement that sought to ensure conformity of belief or practice. While the statement identified those who owned the convictions as "Christian" – with explicit references to Christ, the Holy Spirit, the church, Christian Scriptures, and various religious rituals – it did not provide any substantial advance on MCC's previous "rusty nail" mission statement (discussed earlier in this chapter). With seven quite general statements, the Shared Convictions remained much less specific and extensive than CAM's weighty list of twenty-three edicts. By adopting this statement MCC continued to be sacralized in similarly vague sorts of ways, as had previously been the case.

Second, the statement was clearly not intended to provide meaningful direction for MCC's field programs. The statement itself was adopted verbatim from the Mennonite World Conference (MWC), the global umbrella group of Anabaptist-Mennonite churches, which in March 2006 introduced the statement as its own Shared Convictions document. This was the first statement of belief to be adopted by leaders of the global Anabaptist church.[59] Given this earlier formulation, the statement was not formulated with the goal of providing guidance to Mennonite service or mission organizations. Like MCC, most Mennonite and Anabaptist churches and organizations were able to adopt the statement without adjustment. It did not, therefore, require changes in practices. This was not "a missiology for MCC" or a "theology of service" in the same sense as Brubacher had initially intended.

Third, given that it would not ensure theological homogeneity or provide guidance for MCC practice, the adoption of the statement should be seen as a political strategy of enrolment. At the time of adoption one of the most pressing issues facing MCC as an organization was that of internationalization. This was closely related to (theological, organizational, and ecclesial) attempts to broaden the understanding of the Mennonite "peoplehood" beyond North America and beyond "ethnic" Mennonites. Questions about whether MCC should be made accountable to a global Anabaptist body – and the Mennonite World Conference was the only viable candidate for this – rather than only to Canadian and American Mennonite churches were actively discussed in the organization. During interviews in North America and Indonesia this issue frequently emerged as a prominent concern. Many senior leaders within MCC felt a strong moral imperative to enact non-coercive approaches to global partnership. These included active attempts to rethink how a North American entity (including the "donors" who controlled the money) could interact positively and Christianly with partners and communities in developing countries (the "recipients"). The adoption of Shared Convictions was symbolic of this wider process of attempting to realign MCC's relationship with global Anabaptism. These dynamics are made clear in an article by an MCC staff writer who reports that, soon after Shared Convictions was adopted by MCC, it was also proposed that MCC would "facilitate relationships between and among Anabaptist service agencies worldwide."[60] This implicitly raises the question of global Anabaptist ownership. However, the writer goes on to describe how this goal was downgraded so that, at the time of writing, MCC was merely seeking to participate in a "Global Anabaptist Service Network." This shift in language suggests that the question of ownership was resolved in favour of MCC's constituency remaining a North American affair. In fact, the dynamics of ownership were adjusted in the opposite direction in a movement towards greater *localization*. The same report outlines the decision to abolish MCC binational altogether such that MCC would be "collaboratively led by both MCC Canada and MCC US."[61] These tensions between whether MCC required further embedding in North American Mennonite communities or whether it should operate under a mandate from a global Anabaptist constituency mirror debates about perceived needs to expand or contract the identification of the Mennonite peoplehood. Regardless of the outcome of the Wineskins process, the adoption of this theological statement was primarily a mechanism of political recruitment and a means of realigning MCC with other organizational shifts. The theological content of the statement was largely insignificant compared to the work of constituency building that it signalled.

IS GOOD THEOLOGY UNIMPLEMENTABLE?

This chapter does not argue that MCC is theologically vacuous or devoid of theological imaginations. I show that Mennonite Christian theology, spirituality, and ethics permeate the organization. They constitute a crucial dimension of the habitus within which MCCers carry out their work. Challenges to this pervasive Christianity, such as the case of "strategic Pancasilaism" noted in the previous chapter, are exceptions that prove the general rule. The religious saturation of MCC's work and practices can be tacit or perspicuous, intermeshed with even the apparently most mundane actions or bureaucratic procedures. Rather, in this chapter, I examine articulations of theology-as-policy – the formal, official, and sanctioned theological representation of the organization. These have been consistently vague and ambiguous. While alluding to a Christian identity, the content and meaning of this has been left largely indeterminate. MCC is not non-theological, but it has consistently disarticulated an organizational theology of service. This disarticulation has been part of an ongoing strategy to enrol a theologically diverse constituency in North America as well as its own theologically diverse personnel.

While MCC practices in their field programs around the world invariably take on quite different formations and trajectories as they become enmeshed in local social and political ecologies, this chapter highlights how such diversity is not simply a matter of multiple transformations of a relatively static "source." MCC's disarticulation of a clear organizational theology of service ensures that not only are church planting, cooperation with the Department of Transmigration, shipping canned meat, and channelling CIDA funds all plausible practices, such diversity is veritably inevitable. Each of these practices can be framed as a valid translation of MCC's enigmatic theological policy. This is not to say that the range of possible translations of MCC is boundless but, rather, that the substantial room for manoeuvre available to MCC field leadership, discussed in the previous chapter, ensures the high probability of multiple and diverse organizational incarnations.

This has a number of further implications for MCC's field practices. First, one of the most fundamental translations within MCC is from vague and indeterminate policy into materialized and embodied practices of service within specific historical, spatial, cultural, and political junctures. The amorphous is thereby made definite and specific. Second, because none of these materialized embodiments can claim definitive theological legitimacy, each remains inherently contestable. Indeed, conflict between differing expectations is ingrained in MCC praxis. Third, because MCC field practices are contestable, they are also transitory. The remarkable stability that can accrue around certain donor practices in North America, whereby, for example, communities come to own their canned meat operations or their relief sale over the course of generations, is not the case for field programs. In the field, regular changes in service worker personnel, and especially transitions in the in-country leadership, ensure that practices are highly transient and provisional.[62] Finally, to understand MCC's field practices it is therefore necessary to pay attention to the people involved. The question of *how* MCC is practised is intimately associated with the question *who* the MCCers are. Relationships, personalities, idiosyncrasies, and particular individuals' vernacular theologies deeply inform MCC practice. The theologies espoused by the MCC Reps are not determinative for all that takes place in MCC Indonesia. Wider factors of political economy are also relevant, and other translators are always involved in enacting programs. However, the MCC Reps are located at a pivotal point around which translation relationships turn.

Stanley Green and James Krabill, both of whom work for Mennonite Mission Network, argue that MCC's failure to express a clear theological identity is a serious theological error that should be corrected.[63] Observing the multiple existing "operative" missiologies that are at work within MCC, they seek to "make some assessments regarding our sense of which of these is most closely aligned with God's purposes." Similarly, in concluding a comparative study between the development perspectives of MCCers and "evangelicals," Kristen Grace, Merril Ewert, and Paul Eberts argue that MCC and other organizations engaged in "religious intercultural ministry" should aim to develop "a clear theology that guides why and how they do development so that both word and deed promote a consistent witness."[64] They therefore mirror Brubacher's initial call for a missiology for MCC, as was published in *Intercom*. Based on the argument presented in this chapter I want to close by asking: Is good theology unimplementable?[65] Answers to this question hinge on what theological articulation is supposed to do. The task of constructing a centralized, organizational theology that guides MCC practices proved, for Heisey and Brubacher, a task mired in insurmountable difficulties. Not the least of these was their own growing doubts about whether the task was theologically and practically worthwhile. However, this failure may well be the genius of MCC. Theology does not need to be articulated as policy to be implemented in practice. It is within MCC practices, therefore, that the theologies of MCC must be examined.

5

Peace and Friction

PEACEBUILDING IN THE SHADOW OF 9/11

11 September 2001 was a pivotal moment in the representation of "religion" in the West. The terrorist attacks were not, however, so much a change of script as an accentuation in the popular imagination of ideas that were already widely disseminated in media and academic publications. It was widely portrayed as spectacular and incontrovertible evidence of a global "clash of civilizations" – another instance of violence in the enduring conflict of competing and incommensurable worldviews.[1] Such ideas gained yet further traction, and not just in the West, by the military response of the US government under President George W. Bush, which invaded Afghanistan in October 2001 and Iraq in March 2003. These conflicts – and the others that they helped ignite – remained fixtures in North American media coverage over the next two decades.

In the aftermath of 9/11 Islam was widely disparaged, if not demonized, in North American public and political discourse.[2] Bush's notorious "axis of evil" insinuated connections between Islam, miscellaneous "rogue states," and perennial menace to American identity and nationhood. Indeed, the ensuing invasions were framed as a "new Cold War" between the liberal democratic "free world" and Islamic fundamentalists.[3] Analyzing these discourses and modes of political violence, Saba Mahmood argues that the situation resembles "a secular-liberal inquisition before which Islam must be made to confess" in "the court of international public opinion" for its failure to remain within "the supposedly 'normal' domain of private worship."[4]

Against this backdrop of geopolitical violence and heightened animosity MCC sought to realign its work by initiating a range of peacebuilding projects.[5] In 2006 MCC launched a five-year "key initiative" of interfaith bridge building with a prominent focus on Muslim-Christian relationships. The goal was to construct bridges of understanding and relationships through projects that crossed religious divides.[6] Peacebuilding efforts by American and Canadian organizations like MCC did not capture much media attention. The visual politics of suffering and conflict are such that they compel media attention in ways that the complicated and messy quotidian practice of peace does not. But the dynamics at play in initiatives for peace pose compelling demands on anthropologists and religious studies scholars for careful analysis and explanation. MCC's peace programs after 9/11 attempted to translate vernacular Mennonite theologies of peace into practices of peacebuilding in Indonesia. This peacebuilding work was infused with theological ideas and identities.

To explore the workings of and for peace in MCC I make use of Anna Tsing's concept of friction.[7] Friction describes how cross-cultural connections work by both relying upon and transcending cultural difference. Friction denotes the "awkward, unequal, unstable, and creative qualities" of these interconnections and differences. Central to the workings of friction is that difference is profoundly generative. It is not inevitable that differences lead to antagonism or hostility. In fact, all kinds of collaborations are formed through interconnections across difference. Tsing explores the productivity of difference through analogy: "The wheel turns because of its encounter with the surface of the road; spinning in air it goes nowhere. Rubbing two sticks together produces heat and light; one stick alone is just a stick." Through "sticky engagements" collaborations are formed and build momentum. Tsing frames this as a question of scale. "Universals" and "globalisms" travel not by erasing difference but, rather, by working through difference. For Tsing, "actually existing universals are hybrid, transient, and involved in constant reformulation through dialogue." Because differences persist, collaborations are also always precarious. Even the most apparently obdurate global formation is therefore actually fragile, vulnerable: "tiny cracks might yet break open the dam."[8] Friction, for Tsing, is therefore something to be celebrated. The ambiguity it engenders creates possibilities for unexpected change and therefore also for hope.[9]

Friction frames my analysis of the ways in which Mennonite and Muslim identities are generated and made precarious by MCC's peacebuilding initiatives. The perceived geopolitical tension between Islam and Christianity provided the context out of which MCC's peacebuilding programs in Indonesia emerged. However, these programs sparked further frictions that both threatened and further propelled the work for peace. This chapter examines the frictive dimensions within the North American Mennonite peace witness and then turns to explore two distinct MCC programs engaged in interfaith peacebuilding. First, I examine the high-profile and controversial series of interfaith dialogues that MCC helped organize with President Mahmoud Ahmadinejad of Iran, focusing particularly on the furor surrounding the New York meeting in 2008. Second, I trace the partnership between MCCers and an Indonesian Mennonite pastor involved in interfaith peacebuilding with Muslim leaders and Islamic militants in the Central Javanese city of Solo. These narratives allow space for exploring another dynamic, that of friendship, which operates as a kind of parallel or lateral axiom to that of friction. I argue that attention to friendship is essential for understanding MCC's peace practices.

PEACE SHALL DESTROY MANY

MCC's involvement in peace concerns emerged from the tradition of North American Mennonite theological discourses and practices. In turn, MCC's peacebuilding work has informed and helped reshape these discourses and practices. This sense that peace and MCC belonged together was expressed during an orientation for new staff that I attended in Akron, Pennsylvania, in mid-2008, during which a senior administrator told the group that peace was part of the organization's "spiritual DNA."[10] Evoking this genetic metaphor was clearly intended to demonstrate that peace was an indispensable and non-negotiable feature of MCC projects, planning, and activities. The description of this as "spiritual" located peace right in the sacred centre of the organization. Peace is here understood as the essence of MCC's work.[11]

As one of the Historic Peace Churches, Mennonites have long emphasized the moral imperative for a radical departure from practices of violence on account of a particular reading of Scripture. For many Mennonites in both the US and Canada the practice of seeking to live without violence is inseparable from their understanding of what it is to be a Christian. According to Karl Koop, "virtually all official teachings of present-day Mennonite denominations affirm a form of nonresistant or peace position."[12] A window into this Mennonite peace tradition is vividly provided by Canadian Mennonite Rudy Wiebe in his novel about "Russian" Mennonites in rural Saskatchewan during the final years of the Second World War.[13] Wiebe narrates how, while ploughing a field, Thom Wiens is startled by the roar of Royal Canadian Air Force planes overhead practising manoeuvres. Initially condemnatory of the "heathen" and their "godless" preparations for war, Thom's conscience is then stirred by memories of a recent sermon delivered at his Mennonite church by Brother Goertzen:

> We are to follow Christ's steps, but we do not have pride. By God's grace we understand what others do not. As we cannot imagine Him lifting a hand to defend himself physically, so we, His followers, conquer only by spiritual love and not by physical force. Always only love: for those who love us, for those who would kill us, which is the same thing; all are included when He says, "This is my commandment, that you love one another even as I have loved you."

Wiebe discloses that Thom "had grown up hearing these statements and if someone had asked him when he had first known that Christ bade his disciples love their enemies, he could no more have answered than if he had been asked to consciously recollect his first breath." Here again, a biological metaphor is evoked to illustrate the ways in which ideas and practices of peace constitute the very habitus of Mennonite life. Brother Goertzen's sermon, and myriad other discourses, formed part of a vernacular theology that shaped and disciplined Mennonite imaginations, legitimating certain practices and invalidating others. It is these vernacular theologies and practices that have helped shape what Sally Engle Merry calls the "distinctive culture" of Mennonite peacebuilding.[14] The theological basis of Mennonite peace concern has been repeatedly emphasized in Mennonite sociological, historical, and theological writings.

The idea of "peace" among Mennonites, however, has been substantially reworked over time, and differences of perspective over the languages and practices of peace have been matters of considerable tension and conflict. Mennonite tradition is dynamic and contested, and this includes the traditions of peace. Prominent contemporary forms and modes of Mennonite peacemaking are relatively recent innovations that were developed during and after the Second World War. Set during this tumultuous period of change, Wiebe's novel, discussed above, is a reflexive and nuanced meditation on the demise of a prior consensus on peace as a result of intrusions from beyond the "bush," Wiebe's evocative metaphor for non-Mennonite outsiders. The title of Wiebe's (1962) novel, *Peace Shall Destroy Many*, neatly captures the highly ambiguous and deeply contentious nature of this politics of peace.

The watershed of the Second World War had far-reaching effects on Mennonite communities and their understandings of peace. It was during this period that there began a marked shift away from a stance of quietest nonresistance to that of activist peacemaking.[15] For centuries nonresistance had been a defining feature of Mennonite identity. The notion suggested a passive stance and was semantically parallel to "defencelessness." It was often used in tandem with the idea of "nonconformity." Nonresistance separated Mennonites from mainstream North American Protestants, few of whom prior to the 1950s held to a pronounced general ethical critique of coercion and violence. The framing also differentiated Mennonites from the growing pacifist movement after the First World War, which tended to be regarded as too liberal and "modern" for Mennonite sensitivities. The Second World War profoundly disrupted this earlier consensus through a series of overlapping factors. The traumatic experience of negotiating the Canadian and American military draft saw many Mennonite men enter military service against the outspoken will of church leaders. The draft also spurred the establishment of Alternative Service camps for conscientious objectors, which served as a kind of melting pot for exchanges among the youth of the Historic Peace Churches.

Also pivotal were the experiences of young Mennonites in MCC's European relief work, accelerating Mennonite urbanization, rising prosperity (on the back of agricultural war prices), increasing participation by Mennonites in higher education, and the articulation of new theological formulations such as Harold Bender's influential "Anabaptist Vision."[16] Collectively, these instituted far-reaching transformations and, for many Mennonites, profoundly destabilized earlier expectations that peace equated to practices of separation and passive nonresistance. Processes of transformation in peace logics initiated at this time were soon met by a series of further challenges and inspirations in the 1960s and 1970s, including engagements with the counterculture movement, civil rights activism and protests, and mass mobilization against the war in Vietnam. Leo Driedger and Donald Kraybill argue that MCCers returning from volunteer overseas assignments and key institutions, such as the MCC peace section, were key "change agents" in spurring more activist Mennonite practices and theologies of peace.[17] These former MCCers coaxed other Mennonites into more proactive engagements with the American and Canadian states. This overarching trajectory of change in Mennonite peace theologies and practices towards greater levels of activism was not equally shared among Mennonite groups. The fragmented nature of the Mennonite peoplehood ensured that different groupings responded in very different ways to the possibility of change, whether that be the embrace of new logics or the reinforcement of older traditions. Because of uneven reception this process of change was not necessarily tranquil; instead, it was frequently accompanied by divisions, schisms, and "tribal squabbles."[18]

Fred Kniss, in his wryly entitled *Disquiet in the Land*, provides an in-depth sociological study of what he calls the "surprisingly conflict-ridden character of Mennonite history."[19] Kniss examines the patterns of conflict in the (Old) Mennonite Church in four US states between 1870 and 1985. He argues that the nature of these conflicts shifted over time because of internal organizational and ideological change and because of the influence of wider dynamics in American society. While Mennonites traditionally sought to maintain a "closed system" with rigid boundaries separating them from the outside world, Kniss argues that these have, in fact, always been highly "flexible, fluctuating and porous."[20] The roles of logics and practices of separation have tended to be somewhat overestimated, both by insiders and observers. A central thesis in Kniss's argument is that the Mennonite experience in the US has been profoundly shaped by persistent "dynamic tension" between two ideological paradigms that "produced frequent, if not continuous conflict." He labels these two paradigms "traditionalism" and "communalism," with the former concerned with the locus of moral authority and the latter with enacting moral projects:

> For Mennonites, traditionalism has meant stressing traditional moral and spiritual values, the importance of family, biblical and communal authority, and denial of individual interests in favor of the collectivity. Communalism has entailed a concern for egalitarianism, social justice, pacifism, stewardship of the environment, mutual aid, and a focus on religious congregations as primary communities for their members. The two paradigms pull in different directions, especially in American political culture, where the former looks toward the right while the latter has affinities with the left. With respect to Mennonites' position in the world, traditionalism supports a sectarian, separatist stance, while communalism supports a more activist, socially progressive stance.[21]

Kniss maintains that MCC has been firmly aligned with one of these poles as the "primary institutional carrier of communalist concerns."[22] MCCers have certainly often been at the forefront of activist approaches to peacebuilding, and it is equally often regarded by MCCers as the Mennonite bastion for left-leaning political inclinations. However,

Kniss's description is clearly more accurate for some parts of MCC than for others. As a peoplehood movement MCC has always actively enrolled a wide spectrum of Mennonite groups, including those Kniss would label as staunch "traditionalists," into participating in the organization. Nevertheless, his analysis is helpful for locating MCC within the politics of peace and conflict among North American Mennonites. While clearly a sociological reduction, his bipolar approach displaces notions of a static, unchanging, essentialist, North American Mennonite identity and locates vigorous (and, possibly, endless) argument at the heart of the Mennonite tradition.

This (very brief) retelling of the history of Mennonite conflict over peace illustrates the ways in which the two are intimately interwoven, including within MCC discourses and practices. As modes of interconnecting across difference both relationships of conflict and peace are characterized by an inherent ambivalence between generative and endangering dynamics. They spark possibilities and threaten to unravel. Conflict creates the possibilities for active peace work; it is a necessary precondition. But peace can also generate conflict, as with perennial Mennonite arguments over the appropriate ways to enact peace. Even the most delicate and nuanced peace intervention can instigate antagonism that threatens collaborations and unravels relationships.

Central to matters of peace and conflict is the practice of identification, a process of constructing identities that involves discerning differences and similarities.[23] These differences and similarities are not simply waiting to be uncovered, however, but, rather, are produced through actual encounters. Through interactions difference and similarities are imagined, reconfigured, and inscribed. Identities are formed and reformed comparatively in relationships within and beyond (imagined) communal boundaries. Questions of with whom peacemakers seek to make peace, and with whom they experience tension, are therefore intimately interwoven with the politics of identity. Lamin Sanneh is insightful on this point: "you do not fight with a perfect stranger but only with someone with whom you have something in common."[24] Conflict can therefore propel the dissolution of relationships, but it can also help illuminate the dynamics of belonging and mutuality. Likewise, while peacebuilding can be indicative of connectivity and relationality, it can also operate as a demarcating impulse in which others are kept at a distance and through which divisions are replicated and reinforced. The following narratives examine these processes of identification, and the frictive entanglements of conflict and peace, in two MCC peace programs.

AHMADINEJAD AND "MARY KLASSEN"

In late September 2008 a number of Christian organizations, including MCC, organized and hosted a high-profile dinner and dialogue in New York with Mahmoud Ahmadinejad, at the time the hard-line president of Iran.[25] Remarkably, this was the fourth such meeting between MCCers and Ahmadinejad since 2006.[26] Ahmadinejad's pariah status in the US ensured that each of these meetings attracted controversy. But more than any of the others, the 2008 dialogue became embroiled in heated conflict. In large part this was because it attracted much more extensive media coverage than had the previous meetings, and much of this was markedly hostile. Here, therefore, MCCer attempts at building peace became a source of conflict.

On the surface the dialogues appear counterintuitive and contrary to "typical" Mennonite peacemaking practices, with their emphasis on small-scale initiatives and their propensity for avoiding the media spotlight. Indeed, much of the academic literature on the topic of Mennonite peacebuilding locates this "quietist" model as the standard version of Mennonite peacemaking, with a concern for small-scale projects and an emphasis on grassroots engagement and relationality.[27] Sandrine Lefranc argues that Mennonites specialize in a distinctive mode of doing peacemaking from below by deploying strategies of *relationnisme*.[28] For Lefranc, this depoliticizes Mennonite peace work by eschewing high-level interventions with political elites.

Keith Graber Miller's analysis of the advocacy work of MCC's Washington office calls attention to some reasons for this political aversion.[29] While the Washington office was established in 1968 specifically to monitor the activities of the American government and, when necessary, to represent Mennonite interests to the state, MCC staff have had to tread very carefully with these political engagements on account of sensitivity about their work among MCC's constituents. Those Mennonites holding to a "two kingdom" theology (see chapter 1) are deeply apprehensive about the transgression of a decisive church-state split. Although other Mennonites, and many MCCers themselves, have been influenced by more activist ideologies and modes of peacemaking, alongside more outspoken engagements with the state, MCCers at the Washington office have nevertheless remained cautious about ostracizing the conservative parts of the organization's constituency. Graber Miller deploys the metaphor of the Amish bundling board to describe the constraining role of constituent beliefs and practices. This refers to the Amish practice whereby a courting couple will lie together in bed "with their clothes on and sometimes with a board between them – purportedly for mutual edification and fuel conservation."[30] Accordingly, Mennonite beliefs and practices have forced the Washington office to keep its distance from the rough and tumble of American politics; although, like the actual bundling board, this is not always an effective mechanism for encouraging abstinence.

Given the penchant for grassroots activity and inhibitions pertaining to engaging with American and Canadian political elites, MCC's involvement in dialogues with Ahmadinejad does indeed seem thoroughly contrary to usual practice. This is apparent in the discursive strategies deployed by MCC leadership, which illustrate that it, too, saw a disjuncture between purported preference and (highly visible) reality in that this conundrum required careful attention and legitimation. MCCers consistently sought to portray the meetings as being in direct continuity with its grassroots and relational focus. To make this connection they delved into history. MCC's work in Iran began nearly twenty years earlier with the provision of relief supplies following the 1990 Manjil-Rudbar earthquake in northern Iran. Since 1998 MCC had sponsored ongoing academic exchanges and, since 2002, regular theological conferences between North American Mennonites and Shi'ite clerics from the Imam Khomeini Education and Research Institute in Qom, Iran.[31] The elite-level meetings with Ahmadinejad were praised by MCCers as affirming the sorts of results that grassroots, relational work could help produce. Reflecting on the Iran-Mennonite dialogues in 2007 Ed Martin, an MCC administrator, stated:

> The nurturing of personal relationships over seventeen years resulted in the unexpected meetings with the President of Iran ... Finding ways for people of the two countries to meet and learn to know each other as fellow human beings is essential to breaking down the stereotypes and dispelling the misinformation fostered by government rhetoric and the news media. One never knows where relationships built on mutual respect will lead.[32]

This grounding of the dialogues in a relational foundation – a perfect rendition of the process of rendering relational outlined in chapter 2 – was important to enable MCCers to celebrate them. And celebrate they did. Robb Davis, MCC executive director, was quoted as saying that the dialogues were "the kind of thing... MCC should be all about."[33] Throughout my fieldwork in Indonesian, Canadian, and American contexts, MCCers would frequently express to me their sense of excitement over the dialogues and their belief that these were among the most important and momentous peacebuilding activities undertaken by Mennonites in recent years. Narratives about the meetings spread rapidly throughout the organization and were frequently noted in formal settings and casual conversations. The interfaith peacebuilding initiative with the Iranian president clearly animated many MCCers.

But the discursive work of relationally grounding the high-level dialogues shouldn't be overstated. At least as important for explaining the reception of the dialogues among MCCers was the fact that these meetings enacted a stark alternative to mainstream North American politics, and particularly to the antagonistic, hostile, and militaristic bravado at that time emanating from the US government. At the time US-Iran tensions were escalating. Iran had been clumped in within George W. Bush's "axis of evil." Mainstream opinion was apparently unanimous in contending that Iran was an international threat. Both Ahmadinejad's and Bush's rhetoric had escalated as they traded verbal attacks. Opposing this polarizing discourse, Arli Klassen, who followed on from Davis as MCC executive director, argued for an alternative kind of intervention: "Right now the US and Iran are defining each other as enemies and so, as Christians, we are trying to promote dialogue, understanding and bridge building, rather than leading to war."[34] MCC sought to enact a different and specifically Anabaptist Christian way of behaving towards "enemies" by rejecting hostility and seeking peace. This same logic undergirds Mennonite theologian Thomas Finger's account of the intent of the various peacebuilding interconnections with Iranian Muslims as a movement from "demonization" to "dialogue"; others might indulge in hate speech, but Mennonites pursue alternative and constructive approaches.[35] Mary Ellen McNish, general secretary of the American Friends Service Committee and a participant in the September 2007 dialogue with Ahmadinejad, articulated succinctly the generative nature of conflict for these initiatives: "You make peace with those with whom you disagree, not your allies."[36] As with Klassen's framing, the presence of hostility was the fertile ground upon which peacemaking should emerge. The tensions between the US and Iranian governments, and "the West" and "Islam," as well as a sense of difference to that of mainstream North American political opinion, helped produce a proactive attempt to make peace through dialogue.

This same tension-filled context meant that such meetings were highly susceptible to critique. Here the paradox of friction – both generative and threatening – is apparent. In the wake of early publicity about the meetings with Ahmadinejad, Christian news outlets were overwhelmingly scathing, with the participants coming "under fire" from all quarters.[37] An online magazine article carried the title "Dining with the Devil," and many others followed suit.[38] One particularly potent example is a jeremiad by Richard Land of the Ethics and Religious Liberty Commission of the Southern Baptist Convention:

> The disgraceful meeting between religious leaders and President Ahmadinejad has been described as a "conversation about the role of religions in tackling global challenges and building peaceful societies" with "His Excellency" Ahmadinejad as the guest of honor. You can put lipstick on a pig, but it's still a pig. And you can call a murderous dictator "His Excellency," but he is still a murderous dictator. I am appalled at the moral obtuseness of people, some of whom come from historically pacifist religious traditions, who are so eager to talk with a man who advocates the annihilation and destruction of Israel and America … When I watched Ahmadinejad give his speech at the United Nations, I couldn't help but feel that he was channeling the spirits of Hitler, Himmler, and Goebbels.[39]

Land's evocation of haram swine and his analogous linking of Ahmadinejad with Nazi leaders was clearly intended to be deeply and profoundly offensive. Similar vehement attacks were also launched at the September 2008 dialogue venue itself where, as guests entered the hotel, protestors shouted out names and hurled insults.[40] The 2007 Mennonite-Muslim theological conference at Conrad Grebel University College in Ontario had also been confronted by protestors who "shouted down" the meeting, claiming that the Iranian clerics were "murderers" and "terrorists." Commentators labelled this theological conference "naïve" and portrayed MCC as "being used" by manipulative and cynical actors.[41] The theological dialogues have also been derided as "fetishized" and "commodified."[42] MCC's interfaith peacebuilding was the cause of further tensions, stimulating and energizing vociferous critique.[43]

Inside the theological dialogues some of the participants experienced the awkwardness of relating across differences. In a news article posted on the MCC website Ron Flaming, MCC's director of international programs, compared the perspectives of the Iranian Muslim religious leaders and the North American Christians who participated in a 2007 delegation to Iran. Flaming saw these two groups as separated by a sharp disjuncture: "I think the delegation was keenly aware we sat between these two narratives and found how difficult it was to make the bridge."[44] While much of the conversation was characterized by pleasant exchange, tensions were also apparent.

The critiques of MCC's high-profile peace work, noted above, are hardly surprising given the geopolitics surrounding the event. But, because of the sense that the organization is owned by a specific constituency rather than a general Canadian or American public, such criticisms were unlikely to significantly influence the actions of MCCers. The more important issue, therefore, was how MCC's own constituency responded to the dialogues. According to informants who were volunteering in MCC's Akron office at the time, the telephones ran hot for days. MCC was obliged to put extra staff on the phones simply to be able to receive all the calls. Most of the callers were highly critical of MCC's work, some were caustic. Many "two kingdom" Mennonites were deeply wary of MCC crossing the church-state boundary. This wariness was further exacerbated by the fact that the dialogue was with an infamous and controversial figure, an ardent critic of the West, and a holocaust denier. A small minority, however, expressed staunch support. Among this group were several prominent church leaders. Still other callers were thoroughly confused by what they were reading and simply wanted more information. Regardless, each of these calls was indicative of ownership. By taking the time to call the MCC office and express their disappointment and/or support, Mennonites symbolically participated in *their* organization and thereby claimed ownership of it. However, the angry phone calls were not without ambiguity. Implicit in their condemnation, and sometimes also explicitly articulated, was the threat of the possibility of disownership and abnegation. The tension here therefore leaned towards both the possibility of belonging and the possibility of separation.

The distance between many MCCers' passionate support for the dialogues and the suspicion or outright opposition of large portions of MCC's constituency threatened to unravel the peace work. MCCers were forced to go on the defensive. Senior MCC leaders sought to counter the criticisms and reassure the constituency by publishing a series of articles in Mennonite newspapers and magazines and posting material on the MCC website.[45] The felt need to engage in a proactive defense within specifically Mennonite publishing networks illustrates the desire of MCC leadership to connect with its denominational constituency. As a peoplehood movement, MCC is accountable to those who "own" the organization, and this relationship continued to operate as a "bundling board" with its engagements with high-level politics and political elites.

The gravity of this relationship was made clear to me when MCCers in the Akron office divulged to me that a key guiding question in initiating new programs or making changes to existing ones was: "What would Mary Klassen think?" Mary Klassen, in this image, is a fictional personification of the constituency. She is an imaginary Mennonite grandmother, a representative of MCC's conservative or (to evoke Kniss's categories) "traditionalist" Mennonite support base.[46] And yet the logical answer in this case, as indicated in the critical phone calls made to MCC, was that Mary Klassen had major qualms about these dialogues with the Iranian president. Moreover, MCC administrators would certainly have known and anticipated Mary Klassen's sensitivities prior to the dialogues taking place. The history of the MCC Washington office having to tread carefully around constituency predilections in the US would have, on its own, given ample warning.

I suggest that in organizing and facilitating the dialogues MCCers saw themselves as engaging in a "prophetic" role vis-à-vis their constituency. They sought to push the edges of acceptability *despite* "Mary Klassen's" assumed hesitancy and reluctance. Keeping the constituency on side was important, but this was not the only, or perhaps primary, goal of MCC activities. Of course, keeping Mary Klassen happy was never going to be easy given the plurality of perspectives among fragmented Mennonite groups and the internal (communalist-traditionalist) tensions that lie at the heart of the Anabaptist tradition. MCC remains a precarious and yet surprisingly durable collaboration produced and reproduced in such frictions, and it is within these frictions that MCC's peace work takes place.

Anticipated conflict therefore provided the grounds for MCC's peace work. Ahmadinejad, the leader of an Islamic "pariah" state and in many ways the ultimate Other to North American Protestant Christians in the twenty-first century, was actively engaged in courteous conversation. The cultural distance that separated the players in these dialogues were overcome, even if only temporarily. Or, rather, the cultural gaps were generative of the desire among MCCers (and possibly also Iranian clerics and Ahmadinejad himself) to proactively engage. The rejection of conforming to mainstream media opinions, which overwhelmingly condemned the dialogues and thereby enacted Mennonite countercultural difference, was also productive. This hostility operated as an implicit confirmation of the alternativeness of their approach. Moreover, an uneasy Mary Klassen may have further stimulated the peace work on account of an imagined prophetic role that sought to nudge her into a more proactive peace ethic and "communalist" orientation. But the peace work was also made precarious through these conflicts. Particularly important here were the views of Mary Klassen and MCC's response to them. Mary Klassen was not comfortable with MCC's high-profile engagement with Ahmadinejad. The active articulation of disappointment in hundreds of phone calls threatened to unravel the collaboration between MCC and a segment of its supporting constituency. By proactively engaging with these tensions through Mennonite media and online articles, MCCers sought to solicit and re-enrol their constituency so as to provide ongoing support. The critical responses from Mennonites to the Ahmadinejad dialogues necessitated active "peacemaking" attempts directed toward MCC's own constituency.

PEACEBUILDING WITH MILITANTS IN JAVA

An imagined political clash of "Islam" and "the West" furnished the backdrop for the Mennonite dialogues with President Ahmadinejad. MCC's "key initiative" of interfaith bridge building was established within this context of the growing animosity that characterized the years following 9/11. Likewise, this provided an impetus for a reorientation of MCC's programs in Indonesia to prioritize interfaith peace work. Prior to the late 1990s MCC had few, if any, specific peace programs focused on engaging with Muslims. But in addition to shifts in the geopolitical imaginary there were also thoroughly Indonesian dynamics that facilitated MCC's refocusing on interfaith peace work. The collapse of the New Order state in 1998 saw a series of dramatic changes to Indonesian society, including the extraordinary proliferation of civil society organizations after thirty years of tight state regulation and control. Various civil society organizations emerged at this time, including those that dedicated themselves to proactive interfaith peacebuilding. The presence of such groups opened new space for partnerships with international donors. Simultaneously, newly arrived MCCers brought with them a much stronger interest in interfaith concerns and a more proactive stance towards forming partnerships to engage in peace programs. Of particular importance in this regard were the MCC Representatives in Indonesia. MCC Indonesia had already initiated a number of peace programs before Anna and Jake Friesen arrived in Indonesia to take up the country leadership role in 2001. Their strong interest in interfaith concerns and their proactive stance towards peace built upon this recent shift, while also moving it in new directions.

The new possibilities for peace work opened in parallel with, and in response to, an extremely turbulent period of change. Over a decade from the late 1990s the renegotiations of political realities in Indonesia erupted into episodes of violent communal conflict in different locations across the archipelago.[47] Some of this violence took place along Christian-Muslim lines. In part this reflected a reification of religious identities. There was also a mushrooming of "hardline" Islamic groups at this time that actively sought to defend Islam against perceived threats, whether in the form of "proselytizing" (In. *kristinisasi*) Christians or "deviant" Muslim groups (In. *aliran sesat*).[48] However, the rise of militant Islam was only part of the broader political terrain. Each episode of conflict was complex and often ambiguous. Religion always merged with other identities and political processes, including ethnic affiliation, economic disparities, military manoeuvres, and inter-personal hostilities. Violence was concentrated in particular areas, including the Malukus, Ambon, Poso, Kalimantan, Aceh, East Timor, and Papua, and there were also the widely publicized bombings in Jakarta and Bali. But these were manifestations of growing tensions felt throughout the archipelago during these years. Paralleling the felt impetus among MCCers to pursue dialogue with Ahmadinejad at a time of growing tension, the perceived need for peacebuilding initiatives in Indonesia emerged out of this national context of emergent conflicts. My analysis of MCC's peace work in Indonesia centres on partnerships between MCC and local organizations that sought to relate across Christian-Muslim identities.[49]

In the late 1990s "Pasukan Islam" was re-established as part of a wider surge in growth of hardline (In. *garis keras*) Islamic groups.[50] This paramilitary group traced its history back to independence struggles against the Dutch in the 1940s. In the decades after independence the group had been suppressed by the state. Taking advantage of the new political space available due to the collapse of the New Order regime the group quickly grew in size. Its headquarters were located in Solo, more formally known as Surakarta, but it had membership in various urban centres across Central Java.[51] The leader of Pasukan Islam, Rachmad, led the group in carrying out "sweepings" against perceived immoral activities in Solo in the early 2000s.[52] Rachmad and others in the group also joined with Laskar Jihad combatants sent from Java to fight in the bloody conflicts in Ambon and Poso between 1999 and 2001.[53] Pasukan Islam especially appealed to those from lower socio-economic strata who found that membership in the militia provided a renewed sense of purpose and identity. This was procured not just from regular military training drills (In. *perlatihan militer*) but also from a series of other communal activities including, for example, active provision of relief services after floods in the region. Pasukan Islam also operated a radio station to promote its message of reformed Islam. In 2003 this radio station became embroiled in a protracted, though non-violent, dispute with another Muslim radio station that shared a similar frequency but that had a widely differing vision of what constituted authentic Islam in Indonesia.

It was at this time that Rachmad first met Lukas. Lukas was the manager of a Christian radio station called Radio Emanuel. It was in this role that he was asked to help mediate between the two Muslim stations. Lukas was initially very nervous about this prospect. Lukas was a Mennonite pastor from Gereja Kristen Muria Indonesia (GKMI) and was ethnically Chinese. He was acutely aware of growing religious and social tensions in Solo over the preceding decades, including the rise of extremist and radical Islamist groups and their use of vigilante coercion to impose conformity of belief.[54] Only a few years earlier, Solo had been the site of major riots, many of which had a strong anti-Chinese tone and, due in large part to the conflation of "Chineseness" and Christianity, an anti-Christian dimension.[55] Lukas therefore approached his meeting with Rachmad with great uncertainty. He told me that he had no idea how he was going to be received by the Muslim militants. However, the mediation process went well and, over time, anxieties diminished. Slowly a tentative working relationship began to form between Rachmad and Lukas.

Around this time leaders from a number of different religions in Solo began planning a large-scale, public event to demonstrate solidarity across ethnic and religious divides. This collective action was imagined as a local response to the recent US-led invasions of Iraq and the then impending threat of an invasion of Afghanistan, both of which were widely criticized by many Indonesian Muslims as a modern Christian crusade against Islam. Calling themselves Forum Adem Ayem, after the popular Javanese restaurant in which they had their meetings, the group organized a demonstration to pre-empt any potential rising tensions in Solo.[56] Lukas, the GKMI pastor, was among the key Christian leaders in this group. Another prominent leader was Agung, a Muslim entrepreneur and an influential member of his neighbourhood mosque, a twice Hajji (having engaged in the pilgrimage to Mecca on more than one occasion), and an active member of the traditionalist Indonesian Islamic organization Nahdlatul Ulama (NU). Since the early 1990s, NU had been a prominent Indonesian voice for democratic reform and religious pluralism.[57]

Forum Adem Ayem's strategy was to present a united visual spectacle of inter-religious solidarity. To do so the group sought funding from external sources to help cultivate the desired performative aesthetic. Lukas connected the group with the MCC Reps, whom he had known through Mennonite church connections for several years. Forum Adem Ayem asked MCC for funds to purchase T-shirts that would be worn by all participants. Anna and Jake were initially hesitant about whether such expenditure fit with MCC's priorities. However, they agreed to support the initiative because they trusted Lukas and wanted to support the budding inter-religious dynamic that this group was pursuing in the context of growing religious tensions.

After the march for peace, which was regarded as a success from the point of view of the organizers, Forum Adem Ayem morphed into a more explicitly inter-religious (In. *antaragama*) group and, in the process, assumed a new name: Interfaith and Intergroup Forum for Peace (In. Forum Perdamaian Lintas Agama dan Golongan, FPLAG). Lukas and Agung took up key leadership roles in this new organization, supported in ad hoc and loosely knit ways by a range of religious leaders and community activists. FPLAG – again through the connection between Lukas and Anna and Jake – continued to receive financial support from MCC to undertake community-level peacebuilding activities in Solo. One such initiative supported by MCC was a series of peace trainings that FPLAG organized with members of Pasukan Islam. The opportunity to undertake this training was created through the slowly developing friendship between Lukas and Rachmad.

An MCC-sponsored publication by Jeanne Jantzi narrates an occasion when Lukas and Rachmad visited Aceh together sometime after the December 2014 Indian Ocean Tsunami had devastated the coastline.[58] Lukas, a veritable organizational entrepreneur, had helped initiate another organization that partnered with MCC in undertaking tsunami relief work. During their stay in Aceh, Lukas and Rachmad met with a group of Americans and Canadians participating in a tour of MCC's tsunami response. Rachmad was asked to speak to the group, but after just a few words he choked up and was only able to express a few words of thank you. Later, Rachmad talked with Lukas about the reasons for his tears:

> I don't know. It was coming from my heart, and I couldn't block it or stop it. I remember when I chased out the Americans. I hated them. I made war against Christians. Why are they the ones that sincerely help our brothers and sisters in Aceh? I am truly touched. I know that Americans and Christians are not like what I had thought up to now.[59]

Jantzi then considers the theological implications of transformation and reconciliation that she finds apparent in Rachmad's confession. She writes:

> I believe that the more points of connection with people of other faiths, the better. We know that we are called into relationship with others who are created in God's image … [and] we seek to bear

> witness to the reign of Christ in our work and relationships … We seek to join in faithfulness to what God is doing in Indonesia. We trust that God is at work in those interfaith relationships. We recognize that we are not in control of the results. In many cases, we do not even have enough imagination to visualize the possibilities of the work of the Holy Spirit.[60]

Here again the grassroots and relational orientation of MCC peace programs is foregrounded and celebrated. It is through relationships that "faithfulness" is enacted and embodied. Through relationships one can "bear witness" to the Christian faith. At the same time inter-religious relationships are celebrated ("the more … the better") in a Mennonite cosmopolitan ethic that embraces religious diversity. Without religious others, the sacred practice of Christian relationality wouldn't – indeed couldn't – be enacted.

As Jantzi's chapter illustrates, this story of peacemaking relationships was celebrated in Mennonite circles, both in Indonesia and North America, although it never received the level of attention that the meetings with Ahmadinejad attracted. Its thoroughly quotidian nature, however, is a rich space for ethnographic analysis about the politics of inter-religious identities and the frictions of difference.

Most Mennonite renditions of this story that I heard celebrated decreasing animosity because of small, relational acts of reaching across religious boundaries. This movement towards peace was narrated as a journey rather than as a rapid change. But it was nevertheless considered radical and transformative, even if tensions and ambiguities remained. Pasukan Islam ceased to participate in the "sweepings" of the early 2000s. Rachmad clearly changed his language of confrontation, though he didn't entirely renounce coercion as a possible strategic option, and he told me that he continued to organize military training drills for his members. The changes in Pasukan Islam, however, followed a similar trajectory to other hardline groups in Solo, which suggests that the political room for manoeuvre for Islamic militant groups had shifted. Indeed, new police and military operations worked to suppress "terrorist" activities, and new patterns of governance restricted the social and political space previously afforded to hardline groups.[61] Even transformative relationships take place alongside and within political and institutional configurations. These configurations remain influential, although not determinative.

Each of the actors in this peacebuilding initiative was affiliated with a religion (In. *agama*). These identities are signalled in the preceding narrative. As discussed in chapter 3, all Indonesians are required by law to have an *agama*. Since the collapse of the New Order, the original five – Islam, Buddhism, Hinduism, Protestantism, and Roman Catholicism – have been expanded to include Confucianism. Although having an *agama* is obligatory, the level of influence such identities have on practices and relationships is, unsurprisingly, highly variable. In this case, however, the religious identities of the actors were pivotal to how the different figures related to each other.

In the case of FPLAG the "inter-religious" identity of this group embedded *agama* as the basis of their collective action. These religious identities were plural: an inter-religious forum requires religious diversity. The forum celebrated and reinforced differences between traditions in ways that frequently bordered on reification. But while each religious representative self-located within a particular tradition – "Muslim," for example, was presented as an identifiable group – all those involved in this forum were acutely aware that each of their traditions was permeated by fractures and divisions. None of the religious leaders in this group were under any illusion that these *agama* identities were homogeneous. Key fissures were both within and between "Muslims" and "Christians."

The Mennonite identity shared by Lukas, Anna, and Jake was vital for animating the partnership between FPLAG and MCC. MCC's work in Central Java was a direct consequence of an imagined transnational denominational community that facilitated global connections between American, Canadian, and Indonesian Mennonites. MCC was one of the organizations that provided an opportunity for these different national churches to interact. I once asked Matthew, a senior administrator in MCC's Akron office, if MCC's work in Indonesia was primarily to facilitate connections across religious boundaries with Indonesian Muslims. Matthew told me that, while these interfaith relationships were important, they were not the primary impetus for the presence of MCC in Indonesia. He told me that the most important factor that legitimated, and almost demanded, MCC's ongoing presence in Indonesia was the link with the Indonesian Mennonite churches. Matthew said that this was the fundamental reason Indonesia would remain an important location for MCC's work in Asia for the foreseeable future. This was despite his own qualms about whether Indonesia faced the sort of pressing poverty found elsewhere in the region. The relationship with Indonesian Mennonites was MCC's raison d'être in the country.

Consequently, Lukas's identity as a Mennonite (GKMI) pastor situated him as an ideal partner for MCC. Perceived commonalities and shared interests between the MCC Reps and Lukas propelled this relationship. This was particularly so because Lukas's articulate and proactive interest in peacebuilding across religious divides was not shared among all his fellow pastors. The relatively few Indonesian Mennonite pastors who actively engaged in peacebuilding tended to attract North American Mennonite attention far more readily than did their colleagues. This was candidly acknowledged by Jake and Anna when they told me that Lukas was a "poster child" for MCC. Lukas's active pursuit of peace as an Indonesian Mennonite was therefore key, and his work was widely discussed and highly praised within the organization. Like the Ahmadinejad dialogues, stories of Lukas and his work circulated throughout MCC's transnational networks. In these narratives Lukas's "Indonesian" and "Mennonite" identities were always emphasized. Sometimes his ethnic identity as "Chinese" was also highlighted, though ethnic difference was generally less prominently situated, presumably because ethnic difference in Java was considered less intuitively legible for a North American audience than that of religious difference. But as the qualifier "Indonesian" indicated, there were significant identity separations between Lukas and North American MCCers. Lukas was not the same kind of Mennonite as American and Canadian Mennonites, and the partnership was predicated on the difference of nationality. The MCC logic of partnership located the organization as a foreign North American entity, derived from the ethnic Mennonite peoplehood, which worked in collaboration with local partners.[62] It was therefore Lukas's status as both Indonesian and Mennonite that rendered him a viable and compelling partner.

Throughout my fieldwork the differences separating Lukas from MCCers were rarely discussed as sources of tension. Significant rhetorical work was undertaken to lubricate the relationship and to downplay possible disruptions. Even when an organization that Lukas headed failed to adequately account for significant MCC funds, the partnership continued unabated. Anna and Jake believed that the funds were inadequately reported rather than misspent. Just before I left Indonesia FPLAG began exploring possibilities of gaining access to USAID funding. While this would have greatly increased the level of funding available for the forum, USAID funding was also seen as a moral mistake, if not thoroughly repugnant, within MCC in Indonesia and elsewhere.[63] Yet this possibility did not disrupt the partnership. Lukas continued to receive trust and support. Issues that could well have caused dissolution were smoothed over in active attempts to dispel contention.

Throughout my research I rarely came across incisive critiques of MCC by its Indonesian partners. Most staff and personnel of partner NGOs had outright praise for MCC's affable, adaptive, and conciliatory work.

I was initially reluctant to take these comments at face value, attuned as I was to the idea that conflict was pervasive in the functioning of "partnerships" in the contemporary development industry – a repeated theme in the scholarly literature on the subject.[64] So, out of earshot of MCCers themselves, I sometimes probed further, seeking to elicit some more critical commentary. Rarely did I learn of hidden or suppressed antagonisms.[65] While MCC required written reports and financial accounts, and this was sometimes seen as a burden or inconvenience, MCC did not demand the same sort of tedious, and largely vacuous, monitoring and evaluation procedures required by major international NGOs. Because MCC had a presence on the ground in Indonesia through both North American and Indonesian staff, partners had frequent opportunities to work through issues as they arose in face-to-face conversation. The discussions between MCC and partners that I attended were almost always cordial and amicable. These interactions reflected Anna and Jake's partnership model, which stressed mutuality and flexibility and thereby militated against heavy-handed or unilateral approaches. This partnership model relied on the recognition and inscription of differences between foreign and local.

Differences animated and energized MCC's involvement in peacework in Indonesia, whether these were intra-Mennonite or inter-religious. However, the friction of these differences was not the only propelling dynamic. Operating alongside difference was a powerful and mobilizing conviviality. Affection and enjoyment were not inevitable features of MCC partnerships, nor were they programmable outcomes. But where friendship emerged over time and in particular relationships its effects were far-reaching for how MCC carried out its work. This was certainly the case in the relationships Lukas shared with Anna and Jake, which were characterized by mutual warmth, generosity, and enjoyment. Over many visits and meetings, through regular phone calls and text messages, and over hundreds of cups of sweet tea (In. *teh manis*) and shared dinners, this relationship enacted a convivial Mennonite cosmopolitanism. As I sat in on meeting after meeting, and as I interviewed each of the actors involved in this partnership, it became clear to me that an adequate ethnographic description of how this network worked in practice would require attention to their shared affective relationships. Their friendship provided a powerful impetus for facilitating MCC's support for FPLAG's peacebuilding in Solo.

According to Nicholas Lash the concept of friendship carries a density and weight that is rarely sufficiently acknowledged. Indeed, his theology locates friendship at the heart of the Christian gospel; friendship, for

Lash, is the human instantiation of divine love.[66] Friendship does not require either the suppression of difference or a complete aversion to conflict; rather, friendship is a particular mode of relating across difference that allows difference to be received as gift. Lash's friendship and Tsing's friction are not opposites. Like friction, friendship is a pervasive and social force. It mobilizes, animates, and propels social interactions. Friendship is also a mode of "sticky engagement" that generates networks and builds momentum. The workings of friendship have received limited attention in anthropological studies of development. I argue that attention to affectionate relations was vital in accounting for the routes along which MCC's peacebuilding partnerships were formed and practised. That friendship played such an important role was in part due to the privileging of relationships as domains of intervention in widely circulating moral and theological discourses in MCC. The tendency to "render relational" within MCC elevated friendship into a sacred domain of Christian praxis.

Conviviality provided an animating impulse for the forming and lubricating of MCC's peacebuilding partnerships in Solo. Two additional programmatic effects emerged out of this politics of affection. First, as friendship is interpersonal, the relational subsumes organizational and administrative processes. Relationships are idiosyncratic, involving non-fungible personalities and interactions. That is, changing the personnel in any part of the partnership is highly disruptive, potentially dissolving programs and projects. The relational, affective basis of partnership is one of the primary reasons a change in the MCC Reps in Indonesia, or the change in the head of a local partner, could prove disastrous for ongoing collaboration. Second, friendship operates as an alternative momentum to that of "outcomes" or "impacts" in propelling partnerships forward. This does not necessarily relegate to irrelevance the formally stated ends of any given program, but it raises the prospect that they might not be determinative for decision-making processes. The privileging of affective relationships can furnish a partnership with longevity, just as it could also make the same partnership precarious.

While friendship was given a particular valence within MCC it is not, of course, just a Mennonite thing. Indonesians and expatriates who worked in other NGOs in Indonesia told me stories about close friendships in their networks that had facilitated long-standing organizational partnerships. They also noted cases in which partnerships quickly unravelled when key personnel changed. This suggests that friendships are often animating forces across the development sector. Inter-religious friendships were also important for the Solo peacebuilding work supported by MCC. Lukas's friendship with Rachmad, the militant leader from Pasukan Islam, and also Agung, a member of the pluralist Muslim mass organization Nahdlatul Ulama, were also central to the workings of these partnerships. Lukas told me that, as a Chinese Indonesian Christian pastor, he thought it was easier for him to engage in friendships with both Muslim leaders than it was for them to do so with each other. This was because Rachmad and Agung represented very different positions within the spectrum of Indonesian Islam, and their respective wings were frequently at cross-purposes.[67] In fact, according to Merle Ricklefs, in a particularly heated episode during Ramdan in December 2000, the Nahdlatul Ulama youth organization Ansor threatened to mobilize thousands of its own people to barricade Surkarta *against* militant Islamic groups such as Pasukan Islam. While Agung clearly played a key brokering role in vouching for and endorsing Lukas and North American Mennonites to Pasukan Islam, a shared Muslim identity by no means negated the potential for sharp differences. As Lukas pointed out, it is sometimes easier to relate to the religious Other than to a fellow believer.

Importantly, the actors in this narrative did not actively seek to diminish or reduce the distinction between Mennonite and Muslim. This is noteworthy because within both Islamic and Christian theologies there exists a latent potential for breaching boundaries with the religious Other via practices of conversion, including evangelism or *da'wa* (In. *dakwah*). Tsing specifically notes this propensity towards universalism in both Christianity and Islam, and she regards these "world religions" as historically among the most successful in claiming universality.[68] Indeed, Webb Keane argues for the theological origins of notions of "the global."[69] He points out that "the very possibility of evangelization seems to depend on some sort of assumption about human unity." But to proselytize is an inherently ambiguous enterprise. On the one hand, it situates the target of the message as Other, as beyond the fold of the believers and requiring transformation to enter the community of believers; on the other hand, it simultaneously acknowledges the potential for commonality and the collapse of the boundaries of differentiation. For proselytizing to take place the Other must be seen as being capable – upon acceptance of the promoted faith – to be embraced within the fold. Conversion out of Otherness is a distinct and realizable possibility. Evangelism and *da'wa* assert divisions and simultaneously offer the possibility of superseding them.

Conversations about the possibility of Muslim conversion to Christianity arose occasionally among MCCers in Indonesia. Given debates about "mission" within MCC and among constituents, and given that MCC had previously participated in planting churches in West Kalimantan, this is hardly surprising. On one occasion over lunch MCCers discussed whether it was conceivable that Rachmad would ever convert to Christianity. The answer was clear: "it isn't possible." On one level this negation was a frank acknowledgment that Rachmad's conversion was not an intended goal of MCC's involvement in the peacebuilding in Solo. The funding of the peace work was not a surreptitious "Trojan horse" aimed at *really* producing conversion when the stated goal was the building peaceful relationships. I never got any sense that MCCers were engaged in deceitful attempts to do something other than what had previously been publicly expressed to Rachmad and his militant colleagues. A devious smuggling in of evangelism would not just have countered the intention of peacebuilding but could easily have jeopardized the entire process. To collapse difference through conversion could result in two undesirable outcomes. First, it could ignite Muslim anger over Christian proselytization. As discussed in chapter 2 and chapter 3, concern about Christian evangelism (In. *kristenisasi*) is widespread throughout Muslim Indonesia, and the conversion of a well-known Muslim leader such as Rachmad would have had far-reaching ramifications.[70] The dissolving of difference could increase visibility and tension in undesirable ways. Second, to decrease the difference between Lukas and Rachmad would be to diminish a highly productive dynamic in which that relationship performed and modelled an exemplary peaceful interaction across *agama* identities.

One further ambiguity also connected with the issue of conversion was at work within this partnership for peace. The collaboration between MCC and FPLAG brought each organization into an acknowledged close association. Staff from both MCC and FPLAG used the names and identities of the other to enhance their respective, but clearly overlapping, projects. The intimacy of friendship, as noted above, was clearly apparent in their casual interactions in both formal and informal settings. However, MCC's relationship with Pasukan Islam was completely different. MCCers took active, clear, and firm steps to separate themselves from Pasukan Islam militants. This caution and vigilance included both MCC's internal and public communications about the partnership with careful self-monitoring of e-mail and phone conversations and the deployment of pseudonyms for Rachmad in all communications, whether public or otherwise. MCCers were also active in self-disciplining to delimit the boundaries of the relationship with Pasukan Islam. This included extreme caution with finances so that none of MCC's finances could ever be construed as having been transferred to Pasukan Islam members. MCCers were careful in monitoring these relational and financial flows to ensure that FPLAG was their sole partner and so that Pasukan Islam could not be construed as a direct beneficiary of MCC programs.

The opportunity to work with the militant Islamic Other was a powerful animating impulse for MCC's involvement in the peace work in Solo. However, the threat of possible accusation of connection with "terrorism" by the US government, no matter how tenuous, furnished MCCers with an equally strong impetus for separation. This highly cautious approach was based on the knowledge that the US State Department had taken active steps to shut down registered American charities based on suspicion of involvement in financing terrorism.[71] MCC's connection with Pasukan Islam was therefore strategically distanced. Partnership processes removed MCC from the work on the ground and from direct relationship with Islamic militants; it cocooned MCC from unsavory tensions. Here, therefore, is an example of active steps being taken to counter coercive American political threats through drawing a clear line between MCC and Pasukan Islam and, reminiscent of the work of the Mennonite Scholarship Commission in chapter 3, ensuring that FPLAG was deployed as a buffer between them.

CONFLICTED PACIFISM

In analysis of inter-religious encounters, it is often tempting to assume a Huntingtonesque prospect and, from some lofty and distant peak, survey the landscape of different religious blocks as they meet in a "clash of civilizations." This temptation should be resisted. It is not that civilizational thinking is not relevant to attempts to build transnational movements and to mobilize networks but, rather, that these globalisms rarely have a monopoly over identity constructions. Drawing on ethnographic analysis of Mennonite peacebuilding, this chapter explores how MCC's collaborations were inflected with friction, the generative yet precarious process of interconnection across difference. It is through frictive encounters that peacebuilding initiatives were formed, reshaped, and enacted.

The presence of conflict and the work for peace in MCC and its partnerships reveal a complex and dynamic relationship between senses of commonality and difference, belonging and otherness. Rather than poles on a binary continuum they are better seen as operating in dynamic interaction. For example, during my fieldwork I had to tread very carefully around the tsunami relief operations in Aceh because of the extensive interpersonal conflicts that pervaded MCC's work there. These tensions emerged in the high-stress start-up period for MCC's tsunami-relief program in early 2005, and the relational tensions stretched between Aceh, Central Java, Akron, and Winnipeg. I found it challenging to understand the issues at stake as these conflicts tended to flow along subterranean routes and were expressed in indirect ways.[72] These pervasive interpersonal conflicts simmered in the background, almost as a shadow effect of the strong organizational affirmation of friendship.

At one point I became embroiled in these tensions. Early during my fieldwork, I was invited to contribute to the MCC tsunami evaluation team that was set to tour Indonesia, Sri Lanka, and India. While sorely tempted, I decided that the timing did not suit my research plans, and, as I had been recruited without my direct consultation, I assumed it would be simple enough to decline involvement. I communicated my decision to Anna and Jake, the MCC Reps in Salatiga, who were very understanding. However, information soon began filtering back to me that some personnel involved in the evaluation process, whom I had never met or communicated with, were "POed" with my "pulling out." I also learned that some MCCers in North America had speculated over e-mail about my apparent resentment at not being offered the lead role in the team. Later, when the evaluation team toured Indonesia, Anna and Jake invited me to sit in as they made a presentation about MCC's tsunami response. Just before they began their presentation Jake took me aside and, very apologetically, asked me to leave the room as a member of the evaluation team had expressed concerns to him about my presence. Given my almost complete separation from the situation and my lack of any kind of relationship with almost all who were involved, the tensions directed at me seemed uncanny. I concluded, however, that I was not so much a target of critique as I was a pawn in wider MCC battles. My potential insertion into the evaluation process – which was heated and tense because the tsunami relief operations had frequently been heated and tense – meant that I was immersed in a highly contested political and relational terrain.

In my experience tensions between MCCers rarely resulted in complete rejection of the organization, although this remained a possibility; rather, through their arguments MCCers registered themselves as full and rightful members of their organization, and they tested their place within the wider arena of MCC authority structures. Much like the angry and passionate phone calls of constituents over the Ahmadinejad dialogues, conflicts within MCC were indicative of enthusiastic commitment and belonging. Accordingly, throughout my research in Indonesia, Canada, and the US, the most profound, far-reaching, and perceptive critiques I encountered pertaining to MCC's work came from those most intimately associated with the organization: North American Mennonites, many of whom were former or current MCCers. Time and again interviews with American and Canadian Mennonites encapsulated a passionate commitment to MCC coupled with strident critique. An interview with Todd Erb, a retired Mennonite academic in Harrisonburg, Virginia, exemplifies these encounters. Todd told me that, although he had never actually worked within MCC, his whole life had been "interlaced" with the organization: he was an "MCC alumnus without ever being an alumnus." His litany of complaints and criticisms regarding the organization were extensive: the Damascus Road anti-racism trainings had been an "unfortunate chapter"; there were major challenges involved in maintaining a clear and shared focus within the organization; the early departure of executive director Robb Davis (the first non-ethnic Mennonite to head the organization) had highlighted major organizational failings; ongoing US-Canada tensions were troubling. Yet Todd concluded the interview by emphatically stating: "I love MCC!" Todd's criticisms of MCC were not attempts at distancing himself from the organization but, rather, articulations of ownership and affection. Within MCC, conflict and love frequently formed an intimate embrace. Just as peacebuilding can serve to demarcate self from Other, so too conflict can help bind a peoplehood movement together.

6

Orienting Guesthood

DRINKING TEA WITH THE LOCALS

In *Nurturing Doubt*, an autobiographical account of his conversion from Mennonite missionary to secular anthropologist, Elmer Miller refers frequently to his habit of drinking *maté*, a kind of herbal infusion, with the Indigenous Toba of Argentina. While he continued this practice during his ethnographic fieldwork it was especially prominent in his account of his years as a missionary. Miller narrates that he spent inordinately large amounts of time sitting, listening, and drinking *maté* in Toba homes. According to Miller the "social significance" of *maté* for Toba life "can scarcely be overestimated."[1] Yet, it is the social significance of *maté* to Miller that is particularly pertinent for my argument in this chapter. Although he worked with a mission board, Miller's experience as a Mennonite missionary closely resembles normative ideals within MCC. Miller's missionary approach – frequently drinking *mate*, cultivating relationships, providing a listening ear, visiting Toba homes, treading softly on matters of Toba culture – also epitomizes MCC ideals of relational service.[2] During my field research I frequently encountered expressions and celebrations of a particular image of expatriate service directly paralleling Miller's account that operated as a normative ideal within the organization. This image was of an MCCer sitting down in a mud hut in Africa drinking tea with the locals. It is a picture of simplicity: the technology, materiality, and affluence of white North American middle-class life is peeled away for a rustic and poignant embrace of genuine camaraderie with poor villagers in the Global South. The image implicitly, although sometimes also quite explicitly, served as a discursive backdrop for MCC's work in Indonesia. It was an influential organizational myth. Three issues relating to this image are key themes in this chapter.

First, drinking tea, *mate*, or other local equivalent highlights MCC's ideal of a non-coercive and profoundly relational approach to international service. It is an attempt to enact an ethics of peace in the course of service. Drinking tea is less about doing something *for* those living in the mud huts, and thereby exercising one's power on or over them, than it is about engaging *with* them and receiving *from* them. The ideal of "drinking tea" is therefore a counterbalance to the objective of canned meat discussed in chapter 1. Whereas canned meat is imagined as a matter of delivering protein to the needy, drinking tea celebrates meaningful and intimate conviviality. The notion of drinking tea dislodges concrete acts of "aid" from being the sole or ultimate goal of MCC service assignments. It also conjures images of conversation between parties for whom a considerable amount of translation is required. In this chapter I argue that concerted attempts are made within MCC to encourage self-reflexivity and to displace the privileged positions of North American expatriate service workers.[3] This displacing of power was considered a necessary precondition for being able and willing to engage in the relationality of drinking tea.

The second and third points form an apparent paradox that lies at the heart of my argument. On the one hand, "drinking tea" speaks of *association*, suggestive of warm relationships involving reciprocity and friendship. It also expresses an ideal of expatriate MCCers living with and alongside the locals, communicating in the vernacular, and taking time to form caring and enjoyable friendships. However, and this is the third point, the very concept of "the locals" relies on a logic of *disassociation*. On the other hand, therefore, the image of drinking tea situates the expatriate MCCer as someone who is serving not in their own place but, rather, as a foreigner away from home. Expatriate MCCers carry out their work within the politics of these competing logics of association and disassociation.

This normative myth of drinking tea with the locals is a useful entry point into exploring an ideology of guesthood that provides a distinctive imagining for MCCers for their work in Indonesia. Ideology here is used in the same sense as it is by Webb Keane, who describes ideology as "animating ideas" through which actions are made "inhabitable and practicable."[4] As with many of the ideologies that circulate within MCC, guesthood derives from North American Anabaptist theology. Indeed, guesthood strongly resonates with prominent themes in Mennonite ethics, such as with the traditional emphasis on Mennonites being "The Quiet in the Land" (Pl. *Die Stillen im Lande*), with its connotations of non-coercive quietude, and also with Anabaptist ideals of "pacifism, humility and service."[5] Guesthood can be seen as an embodied recapitulation of a theology of "not being in charge" espoused by Mennonite theologians.[6] Guesthood is therefore a particular translation of certain strands of a Mennonite ethico-theology. It neatly encapsulates the logic of partnership-as-mutuality and the practice of rendering relational, introduced in earlier chapters.

"Guesthood" is also an alternative term to a cluster of other buzzwords currently popular in mainstream development discourse. Among the most prominent terms in this professional vocabulary are "empowerment," "participation," and "partnership."[7] These terms are aimed at various targets, imply different intended effects, and are accompanied by their own technologies of implementation. What they all share with guesthood, however, is their deployment to negate or counteract potential or actual accusations of the coercive use of power in international development. The context in which international NGOs operate is increasingly beset by pervasive critiques from within and beyond the development industry that question the legitimacy of development interventions and highlight negative effects. The goodness of NGOs can no longer be taken for granted. Indeed, according to some commentators "NGO bashing" has become increasingly trendy right across the political spectrum.[8] Guesthood draws on a different genealogy from these other terms. It has roots within and draws upon a particular moral tradition. It is shaped by MCC's peripheral location vis-à-vis mainstream development. It is also infused by a specific theology. But, like the other buzzwords, guesthood is also an attempt to respond to this same context of pervasive critique. The articulation of guesthood serves as both justification and normative ideal for MCC's service in relief, development, and peacebuilding.

Notions of "guest," and its correlate "host," have had little resonance in the anthropology of development. This contrasts with anthropological studies of tourism, in which the guest-host dyad has a long history among anthropologists.[9] Addressing the tourism literature, Darlene McNaughton critiques the limitations of a guest-host research framework on the grounds that a rigid dichotomy should not predetermine a researcher's approach to the study of tourism relationships.[10] A blanket application of a guest-host framing of development interactions would clearly also be unhelpful. However, when development actors within any given context articulate their roles through guest-host language they make use of a "cultural logic" or "moral framework" that should be analyzed carefully.[11] MCC's guesthood ideology is a framework that locates expatriate MCCers as "guests" in relationship to both "home" and "hosts" in particular ways.

This chapter explores the ways guesthood is articulated and disciplined through orientation events at MCC offices in Akron, Pennsylvania, and in Central Java in Indonesia. Collectively, these highlight the paradox of simultaneous and competing logics of association and dissociation that ensues from attempts to encourage expatriate MCCers to behave as good guests. Following on from these orientations, I then present biographical sketches of two MCCers in Indonesia that draw attention to how the logics of (dis)association work in the everyday lives of MCCers.

DISPLACING PRIVILEGE

Organizational orientations are rich spaces for anthropological analysis. These are events in which organizational "elders" represent the goals and mission of their institution to neophytes for the express purpose of cultivating a certain kind of membership. Communication is carefully framed and crafted, though sometimes also contested. Orientation events are initiation rituals or *rites de passage*.[12] They mark points of entry into liminal spaces of transformation for roles, responsibilities, and standing. Because orientation rituals are primarily designed for internal communication they potentially proffer very different modes of discourse from those communications produced for a more general audience, such as policy statements, fundraising appeals, and newspaper reports.

The first orientation I examine took place in MCC's binational headquarters in Akron, Pennsylvania.[13] The location of MCC's head office in this tiny rural town seems, at first, quite peculiar. MCCers frequently joke that visiting international VIPs often arrive in Akron expecting a global cosmopolitan hub and are instead shocked to encounter a sleepy one-traffic-light country town of about four thousand people, complete with white picket-fences, neatly trimmed yards, roadside fresh produce stands, spacious cornfields, and the occasional passing of a horse-drawn Amish buggy. Most major international NGOs situate their head offices for accessibility to important transport nodes and in close proximity to the corridors of power. MCC's office was located in Akron because, when Orie O. Miller was appointed secretary in 1935, the office shifted from the house of the previous secretary, Levi Mumaw, who resided in Scottdale, Pennsylvania, to his own. Miller resided in Akron, having moved there when he married his wife, Elta, to work in his in-law's shoe-manufacturing business. Because Miller was such a dominant force throughout these early decades – he was "Mr. MCC" – the organization grew around him. In 1958, MCC carried out a study to adjudicate whether the MCC office should remain in Akron or be moved elsewhere. The findings indicated that the office was "well located" for, along with being within driving distance of various major cities, it was situated in "a dense Mennonite population, conservative but very active."[14] It was not, therefore, by accident that the MCC head office was located square in the middle of rural Lancaster County, "Pennsylvania Dutch" country, which had long been a heartland of the ethnic Mennonite peoplehood in the US. As a peoplehood movement it made sense to be located near the "corridors of power" that mattered most for Mennonites.

The intimate connection between MCC and the Mennonite peoplehood was expressed on the very first day of the orientation in a session providing an overview of the organization. The presenter, a senior leader in MCC binational, posed the question: "Who owns MCC?" The first and primary answer was that, in MCC, the Mennonite and Brethren in Christ churches in Canada and the United States were known as "the constituency." She went on to say that these churches "created MCC," that they continue to "support MCC," and that, as a result, "they own us."[15] Despite MCC having worked continuously in Indonesia since 1948, it remains organizationally, legally, and in its workers' self-identification, indelibly connected with this North American peoplehood.

The Akron orientation took place over a two-week period in July 2008. In attendance were international service workers due to embark for various parts of the world and also, though only for the first week, new staff starting work in Canada and the US. Most of the attendees came from North America. International service workers are volunteers and, for the duration of their service assignments, receive no salary, though their living costs are covered by MCC. Three or more such orientations took place the same year with generally between forty to sixty participants in each.

Prior to discussing various activities that took place in this orientation, it is important to note a key absence. There were no workshops or training sessions in the sorts of "toolbox" approaches so liberally invoked in the mainstream development industry. In Aidland development fieldworkers learn how to use participatory rural appraisal (PRA) approaches, logical framework analysis (Logframe), micro-enterprise credit schemes, and monitoring and evaluation processes. The reason for this absence is that few MCC service workers were required to use these approaches in their work. Assignments that awaited this group of orientees included a diverse range of positions, such as being the hostess of a retreat centre, lecturing in a university, and teaching English as a second language. Rather than development professionals trained for participation in technocratic Aidland, most of the service workers were being prepared for roles that fit tangentially to the technocratic development industry. The lack of attention to mainstream development tools and techniques reflects a broader disconnect between Aidland and the work expected of expatriate service workers.

One of the sessions at the Akron orientation was entitled "Theology of Service and Peacemaking." While the title suggested it might do otherwise, no systematic "theology" was offered by the experienced MCCers who ran it. This was in keeping with the disarticulation of an organizational missiology examined in chapter 4. The session took place on the fourth day of the orientation. After a brief introduction to the topic, all the participants were split into groups and asked to go outside onto the grassy lawn to undertake an "unofficial power survey." Questions were called out by the leader and, depending on one's response, participants would step forward, stay still, or step backward. In so doing they embodied their answer. It was explained that, while the survey was not exhaustive, the exercise was designed to address issues of "structural inequality" and "power imbalances" that permeated American and Canadian society. For example, on the topic of gender, men were asked to step forward and women backward to highlight the privilege of being gendered male. Among the various other categories were questions relating to race/ethnicity, formal education, physical ability, sexuality, and country of citizenship. Once the task had been completed participants were scattered over the lawn. Participants were then invited to discuss their feelings and also whether they would change any of the categories. According to a handout the purpose of the exercise was to recognize that "power is not distributed equally." It went on to explain that "when we are aware, we can be accountable and use the power we have responsibly."

This exercise was immediately followed by a parallel activity that instead highlighted "relational values." This experiment was designed, again according to the handout, "to emphasize sensitivity to relationships that are mutual and respectful, and to build global awareness and community." While the general exercise was the same as the previous one, this time the issues were weighted differently. For example, in the gender category women were asked to step forward and men backwards as this "reflect[ed] the reality that women have traditionally nurtured relationships that are more mutual rather than competitive and hierarchical." Additional categories were added, including language skills (step forward for more than one language), car ownership (step back for each vehicle; step forward for using public transport), the ethnic diversity of one's church and/or neighbourhood (step forward if diverse; step back if homogeneous), and so on. Unsurprisingly, the spread of participants was a near mirror image of the earlier exercise.

This occupied a couple of hours of orientation time. It was not, however, the only such exercise. In another session, provocatively entitled "Sex, Lies and the Global Economy," participants were invited by a different facilitator to fill in an "economic privilege grid" to provide an indicator of relative advantage as a result of family history, upbringing, ethnicity, opportunities, and so on. Having filled in some 104 separate questions and allotted ourselves positive or negative scores, we lined up in a row from the highest scorer (most privileged) to the lowest to corporeally visualize our different locations. Yet again, in an entirely different session entitled "Anti-Racism Awareness," led by a different facilitator, participants – many of whom were of "ethnic" Mennonite descent – watched a video that pilloried "white privilege." After the video the group was asked to discuss its contents. A handout given to the orientees even addressed "Why Servanthood Is Bad." This article systematically deconstructed the professionalized provision of social services – such as is carried out by most NGOs – to argue instead for greater emphasis on local, community-based mutual care.[16]

Rather than examining whether these sessions adequately address the complexities of power inequalities, I want to focus on why such activities were such an important part of the MCC orientation process. Collectively the sessions amounted to a forthright critique of privilege. The goal was to facilitate self-reflexivity about participants' privileged backgrounds to cultivate intentional efforts to displace this inherited power. The activities were a communal, ritualized, corporeal confession designed to produce what Michel Foucault calls "intrinsic modifications" within the participants' subjectivity.[17] They sought to produce a modified conception of the self through inculcating new forms of self-reflexivity. The tasks worked through corporeal spectacle to encourage a sustained negation of potential inclinations among service workers towards assuming a "messianic complex" in which their efforts would be construed as heroic and salvific. The Akron orientation undercut privilege to create space for non-coercive and mutual engagement during the course of their field assignments. This displacing of privilege and promotion of self-reflexivity were preliminary steps in preparing MCC candidates for service, with the intention of facilitating a particular sensibility among MCCers during their terms of service. It was based on this sensibility that an ideology of guesthood was espoused in Indonesia.

While not a fully formed "guesthood" logic in itself, this prior preparedness helps explain why guesthood was readily affirmed by expatriate staff upon their arrival in Indonesia.

LOCATING EXPATRIATE GUESTS

In addition to a pre-departure orientation expatriate volunteers in MCC Indonesia also participated in an orientation after their arrival. This orientation introduced new service workers to MCC's many different programs in Indonesia and addressed questions about the Indonesian contexts of their assignments. The responsibility for running these post-arrival orientations lay with Anna and Jake Friesen, the MCC Reps and the most senior managers based in Indonesia. In Indonesia the MCC Reps have always been North Americans from Mennonite or Brethren in Christ backgrounds.[18]

In chapter 3 I discuss the diversity of MCC's programs across different countries as well as the common understanding that MCC Indonesia was quite distinctive in terms of program implementation and in regard to leadership structure, group dynamics, and team interactions. Among the distinctives for MCC Indonesia was that most of the international volunteers, up to a peak of about thirty, worked in education. During their assignments they were seconded to local schools or universities to work as members of those institutions' staff teams. Such secondments were particularly compelling in MCC Indonesia because of the ready availability of visas for the education sector. The primary exception to this focus on education was the disaster relief and reconstruction work in Aceh following the 2004 Indian Ocean tsunami discussed in chapter 2. The Aceh program, however, was a temporary aberration of business-as-usual, necessitated by the deluge of funds donated to MCC for tsunami relief and reconstruction and made possible by the availability of visas through alternative mechanisms opened by the Indonesian government to facilitate NGO access for the duration of the disaster relief process. Although education secondments took place in other MCC country programs, the education sector was especially prominent in Indonesia.

A certain programmatic idiosyncrasy was also apparent in the way in which orientations were run in MCC Indonesia. In MCC Indonesia Anna and Jake had held the role of MCC Reps since their arrival in the country in 2001. They were unusual in the extensive duration of their field service with MCC. This meant that they also had considerable experience in designing and implementing introductions for new expatriate volunteers. In this section I focus on two orientation sessions. Each took place over the course of two days. The first was specifically for four participants in the Service and Learning Together (SALT) program, an eleven-month "exchange" for North American young adults.[19] The SALT assignment includes three core components: living with an Indonesian host family, participating in a local church, and volunteering in a local organization. For this last component, most SALTers were assigned to teach English as a second language in high schools (Sekolah Menengah Pertama [SMP] or Sekolah Menengah Atas [SMA]). SALTers had a week-long orientation in Akron prior to arriving in Indonesia, but here I examine the additional orientation provided once they had arrived in Indonesia. The second orientation I discuss was attended by eight recently arrived MCC expatriate service workers who had previously participated in a two-week pre-departure orientation in Akron, Pennsylvania. The members of this group were all adults, including some parents of young children and some who had come to Indonesia as grandparents. Some had previous experience with MCC in other contexts. All were married couples. Two couples were accompanied by their young children. Most of these orientees were assigned to work in academic positions in Indonesian higher education institutions in Central Java and Papua.

When I asked Anna and Jake about their approach to orienting new staff, I was given a booklet by Thomas and Elizabeth Brewster entitled *Bonding and the Missionary Task* and published by the Summer Institute of Linguistics (SIL).[20] While this came from a non-MCC source and its recommendations were adopted selectively, it nevertheless articulated certain philosophies that were seen as valuable and influential. It was often handed out to expatriates before or immediately after their arrival in Indonesia. Critical of the "foray approach," the Brewsters argue that "bonding" – intimate relationships "at a very deep level" between expatriate missionary and locals – as well as a sense of "belonging" to the new culture/people are vital for new missionaries. The booklet focuses on strategies regarding how this can be achieved, including a strong emphasis on attaining fluency in the local language. As well as developing bilingualism, the missionary should also develop a new "bicultural" identity. The text outlines the "imprinting" theory developed by naturalists to explain why, immediately after hatching, ducklings, in a heightened state of alertness and apparently ready for relational commitment, attach themselves to the present biologist instead of the absent mother duck. According to the Brewsters, missionaries going through the process of entering a new culture are similarly ready for imprinting. It is vital, therefore, that during this initial entry period missionaries bond with the right people – "the local people." This initial experience will enable the newcomer to learn about insiders' attitudes and society as well as to consider "adopting [their lifestyle] for himself and his own family."

During the orientation for the SALT volunteers, Anna and Jake flatly dismissed the gendered language of the booklet as anachronistic and annoying. They also indicated their discomfort with the "missionary" terminology employed. Nevertheless, the "bonding" the Brewsters advocated was promoted as the sort of relationship that Anna and Jake hoped expatriate MCC volunteers would assume with Indonesians.

The SALTers were also told that, after their structured language learning had finished but before they were sent to their assignments, they would receive mobile phones that were intended primarily for safety purposes and communication with the MCC team rather than for communication with friends and family back home. The justification for this advice was that they were to bond with their local host family, church community, and colleagues and look to them for emotional support and care rather than relying upon distant supporters. This point was made forcefully in this orientation because, over the preceding years, the issue came to be seen as increasingly significant. Widespread and cheap access to mobile phones and internet usage in Indonesia had resulted in a significant increase of SALTers communicating with friends and family back home. Some SALTers had talked with family members in the US and Canada almost every day. That some communication would take place was regarded as natural and was encouraged by the MCC Reps. However, the norm of seeking emotionally fulfilling relationships with Indonesians during their time of service was promoted as ideal, and guidelines for the use of mobile phones was intended to facilitate this relational orientation.

While the temptation to rely upon support from home was often present, another tendency was to attempt to operate as an atomized individual. SALTers were therefore advised that "we come as Westerners to this place wanting to be self-sufficient. But it is good to be vulnerable [with our hosts]." Certain topics were intentionally avoided during orientations. One example of an occluded topic was contemporary Indonesian politics. The reason for this was to enable SALTers to learn about politics "through Indonesian eyes" rather than from a "Western" perspective. Through encouragement and advice, as well as through intentional absences, SALTers were counselled to learn primarily from their Indonesian hosts.

The focus on bonding was also expressed in the orientation for service workers, where it was framed by the concept of "relationships." About halfway through this orientation session Anna asked whether anyone could remember the content of the discussion on MCC's values that had taken place during their Akron pre-departure orientation. No one could. She then reminded the group of the priority given in MCC to the value of relationships. This value, it was explained, provided the justification for MCC bringing North American volunteers to Indonesia. It wasn't that Indonesia lacked skills or capabilities and was therefore somehow deficient. Nor was it that MCCers had the solutions to Indonesian problems that would locate them as foreign "experts." Rather, MCC was in Indonesia to facilitate "exchange" and for "building relationships." It was important for MCC's partners in Indonesia that MCC not be seen simply as an organization "across the ocean, writing letters" but, rather, that "we are here as the face of MCC." The service workers were therefore encouraged to render relational their own secondments and to imagine them primarily as opportunities for engaging in warm and mutual friendships.

Ideologically, the Brewsters' philosophy for entering a new culture justified two specific practices that were applied in orienting new MCCers to Indonesia. The first was the practice of staying with an Indonesian host family during their first week in the country. This immersion experience in a local home was held out as a means of facilitating learning about Indonesia from Indonesians. Much effort was made to ensure that these homestay experiences were neither too comfortable nor too awkward. Often these initial experiences were looked back upon with considerable pleasure, or at least with good humour regarding the common mishaps and mis-communications. The opposite response, however, was also possible. One couple in their sixties, who had a week-long homestay in Papua, came back to Central Java for a period of language study tired and exhausted from the rustic conditions. To make matters worse, one of them had contracted malaria during the homestay, which significantly dampened their enthusiasm for the experience.

The second orientation practice that connected closely with the Brewsters' booklet was the emphasis on language learning. During my fieldwork in Indonesia, all new MCCers studied at the same small language school in Central Java run by a young Javanese man and his small staff. It was a bespoke model of language learning, often catered to individual needs, rather than a formulaic and rigid process facilitated by some of the larger language schools. Service workers who were on three-year terms in Indonesia spent about three months in full-time language study. Due to their shorter stay, SALT participants were allocated six weeks. Most had no Indonesian language before arriving in Indonesia and, therefore, attaining proficiency in that time was impossible. Nevertheless, this period often gave sufficient foundation for many MCCers to eventually become thoroughly fluent. The language learning laid the foundations for daily practice and full immersion in workplaces and environments in which Indonesian was the primary or sole language of interaction. In the SALT orientation, Jake justified the language learning process by pointing out that "your ability to have relationships in Indonesia is based on language."

In *Transnational Lives*, an ethnographic analysis of corporate expatriates in Jakarta, Anne-Meike Fechter argues that expatriates structure their interactions with Indonesians through powerful and pervasive boundary constructions.[21] Through a myriad of separations expatriates distance themselves from Indonesians. The ideology of guesthood operating in MCC Indonesia starkly contrasts with Fetcher's observations about sharp differentiation. The norms and intentions in MCC are profoundly different from those of corporate expatriates in Indonesia. MCC discourse consistently encouraged "bonding," immersion experiences, and language learning among expatriate staff to bridge cultural divides. MCCers were also actively dissuaded from acquiring any sense of superiority. Myths of the "lazy native" or the "expat expert," which Fechter saw as pervasive among corporate expatriates, were completely absent among MCCers.[22] A sense of being a "victim" was also very rare.[23] Revealingly, too, the sorts of metaphors that Fechter found in frequent use in Jakarta – the expatriate "bubble," "frontier," "bunker," "ghetto," "hot house," and "Disneyland" – were never articulated in my casual discussions or my interviews with expatriate MCCers.[24] MCCers had very little in common with the discursive framings of the expatriates Fechter encountered in Jakarta. They were, rather, encouraged to live up to the ideal of "drinking tea with the locals," a metaphor with profoundly different implications.

However, during the orientation for expatriate service workers a casual conversation hinted at a complex paradox at work in these matters. At one point Anna noted: "As guests in Indonesia, we can't just criticize things here. But I can criticize the [American and Christian] international school that my children attend. I bottle it [my criticisms] up and let it out on the international school." Anna framed her withdrawal from explicitly criticizing Indonesian actors as a direct consequence of being a "guest." Here there is intentional distancing from Indonesian contexts and, therefore, a kind of separation *is* drawn. It is not the case that opinions are unformed but, rather, that they are *withheld* or "bottled up." According to the cultural logic at work here, guests should not criticize. They should behave in a manner appropriate for those who are "visiting." This withholding directly contrasts with Anna's relationship with the American international school her children attended. Where MCCers could assume a non-guest identity, of being "at home," they were free to engage in a proactive politics of influence, participation, and critique. Anna could get involved and could express her unease or unhappiness with what was going on at the international school because in that context she was no longer a guest. The guest identity was deactivated within her relationships in this space. Guesthood, therefore, also operates as a *disassociative* impulse. By refraining from criticism, a medium that, as I suggest in the previous chapter, can also express a passionate sense of belonging and ownership, her status as foreigner is established.

Accordingly, many MCCers adopted a form of bifurcated involvement. While they frequently commented on perceived North American Mennonite "failings," noted their disappointments and occasionally expressed considerable anger with MCC as an institution, and actively engaged with their home country's national politics, they simultaneously tended to refrain from critiquing perceived failings in Indonesia and avoided actively or publicly participating in Indonesian political processes. They thus embraced a cultural logic of demarcated domains of relationality, with "home" differentiated from "away," "insider" differentiated from "outsider," and "host" differentiated from "guest." This guesthood ideology therefore helps elucidate the relational routes of peace and conflict addressed in the previous chapter. While the stated goal was to bridge these divides through bonding, the attempt to bridge the gaps in a non-coercive manner through behaving as good guests simultaneously reinscribes those same distinctions.

The cultivation of a guesthood relationality bridges cultural gaps and instantiates them.[25] Guesthood inspires a powerful logic of association with Indonesia and Indonesians. It enacts the normative myth of "drinking tea with the locals," holds up an intimate sense of bonding as the organizational ideal, and animates the practices of MCCers in their forming of relationships with Indonesians. However, guesthood also facilitates a sense of differentiation and situates guests as foreign from "the locals" in the tea drinking myth. A sense of demarcation therefore remains. The guesthood paradox is that it is simultaneously associative *and* disassociative.

SITUATING INDONESIAN STAFF

The orientations already discussed in this chapter were designed for and attended by expatriate or North American MCCers. But few international NGOs rely solely on expatriate staff. Local staff members are crucial for MCC given the organization's reliance on a three-year term as normal operating practice for its expatriate service workers. MCC's Indonesian staff are crucial mediators and brokers who play vital roles in making MCC work. This is readily acknowledged by their expatriate colleagues. Whereas most expatriate service workers are seconded to other Indonesian organizations, all Indonesian staff members are employed directly by MCC and work within the organization. The roles of Indonesian staff vary considerably, but they generally involve administrative tasks (finances, government liaison, etc.) and/or partnership advisor roles.

In June 2007 Anna and Jake decided to hold a two-day orientation for the small Indonesian office staff team working with MCC in Central Java. This was triggered by two recent changes. First, the office team had undergone unusually high staff turnover in the previous two years. It expanded by adding an additional staff member to keep up with the greatly increased administrative workload associated with the tsunami relief and reconstruction work in Aceh. Further, in early 2007 a long-time staff member was asked to leave the organization and soon after two new staff members were appointed to partnership liaison roles to fill the personnel gap. The new staff members made up most of the four-person local staff team. One of these new staff was very familiar with MCC, having come directly from the MCC team in Aceh and having previously participated in MCC's International Visitor Exchange Program (IVEP). The other staff member's knowledge of MCC was much more limited. Regardless, it was felt that a deliberate introduction to the organization would be advantageous for all the Indonesian staff members. The second trigger was my arrival along with my wife, Iris, who volunteered with MCC as a service worker based in the MCC Central Java office for the duration of my fieldwork. At that stage, due to our unorthodox entry into MCC (i.e., I was a researcher), neither of us had been through an orientation in Akron. Although Anna and Jake spent considerable time trying to bring all the new arrivals up to speed with the organization, they felt that we would all benefit from something more systematic.

The orientation was almost entirely in English. This was the language of choice for team meetings in Central Java for both the MCC Reps, who found it easier to communicate with, and the Indonesian staff, who all wanted to continue to enhance their fluency in English through regular and sustained practice.[26] This session was the first such orientation event for local staff in the past decade and perhaps in the whole history of MCC Indonesia – a fact that was the subject of frequent convivial jokes among the attendees.[27] Various participatory activities, including Scripture reading, devotions, and autobiographical storytelling, were incorporated into the orientation sessions. The discussion of MCC was wide-ranging and very thorough. Anna and Jake clearly intended to furnish their staff with the organizational knowledge necessary for their work. The whole event was, of course, an ethnographer's dream. It is hard to imagine a better way to begin learning about the intricacies of MCC's structures, politics, and values than through this systematic emic experience provided over a couple of days of conversations.

As with the Akron orientation, a strong case was made for "ownership" of MCC by North American Mennonite and Brethren in Christ churches, with "the constituency" being identified unambiguously as the primary raison d'être for MCC. But the constituency was not imagined as beyond critique. Anna discussed a recent experience when she visited the Ohio Relief Sale and was shocked to see a tractor-pulled "train" prominently adorned with the red and white stars and stripes of the US flag. She told the orientation group that she had never before seen such a prominent display of American nationalism at an MCC-sponsored event. This flagrant patriotism was clearly imagined as a moral and political failing, and Anna's criticism was pointed and acute. Anna also told the group that she was shocked to learn of support among American Mennonite congregations for the American military during the Second Iraq War.[28] She told the group that, as a Mennonite peace organization that drew on the long heritage of Anabaptist and Mennonite peace theology, MCC had roundly and publicly criticized American bloodshed during the war and that Anna and Jake fully agreed with these critiques.

As already discussed, critique can be an expression of belonging as well as an act of distancing. In this instance, through criticizing American nationalism, Anna and Jake performed their American citizenship and thereby inhabited an at-home or non-guest identity. Throughout my field research I frequently heard Anna and Jake criticize the American government or the behaviour of fellow Americans. For example, a few days after the local staff orientation, while enjoying a picnic at a nearby waterfall, Anna asked me pointedly: "What is it like being part of a nation that you are not ashamed of?" Just a few days prior to the orientation, during a car ride between partner visits, Jake and Anna joked about George W. Bush's appearance and compared his ears to those of Pat Robertson, a prominent and (among American Christians of a non-fundamentalist bent) notorious Southern Baptist media mogul. These sorts of critiques and light-hearted comedic engagements were common among virtually all American MCCers in Indonesia.[29]

This approach contrasted sharply with Anna and Jake's political engagement in Indonesia. In the local staff orientation, Jake mentioned that MCC frequently faced questions about whether it should be more active with regard to advocacy over human rights abuses by the Indonesian state. In accordance with legal restrictions on MCC as a foreign NGO in Indonesia, MCC had refrained from doing so. Anna added to this by pointing out that MCC had an agreement with the Indonesian government not to become engaged in political actions. Because MCC's "niche" in Indonesia was to engage in "face-to-face relationships" it was unable to proactively engage in political concerns to the same extent as could those advocacy organizations that did not have a presence in the country.

Partnership was also in focus at the local staff orientation. Anna and Jake talked about how they had sought to ensure that MCC only carried out its work through partnerships. They stressed that it was important to recognize that "we have different identities" because "MCC is a North American Christian NGO" and MCC's partners have their own specifically Indonesian identities. Partnership was neither about getting partners to become a part of MCC nor about making MCC an Indonesian organization.[30] Partnership was a way to ensure that MCC's foreign agenda was not foisted on others, thus enabling local organizations to be the drivers for change in their own contexts. Partnership logic thereby enabled close association – the organizational equivalent to relational bonding – with Indonesian organizations. As previously discussed, MCCers did indeed work hard at facilitating open communication with their partners through frequent face-to-face visits and even more frequent mobile phone and e-mail communication. MCC's partner liaisons were active in providing extensive hands-on assistance and spent a lot of their time drinking multiple cups of sweet tea (In. *teh manis*) with their counterparts. However, as is clear from this discussion, partnership also enabled a sense of differentiation between MCC's North American identity and its Indonesian partners. Partnership discourse was therefore also a way of establishing a carefully demarcated identity for MCC as a foreign guest.[31]

Anna and Jake saw the entire office staff team as an extension of their MCC Rep role. They confessed that in the recent staffing expansion they had struggled in deciding whether it was appropriate to hire Indonesian staff to work in a North American organization. They thought that, as a rule, it was more suitable to have Indonesian colleagues working within Indonesian organizations because, as Jake put it, "you [Indonesian staff] must put on a North American mindset" while working within MCC. Further, "you folks are in a difficult position to represent weird North American ways of thinking to partners." A variety of structural concerns were also discussed with honesty and candour. Whereas with expatriate service workers both spouses (in the case of a married couple) were MCCers, and, while voluntary, all expatriate MCCers and their families were provided for on the basis of a "simple" or "appropriate" standard by MCC, local staff were hired individually according to a fixed salary.[32] For Anna and Jake this raised important questions about equity between the two groups. Here, therefore, just as MCC was situated as a "guest" in Indonesia, so too local Indonesian staff were located as "guests" in MCC and were structurally displaced in the organization. The need for improving equity was a frank acknowledgment of its absence or deficiency. Anna and Jake actively sought to address these issues in the local staff orientation and in other forums and on other occasions, and they frequently encouraged feedback from their staff over any concerns they might have had. However, the expatriate-local split proved difficult to renegotiate because it rested on the different status each group had within the organization as a consequence of employment contracts and work contexts.[33] Interestingly, while Indonesian MCCers on occasion did discuss with me a sense of feeling marginal in the organization, it was rarely expressed as resentment. Indeed, MCC seemed to have a long and permanent queue of Indonesian Mennonites hoping to be employed within the organization, and working within MCC was widely regarded as an attractive possibility.

LIVING GUESTHOOD: (DIS)ASSOCIATION IN PRACTICE

The different orientation events illuminate Anna and Jake's approach to guesthood and also point to continuities between their articulation and wider organizational myths, structures, and norms. But how were these ideologies enacted in lives of MCCers themselves? I turn now to explore the biographical narratives of two MCCers to examine how the ideology of guesthood informed their everyday lived experience. While guesthood is grounded in and propelled by an attempt to displace expatriate MCCers' sense of privilege, it also results in displacing Indonesian staff within the organization. Guesthood reinscribes distinctions that bonding seeks to bridge by excluding Indonesian staff from full participation within MCC. My research with MCC has led me to conclude that this displacement was an unintended consequence of guesthood. What makes it so interesting is that it derives from the desire to pursue a non-coercive approach to Christian service.

Frank Kauffman, in his twenties, was born in Africa while his American parents served with a Mennonite mission agency. His family name is well known as Swiss-German Mennonite. Numerous relatives, including his parents, are deeply involved in Mennonite church institutions. He studied in Mennonite schools and attended an Anabaptist-affiliated college where he met Lydia, his wife. After he completed a master's degree in English literature and taught briefly at a community college, Frank and Lydia volunteered as service workers with MCC. They chose placements in Indonesia because the position description indicated what looked to be interesting and relevant work. Their assignments were to teach in a Christian university in Central Java. Like most North Americans they knew little about Indonesia before arriving in the country, although, uniquely among his fellow MCCers, Frank had read Clifford Geertz's classic *The Religion of Java* as an undergraduate, having stumbled upon it in the library.

Both Frank and Lydia had attended an orientation session in Akron, and Frank mostly appreciated the content, though when I talked about it with him a few years later the details were blurred. Nevertheless, he considered the various activities appropriate, meaningful, and useful as they prepared to head out. Upon arrival in Central Java they were greeted at the airport by a Javanese family who hosted them for the first week of their stay in Indonesia. Despite limited communication capabilities Frank enjoyed this time as it gave him a relaxed opportunity to wander around the town that he would live in for the next four years. He also read a lot of novels. This first taste of Indonesia was appreciated, and years later he would still occasionally visit the family that had hosted him.

Their in-country orientation took place over a weekend. Though brief, he regarded it as sufficient. Frank hadn't come to learn about Indonesia from expatriates but, rather, from Indonesians. Three weeks after arriving in Indonesia Frank and Lydia started their teaching assignments at their university. This was considered unusually short, but there was no sense of regret. Again, Frank explained that he had come to build friendships with Indonesians and was glad that he was able to do so without significant delay. They soon began intensive language learning working with a Javanese tutor. This continued for a few months, although it became increasingly ad hoc. Although Frank taught all his classes in

English, as requested by his university, he became fluent in Indonesian and used it regularly in most of his relationships with Indonesian colleagues, neighbours, and friends.

When I began my fieldwork in early 2007 one of the topics that was extensively discussed in MCC Indonesia concerned the need to build a stronger felt community within the organization. But Frank didn't share this sentiment. He enjoyed his friendships with other MCCers, but he considered his university colleagues as his "primary community" in Indonesia. Although Frank lived in Salatiga, also the location of the MCC Indonesia office, he rarely visited and felt that he had limited knowledge of its daily affairs. The two annual country-wide gatherings of MCCers were important events in his calendar but were considered only a brief if enjoyable interlude from his everyday life. Likewise, while he regularly played basketball at the nearby international school with other expatriates, the friendships he made there remained peripheral. Frank and Lydia attended an Indonesian Mennonite church in which the services and sermons were entirely in Indonesian. Despite feeling disconnected from the kinds of spirituality and ritual practices that took place there, he attended church every Sunday.

Frank understood that one reason he was valued and appreciated at his university was his status as a "native speaker" of English. For governmental accreditation purposes English language departments in Indonesia benefit greatly by having a native speaker on their faculty. Each time a government official came through the department Frank was on the list to meet with them. Initially, Frank was asked by his department to teach English language courses, but this did not excite him. Prior to starting his assignment, he had been under the impression that he would take up a position teaching literature. This disjuncture between his expectations and the department's priorities was disconcerting at first, but over time he managed to progressively shift his teaching more towards his interests and training. Frank did not manage any staff in his department and his supervisor was Indonesian. He participated along with other colleagues in staff meetings. This participation increased with his developing language skills and his knowledge of the context.

As arranged by the MCC Reps with their university, Frank and Lydia's housing and visas were provided by the university. However, MCC provided all other living expenses, including food, holidays, a low-cc motorbike colloquially known as a *bebek*, health care, and domestic help (In. *pembantu*). At first Frank found the relationship with their *pembantu* awkward as it felt layered with class and hierarchy. He was particularly uncomfortable when she cleaned in the same room in which he was working or relaxing. She enacted Javanese patterns of deferral to social superiors through visual cues or verbal exchange, and these also made him feel awkward. Frank and Lydia tried to treat their *pembantu* as a member of the family and have lunch with her on a regular basis. They often chatted in Indonesian with her and expressed an interest in her family. Although he thought their friendliness was appreciated, he also thought she was uncomfortable with attempts to flatten or dissolve the hierarchy. Frank justified hiring a *pembantu* by saying that it provided someone with employment, and they ensured she was paid at a higher rate than were other expatriates and Indonesians they knew. However, when Frank and Lydia had their first child, a baby boy delivered in a local hospital, they found their *pembantu* became invaluable with regard to helping manage their house and assisting with childcare.

Frank and Lydia regularly wrote newsletters home to supporters to explain their work and to provide updates. On one occasion they mentioned that they missed eating good chocolate and a few weeks later were inundated with chocolate sent from family and friends in the United States. Frank also kept up with family on the phone and, once they had installed broadband in their home, over the internet. He paid close attention to American politics and was a keen Obama supporter. Members of both Frank's and Lydia's families visited them in Indonesia. After two years in Indonesia Frank and Lydia decided that they would extend their initial three-year commitment to four years. This gave them the chance to take "home leave" for two months back in the US. They spent their leave largely in Pennsylvania between the houses of both sets of parents. During their stay they had numerous speaking engagements with Mennonite churches and schools. For these events they told stories of their time in Indonesia and sought to provide a glimpse into Indonesian lifeworlds. On occasions this involved a *National Geographic*-type description of some of the flora, fauna, cultures, and religions of the archipelago.

Frank felt some ambiguity due to his two roles – namely, a lecturer in his university and an MCC service worker. For example, Frank expressed a disconnect between what he had been told since childhood about MCC's identity – "relief, development, and peacebuilding" – and his actual role of teaching English literature, which he saw as only tenuously connected with MCC's stated goals. He sought to lessen this disconnect by associating more closely with his university than with MCC. But Frank also talked about how being a service worker in MCC gave him a sense of ownership and belonging to the organization. By working within MCC he found that it became his organization. Although his secondment meant that he did not work directly within MCC organizational structures, and while he felt removed from the routines of the MCC Indonesia office, he was animated in talking about some of the large-scale changes taking place in the organization.

When Frank and Lydia finished their service assignments with MCC they returned home to Pennsylvania. Again they did a round of itinerant speaking engagements during which they spoke at numerous Mennonite churches, schools, and community events. They started attending Lydia's parents' Mennonite church and remained open to further involvement with MCC as supporters. Frank began his doctoral studies at Penn State. Although the four years in Indonesia were seen as a life-defining experience, he was glad to leave Indonesia when he did and to head back home where he would be close to family and familiar features of life. He felt confident that his experience in Indonesia would continue to shape his identity, but he also acknowledged that the geographical separation from Indonesia was a temporal demarcation that brought that season of life to a close. Having been a guest in Indonesia for four years, Frank came back home.

Paulus, a Javanese man in his thirties, was brought up in a tough neighbourhood in Semarang, Central Java. During the notorious "Petrus" operations in the 1980s, in which the Indonesian government commissioned extrajudicial assassinations of "gangsters" (In. *preman*), a number of Paulus's near neighbours had been targeted and executed. Paulus told me that his neighbourhood had such a bad reputation that even police were afraid to go there. Still, he managed to gain a good education and was able to move out of that neighbourhood. Paulus's family were members of the Gereja Kristen Muria Indonesia (GKMI) Indonesian Mennonite church.

After finishing high school Paulus worked as a graphic designer and eventually set up his own business. He had an entrepreneurial streak and was good at his work. For a few years in the late 1990s he was hired by his church's Synod office and through this connection heard about MCC's International Visitor Exchange Program (IVEP), which provided opportunities for Indonesians to live in North America for eleven months. He applied for the program and was surprised when he was accepted. Paulus spent a year in Canada with IVEP from mid-2000 until mid-2001. This was his first significant personal connection with MCC and North American Mennonites. He really enjoyed his stay in rural Ontario. It was socially fulfilling as he interacted with Canadians and fellow IVEPers who came from all over the world. His work experience also provided an opportunity to learn a variety of new skills, and his English language skills improved considerably. It was during his time in North America, he told me, that he learned what it really meant to be Mennonite.

After returning home to Java, Paulus continued working in graphic design. In December 2004, when the Indian Ocean tsunami devastated coastal Aceh, he talked with friends about the possibility of going there to help in some way. The opportunity to do so opened for him in January 2005 when his church office was called by MCC to find out if they knew of anyone willing to work in MCC's newly established relief work. The church office suggested Paulus. At this time Aceh was like a "battlefield," and many Indonesians were unwilling to work there. When Paulus was called and was offered the chance to join the MCC team in Aceh, he was given just two hours to make up his mind. Remarkably, he decided he would take it up. His self-employed status and the fact that he was not yet married gave him the flexibility to do this. The next day he was on a flight to Jakarta for meetings with other NGOs, and by early February he was posted to Aceh. Initially, he committed to just one month, but this kept being extended. Paulus ended up working in the MCC office in Aceh until MCC closed its tsunami relief program in 2008.

During the early months of the relief work in Aceh there were five management transitions in the Aceh office. Each new manager came from North America. There was a similarly high turnover of short-term expatriate staff. This situation eventually stabilized with more enduring appointments. Paulus's early tasks included looking after the logistics of housing, transport, and food for the rest of the MCC team in Aceh. This role soon shifted to partnership liaison. However, he had no job description and was unclear what his exact responsibilities were. During his time in Aceh he carried out a wide range of tasks. His work in administration and interacting with partners was typical of the roles held by local staff as they played the roles of brokers and translators. Unlike some of his Indonesian friends in other NGOs, Paulus had no specific background in the development or relief field and received little formal training from MCC to do his job, although some supervisors worked closely with him on various tasks. Paulus never received any orientation to work with MCC, either in Indonesia or in North America. The lack of an orientation was not considered unusual among Indonesian staff, although the high pressure of the tsunami response work also militated against a more structured and orderly introduction to the work.

When Paulus arrived in Aceh he felt like a complete "stranger." He didn't know the Acehnese language, had limited access to transportation and therefore limited mobility, and felt that many Acehnese resented the presence of Javanese aid workers.[34] He had to learn entirely new cultural norms and tried hard to pick up some Acehnese language skills. He also felt that his status in MCC was ambiguous for, although he was Indonesian, he felt like a foreign visitor, just as much an "expatriate" as his North American colleagues.[35] Like them, he too was a volunteer rather than salaried. His work was often similar to that of his colleagues, regardless of their country of origin. For the first eight months of his work in Aceh he worked and slept in the same rented house as did all the other MCCers, a situation that created a certain communal equity among the team. However, this ambiguity – was Paulus "local" or "expatriate"? – was progressively resolved through two processes. First, after three months of working in Aceh, Paulus shifted from being a volunteer to being employed. This reinforced the traditional distinctions in the organization between expatriate volunteer service worker and local salaried staff. Paulus considered the remuneration to be fairly generous. Second, as mentioned above, it became increasingly clear that Paulus's role was as a partner liaison. Again, this role was traditionally held by local staff and distinguished him from most of the expatriate volunteers who were seconded to other local organizations. These shifts weren't seen as inherently negative, but one of their consequences was that Paulus was reinscribed as a local staff member, while his feelings of being out of place in Aceh continued.

Simultaneously, another important change of identity took place. Paulus became increasingly aware that the organization "exists for North Americans." He came to this awareness through learning more about his place within it. While he was initially involved in making decisions about the relief operations in Aceh, changes in supervisors resulted in changes in the tasks given to him. He told me: "We [Indonesian staff] are 'ground' people. We don't know what is going on upstairs with the politics and decision making." Over time he felt like his participation in decision making decreased. He also felt he rarely received all the information he needed to do his job properly. This sense of MCC not being his organization was particularly apparent to him during the two annual gatherings of the whole MCC team. He felt that the discussions often revolved around the interests and concerns of the North American staff members – especially the service workers – rather than the issues that he had to deal with as a Javanese staff member in Aceh. I never heard Paulus express a sense of ownership over MCC.

In Aceh, Paulus met his Indonesian wife, who also worked for an international NGO doing relief work. They married and soon after had their first child while they were still based in Aceh. At the end of three years of relief work, the MCC Aceh office closed down. Paulus, his wife, and newborn child subsequently moved to the Indonesian capital, Jakarta, where he returned to entrepreneurial graphic design work. He looked back upon his experience with MCC positively and thought that it had freed him from fear by exposing him to previously unconsidered opportunities. He also thought that it helped expand what was possible in terms of both vocation and his own personal abilities. He appreciated his experience with MCC and spoke well of other MCCers. He knew that his time with MCC was only for a certain period – and that time had come to a close.

These two biographical narratives highlight the paradoxical associative and disassociative impulses of the ideology of guesthood in MCC Indonesia. Frank's prioritizing of relationships with his Indonesian colleagues and neighbours epitomizes the ideal promoted within MCC for service workers – an ideal that was frequently celebrated in the organization. Frank cultivated close and convivial relationships with Indonesians. However, these relationships were spatially and temporally bounded. Discussions of "home leave" and "returning home," as well as ongoing accountability to and communication with "home," continued to inscribe a crucial distinction: Indonesia was "away." In Indonesia Frank located himself as foreign guest. He came from the North American Mennonite peoplehood and he returned to that same peoplehood on the conclusion of his assignment. Further, the awkwardness of relating to the *pembantu* illustrates the tensions involved in attempting to enact non-coercive relationships. When the Javanese domestic worker adopted a subservient position in her role (as she assumed she should), this caused discomfort and initiated attempts to diminish the hierarchically structured power relations. That these attempts were eventually unsuccessful should be seen as Frank's acceptance that his own framework should not be forced on the lives of the Indonesians with whom he interacted, even when this caused him discomfort. Frank was the archetypal "good guest."

While Frank, like most other expatriate service workers, was seconded to an Indonesian organization for the duration of his service, Paulus, like all other Indonesian staff, was directly employed by and worked within MCC. Paulus felt that his identity in Aceh was, initially at least, thoroughly ambiguous. He certainly felt "foreign" in that, while he shared the same nationality with Acehnese, there remained considerable linguistic and cultural differences that marked him as an "outsider." He often felt like he was treated as such by Acehnese. Another of MCC's Javanese staff members told me that she thought that it was much harder being

Javanese in Aceh than being a *bule* (white foreigner). She thought that *bule* at least were given respect and prestige, whereas Javanese were seen as taking jobs that should have gone to Acehnese. While Paulus continued to feel the tensions of this ambiguity, the situation was eventually "resolved" as he was increasingly ascribed a "local" identity within MCC. His growing understanding of MCC as a "North American" organization showed his sense of distance from it. As an Indonesian, Paulus came to feel that his participation in MCC was more constrained than that of his expatriate colleagues, and he saw himself as displaced from full participation and ownership.

A certain parallel between Frank and Paulus is therefore apparent: just as Frank was seen to be a guest in his work in an Indonesian institution, so too was Paulus seen as a guest as a local staff member in MCC. The ideology of guesthood situates MCC's work in Indonesia as away-from-home. This resulted in particular social dispositions, forms of behaviour, and expectations. One key consequence is that this necessarily situates local staff as being away-from-home while they are within MCC structures. MCC is not an Indonesian organization; it is not *their* organization. Their ability to belong within this North American "peoplehood movement" is constrained, if not hamstrung. As guests in MCC, local staff are welcomed and relied upon but are ultimately refused full participation in the politics of belonging within the organization. Local staff members were expected to adapt to the culture of MCC – as noted above, Indonesian staff were required to "put on a North American mindset" – in the same sort of way that MCCers were expected to adapt to Indonesia. Therefore, while the stance of guest is taken up by expatriates as they begin their voluntary service in Indonesia, it is also ascribed to local staff in their work within MCC. This results in a pronounced expatriate-local split within the organization. The ideology of guesthood, premised on expatriate bonding with Indonesians, both enabled the transcending of boundaries and their simultaneous reassertion.

PEOPLEHOOD AND GUESTHOOD

Through orientation rituals and biographical narratives this chapter traces a distinctive ideology of guesthood in MCC. This articulation of guesthood was Anna and Jake's philosophy of service. As the MCC Reps in Indonesia, they played a crucial role in shaping the expectations, interactions, and "locations" of both local and expatriate staff in the organization. The orientation events I describe were moments in which they intentionally and systematically sought to clarify these issues and their expectations. But the idea of an MCCer-as-guest was *not just* Anna and Jake's. The "drinking tea with the locals" myth has wide currency among North American volunteers in MCC, and guesthood in Indonesia evoked these ideas to legitimate its practice. The Akron orientation, while not locating expatriates as guests per se, nevertheless provided the sorts of frameworks amenable to guesthood: the displacing of privilege, articulation of ownership of MCC by North American churches, and identification of MCC as a "peoplehood movement." The structural displacement of local staff within MCC was not peculiar to Indonesia but, rather, was widespread in the organization. Anna and Jake translated values, stories, and theologies that circulated around and within MCC into a guest logic that operated as normative in MCC Indonesia.

This Mennonite ideology of guesthood was shared with MCCers in other contexts. In chapter 4, I discuss Joseph Liechty's letter to Ray Brubacher regarding the proposed project of developing a missiology of service for the organization. Writing in 1991, Liechty described how a senior member of his MCC Europe team was "so consistent with his 'guest' logic that he doesn't think MCC can invite people to a meeting." As Liechty also pointed out, this guesthood approach was but one among a number of different paradigms that were held by his fellow MCCers. "Guesthood" was not universal and unquestioned within the organization. Indeed, in response to an earlier version of this argument a Mennonite sociologist friend wrote to me outlining guesthood's genealogy within MCC.[36] The guest model, he suggested, initially took root in MCC teams in Africa in the 1970s and 1980s. It was here that an emphasis on mutuality and the sense that foreigners should tread softly was most pronounced within MCC. Parallel logics with sometimes quite different nuances had been articulated elsewhere. In Latin America guesthood generally took "the form of solidarity" with radical groups involved in the various insurgencies at that time; "volunteers were still guests, but they were clearly guests at a particular party," which necessitated specific political commitments.[37] Guesthood as articulated in Indonesia was not the sole or inevitable framing for MCC practice but was adopted from a wider "discursive repertoire."[38]

Yet guesthood wasn't arbitrary either. Guesthood should be located as a Mennonite discourse grounded in the concept and practice of the North American Mennonite peoplehood. Guesthood resonates with the prominence of peacefulness and simplicity in much vernacular Mennonite theology and ethics. It should be seen in relation to the traditional conceptualization of Mennonites as "the Quiet in the Land" in North America; guesthood guides "quiet" behaviour when in someone else's land, which, in this case, could be translated to *Die Stillen im Indisch*. Further, as a consequence of this conceptualization of the peoplehood, and the national territories of Canada and the US being "home," MCC's work in Indonesia was understood as being "away." Guesthood is therefore one possible refraction of MCC's identity as a "peoplehood movement."

During interviews with MCCers in North America a frequent topic of conversation was MCC's relationship with the Mennonite peoplehood. One such interview with an academic in a Mennonite higher education institution was particularly relevant to the themes of this chapter. Tobias Day had a PhD in social sciences, had previously worked with MCC in Asia, and had been involved in Mennonite institutions for almost two decades. Yet when we sat down in his office to talk about MCC he almost immediately divulged, without any prompting from me, that "there is a glass ceiling above my head, that's why I slouch in my chair." His name was not part of ethnic Mennonite history. He was, he told me, an "OTM," Other Than Mennonite. As a "non-ethnic Mennonite" he felt profoundly disempowered in the Mennonite world in North America, which he characterized as imbued by a "culture of ethnicism" replete with "institutional bias" and "discriminating" dynamics. While he had loved working with MCC in Asia, his experience among Mennonites in the US disturbed him: "It comes as a shock and hurts me to know that my colleagues [at my Mennonite college] think that I should behave here [in the US] as I did in [Asia] where there is a clear difference between insiders and outsiders." Tobias drew a circle for me and indicated that, during his MCC service, he was never in the circle and part of his host culture but only ever a "hyphen" or "tangent." Likewise, "I'm welcome here [at his educational institution], but I'm either a hyphen or a tangent, never more than that." His attempts to become a part of "the circle" had been consistently curtailed. If he had had the right last name – a recognizably Swiss-German or Dutch-Russian Mennonite one – he was sure the situation would have been different. Tobias took a book and placed a piece of paper on it, and he instructed me to place both book and paper on the top of my head. "Draw a picture of a snowman," he instructed me. My picture was, predictably, an indecipherable scribble. "This is what it is like to be autistic," I was told. It was the same for OTMs within MCC: "A non-Mennonite following the MCC way follows instructions. They are *diff*abled, but they are treated as *un*abled." OTMs were seen as autistic and were never given the ability to fully participate and belong in the organization.

Tobias's sentiments were not replicated in every interview I had with OTMs in MCC. One interviewee talked about how, in her experience, every institution has a particular "culture" and that MCC's was no more thick, complicated, or difficult to access than any other. Another OTM in Akron talked about how there were ways to do Mennonite politics and ways not to, the trick being to know the difference and respond accordingly. Those who found themselves marginalized, I was told, did it of their own volition by refusing to learn and adhere to the rules. A certain ethnographer's nose was therefore needed to figure out the tacit rules and work within or around them. Yet a significant number of other OTM's reflected key elements of Tobias's experience when they told me their stories. Tobias's narrative of feeling the need, when among North American Mennonites, to behave in the same way that he behaved during his MCC term in Asia – as a "hyphen" or "tangent" to the in-group – is thoroughly congruent with a guesthood logic.

Some ethnic Mennonites were aware of the challenges faced by OTMs. Albert Regehr, an ethnic Mennonite and a Canadian MCCer in Indonesia, told me that he was "sympathetic to the situation of non-Mennonites in MCC." To which he added: "But I always wonder: why would non-Mennonites want to be a part of MCC?" Albert rejected an exclusionary impulse. Yet the rhetorical question reasserted the nature of MCC as a "peoplehood movement," intended primarily for a particular group and therefore, implicitly, not for others. Lucy Krehbiel, a Mennonite academic from Harrisonburg, Virginia, and a passionate long-time MCC supporter, also once remarked to me: "Can someone who is not raised in *the milieu* –Thrift Shops, [Ten Thousand] Villages, Relief Sales, SALT, three-year terms, Mennonite churches – make it in MCC?" For Lucy this remained a live question. "The milieu" that Lucy describes maps neatly onto the ethnic Mennonite peoplehood.

In his history of American Mennonites, Paul Toews, reflecting a prominent theme in wider Mennonite historiography, describes the boundary maintenance mechanisms Mennonites deployed to seek to ensure their status as "a distinct and separate people" in the face of dissolving visible and spatial markers of difference in the years after the Second World War.[39] While expanding Mennonite horizons and bringing Mennonites into contact with the "farflung corners of the world," Toews frames MCC as very much a part of "the core of a refurbished Mennonite identity" that located Mennonite distinctiveness as involving an "altruistic vigor" by a "servant people." Guesthood, I argue, was an extension of the paradox that Toews identifies in MCC: it enabled the transcending of difference while simultaneously reinscribing it.

Notably, the ideology of guesthood was largely accepted by both Frank and Paulus. It enabled Frank and other expatriate MCCers to see their volunteer work as legitimate and worthwhile. Through performing a "good guest" identity, expatriate MCCers in Indonesia negotiated the moral politics of development. It operated as an ethical compass through which to navigate a complex and fraught ethical terrain. It encouraged the sort of stance – listening, learning, participatory, and infused with a sense of mutuality – that militated against overbearing (or over-complaining) behaviour. Paulus also did not resent the knowledge of his own marginality within MCC. Although MCC was not *his* organization, he was glad to have worked with it and was grateful for the opportunities that MCC provided. He enjoyed his friendships with MCC service workers and his fellow Indonesian staff members. The paradox of guesthood offered a way for each of them to locate themselves within the organization.

7

Everyday Embodiments

> It's risky business, embarking on a cross-cultural venture. You never know what will hit you momentarily or transform your perspectives forever. The only guarantee is that you won't come back the same person
>
> Dorothy Jean Weaver[1]

The pattern of expatriate service found in MCC Indonesia today derives from one established during the Second World War in American and Canadian Mennonite experiences of "alternative service," which saw conscientious objectors enacting non-violent alternatives to participation in the armed forces. In early 1941, two years after Canada entered the war, Canadian Mennonites successfully negotiated with their government to establish Alternative Service Work camps in which conscientious objectors were put to work on state-directed projects. American Mennonites likewise negotiated with their government for exemption from active military duty.[2] The resulting Civilian Public Service (CPS) scheme, which ran from 1941 to 1947, was entrusted by American Mennonites to MCC for oversight and management. The service of conscientious objectors was intended to match those of their fellow citizens who had been conscripted into the military. Not all Mennonite young men from Canada or the US opted to participate in these alternative service arrangements.[3] For the many who did, it was conceptualized as a direct, positive parallel to involvement in war. Just as other young men put their bodies on the line for the nation, so too Mennonite young men would embody an alternative to violence. Mennonite service through CPS was a "moral equivalent for war" based on a "philosophy of the second mile."[4] The deployment of physical bodies was crucial. This was not simply a financial off-set for non-participation in war: the alternative service of Mennonites was performed through Mennonite flesh. Their bodies enacted Mennonite difference.

In his history of a CPS camp in Nebraska, Marvin Hein describes the CPS experience as "involuntary servitude" and a kind of "captivity."[5] It is ironic therefore that it was the voluntary nature of choosing not to participate in war that was one of its most durable legacies. This was particularly apparent in the "new concept of service" that emerged from CPS camps:

> Most of us entered CPS largely because we had little choice. We exited CPS persuaded that a life of voluntary Christ-followership demands constant service to other people. For two years we had served our national government, the church and each other. Somehow the conviction that our lives were not our own was translated into an unshakable belief that we were destined as God's people to serve the world.[6]

For Hein, the transformative nature of service within CPS was dual. He emphasizes changes in "conviction" and "belief" during the CPS experience that served as a powerful impetus for further action. Hein situates these transformations as emerging from enacted and embodied behaviour. The physicality and materiality of practice thereby merges with ideas and theologies into a potent source for action. The dramatic changes instigated through CPS are captured in the parturitional metaphor in the title of Hein's book, *A Community Is Born*.

Hein did not overestimate the impact of CPS on American Mennonites. For Perry Bush, CPS contributed to the "redefinition of Mennonites as a people of service" through providing "an opportunity to physically demonstrate love in a world seemingly lost in hate."[7] Likewise, Paul Toews judges CPS to have been a definitive "Mennonite university experience" with profound effects on Mennonite identity, particularly around newly prominent ideals of service.[8] The distinct pattern of service that was birthed at this time included widespread commitment to undertaking a two-to-four year term of voluntary service, the physical presence of workers sent outside their home communities, and inter-Mennonite ecumenicity and interaction. Although the idea of volunteering to outmatch conscription lost some of its potency after the draft was discontinued in the US in 1973, the pattern of seeking to approximate the sacrifices of those conscripted to the military remains influential. Among the most important legacies of this time is the Mennonite sacralization of embodied service.

This sacralization is apparent in the rising popularity of the story of Dirk Willems, a Dutch Anabaptist who was burned at the stake in the

Figure 7.1 | Jan Luyken's 1685 etching of Dirk Willems

city of Asperen in 1569. The story of his martyrdom is included within the *Martyrs Mirror*.[9] The 1685 edition of *Martyrs Mirror* was accompanied by the now iconic copper etching by Jan Luyken (see figure 7.1). The image is widely reproduced across contemporary Mennonite publications and in church imagery. Van Braght's account narrates the valiant actions of Willems, who, while fleeing persecution from Roman Catholic authorities, turned around to save his pursuer from drowning in a frozen pond. This action led to his capture and violent martyrdom and, subsequently, to his memorialization among Mennonites as a faithful witness to following Jesus.[10] David Weaver-Zercher's rich social history of the *Martyrs Mirror* notes that references to the story of Dirk Willems were "practically nonexistent in nineteenth- and early-twentieth century Anabaptist sources" but that they rapidly grew in ascendance such that by the end of the twentieth century Willems had become the most well-known Mennonite martyr.[11] The growth of interest in Willems was in response to the increasingly activist orientation of North American Mennonites, fuelled by the experience of conscientious objectors during the Second World War, which saw in this martyr a model of "service to others." The story of Dirk Willems today is retold as an affirmation of a theological conviction about the imperative for embodied, costly, and sacrificial service.

The birth of an activist Mennonite service ethic in the experience of conscientious objectors within alternative service camps in Canada and the US continued to shape the expectations and models of service within MCC during my fieldwork. The ongoing strength of the concern to send Mennonites to embody and enact service was highlighted during MCC's 2008 Annual General Meeting held at Conrad Grebel University in Waterloo, Ontario. During this meeting a speaker noted that the number of personnel that MCC sends overseas peaked at around five hundred service workers in the mid-1980s. It had steadily declined since then to just under three hundred.[12] This was addressed as a cause of considerable concern, specifically because MCC remained committed to sending people and not just finances.

The priority of embodying service has been addressed by Donald Kraybill, who proposed that, under the auspices of MCC, "uneducated farmer and sophisticated philosopher alike are able to translate the virtues of Anabaptist conviction into concrete expressions of care 'In the name of Christ.'"[13] MCC is therefore a "tangible embodiment," a "concrete expression," and an "incarnation" of the core Mennonite values of discipleship, service, and peacemaking. A similar line of argument was explored in a conversation I had with two former MCCers who were both academics – an anthropologist and a sociologist – on a car trip from Virginia to New York State. My friends told me that Mennonites have historically underplayed the sacramentalism of high church traditions, such as the ritual of Eucharist. Instead, the primary Mennonite sacrament is the action of embodied service. For J.R. Burkholder, embodied acts of service comprise a distinctive, embodied Mennonite "liturgy" that imbues a theology of ethical discipleship as an act of worship.[14]

This chapter analyzes the liturgy of everyday embodied service by expatriate MCCers in Indonesia. By emphasizing embodiment I mean to point to the fleshed materiality of corporeal bodies, the phenomenology of lived experience, and the composition of selves through relationships or intersubjectivity. It recognizes that international volunteers in MCC are travelling bodies. Michael Cronin argues that, when someone goes on a journey, they embody processes of translation such that "languages and cultures physically meet in, are inscribed at some level on, the body of the traveler."[15] Through their relocations and movements MCCers become the meeting points of different cultures, the blending of which could be both profound and challenging. Service is an amorphous if also powerful moral ambition that, to be put to work, must be enacted into practices and relationships within specific lives. Previous chapters analyze the role that brokers and translators play in making MCC "work" in Indonesia. These mediators play pivotal roles in enacting theologies, identities, relationships, and programs. Translation involves both transferring and transforming these ideas through dynamic and creative processes. In this chapter I analyze the ways in which embodied service is translated into Indonesia. In doing so, I focus on MCCers as themselves in translation. In the following sections, I analyze the experiences of embodying service through international travel in MCC. This includes experiences of disjuncture and rapprochement as MCCers travel into Indonesia as well as processes of reverse translation when, at the conclusion of their terms of service, they return back home.

TRAVELLING BODIES

Bodies are not easily or seamlessly translated into new contexts. The bodily adjustments necessary for international travel can be exacting. Travel involves corporeal, relational, and intersubjective encounters. This section examines the corporeality of travel. Drawing on selected examples I illustrate how MCC volunteers encountered new experiences, including new perceptions of their racialized and gendered bodies and changing understandings of their Christian faith.

The experience of travel as transformative is not, of course, unique to MCC volunteers. International MCC service has strong parallels with other international migrants, including pilgrims, tourists, refugees, and other volunteers or development workers. They also offer striking parallels with the experience of anthropologists carrying out ethnographic fieldwork. Anthropology has a long-standing emphasis on the importance of "being there" in anthropological fieldwork. The circulation of physical anthropological bodies has been regarded as vital for enabling new relationships and new understandings of the world. The fetishization of the field within anthropological research is well known and theorized in the discipline.[16] In the corridors of anthropology departments or on the sidelines of conferences I have often heard fieldwork being referred to as a kind of sacred pilgrimage. Ethnography is a liminal space that a neophyte anthropologist must traverse in order to return, triumphant, as a fully fledged member of the guild.[17] The power of ethnography stems directly from its corporeality. The doing and being of ethnographic fieldwork and the experience of volunteering for service in MCC are both embodied experiences that facilitate transformations within the traveller. While not all anthropological fieldwork and not every MCC volunteer travels internationally, in both contexts the image of the international fieldworker remains a stubborn archetype.[18]

Travelling bodies must adapt to new conditions, resulting in physical and sensorial adjustments. For most expatriate MCCers, travel to Indonesia was a baptism into the unknown. The languages, cultures, politics, histories, economics, and religions of Indonesia were little understood by expatriate MCCers prior to their arrival in the country. Some MCCers confessed to me that, prior to their imminent departure for Indonesia, they had no idea how to locate Indonesia on a world map. This reflected wider North American imaginative cartographies in which Indonesia is rarely foregrounded within media discourses.

MCC anecdotes are rich with stories about new tastes, smells, sounds, and sights. Expatriate MCCer mouths and tongues had to learn to move differently to form new sounds to effectively articulate the Indonesian language, including especially the ubiquitous "nga" syllable, which often stumped North American accentual palettes. Nostrils sniffed entirely new smells, not all of which were regarded as pleasant. The formidable durian, the Southeast Asian "King of the Fruits," was often regarded as especially provocative.[19] MCCer taste buds accommodated unfamiliar flavours, which could be particularly difficult for those unaccustomed to spicy cuisine, and textures, such as the slippery *papeda* (In. sago congee) for those living in Eastern Indonesia. Even if mouths were able to consume the barrage of new tastes, stomachs were sometimes less able to adapt; stomach upsets and awkward toilet encounters were common among new arrivals, and most expatriate MCCers accumulated numerous scatological stories after even just a few weeks.

Another feature of the corporeality of travel that produced animated conversation were changes in body mass for recent expatriate arrivals in Indonesia. These changes followed different trajectories, depending on the conditions in which the volunteers found themselves. Anna Friesen, one of the MCC Reps, observed that Service and Learning Together (SALT) volunteers tended to quickly put on weight. Because SALTers reside with host families as part of their eleven-month exchange program, they tend to lose control over their diet. As guests in other people's homes, when they are offered food they feel obliged to eat it, even if it comprises unhealthy deep fried snacks. They also lose control over their exercise regimens. Combined, these changes result in weight gain. However, service workers tended to experience the obverse. Service workers, and especially those with families, were generally allocated their own accommodation, and this facilitated greater independence, although not complete control. They were rarely able to obtain preferred food items due to communication challenges. They also often had to engage in more exercise than they were used to back home. This often resulted in weight loss. One service worker lost twenty pounds in his first few months in Indonesia. In her observations Anna astutely connected weight change with social processes, including encounters with the unfamiliar and a reduction in control over diet and exercise. The contrasting situations between SALTers and service workers produced different outcomes in changes to the weight and shape of their bodies.

Travelling bodies enter new webs of relationships. Michael Jackson describes ethnographic research as "a kind of controlled experimentation on oneself whose object is an enlarged understanding of what it means to be human."[20] This experiment involves situating oneself within new relationships thereby exploring different ways of being in the world. Humans are composed intersubjectively through our relationships and, therefore, travelling to live in a new culture can "change us utterly," resulting in a reconfigured sense of the self.[21] For Jackson, this is the risk and promise of ethnographic research. The embodiment of transnational service in MCC is similarly utterly transformative. Shaped by expectations of being a good guest who seeks to live alongside one's hosts and learning the vernacular, and guided by moralities of relational prioritization, MCCers plunged into the social worlds of their Indonesian hosts.

All expatriate MCCers in Indonesia experienced being regarded as foreigners on account of their racialized bodies. In their orientation sessions before coming out to Indonesia, Canadian and American MCCers went through the Damascus Road anti-racism training program, facilitated by MCC US.[22] This program confronted volunteers with the history of racism within contemporary North American society. Damascus Road training was orientated towards addressing issues of racism within North American Mennonite congregations, and it did not seek to assist volunteers to respond to their own experiences of racialization in their countries of assignment. The experience of being exposed to what Anne-Meike Fechter calls the "gaze of the Other" was, for many MCCers, an uncomfortable one.[23] While the gaze was unwelcome, MCCers were limited in their ability to conceal their conspicuousness. The relational orientation of MCC service celebrated the value of encounter and thereby necessitated visibility and exposure. MCCers also lacked the financial resources necessary for effective concealment measures, such as private cars, high-rise apartments, or living within "gated" communities.

Cherie, a white Canadian SALT volunteer in her early twenties, talked with me about a common experience for many MCCers in Indonesia. When she walked along the streets of her small Javanese town, groups of boys would frequently call out to her with "hey mister" or "Landa."[24] Peter, an MCC service worker in his twenties, told me that he loved visiting Bali because, with so many tourists around, his whiteness and American accent were hardly noticed. For his assignment in rural Aceh, he always attracted unwanted attention. The experience of visiting Bali made him wonder what it would be like returning to the US. Would he suffer from "reverse celebrity shock" when he returned home, when no one would regard him as noteworthy?

Joyce Wiebe was also a white American service worker. She and her husband had adopted daughters from China some years before coming to Indonesia on their MCC assignments. Joyce told me that the experience of taking her children to a restaurant in Indonesia contrasted sharply with their experience back home in the US. In an American restaurant her children were noted as "Asian" and were frequently complimented and given enthusiastic attention. In Java, however, "Asian kids are uninteresting." This contrasted with her observations of how white children were treated in Indonesia: they often attracted restaurant staff who would spend the evening "fawning" over them.

New experiences of whiteness were common among MCC expatriates but, as with Joyce's children, not all MCCers were white. Sipho and Dumisani, two Ndebele volunteers from Zimbabwe, came to Indonesia in mid-2008 with the Young Anabaptist Mennonite Exchange Network (YAMEN!), a South-South exchange program operated by MCC as a parallel with SALT and IVEP. When Sipho and Dumisani wandered the streets of their small towns in Java they were also frequently greeted with shouts from groups of boys.[25] However, unlike Cherie's "Landa," Sipho and Dumisani were addressed with shouts of "Obama." Barack Obama was at the time still just an American presidential candidate. The term was clearly racialized and marked the Zimbabweans as black even if Obama, who had spent part of his childhood in Jakarta, was a popular figure throughout the archipelago.

In his ethnography of the Central Javanese city of Solo in the 1980s, James Siegel analyzes interactions with foreigners. Siegel argues that beggars, transvestites, and wanderers were largely unnoticed and uninteresting for residents of his Solo neighbourhood. Their difference was only in terms of social rank, and therefore they were deemed "dismissible." When passing by a Javanese stranger, the appropriate etiquette was to avoid speaking and interacting with them. This contrasts with behaviour towards foreigners, who were located outside of Javanese sociality. Siegel suggests that foreigners are seen as objects of "contempt" and, simultaneously, as "extremely attractive." Their perceived outsider status meant that the usual rules of behaviour could be suspended. For Siegel, the very act of calling out to a stranger inscribed the foreigner as beyond sociality: the "result of addressing foreigners is not to include them but to exclude them."[26] Accordingly, the calling of names can be regarded as a sonic strategy for inscribing boundaries between the familiar and the foreign.

Siegel also notes that these interactions were gendered, with women frequently being treated as sexual objects. MCCers often found themselves being referred to through the use of sexual language. Young MCC women were particularly prone to unwanted sexual attention. Single expatriate MCCers adopted strategies of caution and disinformation to exit from awkward situations. Phoebe, an American single white woman who lived in Eastern Indonesia, talked with me about her experience of facing repeated sexual harassment. We talked a few months before she departed to return home. Throughout her term of service she had endured frequent cat-calls and verbal sexual abuse when walking on the street, and this made her feel violated and dirty. She learned to deflect male advances by saying she was a Roman Catholic nun or that she was married with several children. On one occasion a young Indonesian man smiled at her, raised his eyebrows, and ran his eyes over her, and Phoebe was furious: "I blew up and spouted venom. It felt so good!" She felt that the repeated sexual abuse was changing her. She began feeling angry towards men in general. For some time whenever she walked down a street alone she would flip open the lid on her can of mace and look for an opportunity to use it. She became increasingly wary about interacting with men, including her male MCC colleagues. She told me she was no longer sure what a healthy relationship with a man looked like.

She felt supported and cared for when she addressed these concerns with the MCC Reps, her immediate supervisors. She found it particularly helpful when men expressed anger about her situation. Phobe struggled with how to communicate these experiences to friends and supporters back home in the US. She tried to discuss the harassment in her regular letters to supporters, but she didn't find this easy to do. She "didn't want to tell ugly things" and so she told "the more *halus* [In. polite] version." This included narrating her sessions sitting and talking with her "mamas," an informal group of older women who were her mentors and talented storytellers. Phoebe felt safe in their company, and she described their friendship as experiencing the presence of God. Phoebe's filtered messages home dwelt on those parts of her assignment that involved warm and caring relationships, and she avoided the painful experiences of sexual abuse.

MCC workers experienced significant changes in their Christian faith, which also had embodied dimensions. While embodying service was a Mennonite sacrament, theology also required translation. The extent to which faith was an embodied and intersubjective experience was made apparent in a conversation I had with Joyce Wiebe, an academic theologian who was assigned as a lecturer in religious studies at a prominent university in Java. Three months into her term of service Joyce had come to the startling realization that she had stopped theologizing. This was surprising because she was trained as a theologian and, up to that point, she had always found that theological thinking had come "naturally." She told me that, since coming to Indonesia, she no longer comprehended events, relationships, and encounters in theological terms. Joyce had reflected on the reasons for this new predicament and had come to the conclusion that, as a Mennonite, she had always understood that theology was done within the context of "a faith community."[27] The problem was that she did not have a clear sense of who this was for her now. Was it the MCC team? But secondment out of MCC to an Indonesian university meant that her interactions with most other MCCers in Indonesia was limited. Was it her Indonesian church or her Indonesian colleagues? But language and cultural divides were seen as significant and limiting. Joyce worried about what this meant for the remainder of her term of service: "I cannot conceive of getting to know the Indonesian context well enough in the next three years to be able to do my theologizing in it."

Hank Toews also experienced a shift in his religiosity. He told me that he had joined the SALT program because he regarded MCC as the "most liberal" Mennonite international organization. Initially he wanted to go to Latin America to work on his Spanish, but last-minute changes saw him being reallocated to Indonesia. He was told by administrators at the time that one of the reasons for this was that his application had not been "evangelical enough" for Latin American Christian sensibilities. Indeed, his application had been blunt about his theological inclinations as he had written: "I don't actually believe that Jesus Christ was the Son of God. I believe he was a human being only." He told me that he knew that this would ruffle feathers but that he "wanted to be honest." Even so, he said, "I wasn't completely honest [because at that point] I was almost ready to consider myself an atheist."[28] Hank's desire to participate in MCC, despite his dissonance with the Christian faith, flowed from his self-identification as Mennonite. He had a Dutch-Russian Mennonite family name, he had attended an American Mennonite college, he had been brought up in a Mennonite church, and he warmly embraced the sense of tradition, which included "potlucks" and a commitment to peace and service.

Halfway through his SALT assignment I asked Hank how he now stood in regard to his previously stated atheist proclivity. "Now," replied Hank, "I *am* an atheist. Previously I was agnostic and open to changing my mind, but now I am more aligned with atheism." A few months later we met up in the US. Hank had just arrived back home and was going through the debriefing process at MCC's Akron headquarters. Hank told me that, in his end-of-year report, he had written: "maybe as a result of engaging in Indonesia with Javanese mysticism and blind dogmatism or maybe because I had a chance to think more about it, the SALT year reinforced my stance on the value of science, critical thought, and secular compassion." Yet he did not perceive this as a rejection of his Mennonite identity, which remained important for him. Hank's embracing of an explicit atheism was unique among the MCCers with whom I talked. Other theological reconfigurations were also possible, including some who further embraced a Christian identity and others who found their experiences in Indonesia left them with many questions and few clear answers.

NAVIGATING DISJUNCTURE

In his analysis of development processes David Mosse argues that different parts of any given project system – including policy makers, management personnel, field staff, consultants, and "recipient" communities – operate with considerable autonomy from each another, such that they each constitute a separate, although not rigidly bounded, "interpretive community."[29] As various parts of this system interact, as they necessarily must, a common outcome is misfit and disjuncture. Similarly, the MCC "patchwork quilt" brought together diverse interests and agendas. This section analyzes how expatriate MCCers navigated the disjunctures between them. As addressed in previous chapters, MCC policy and structure provides a discursive repertoire that affords a range of visions about what MCC is, or should be, as well as diverse programmatic incarnations. Expatriate MCCers arrived in Indonesia, therefore, with expectations about the ethics and practices of the organization that didn't always match the arrangements established on the ground. This was further complicated by the practice of secondment. As with Frank

Kauffman in the previous chapter, most assignments for expatriate MCCers involved being seconded to a partner organization. This created a dual identity in which the volunteer was simultaneously an MCCer and a member of a local organization. Being positioned within multiple parts of the MCC patchwork quilt meant that MCCers embodied the disjunctures between them.

This sense of disjuncture was clearly articulated by Joyce Wiebe, the MCC service worker who was assigned to lecture in religious studies at an Indonesian university. Some months into her term of service Joyce wondered whether what she was doing was actually "MCC service." She had recently browsed one of her MCC cookbooks and had flicked through various stories, scattered among the recipes, describing the work of expatriate MCCers around the world.[30] She was struck by how much each of these narratives contrasted with her own daily experience. In the cookbooks MCC had what she called "a particular profile and image," which she felt "did not represent reality at all; or at least not very closely." Joyce continued: "Before I came to Indonesia I *got* my assignment much better than I do now. At orientation in Akron, I *got* what I was to do and why I was to do it. But here …," she paused, "What am I doing? What do I do here? Why am I doing it? This is all much less clear to me now than it was before I got here."

A few months later we had another conversation. Joyce continued to feel her service with MCC was peculiar or unusual. When she had applied for MCC with Carl, her husband, who had a medical background, they had both presumed that he would hold the primary service assignment. At the time Joyce thought that MCC service was all about sustainable development, appropriate technology, and "digging wells." She had a doctorate in theology and her research engaged with feminist, systematic, and Mennonite theologies – all of which she thought would be thoroughly irrelevant for MCC service. "I thought I would be useless to MCC," she told me. So, when an academic assignment in her field was advertised, one that involved teaching religious studies, she was shocked. "This is not what I had envisioned MCC to be about." She continued to think that her assignment was probably an anomaly. She presumed that MCC's work in other countries was more aligned with her prior preconceptions. Regardless, she felt that she had better try to "come up with something" quickly to justify herself as a bona fide MCCer.

Experiences of disjuncture were felt by other MCCers. Hank Toews, the atheist Mennonite, told me he ended his SALT term feeling disillusioned. He had been assigned to assist a Javanese English language teacher in a secondary school in Java but had found few opportunities to undertake actual teaching tasks. Instead, he thought that, "just like the SALTers before me," his primary role had been as a "mascot," "celebrity," and "icon" for his school. The realization that his service to his school was entirely predicated on his status as a white foreigner, rather than due to any skills, knowledge, or character that he brought to the tasks assigned to him, was thoroughly disorienting.

Emily Martin, another SALTer in Central Java, was shocked at her living conditions during her assignment. She had expected a simple, rustic home – the Indonesian equivalent to the "mud hut" in Africa discussed in the previous chapter. She imagined that she would feel uncomfortable because of her proximity to poverty. But her expectations were completely confounded. She was placed with an affluent Chinese Indonesian host family who provided a newly constructed stand-alone two-story apartment for her personal use. It came with its own kitchenette, living room, TV, air conditioning, and modern bathroom. Her host family employed numerous domestic workers who did all her cooking, cleaning, and washing. Emily told me about an occasion when relatives of her host parents visited the house. These relatives owned a jewellery boutique, and they brought with them a selection from their shop for sale with an attractive family discount. Invited to browse over the glittering display, Emily was shocked at the cost of each item. She politely declined to buy any items and sought to escape the uncomfortable situation. A few days later Emily grumbled to her MCC colleagues: "I did not do SALT to get diamonds!"

Most expatriate MCCers shared Emily's sense that the ideal of embodied service did not include indulging in the trappings of elite, bourgeois luxury. Jokes about "suffering for Christ" after having a pedicure, or how to write home about Javanese cream baths (a beauty treatment) and Bali beach holidays, were bantered around MCC social gatherings. Emily's combination of SALT and diamonds was similarly comical in its imagined contradiction. This humour acknowledged and alleviated the awkwardness of disjuncture. Erika Yoder's situation was regarded as similarly incongruent, but it wasn't very funny.

Erika's SALT assignment was to teach English language in a private, wealthy Christian high school in Semarang. A fellow expatriate American (though not an MCCer) headed up the English department of eighteen Indonesian teachers, all of whom were trained in language teaching and were fluent in written and spoken English. Erica was not a trained teacher. Without teaching skills or qualifications Erika ended up without much in the form of actual work, and she was extremely bored. She spent most of her worktime colouring posters. Erika's host family was very wealthy. Her Chinese Indonesian host father owned a water bottling industry and had a side business in the transnational trade in swallow nests. When they were home her host family kept their bedroom doors shut to keep the air-conditioned cool air locked in. For leisure Erika's host family browsed the latest in Indonesian fashion in Semarang's shopping malls. During their "shopping sprees" Erika felt pressured to purchase items that she couldn't afford. Before coming to Indonesia, she had been passionate about social justice and global inequality. She was an eager supporter of fair trade and described herself as "anti-American." Motivated to live out her globally minded service, Erika had signed up to SALT as soon as she was old enough to do so. However, the actual lifestyles she encountered in this part of the "developing world" were considerably more ostentatious than her lifestyle back home. Lonely and isolated, Erika spent much of her free time chatting over Skype with her parents and friends in the US.

Over a period of about a month the MCC office staff in Salatiga discussed and analyzed Erika's predicament. During a car journey I shared with Adi, a Javanese member of MCC's staff, our meandering conversation eventually and inevitably came to Erika. For Adi, the socio-economics of Erika's host family merely reflected the reality of many other Indonesian Mennonites. They simply weren't poor. The expectation that Indonesian Christians were poor was, he thought, the primary problem. Adi argued that the burden of initiative rested on Erika to try to fit in with her hosts and to work with their priorities and lifestyle. A few weeks later a decision was made for Erika to change assignments; she would shift to a rural Javanese village to live in a modest house and work alongside a local NGO and nearby church. This assignment would be practical, grounded, and very simple. Adi told me at the time that he was unsure whether it would work out. His doubts proved prophetic. Not long afterwards Erika "early terminated" her SALT year and returned home.

"Early termination" is the term used within MCC for premature departure from a fixed-term assignment. It was not a common occurrence in MCC Indonesia but, as with Erika's case, it wasn't unknown. It was one of the strategies available to MCCers who really struggled during their assignments. While some early terminations were perceived by fellow MCCers as necessary, I never heard anyone describe premature departure as a successful outcome. Early termination was an implicit negation of the logics of relationality within MCC. It involved the irreversible and unilateral rupturing and dissolution of relationships, and it was these relationships that were regarded as the primary purpose for sending MCCers around the world. In Erika's case, early termination provided an uncomfortable resolution for the disjuncture she experienced between what she had imagined MCC service would be and actual practice in Indonesia.

Unexpected luxury was not a problem all MCCers faced. Upon first arriving in rural Aceh to undertake tsunami relief work, Peter and Jed, two young American MCCers, were allocated bedding in a single room in a shared house that was also occupied by their Acehnese NGO colleagues. The heat, humidity, heavy smoking of clove (In. *kretek*) cigarettes, cramped conditions, and absence of any personal space were challenging. Dumisani, a Zimbabwean YAMEN! participant, lived in a small rural Javanese village for his assignment. His experience was the opposite of that of Emily and Erika. Dumisani's host family lived in a simple concrete house typical of many Javanese towns. Dumisani's main struggle was the fact that his hosts had no internal bathroom; instead, they used public facilities. Showering in the public washroom was very uncomfortable for him and left him feeling exposed. The occasional rat in his bedroom offended his sense of hygiene. The most challenging issue, however, was the use of the kitchen washing area as a urinal at nighttime. This pushed him way outside his comfort zone and was a topic of animated concern for months. In the end, after lots of discussion, MCC Indonesia took the unprecedented step of building a bathroom for Dumisani's host family to help him feel more comfortable.

While all MCCers lived the disjunctures, most managed to see these through to learn to enjoy their term of service. This conciliation was clearly held as the goal of embodied service in MCC. In her analysis of the interactions between middle-class NGO workers and rural villagers in Nepal, Celayne Heaton Shrestha observes a bridging of cultural worlds, resulting in "a kind of rapprochement, a convergence of worlds."[31] This rapprochement emerged as a consequence of embodied everyday encounters in the course of daily meetings and recreation activities. As a consequence of sharing time and space, perceived differences diminished, commonalities were discovered and created, and relationships were formed. The possibility of rapprochement helpfully highlights two key issues. First, rapprochement challenges the assumption that development processes inevitably involve the meeting of incommensurable cultural domains.[32] Differences, or at least some of them some of the time, are bridgeable in practice. Translation always remains a possibility. Second, rapprochement builds upon an understanding of identity formation as dynamic rather than static. Through experiences of cross-cultural interaction identities can be remade and reimagined. Rather than mere outworkings of predefined scripts, interconnections across difference are generative and productive of new identities. Rapprochement facilitates attention to the ways in which identities are reworked through encounters.

For expatriate MCCers their service terms are a potent space for identity re-formation. Through their interactions, learnings, and adjustments, many expatriate MCCers actively sought to accommodate themselves, at least partially, to new relationships and new subjectivities. For those who saw out the full length of their terms of service, some form of rapprochement was probably inevitable. The MCCer who becomes fluent in the vernacular becomes familiar with another form of life, shares close relationships with neighbours and colleagues, and is reshaped by these experiences. "Success" for expatriate service was not simply about enduring adversity but also the ability to learn about and adapt to new modalities, dispositions, and practices. Rapprochement involved a new or altered habitus. Such adaptations often took place by stealth; they were less cognitive adjustments than forms of behaviour acquired through embodied practice. Often the changes became apparent only in hindsight and sometimes with a sense of surprise.

The process of rapprochement was at the forefront of conversations I had with Peter and Jed, service workers who at that time had lived in Aceh for two years. These changes involved shifts in habits and expectations. Having lived in a village in which trouser-wearing was virtually an unquestioned dress code for men, Jed told me he now felt uncomfortable wearing shorts. When he did so he felt improperly dressed. Peter got riled up if someone greeted him with a wave of their left hand. Throughout Aceh the left hand is perceived as impure, and it was never used as a greeting. Peter also told me that when he visited Bali, a predominantly Hindu island in Indonesia, he found himself missing the sound of the Islamic call to prayer, which was broadcast on the loud speakers of neighbourhood mosques across Aceh five times a day. Through repetition the call to prayer had become an ingrained and expected part of his life.

In a conversation with Lydia and Frank Kauffman we explored similar questions. Both were seconded as lecturers to a Christian university in Central Java. Mirroring Joyce Wiebe's narrative, discussed above, when they first arrived three years earlier, they had felt a deep disconnection between their sense of what MCC service was supposed to be about and their actual assignments. They had imagined that MCC work was about social justice and working alongside the poor. However, the university they were seconded to catered primarily to the growing Indonesian middle class, and their daily life was far removed from engagements with poverty. Over time, however, they "resolved [their] tensions" over their assignments. They did so by learning to see their work "as good and helpful to MCC's partner," regardless of whether it fit their expectations of "service."

In another conversation Frank talked about the burdensome obligation of having to endure long speeches, called *sambutan*, a ubiquitous feature of Indonesian sociality. *Sambutan* are an expected part of every function and event held in workplaces, churches, community meetings, state-sponsored gatherings, and national holidays. Virtually all formal occasions necessitated a lengthy *sambutan*. Due to insufficient language proficiency, many newly arrived MCCers struggled to follow these speeches. Those who were able to keep up found the meandering nature of *sambutan* to be confusing or pointless. Frank told me, however, about an occasion that was something like an epiphany for him. Three years into his service term in Java, Frank listened to a lengthy and dreary *sambutan* and was shocked by his own response. The *sambutan* was delivered at the end of a walk-a-thon run by his university. It was mid-morning and, therefore, it was hot and humid. Along with the other walkers Frank waited at the finishing point at the appointed time for the speeches. On this occasion, for the first time, Frank felt like he got it. It wasn't that the *sambutan* was more compelling than previously; rather, Frank felt he now had a sense of appreciation, perhaps even a sense of enjoyment, at the particular rhetorical aesthetic of a meandering and lengthy speech. Frank found it hard to explain what had changed or why he had found a new appreciation for the genre. What was clear was that the communal experience meant something very different for him at that point than it had before. *Sambutan* was no longer a burden but a pleasant aspect of his community relationships.

As a result of their everyday presence, many MCCers learned to embrace aspects of Indonesian life that at first had seemed strange, odd, and confusing. The initial experience of disjuncture, which was part and parcel of being translated into Indonesian communities and workplaces, could, over time, be superseded by rapprochement, accommodation, and newfound appreciation.

REVERSE TRANSLATIONS

Disjuncture and rapprochement are both responses to encounters with difference. They are not opposites or mutually exclusive processes. Rather, as a resolution of disjuncture, rapprochement depends on a prior disseverment. The one is imbricated with the other. Also, while rapprochement was held out as an MCC service ideal, expatriate MCCers were not expected to become "Indonesian" or to remain in Indonesia over the long term. Rapprochement had its limits. Expatriate MCC service involved temporary, fixed-term assignments premised on the anticipation of an eventual return home. However, because embodied service immersed expatriate MCCers in new relationships, and because the processes of disjuncture and rapprochement are generative of new identities and subjectivities, one outcome of being translated into Indonesia is that MCCers' relationships with "home" are also reworked. Effective translation into Indonesia necessitated in turn a reverse translation back home. An illuminating conversation I had with Albert Regehr brought together questions about translation, secondment, and communicating with home.

While sitting in his house in Yogyakarta, Albert talked with me at length about the challenges, pleasures, and opportunities of being an MCC service worker. He was seconded as a lecturer in philosophy to an Islamic university in Central Java. Albert had been awarded his doctorate from a Canadian university. He had previously served with MCC in Africa. He told me that he enjoyed secondment because it gave him an opportunity to work in the university and yet, because he was not a full faculty member, he did not have to conform in the same way as was expected of other members of faculty. He had considerably more freedom than they did in designing courses and preparing teaching material. He also was not burdened with a heavy administrative load. The knowledge that he was only short term meant that much less was at stake for him, and his hosts, than would have been the case had he been a permanent faculty member.

Secondment, however, was also disagreeable in that Albert knew that he was "not really a part of the school." He sometimes found it challenging "to go to work, walk the halls, teach classes knowing that [his] status [was] different, [was] not the same, and so [he was] treated differently. [He was] always other and different." This was "a burden [he felt] more and more." Albert said that he was becoming increasingly aware that his status as Christian – he was, he thought, the only non-Muslim in the whole university – and foreign, Western academic made him a clear outsider. Students would often stop him as he walked around the campus and ask him who he was and why he was there. He came to see these questions as part inquisitiveness and part challenge: to ask them was to assume that he did not belong and that he wasn't supposed to be there. These encounters made him feel awkward and out of place.

The process of secondment helped "bridge" the distance between himself and his colleagues, while also leaving in place a gap: secondment "gets me in the door but also marks me as other." Regardless, Albert thought that secondment was necessary. This was because he was "so outside, estranged" to his hosts that to be required to "fit in" would necessarily have been "long and painful." However, he didn't want to fit in and become comfortable with the operations of his host university. Secondment meant that he didn't have to. Through secondment the most challenging parts of translating oneself into the assignment could be avoided. He thought that this worked for his university as much as it worked for him. It meant that the Islamic university could make use of a foreign academic – and the prestige that went with this – while not feeling obliged to accept him as a regular faculty member or allow him a significant voice in the running of the university. If ever colleagues or administrators felt threatened, the secondee could be easily isolated or expelled. The process of secondment therefore "alleviates tension" through a mix of both separation and connection. It provided both parties with "mutual benefits" through furnishing considerable "latitude and flexibility" to each.

One significant disconnect was that, while Albert thought MCC wanted him to be at his university as an embodied example of what it means to be a Mennonite Christian, he thought his Muslim colleagues weren't in the slightest interested in his Christianity. He hadn't "experienced an iota of interest in people learning about Christianity. Not even a vague suggestion." He thought that this created a problem concerning how he would fulfil his tasks as entrusted by MCC: "At times I feel that I'm not really living up to the MCC part of the secondment, because I can't." While his teaching was going well, seemed to be appreciated, and he got encouraging feedback, he felt this was inadequate. "I'm pretty sure that is not why I was sent to teach here." He felt "forced in this context to move in a direction away from Akron, and certainly away from the majority of Mennonites who support MCC."

Despite this movement away Albert still thought there remained other points of connection. Whenever he taught philosophy he often had in mind the "basic principles that guide MCC," including "peace and justice" and raising questions about violence, and he addressed these from a philosophical perspective, as was appropriate for his classes and expertise. He did not address them through biblical or theological frames. To communicate on these issues Albert translated traditional Mennonite concerns into the language of philosophy. Correcting his own previous uncertainty as to whether he was fulfilling the mandate MCC had given him, Albert added: "I feel I am doing what's being asked of me by MCC. The bugger is how to explain to MCC that what I am doing is what I've been asked to do."

Whereas some Mennonites believed "the message" had to be articulated "in a specific way," Albert thought that "many of the beliefs of Mennonites and MCC can fairly faithfully be translated into another language," such as the discipline of philosophy. For, although "translations always come up short" and remain partial and inadequate, nevertheless "we can translate into different languages." The possibility of translation rested on the ability to recognize in others similarities to oneself. Accordingly, "Islam and Christianity are similar to each other. That kind of translation is particularly awkward for many Christians, especially evangelicals. I understand that. I struggle with trying to find ways of bridging this. I have to admit that I haven't found a satisfactory way of doing that. I don't have a satisfactory way of accounting for the work I do in ways ordinary, regular Mennonites would appreciate."

I asked Albert whether, if most Mennonites found his academic work disconcerting, then what about the wider MCC organization? In response, Albert said, "I am happy to be wrong, but I don't think that MCC sees its guiding values as being translatable into disciplines like philosophy; [nevertheless,] I have a responsibility to MCC and I try to live up to it. However, I struggle to articulate how I am living up to it. I am confident that I am but I struggle in fitting it into MCC's style of reporting." This was not a task that he hoped to avoid: "I don't want to escape my responsibility to MCC. I want to embrace it, because this work is important to MCC. My relationship to [the Islamic university] is important for North American Mennonites. Damned if I could find the vocabulary to use in a church in Lancaster County to explain that though." When I suggested that perhaps he didn't have to find the language appropriate for Lancaster County, he responded emphatically:

> Yes, but I *want* to. Philosophically, I am working out Mennonite beliefs in my role here. But I still haven't found a way I can explain this. If I mention to North American Mennonites that I do "philosophy," unless I say that I do "*Christian* philosophy," I get a similar response to "is that near Japan?"[33] It is off the chart. But I believe it is important to Mennonites, important to the Mennonite world. I can explain in philosophical terms how Mennonite beliefs come out in lectures, but I don't know how to explain in terms that are understandable in the Mennonite church. I haven't got to that. So, I struggle to report to MCC that I'm doing what they want me to do even when many fail to see how.

Albert's secondment in the Islamic university took place within the paradox of connections and disconnections, junctures and disjunctures. A part of his challenge was the question of whether teaching in an Indonesian university was a legitimate embodiment of MCC service. His questions mirrored those of Joyce Wiebe and Lydia and Frank Kauffman. Having concluded that his work was a legitimate embodiment of service, however, Albert then faced the challenge of how to translate his actual work back home. He was unsure as to whether he could show North American Mennonites and other MCCers exactly how his assignment was faithful to the task he had been given. The other part of Albert's problem, therefore, was the challenge of reverse translation. The problem of reverse translation is, again, the question of disjuncture, but this time the disconnect was between the translated MCCer and their home community. In order to reconnect with the Mennonite constituency it was necessary for Albert to attempt a further translation to make his practices comprehensible to those who had sent him. Albert was bewildered as to how he would accomplish this.

Albert's philosophical dissection of these problems was a particularly analytical assessment of the challenges of MCC service as embodied translation. It shares parallels with Phoebe's case, discussed above, in which she, too, struggled with how to communicate back home. While Phoebe had the language to express her situation, she opted for self-censorship in her correspondence. Albert, however, grappled more with how to articulate his activities in an idiom that would adequately convey his situation. The struggle to translate here should be seen as an indication of Albert's commitment to the Mennonite constituency that supported MCC. While he was relieved that he did not have to "fit in" to his host university, he was firmly dedicated to maintaining the links with home.

Homecoming was a crucial dimension of embodied service in MCC. It was structurally built into the organization in the fixed-term assignments for service workers and SALTers. Initial departure was matched with a promised return. The travelling bodies of MCC volunteers involved a circular route. Albert's desire to communicate home presaged his eventual closure of assignment and exit from Indonesia. Because the return home was expected for expatriate MCC volunteers, conversations in Indonesia frequently touched on this theme. On one occasion Joyce Wiebe told me about what she called "MCC types." Joyce said that if she visited a Mennonite church in North America she could always quickly determine whether a person had worked with MCC or not. This was because former MCCers always stood out. For Joyce, MCC types had three characteristics. First, they exhibited a "strong discomfort with North American culture." Former MCCers were ill at ease with the affluence of Canada and the US. They found the lifestyles and work patterns of North Americans strange and unbalanced. They were also generally less prone to expressions of patriotism and were suspicious of the imperial ambitions of their government. Second, they had a "broader perspective of the world" than was typical of North American Mennonites. They had lived in other cultures in places far from the US and Canada. They had learned to see things from a different point of view. They enjoyed other foods, had developed a different sense of aesthetics, and could speak other languages. Third, MCC types experienced deep "discomfort with Mennonite self-understandings." The experience of living apart from their home communities made returned MCCers more critical. They no longer accepted the stories of Mennonite benevolence and generosity; rather, they were prone to rigorous critique.

Joyce told me about a relative that she thought was a "classic MCC type." After completing an MCC service term this relative had searched hard for a job in North America but had failed to secure one. Some of his Mennonite friends concluded that he no longer knew how to work, but Joyce felt otherwise. "He never fit back in." He always struggled to readjust to home life. The translated MCCer, the person who successfully managed to fulfil the task of embodying Mennonite service in other places, emerged transformed and, therefore, also dissonant with the home that sent them out. Eventually, Joyce's relative returned to MCC to continue to work on issues that ignited his passions. Importantly, Joyce knew all this before she departed for Indonesia. It was part of what she sought when she decided to engage in service with MCC. A disjunctive relationship with home, and with the Mennonite community, was a faithful embodiment of service.

Joyce's description of the "MCC type" is what Michael Cronin calls a "translated being."[34] "Translated beings" are migrants that have been so shaped by their experiences of travel that they "no longer have the same attitude towards their country of origin, irrespective of whether they wish to return to it or not, because distance in and of itself leads to a reframing of past experiences." The "daily traces of the hermeneutic work involved in living in another country" become enmeshed in migrants' very selves. Because the process of translation is so "momentous and life-altering" the effects remain embedded in the translator-travellers lives and identities. Just as MCCer translation into Indonesia involves both transfer and transformation, so returning home requires the navigation of the same dynamics.

FAITHFUL AND AMBIVALENT HOMECOMINGS

Alongside the translation of ideas, theologies, programs, and partnerships, so too expatriate MCCers themselves were in translation as they moved between their home countries and their service assignments in Indonesia. As travelling bodies they had to physically adjust to new experiences. Their entry into new webs of relationships resulted in new subjectivities, identities, and habits. Because the process of being translated was transformative, when expatriate MCCers turned to home they faced the challenge of how to translate their experiences in the other direction. Returning home is structurally built into expatriate MCC service. The fixed-term duration of their assignments, as noted in the introduction to this chapter, parallels the military draft. Just as conscripts complete their tours of duty and head home, so too MCCers finish their service assignments and then return to their sending community. But whereas the service of draftees could be seen as concluding with their discharge, the service of MCCers continues. As with CPS, the structural embeddedness of homecoming returns MCCers so that their experiences continue to feed into the wider life of their churches and communities. MCC's service is to and for the North American Mennonite peoplehood.

An interesting comparison with MCC expatriate service is found in Nicole Constable's analysis of the ambivalent and contradictory emotions that Filipina migrant workers in Hong Kong have of their homecomings.[35] Discussing the predicament of migrant workers anticipating returning to the Philippines, Constable notes that, while they left their homes for Hong Kong out of desperation, their experiences in Hong Kong enabled them to carve out "new identities and political spaces." Migrant workers discovered that "it is not always easy to fit back into their old lives and relationships because they have changed and home has been altered by their absence." Constable suggests that they are akin to exiles living in another land. However, she predicts that, because of their profound personal changes, when they go home "they will be, more than likely, in a different space and therefore remain, in a sense, in exile." Exile is certainly a possibility for returned MCCers. The disjuncture that Joyce's relative felt with his home community suggests this possibility. It is not, however, the only possible outcome or the whole story. The transformed MCCer is the migrant who, in the process of their transformation, has nevertheless remained faithful to the task given to them by their home community. Quiet service, mutual sharing, learning the vernacular, working within another's set of rules, forming close relationships – these transformative experiences are all faithful embodiments of the sacrament of Mennonite service.

A different analogy is that of anthropologists returning home after their fieldwork. In anthropology similar practices of relational association, embodied experience, and intersubjective transformation are regarded as fundamental to ethnographic fieldwork. In conducting experiments on themselves in living otherwise, anthropologists simultaneously prove their mettle, and fidelity, to their disciplinary colleagues back home. Anthropologists become anthropologists because and through their field experience, but the process only culminates in the return home. When Canadian and American Mennonites return home from their periods of service with MCC, they likewise show their fidelity to their home communities. The return home is one of their primary acts of service. In the introduction to this chapter, I quote Perry Bush's description of the emerging postwar self-identification of Mennonites as "a people of service."[36] Those Mennonites who complete MCC overseas field assignments – and this was a rite of passage over generations – return home as the epitome of this influential ideal. Returned MCCers are baptized into and through service. While experiences of disjuncture with their home congregations and communities place them in an ambivalent position, even this ambivalence is a consequence and witness to their faithful translation of service.

Conclusion

This ethnography of the Mennonite Central Committee explores the everyday activities of the organization as it is put to work at particular times and places. It has shown that close attention to a case like MCC provides a valuable site to critically evaluate and correct dominant approaches to thinking about the interactions of religion and development. Against the tendency to think of both religion and development as reified categories, this study instead highlights the dynamism involved in the translation of MCC between North America and Indonesia.

MCC is an organization that is composed of contested ideas, theologies, and practices. It is not a stable object with predetermined boundaries and pathways. It is better conceptualized as an ongoing process that is shaped and reshaped by the diverse collection of people that comprise the organization. For any given project, MCCers on the ground in Indonesia, Canada, and the United States draw on a repertoire of options available to them. These are put to work in different contexts only through extensive and sometimes fraught negotiations. These negotiations are both intra- and extra-organizational. Internally MCC is a patchwork quilt, with each different block (piece of cloth) representing a potentially contrasting contribution to the other parts of the whole. But MCC is not the only actor that has the capacity to shape its programs. Externally, MCC is enacted through ongoing negotiations with constituent Mennonite communities, state bureaucracies, and partner organizations among many others. Negotiations between each of these actors can reorient the implementation and trajectory of MCC's operations.

I analyze the negotiations involved in designing and implementing MCC's relief, development, and peacebuilding projects in terms of cultural translation. The frame of translation invites attention to the brokers and translators that operate at the interstices of MCC's organizational patchwork. It also creates space for considering the ambiguous nature of transnational encounters, where what transfers and what is transformed in the process of translation remains continuously in question. Translation concerns the ideas and theologies of service as well as the practices, material artefacts, and personnel that circulate in and through the organization. Translation is more than communication across cultural and religious gaps: it is also a productive space in which differences are inscribed and identities imagined and reconstructed. These dynamic translations help explain why mission statements and other policy documents do not dictate practice in any straightforward way. They also help explain why MCC has assumed such diverse forms. At different times and in different places MCC has been a peoplehood movement, a development NGO, a church-planting organization, an adjunct of Indonesia's New Order state, a repository of technical expertise, a transporter of canned meat, a relational connector, a contractor to the Canadian International Development Agency, a funding agency, a facilitator of academic secondments, and a service agency.

My research into MCC involves a detailed and textured ethnographic study grounded in specific locations and junctures. The research is designed around the conviction that the most important information we can learn about the workings of religious development organizations are found in the complex tangle of actual practices. This methodology can be seen as an anti-taxonomic or anti-mapping exercise in that I seek to avoid freeze-framing the organization, instead focusing my attention on movement and relationality.[1] I seek to understand not only what MCC is but how MCCing is done. Only through careful consideration of quotidian political, cultural, and theological dynamics are we able to formulate better understandings of the interactions of religion and development that take place within religious NGOs. Ethnography is attuned to spatial and temporal dynamics, and so is a privileged methodology for this kind of empirically grounded and fine-grained investigation. *The Service of Faith* is testimony to the analytical and descriptive possibilities available to those who assume an ethnographic stance when conducting research on religious NGOs.

MCC's work has been a vital force shaping North American Mennonite identity since the Second World War. One of the most important roles that MCC plays for the Mennonite peoplehood is to perpetuate a sense of distinctiveness. This imagined shared identity is promoted in the midst of competing versions of what it is to be Mennonite and within a context in which there are many other potential identifications vying for prominence. As the boundaries between "the world" and "the church" grew increasingly murky in both the United States and Canada, MCC helped reshape Mennonite identity around shared practices of activist service. This sense of Mennonite distinctiveness in turn shapes a sense of MCC's exceptionalism, such that for many MCCers their organization is envisioned as unique among other development and humanitarian actors. While MCC is not always as radically different as MCCers imagine, the belief in difference has played an important role in shaping distinctive practices. The narratives of Mennonite service in this book illustrate how the belief in difference can inspire and shape projects for relief, development, and peace.

Service in MCC is simultaneously practical, embodied, ethical, and theological, and these features are intertwined in ways that defy attempts at clear demarcation. Service is shaped and legitimated by vernacular Mennonite theologies. The embodiment of service can be seen as a Mennonite sacrament. Imaginations of Mennonite service as relational, quietist, activist, and peaceable arise out of the history of Mennonite approaches to faith. Nevertheless, like prominent buzzwords in the world of aid and development, service is a capacious concept that can be performed in many ways. A significant part of its use for MCCers is that service does not dictate the substance of activities carried out in its name. A vast array of practices can be legitimated under the rubric of service. This multiplicity of translations of service also occurs because, while important, Mennonite theologies are not the only influences that shape MCC's practices. The embodiment of service takes place amid competing political interests from diverse actors. Moreover, what MCC does and how it works depends on who is involved at any given juncture. Throughout the preceding chapters I highlight the ways in which MCC's service is shaped by particular personalities and their relationships. By focusing on people and not just structures, discourses, or institutions, I argue for the priority of brokers and translators in the anthropology of development.

The nature of MCC service is helpfully illuminated by asking: Who is MCC service for? This question arises at numerous points in this book. If MCC could not change the canned meat label to make it more amenable for consumption by intended recipients in Muslim contexts, then who was the canning for? If MCC structures the service of expatriate volunteers in such a way that the return home is a requirement and fulfilment of their work, then who is being served by this? The answer to these sorts of questions is not clear-cut, and, in fact, this enduring ambiguity helps explain how MCC works. Processes of translation ensure that multiple communities are served simultaneously. It is the precarious, potent, and creative task of the mediators, located in the interstices between different parts of the MCC patchwork quilt, to ensure that the service of MCC continues to benefit different constituencies. A necessary corollary of the requirement that MCCers face in multiple directions at the same time is the acknowledgment that, in this gift economy, there is no clear distinction between givers and receivers. Rather than viewing this as some kind of betrayal of humanitarian rhetoric (with its preoccupation with the distant other), I take this as an invitation to carefully consider how development works in both domestic and field operations. It also remains important to remember that MCC would not work in practice unless its services were multiple.

I show that MCC service is dynamic and changes over time and between places. Over the years since I completed my fieldwork on MCC, the organization has continued to evolve. For the most part, I have not sought to include this ongoing story within this book. I have been content to allow my ethnographic and historical material to speak to the times and places with which I was most familiar. Ethnography is necessarily partial, and this is both a strength and limitation.

MCC now operates within an increasingly complex North American environment. Over the past decade American and Canadian politics have become characterized by growing levels of political polarization and partisanship, driven by changes in the use of social media technologies, declining trust in pivotal democratic institutions, growing inequalities, and cynical instrumentalization of disaffection and anxiety. These fissures have also run through the middle of North American Mennonite communities. Debates over politics, sexuality, and race have risen to the top of Mennonite ecclesial agendas, with churches and conferences becoming places of contentious debates, some of which have resulted in church splits. These tensions raise important questions about the extent to which the Mennonite peoplehood remains plausible as an imagined community. The Covid-19 pandemic exacerbated many of these simmering tensions. In attempting to navigate its relationship with an increasingly disquieted constituency, MCC has often served as an intermediary among Mennonite groups, even while MCCers also sought to provide a prophetic voice calling Mennonites to engage with each other in just, peaceable, and generous ways.

At the same time, MCC continues to carry out relief, development, and peacebuilding around the world within an increasingly volatile geopolitical context. Many of MCC's country programs have been confronted by instability and conflict. While Indonesia has had a relatively stable past decade, the MCC program in Indonesia faced significant new challenges.

Changing political dynamics have constricted the room for manoeuvre available to the organization, resulting in significant reconfigurations in its partnerships. Cycles of personnel changes continued to result in very different versions of MCC becoming enacted. At the same time, the number of Canadian and American Mennonite volunteers committing to serve through MCC has declined. If relationality and presence have been the heartbeat of MCC for most of its history, then changes in the willingness and availability of service workers constitutes a significant reshaping of how the organization is put to work.

During my field research I talked with a Mennonite academic who expressed a sense that MCC was an aging organization reaching the end of its life. This scholar explained to me that organizations have lifespans roughly equivalent to that of humans. The implication, therefore, was that it was nearing the time when Mennonites would need to bury MCC and begin dreaming of new forums and spaces that would carry Mennonite theologies of service into the future. Of course, other Mennonites, and almost all MCCers I talked with, took a completely different tack: while the future is always unknowable, their passion for MCC and their commitment to Christian service within and through it was in no way tarnished by new challenges. MCC had been continuously evolving throughout its history, and many MCCers remained confident that it was robust enough to continue to adapt on into the future.

It was within the context of pervasive tensions and debates that, in 2020, MCC celebrated its centenary. This marked an important milestone in the remarkable history of this organization. Although the Covid-19 pandemic disrupted many of the planned celebrations, events were nevertheless organized across Canada and the United States, with many being live-streamed. The centenary celebrations looked to the past to seek to shore up MCC's future as a major conduit of Mennonite service and as a vital institution shaping Canadian and American Mennonite identities and theologies. The celebratory events also included space for airing stinging critiques of MCC's ethical failures as well as profound moments of confession from its leaders. This bringing together of celebration, critique, and confession has a long and rich history in the organization.[2] The combination has served MCC well over the decades by creating space for new impulses and allowing critical reinventions of how MCC is enacted.

In this ethnographic study of Mennonite service, I am less concerned with celebration, critique, and confession than with the more modest project of description. In the introduction I propose that this book should be read as a contribution to a theological anthropology. The theological impulse shaping this book contends that textured, detailed description is also a kind of service. As an act of service, this ethnography is offered as a gift to those who have dedicated time and energy to serving in and through MCC. It is also offered to others working in or studying international aid and development in the hope that new insights might be gleaned and shared. It is given in the same spirit as I received the stories that I have told. A good description, in my mind, points towards beauty and complexity in equal measure. I have aspired to provide such a description in the pages of this book. In doing so, I have appropriated Aby Warburg's famous dictum: "the dear God dwells in the details." This, for me, is an anthropological article of faith.[3]

Notes

INTRODUCTION

1 Unless otherwise indicated, I use pseudonyms for all personal names. In keeping with common anthropological practice some pseudonyms are also composites.

2 "Pasukan Islam" is a pseudonym.

3 Since the 1980s conspiracy theories concerning Jews have been widespread among Islamist Indonesian groups and more broadly (Van Bruinessen 2013, 261–82; Reid 2010). They gained particular currency after the 9/11 attacks in New York (Burhanuddin 2007). Such views are frequently read through the lens of the conflict between Israel and Palestine (Lukens-Bull and Woodward 2011). Although antisemitic stereotypes are contested by scholars and activists (Ali 2010), speculation about the malicious intention of Jews to disrupt Indonesia and Islam has been disseminated widely, including famously by former president Suharto, who blamed his downfall in 1998 on "Zionists" (Burhanuddin 2007, 53). Rachmad's views reflected these wider circulations.

4 During my field research the Akron office was the head office for MCC "binational," which oversaw the organization's international programs. It was also the location for the national office for MCC in the United States (MCC US), which had responsibility for domestic programs. The convoluted structure of MCC, which also included a national entity in Canada and provincial/regional MCCs, all of which were legally independent, is discussed in detail in chapter 1. On 30 March 2012, after the research for this book was completed, the MCC binational office was dissolved and responsibility for the international programs was passed to the Canadian and US national offices.

5 The distinctive use of wagons has made this feature of Amish life a thoroughgoing cliché in contemporary North American media representations of the Amish (Weaver-Zercher's 2001; Umble and Weaver-Zercher 2008).

6 That is, "Mennonite Urban Professional." See Lesher's (1985) droll *The Muppie Manual*, a masterpiece in self-deprecating Mennonite humour.

7 My use of discursive tradition is indebted to Talal Asad (2009), who draws extensively for his own formulation from Catholic philosopher Alasdair McIntyre. Asad sees tradition as indicating a dynamic relationship with past, present, and future. He juxtaposes his understanding of tradition to notions of static social structure as well as arbitrary, heterogeneous collections. Traditions are internally diverse and permeated with contestation. Yet while a particular representation of any given tradition is always contestable, nevertheless they all "aspire to coherence." Tradition, therefore, does not imply a static or homogeneous entity but, rather, a dynamic, changing, and internally contested process.

8 Concepts of translation and mediation have garnered significant attention in the anthropology of development. My use of these concepts particularly draws upon the work of Mosse and Lewis (Mosse 2005; Lewis and Mosse 2006a; Lewis and Mosse 2006b) who, in turn, are indebted to Latour (1993; 1996; 2005).

9 Cronin (2003, 12). Within recent debates in the anthropology of Christianity concepts of continuity and disjuncture have gained particular prominence. In their research on modern Protestant Christianity Robbins (2003; 2004; 2007a; 2007b) and Keane (2007) advance the case for conversion as radical disrupture, while others critique or seek to nuance this approach, including through attention to other Christianities (Hann and Goltz 2010; see also Chua 2012; Mosse 2012). My treatment of these terms is less focused on conversion than on the broader, if still related, field of translation.

10 Sanneh (2009, 35).

11 See Ruth Coates's (1999, 134–6) reading of Mikhail Bakhtin's carnival, in which the apex and model is Christian agape love. Giving themes of translation a distinctly Mennonite hue, Al Dueck (2002, 78) relates stories of Babel (Genesis 11) and Pentecost (Acts 2) to concepts of translatability, and argues that translation is only possible when enacted through practices of "love … [and] servanthood." See also Tomlinson's (2017) discussion of dialogue via its purported monological opposite.

12 See especially Bebbington et al. (2006b); Green (2009); Markowitz (2001); and Watts (2001).

13 Hilhorst (2003, 2).

14 Rottenburg (2009, 60) describes development as a "black box" that conceals its operations from critical attention. Lewis and Mosse (2006b, 3) have pioneered the study of the "inner workings" of development organizations.

15 Mosse (2005, 8), emphasis in original.

16 My interactionist approach to studying cultural encounters was inspired by van der Veer (2001); Tsing (2005); Rothman (2011); and Keane (2007).

17 Pratt's (1991) influential article argues for a systematic analysis of contact zones. See also Clifford's (1997) discussion and, specifically addressing the context of development, Harris (2005).

18 Rothman (2011).

19 Latour (1993, 123).

20 Green (2009, 400); Quarles van Ufford et al. (2003, 18).

21 Ethnographic studies illuminate this heterogeneity with diverse actors now receiving attention. See, for example: Mosse (2005) and Redfield (2013) on transnational development networks, and also Hopgood (2006), Malkki (2015), Hilhorst (2003), and Riles (2000) on domestic actors within these international networks; Gupta (2012) and Hull (2012) on bureaucracy in South Asia; Rottenburg (2009) on development banks, consultants, and international experts.

22 Lewis and Mosse (2006b, 4).

23 MCC was created in the 1920s as an American consortium to organize disaster relief to distant kin (see chapter 1) and disasters have long had a particular resonance among North American Mennonites (Fountain 2016; Phillips 2014; Wiebe 1976).

24 Fassin (2010, 2012); Adams (2013). Historical studies have reconfigured our understanding of the birth and growth of humanitarianism by attending to the gestation of humanitarianism over the longue durée and by exploring its deep entanglements with religion. See especially: Abruzzo (2011); Barnett (2011); Curtis (2018); Davies (2013); Stamatov (2013); Tusan (2012); and Watenpaugh (2015). But while humanitarianism has a long history, contemporary forms of humanitarianism have been transformed under new political and economic dynamics. See Fearon (2008) and Jamison (2011, 365) for analysis of the exponential growth of humanitarianism after the end of the Cold War. Alongside the far-reaching geopolitical changes at this time, this rapid rise was also due to changes in media technology (Benthall 1993). Disaster events have consequently increasingly operated as a vortex for charitable activity drawing existing

actors into active participation as well as producing new formations designed to ameliorate its effects (Osa 2013). For further analysis of the relationships between religion and disaster relief see the introductions by Fountain, Bush, and Feener (2015b) and by Fountain and McLaughlin (2016) as well as the special thematic issues of which these are a part.

25 Partnership rhetoric began emerging in international development discourse in the early 1990s, but a decade later it was already ubiquitous (Lewis and Kanji 2009, 112–16). This rapid rise culminated in notions of partnership becoming enshrined in the Millennium Development Goals (MDGs) as goal eight when the MDGs were adopted by the United Nations in 2000 (Barnes and Brown 2011). It was precisely at this time that MCC adopted the language of partnership for its own programs.

26 The term belongs to Tsing (1993, 27), who argues incisively for the value of anthropological investigation of the peripheries.

27 On results-based management in MCC see Epp Weaver (2006).

28 Rottenburg (2009, xiv–xv).

29 On post-development see especially Escobar (1995); Sachs (1992).

30 Koop's (2014, 199) discussion of the terms "Anabaptist" and "Mennonite" is instructive for the ways in which they are used:

> The word "Mennonite" may refer to a particular cultural or ethnic tradition with religious roots, or it may refer to a particular religious orientation or church-denomination ... Often, scholars find themselves on a continuum employing the term as may be appropriate to their particular subject matter or disciplinary approach. The way in which the term "Anabaptist" is used may also vary. The English word derives from two Greek words meaning "rebaptizer." The name was given to those in the 16th-century who practiced the rebaptism of individuals, who had already received baptism as infants. In current scholarship, the term is often used to refer to the descendants of the 16th-century Anabaptist movement, such as present-day Amish, Hutterites, or Mennonites.

Koop further notes that recent theological writing increasingly uses terms such as "Anabaptist," "Anabaptist-Mennonite," "Believers Church," or "Evangelical Anabaptist" as a means of greater inclusiveness and to avoid the term "Mennonite," "which in some circles is seen as having a strong ethnic or cultural connotation" (203). Even within organizations such as the Mennonite Central Committee or Mennonite World Conference, where the term is endowed with highly capacious meanings, there is a lingering ambiguity about the ethnic overtones.

31 Fisher (1997).
32 Hilhorst (2003, 7).
33 Cornwall and Brock (2005, 1055). See also Cornwall (2007).
34 Li (2007).
35 Elisha (2011).
36 See, for example, Esteva (1992).
37 Tsing (2005, 7).
38 Robbins (2013, 457–9) commends a "new anthropology" that would "explore the different ways people organize their personal and collective lives in order to foster what they think of as good, and to study what it is like to live at least some of the time in light of such a project."
39 Numerous commentators have noted the remarkable absence of religion in development scholarship up until the early 2000s. See, for example: Ager and Ager (2011); Bornstein (2005); Clarke (2006); Clarke and Jennings (2008b); Deneulin and Bano (2009); Fountain (2013a); Haynes (2007); Hefferan and Fogarty (2010); Marshall (2001); Marshall and Keough (2004); Marshall and Van Saanen (2007); Rees (2011); Selinger (2004); Ter Haar (2011); Tvedt (2006); and Ver Beek (2000). A notable exception to the general rule of neglect was the landmark volume by Philip Quarles van Ufford and Matthew Schoffelleers (1988).
40 For detailed reviews of this literature see: Feener and Fountain (2018); Fountain (2013a); Fountain and Feener (2017); Fountain and Juul Petersen (2018); and Jones and Juul Petersen (2011).
41 Bornstein's (2005) seminal study of Christian NGOs in Zimbabwe pioneered the ethnography of religion and development. A series of studies have since followed, expanding the range and scope of investigation in terms of geographical locations, religious traditions, and developmental formations. A range of Christian (Hefferan 2007; Ngo 2018; Occhipinti 2005; Scheer, Fountain, and Feener 2018; Scherz 2014), Muslim (Atia 2013; Benthall and Bellion-Jourdan 2008; Juul Petersen 2016), and Buddhist (Huang 2009; Weller 1999) actors have since received attention, as, too, have various organizations that are not generally regarded as "faith-based" but that nevertheless are entangled in religious networks and genealogies (Hopgood 2006; Mosse 2005; Redfield 2013). Other studies have expanded beyond a focus on organizations to investigate humanitarian fields (Bornstein 2013), witchcraft (Smith 2008), refugee camps (Fiddian-Qasmiyeh 2014), compassionate communities (Caldwell 2017), "spiritual training" consultants (Rudnyckyj 2010), and materiality (Davidson 2016).
42 Deneulin and Rakodi (2011, 48).

43 Some years back I attended an academic conference in which a representative of the World Bank presented a paper with the aid of precisely such a graph as part of a presentation pertaining to the World Bank's approach to religion.

44 Asad (1983, 1993).

45 Cavanaugh (2009, 59). Other prominent critics of essentialist "religion," albeit coming from quite different perspectives, include: Dubuisson (2003); Fitzgerald (2003, 2007, 2011); Lash (1996); McCutcheon (1997); Milbank (2006); and van der Veer (2001).

46 For further critical analysis of the category of religion in relation to development, and proposals for innovative approaches for research, see: Fountain (2013a); Fountain, Bush, and Feener (2015a); Fountain and McLaughlin (2016); Feener and Fountain (2018); and Bolotta, Fountain, and Feener (2020).

47 Bornstein (2005, 29). Compare, for example, with Atia's (2011) study of "pious neoliberalism" and Islamic charities in Egypt; Benthall and Bellion-Jourdan's (2008, 7–28) description of Muslim charity as a kind of "financial worship"; and Hopgood's (2006; 2013) critical investigations into the "secular religiosity" of human rights.

48 Context is, as Dilley (2002) points out, a "social construct" that can be deployed in many different ways by anthropologists. Emphasizing different contexts enacts and makes some connections and downplays others. This contextualizing of MCC Indonesia as in between, however, is not merely my invention; rather, it reflects the ways in which MCCers themselves contextualized their work.

49 A seminal paper that helped spur this reconfiguration was Gupta and Ferguson's (1997b) classic essay. See also Coleman and Collins's (2006b) edited volume. On multi-sited ethnography see Marcus (1995; 1999); Hannerz (2003; 2004).

50 Watson (1995, 823–34).

51 Flueckiger (2006, 2). See also Flueckiger's (2015) study of popular forms of religiosity in *Everyday Hinduism*. The sociology of lived religion likewise examines forms of spirituality that occur in everyday life (Ammerman 2014; 2020).

52 Consider, for example, theologian and ethicist Michael Banner's (2014) wholehearted embrace of anthropology. He argues that moral theology ought to turn away from a preoccupation with philosophy in order to engage in a sustained and transformative conversation with social anthropology and its concern with how ethical problems are lived out in everyday practice.

53 This approach shares Sheldon Pollock's (2000) focus on the vernacular as action. However, it diverges from Pollock by framing the vernacular as a matter of lay or everyday practice rather than literary culture. I also do not share Pollock's juxtaposition of vernacular and cosmopolitan discourse. Indeed, in many ways, the Mennonite vernacular as practised within MCC is simultaneously parochial and cosmopolitan.

54 For example, Dyck (1970, 262).

55 This framing has similarities with Tse's (2014, 202) notion of "grounded theologies." While the theological for Tse is concerned with transcendence (both religious and secular), their groundedness focuses attention on "immanent processes of cultural place-making, the negotiation of social identities, and the formations of political boundaries" (ibid.). See also Tse (2015).

56 Within MCC two scholarly texts have been especially influential: Harold Bender's (1944) "Anabaptist Vision" and John Howard Yoder's (1972) *The Politics of Jesus*. At various times in the organization's history these have been virtually mandatory reading for MCC service workers. That these have had a far-ranging impact on more quotidian theological expressions speaks to the particular long-standing appreciation of Mennonite scholarly writings within MCC (Fountain and Yoder 2022). Since the 1990s Yoder's work has increasingly fallen out of favour in MCC, and in the broader Mennonite world, with growing public recognition of his sexual abuse. On Yoder's sexual abuse, see Goossen (2015); Roberts (2021).

57 MacIntyre (1988, 12).

58 Cannell (2006a, 1).

59 Robbins (2006). See also Fountain and Lau (2013).

60 Miller (1995).

61 Harding (1991).

62 Bornstein (2005, 30–6).

63 O'Neill (2010, xxvi–xxix).

64 Elisha (2011, 29–35).

65 I did encounter MCCers who identified as evangelical, both as Mennonites and among volunteers who came from other Protestant denominations. MCCers in Indonesia also included a couple of Zimbabwean volunteers who had a Pentecostal orientation.

66 Engelke (2002).

67 After finishing my field research, I found out that I am a descendent of Peter Nofziger, who was an Amish bishop in Ohio in the late nineteenth century. Family lore has it that my ancestor was evicted from the Amish on account of his desire to use brass harnesses for his horses. I haven't yet

been able to verify this story. I also have Swiss ancestry, including from Swiss Hunzikers. Hunziker is a common Swiss-German Mennonite family name. However, I do not know the religious inclinations of this side of my genealogy.

68 Bornstein (2005, 30–6).
69 Kahn (2011).
70 See particularly: Bretherton (2012); Fountain (2013c); Furani (2019); Lemons (2018); Robbins (2006; 2020); Robbins and Engelke (2010); Scharen (2005; 2012).
71 Reck (1983, 8).
72 Thornton (1983).
73 See also Eriksen (2006, 21), who regards the expunging of narration from anthropology to be central for the failure of a vibrant public anthropology.
74 Thornton (1983, 515).
75 Ibid., 517.
76 Milbank (2006, 102).
77 Ibid., 259–60. Milbank continues: "It is supposed, by people who are still temperamentally Victorians, that historiography gathers particular evidence, which is then dealt with by social science in a more universal fashion. Yet something like the converse is the case: there can only be a 'science' of particular, relatively stable formal systems, whereas history is the royal discipline which contemplates the transitions of systems, and so alone approaches, although in a sceptical spirit, the questions of the human as such, human society as such."
78 Jackson (1998, 35).
79 Geertz (1973, 3–30).
80 Geertz's propensity for universalizing was pilloried by Talal Asad (1983), who drew attention to the modern Protestantism of Geertz's understanding of religion.
81 On narrative anthropology see especially Jackson (2002); Bruner (1997); Aunger (1995); Brady (2004); and Ulin (1994). The reference to Aristotle's reading of anthropology in *Nicomachean Ethics* is alluded to by Jonathan Z. Smith (2004, 117).
82 Tsing (2005, 271).
83 Graeber (2009, 509).
84 Ortner (1995, 173–4). See also Tania Li's (2007, 30) detailed study of development projects in Indonesia, which likewise takes Ortner's ethnographic stance as a key point of departure.
85 Mosse and Lewis (2006, 3).

86 Indeed, moral peril is inherent to all ethnographic fieldwork. This is because a fieldworker will invariably be placed, at least at some point during their fieldwork, in situations of moral ambiguity as part and parcel of everyday life. The task of a moral ethnography is not to avoid or overcome such quandaries as the threat of danger is also always an opportunity for learning and discovery (Fountain 2013b).
87 Gingerich and Zimmerman (2006).
88 Lederach (1999, 13). Lederach thereby justifies the priority of narrativization by telling a story about preparing to tell other stories.
89 See, for example, Baniaga and Glick (2005); Dula and Epp Weaver (2007); Dyck (1981); Dyck and Dyck (1991); Kreider and Goossen (1988); Martin (1978); R. Yoder et al. (2004); S. Yoder (1998).
90 As Latour's (2005, 144) dialoguing Professor explains to the enquiring Student: "To describe, to be attentive to the concrete state of affairs, to find the uniquely adequate account of a given situation, I myself have always found this incredibly demanding."
91 I have in mind here the earlier discussion of the appropriateness of the category of religion and also particularly Milbank's (2006, 101–44) critique of the social scientific study of religion, which he regards as a "policing of the sublime." Because of its politically laden nature, and also its perceived inability of offer adequate descriptions, Milbank calls for the sociology of religion to "come to an end" or else redefine itself as a "faith."
92 Stoller (2020, 18–19). Stoller advocates for a Slow Anthropology Movement that parallels the global Slow Food Movement.
93 Supangkat's (2007) history of Salatiga provides useful historical background.
94 The most glaring omission is the absence of significant detail about MCC's work in Papua, which was regarded by many in MCC Indonesia as hosting some of MCC's most interesting work in the country. It is not easy for researchers to gain access to Papua, and, unfortunately, I was unable to visit the province.
95 Gupta (1995, 376).
96 Tsing (2005, x).
97 Gusterson (1997, 116).
98 See Marr (2005) and Fountain and Yoder (2022) for helpful introductions to this literature. Chapter 1 examines scholarship on MCC in more depth.
99 Clifford (1997, 56).
100 Kusenbach (2003).
101 Markowitz (2001, 43).

102 Watts (2001, 295).

103 For example, Hilhorst (2003); Mosse (2005, 11–14); Rottenburg (2009, xxxiv). The term "outsider-insider" was suggested by Bebbington et al. (2006b, 276).

104 With Iris's permission, her name is not a pseudonym.

105 Markowitz (2001, 44).

106 Hall (2009).

107 Nader (1972); Gusterson (1997); and Hannerz (2006).

108 Hilhorst (2003, 94).

109 Gupta and Ferguson (1997b, 1) argue that anthropologists have assumed that fieldwork is vital to the making of an anthropologist.

110 Jackson (1995, 163).

CHAPTER ONE

1 Longacre (1980, 55).

2 For an insightful critique of this approach see Malkki's (2015) anthropology of the "domestic arts" of humanitarianism. Epp Weaver (2020, 9) helpfully draws on Malkki's work to examine the needs and passions that have driven Mennonite involvement in MCC.

3 Gupta and Ferguson's (1997a) seminal, and much discussed, critique of the field as anthropological site, location, and method is indispensable. See also Coleman and Collins (2006b).

4 A terminological note is needed here. "Anabaptist" literally means "re-baptizer." The term "Mennonite" is taken from one of the early Anabaptist leaders, Menno Simons (1496–1561), who had been a Roman Catholic priest. While Anabaptism is often regarded as an overarching term (with Mennonites being located as a kind of Anabaptist along with Amish, Hutterites, Brethren in Christ, and Church of the Brethren), Mennonite and Anabaptist are often used interchangeably in colloquial and scholarly writing alike. Urry (1983, 257) helpfully situates the emergence of "Anabaptist" discourse among Mennonite scholars in the 1940s as part of a rhetorical competition over the writing of Mennonite history. He concludes, however, that the debate over historical essence is "meaningless, for the term 'Anabaptist' was a catch-all phrase for something distinctly 'Mennonite' in theology and church practice. Exactly *what* it was was no longer important, only that it existed and could justify differences between Mennonites and other religious groups in the past and the present" (emphasis in original). The Dutch "Doopsgezinde" and the

German "Täufer" both have extensive histories. In Indonesia, the term usually used today is "Mennonit." I treat Anabaptist and Mennonite as interchangeable.

5 North American Mennonites have tended to be wary of the term "denomination" for theological and ecclesial reasons. Since the Second World War, however, it has arguably become increasingly applicable (Sawatsky 1978).

6 For impressive introductions to North American Mennonite history see the three-volume series Mennonites in Canada (Epp 1974; Epp 1982; Regehr 1996) and the four-volume series Mennonite Experience in America (MacMaster 1985; Schlabach 1988; Juhnke 1989; P. Toews 1996).

7 Winland (1992) intriguingly compares Mennonite and Jewish "native scholarship."

8 Goossen (2017, 200).

9 For useful and accessible introductions to the "radical reformation," see Dixon (2017) and Roth (2002; 2017).

10 For analysis of the debates between monogenesis and polygenesis theories on the origins of Anabaptism see: Deppermann, Packull, and Stayer (1975); Packull (2008); Roth (2002); and Redekop (1989, 3–12).

11 Paul Peachey's (1954) classic historical sociology of the origins of the Swiss Anabaptists traces the social dynamics at work in transforming this urban movement into an increasingly agrarian one.

12 In *Salvation at Stake*, Gregory (1999) shows how persecution of religious dissenters, criminals, and heretics during the early modern period involved a "complex of martyrs" who suffered for their faith across Roman Catholic, Protestant, and Anabaptist groupings. At least as interesting as the violence inflicted against them was the martyrs' willingness to die and their desire to die well.

13 The second edition of van Braght's *Martyrer Spiegel*, published in 1685, was accompanied by copper engravings by Jan Luyken. See Weaver-Zercher (2016) and Roth (2013) on the social history of Mennonite engagement with the *Martyrs Mirror*.

14 Kniss (1997, 42), who discusses the "traditional sectarianism" of Mennonites in the United States.

15 Nolt (1999, 486–8).

16 Cannell (2006b, 44–5).

17 Juhnke (1996, 11) joins a long line of Mennonite scholars who suggest that the belief in Mennonite difference is not always backed up by practice.

18 In a couple of different papers, Burridge (1997; 2007) uses the phrase "separated and peculiar" to discuss Mennonite sociolinguistics in both Pennsylvania and Ontario.
19 Kniss (1997, 8).
20 Redekop (1989, 318) uses the term "quietistic." See also Graber Miller (1996, 1–22) for a discussion of these themes.
21 See Urry (2006, 85–8; 1983) on the history of Mennonite migrations to Russia and from Russia to Canada.
22 Along with the Religious Society of Friends (Quakers) and the Church of the Brethren.
23 For valuable overviews see Driedger and Kraybill (1994) and Sampson and Lederach (2000). Non-violence has never been adhered to with equal tenacity by all Mennonites. For example, in the 2006 Church Member Profile of Mennonite Church USA, the Church of the Brethren, and Brethren in Christ denominations, Conrad Kanagy (2007, 127–30) discusses the declining percentages among American Mennonites who, if faced with the military draft, say they would choose alternative service as conscientious objectors. He also notes that 25 percent of respondents indicated that they supported the war in Iraq. According to Kanagy, such responses indicate that these churches "are being pulled toward an allegiance to the nation that is becoming more important than our allegiance to Jesus Christ ... [and that] like other denominations that began with peacemaking commitments ... Mennonites may eventually abandon the radical peacemaking nature of the gospel."
24 Redekop (1989) explores how social relations have structured American Mennonite society.
25 Kniss's (1997, 65–7) study of shifts in authority over time among American Mennonites argues for a historical trajectory of diminishing powerful and centralized leadership. Such centralized authority reached its zenith with Harold S. Bender and Orie O. Miller, two of the foremost leaders in MCC from the 1940s to the 1960s. However, Kniss also suggests that tensions over leadership are inherent within Mennonite culture (5–9).
26 Redekop (1989, 74).
27 Ibid., 61–75.
28 Bush (1998, 5).
29 Urry (2006, 6).
30 The quotes are from Redekop (1989, 30), Kauffman and Driedger (1991), and Reimer (2008, 15), respectively. See also Loewen (2008); Nolt (1999); and Winland (1992; 1993). In the foreword to an introduction to Mennonites in Canada (Reimer 2008, 9), Urry suggests that the "problem

of too many names and too many varieties of Mennonites for any outsider to possibly comprehend is apparently long standing. In the early seventeenth century, the lawyer and humanist Hugo Grotius noted of Dutch Mennonites that they possessed so many separate groups 'that there is hardly anyone who knows their number, or their names.'"

31 Kniss (1997, 13).

32 For Sawatsky (1991, 171) these two groupings constitute the "two major Mennonite ethnicities," although he also posits the possibility of numerous "sub-ethnicities" within these dominant strains. In contrast, Redekop (1989, 34–5) claims that, while the ethos of each is identifiably different, "the two streams are basically part of the same source – the Anabaptist." Among Canadian Russian Mennonites, this category can be further divided in Kanadier and Russländer, terms that are used to differentiate between migration timings, with the former descending from immigrants who arrived in Canada in the 1870s and the latter arriving in the 1920s. Despite close kinship and denominational ties, the felt difference between these groups can be significant (Urry 1983, 251–2).

33 Urry (1983, 259), emphasis in original.

34 Of note here are roles national identification played within the merger of two of the largest Mennonite groupings, the General Conference Mennonite Church and the ("Old") Mennonite Church, both of which were established in the nineteenth century. Each was composed of various smaller groupings called conferences, and each contained conferences from both sides of the US-Canada border. Steiner (2003) points to Ontario as the first "integrated" Mennonite Conference in North America when, in 1988, three regional conferences amalgamated. Meetings over the next decade between General Conference and Mennonite Church leaders culminated in the merger of both conferences between 1999 and 2002, and also the simultaneous construction of integrated national bodies, Mennonite Church Canada, and Mennonite Church USA.

35 The quotes are from Redekop (1989, 29 and xii).

36 The quote is from Redekop (1989, 31). Although Redekop regards the "non-Germanic" group to be the future of Anabaptism, and perhaps even a more authentic embodiment of the tradition, his sociological study of Mennonite society exclusively focuses on "ethnic" Mennonites. Elizabeth Phelps's (2015; 2020) insightful anthropological study of Virginia Mennonites as they engage with new immigrants from Latin America is a sensitive and careful exploration of this cultural landscape.

37 See Bruno Dyck (2003) for a thorough and insightful analysis of the relational logics of this "game" as practised among Mennonites in Winnipeg.

38 Conrad Kanagy's *Road Signs for the Journey* (2007, 118–23) is a denominationally supported sociological profile of Mennonite Church USA.

39 See Goossen (2017). In an earlier article Goossen (2016, 137) argues:

> Placed in the context of the immediate postwar years, it rather appears symptomatic of a larger effort on the part of high-profile Mennonite leaders across Europe and the Americas to generate and popularize notions of global Anabaptist peoplehood, especially as encapsulated in the discourse of "Mennonite ethnicity." Noting that the vast majority of the world's Mennonites were directly descended from the Anabaptists of the sixteenth-century Reformation, supporters of this project maintained that their church was bound not merely by theological ties but also by an inherited culture, and even, perhaps, by hereditary bonds of blood. Like the members of other ethnically-defined communities – whether whole "nations" and "races" like the Germans, Czechs, or Jews, or smaller "tribes" and "clans" such as Kashubians, Schwabians, and Cherokees – Mennonites' historical experiences or common genes had supposedly predisposed them to exhibit a set of collective characteristics, ranging from emotional qualities such as thrift and severity to proclivities for certain professions and activities like agricultural work and four-part singing. In addition to a host of other factors, the emergence of the racial sciences in Germany and elsewhere directly influenced such thinking.

40 Sawatsky (1978, 237).

41 Heisey (2006). Many of these assemblies were hosted in Europe or North America. However, Mennonite World Conference gatherings have also been held in Brazil, India, Zimbabwe, Paraguay, and Indonesia.

42 Guenther (2011).

43 Heisey (2003, 5–15); Hostetter, Sider, and Steiner (2018).

44 BIC became an official member of MCC in 1940. BIC members participated extensively in MCC-run Civilian Public Service (CPS) camps during the Second World War (Heisey 2003, 10; Heisey 1995, 178–88). This involvement was actively solicited by MCC leadership who worked hard to enrol BIC members into supporting the organization. An important step was the appointment of prominent BIC leader C. Nelson Hostetter, Jr, to be the MCC's chairperson between 1953 and 1967 (see Sider 1982, 159–96). While numerous BIC members have served with MCC overseas and in North America nevertheless some BIC MCCers confessed to me a feeling of

marginality within the organization and the wider Mennonite peoplehood on account of their denominational heritage.

45 Heisey (2003, 12).

46 Sawatsky (1991, 113) cites John Redekop in his discussion of Patrick Friesen's Mennonite identity. By posing the question as to whether "Mennonite" is necessarily a religious category Sawatsky implicitly points to the contours of the category of "religion." Unfortunately, he does not directly address this issue in his argument. See also Urry (1983, 259).

47 For further discussion of the anthropology of Mennonite identity as contested and dynamic, and as caught in the midst of active tensions see Fountain (2020).

48 Urry (2006, 137–42); Epp (1980, 18–20); and Friesen (2018, 4).

49 Reimer and Guenther (2011, 355).

50 This rather innocuous beginning has been much discussed, debated, and mythologized (Dyck 1980a, 9–22; Hershberger 1970; Unruh 1952, 12–16; Juhnke 2011).

51 John Unruh's (1952, 11) early history of MCC, *In the Name of Christ: A History of the Mennonite Central Committee*, frames this initial relief effort as dedicated to serving the "household of faith."

52 Epp (1980, 23).

53 Epp (1980; 1983); Epp-Tiessen (2011); and Marr (2003).

54 Bush (1998, 29); Driedger and Kraybill (1994, 70).

55 Kehler (1970, 298).

56 Marr (2003, 17).

57 Unruh (1952, 17).

58 Mary Jean Kraybill's (2003, 220) memoir of growing up Mennonite in Lancaster County lists the Kratz story as one of the martyrdom narratives that formed the "air that I breathed." Prieb (1990, 59) quotes Hiebert as saying: "Brother Kratz lost his life in the service of suffering humanity. Serving humanity is serving God, and to give one's life for suffering humanity is doing so for Jesus' sake." See also the accounts by Showalter (2001) and King (2001).

59 Patzwald and Kostlevy (2005, 36) suggest that the "death of popular Goshen College student Clayton Kratz while serving as a relief worker in Russia cemented MCC in the Mennonite imagination." Similarly, Toews's (2006, 2) profile of Kratz states that "his sacrifice helped to infuse idealism into a fledgling organization." For Prieb (1990, 59), "the story of Kratz is in many ways the story of MCC."

60 Unruh (1952, 39).

61 Erb (1969, 161).

62 See Kniss (1997, 65–77) and also their respective biographies (Erb 1969; Keim 1998; Prieb 1990; Sharp 2015). Erb (1969, 161) writes: "The development and interpretation of the MCC concept became largely the work of Hiebert, Miller, and Bender, a strong team who supplemented each other and worked well together. They were arbitrary oftentimes, as we view decision-making today. But … they carried on their shoulders a coalition that was precarious, and an open forum would have wrecked the attempt."

63 See Bush (1998, 27–32) for a discussion of the American Mennonite experience during the First World War, and see Shaw (2009, 43–71) for the Canadian experience.

64 Unruh (1952, 230–73); Bush (1998); Charles (2002, 105); Hein (1998); Klippenstein (1998); Marr (2003, 47–55); and Goossen (1997, 15–17).

65 Dyck (1980b, 56).

66 Klets (2018).

67 Thiesen (1999) explores sympathy and support towards German National Socialism among Mennonite colonists who had departed Russia for Paraguay before the start of the Second World War. Redekop (1996) shows that a significant segment of Mennonites in Canada also found National Socialism appealing. Both Thiesen and Redekop begin by noting the apparent paradox of a pacifist denomination engaged in Nazi war efforts. Goossen (2018) argues that Nazi German leaders actively sought to enrol Mennonites into their vision of a racially cleansed Europe and that some Mennonite leaders proactively embraced and promulgated this. Jantzen and Thiesen's (2020) edited volume, *European Mennonites and the Holocaust*, provides a series of careful studies of Mennonite relationships with the Third Reich, including direct participation in genocide of Jews. As Klets (2018), Friesen (2018), and Urry (2006) note, however, Mennonites also collaborated with the Soviet state in a range of complicated ways; and Mennonite identification as "German" was never a straightforward process.

68 For example, Redekop (1980); Unruh (1952, 24–39 and 175–26); Dyck and Dyck (1991); and Regehr (1991). Both Canadian and Paraguayan governments were willing to receive Mennonite refugees. Paraguay offered appealing exemptions for Mennonite refugees to settle in the Chaco region (Dyck and Dyck 1991; Redekop 1980), where Russian Mennonite colonies had been established in the 1920s, also with MCC's assistance.

69 Smucker (2006 [1955], 22).

70 Russian Mennonite migrants to Canada in the 1920s came on credit, with the result that they owed an actual travel debt that had to be repaid to the Canadian Pacific Railway (Epp 1980, 28–9). But the sentiment of owing a reiseschuld that needed to be repaid was shared more broadly. Epp-Tiessen's (2013) history of the Mennonite Central Committee in Canada explores its origins in the Canadian Mennonite Board of Colonization (CMBC), a prominent Mennonite actor engaged in the resettlement of Mennonite refugees. Founded in 1922 to assist with the resettlement of Russian Mennonites, the CMBC merged with the Mennonite Central Relief Committee (MCRC) in 1960, which then merged with six other inter-Mennonite service organizations in 1963 to form the Mennonite Central Committee Canada. This organizational evolution is one of the ways in which MCC was indelibly linked with the arrival of Russian Mennonites in Canada.

71 Unruh (1952); Dyck (1980b).

72 The locus classicus for this new zeitgeist is President Harry Truman's 1949 inaugural speech, in which his famous "Point Four" called for the United States to "embark on a bold new program for making the benefits of our scientific advances and industrial progress available for the improvement and growth of underdeveloped areas." See especially Rist (2009, 69–79). Numerous studies have established a postwar explosion in the NGO movement while also tracing a much longer gestation with multiple and complex entanglements with religion (Barnett 2011; Bebbington et al. 2008; Ekbladh 2011; Stamatov 2013; Davies 2013). On American postwar developmentalism see also Immerwahr (2015); Cullather (2013); and Grubbs (2009).

73 See U. Bender (1969); C.W. Redekop (2001). CPS was succeeded by 1-W Service, over which MCC continued to have responsibility. Pax was the international arm of 1-W Service. Also during this period Voluntary Service (VS) programs were initiated, some of which were entrusted by Mennonite churches to MCC for administration and oversight. VS groups mainly operated within North America (Unruh 1952, 294–309).

74 Mathies (1996, 71–2). See also Eby (1972).

75 Marr 2003 (41–63); Epp-Tiessen (2013).

76 Epp (1980).

77 Heisey (1996, 57).

78 Heisey (1996) offers an incisive critique of the lack of attention women have received in the telling of the MCC story.

79 Marr (2003, 20).

80 Ibid., 85-7.

81 Bender established the legitimacy of his new platform of a newly activist Mennonite identity by grounding it in the history of the radical reformation. Many others have since followed this path in locating the innovations of MCC service as standing in continuity with tradition. One notable example is from Yoder, Redekop, and Jantzi's (2004, 46) *Development to a Different Drummer*, in which they argue that "MCC has tried to practice the faith described by Menno Simons, the sixteenth-century Anabaptist leader after whom the Mennonite Church is named, who wrote: 'True faith cannot lie sleeping, it clothes the naked, it comforts the sorrowful, it feeds the hungry, it shelters the destitute, it cares for the sick, it becomes all things to all people.'"

82 P. Toews (1996, 84).

83 Graeber Miller (1996, 9).

84 Marr (2003, 301). On the impact of Bender's Anabaptist Vision for MCC see also Hershberger (1957); Bush (1998, 64–9); and Kniss (1997, 64–8).

85 For a provocative argument about how understanding key words in any given culture is a powerful mode of socio-linguistic analysis see Wierzbicka (1997).

86 Bush (1998, 75–80).

87 Kraybill (1996, 22–3), emphasis in original.

88 Marr (2003, 265).

89 Epp Weaver (2020, 15).

90 Bush (1998, 78–9); P. Toews (1996, 157).

91 Juhnke (1996, 16).

92 Kniss (1997, 49).

93 Bush (1998, 272).

94 Ibid., 221.

95 Ibid., 29–31.

96 Lewis (2005, 207–9). One such popular periodization is Korten's (1990) famous linear and stadial typology for the successive "generations" of the NGO movement. Korten imagined that eventually NGOs would mature, such that their evolutionary growth would culminate in the triumphant emergence of a "people's movement." In contrast, MCC began as a people's movement by gathering and serving the "household of faith" (Reimer and Guenther 2011, 356).

97 Of course, MCC also receives donations from people who are not members of Mennonite churches, and, as I note below, it has received finances from the Canadian government. However, its primary communication strategies

and the main focus of its fundraising appeals remain directed towards North American Mennonites.

98 From 1968 through to 2013 MCC Canada received numerous significant grants from the Canadian International Development Agency (CIDA) to support projects around the world. Around the time of my fieldwork the CIDA grant component of MCC's international work came to just over US$10,000,000 out of the US$65,000,000 that was donated to MCC in the 2008–09 financial year (Mennonite Central Committee 2009). In 2013 the Harper government merged CIDA with the Department of Foreign Affairs. In 2015 the Department of Foreign Affairs, Trade and Development was rebranded as Global Affairs Canada. MCC Canada has been unsuccessful in attracting Canadian government support for its programs since the demise of CIDA. MCC US has consistently refused to channel US government funding.

99 Redekop (1989, 85) notes that the "entire Mennonite population" is involved with MCC.

100 The staff numbers were provided by the executive director during MCC's annual general meeting at Conrad Grebel College, Waterloo, Ontario, in June 2008. Also highlighted was the corresponding increase in finances during this same period.

101 Mathies (1996, 24).

102 Kraybill (1996, 24).

103 See Estes (1989) and Lehman (1998) for brief histories of the Illinois and Ohio relief sales, respectively.

104 Redekop (1993, 97).

105 In 2021 there were nineteen relief sales operating across the US and Canada, a reduction in part influenced by challenges from COVID-19.

106 Hartzler (2011).

107 Berry (2011, 306).

108 The name was changed to "My Coins Count" in 2016.

109 Hartzler (2011).

110 Redekop (1993, 84). For general introductions see: Hiebert and Miller (1929); Horst (1950); Unruh (1952); Kreider and Mathies (1996); Sampson and Lederach (2000); Yoder, Redekop, and Jantzi (2004); Dula and Epp Weaver (2007); and Epp Weaver (2011a; 2020). Marr's (2005) review essay of MCC historiography is useful. See also Fountain and Yoder (2022) for a discussion of this scholarly and critical habitus. For further historical background to MCC in the US see: P Toews (1996); Graber Miller (1996); and Bush (1998). For historical background on MCC in

Canada see: Epp (1980); Epp (1983); Regehr (1996); Marr (2003); and Epp-Tiessen (2013). Biographical literature on MCCers is also extensive, including authoritative biographies of early leaders Harold Bender (Keim 1998) and Orie O. Miller (Sharp 2015). See also Eby (1972); Erb (1969); Martin (1978); Miller (2015); and Prieb (1990). Dyck and Dyck's (1991) narrative history of MCC's work in Europe during and after the Second World War is iconic and widely distributed. Various MCC country programs have received attention, including Indonesia (S.K. Yoder 1998; see also L.M. Yoder 2006), Bolivia (Glick 1985), Palestine (Epp Weaver and Weaver 1999), and the Philippines (Baniaga and Glick 2005). The series of primary texts edited by C.J. Dyck in four volumes (1980a; 1980b; 1980c; 1981), with a final volume in the series added a few years later (Kreider and Goossen 1988), is collectively entitled *The MCC Story*. See also Redekop's (1993) review essay on this series. A number of special journal issues have been dedicated to examining MCC, including the July 1970 edition of *The Mennonite Quarterly Review* and the fall 1995 edition of *Conrad Grebel Review*. The centennial anniversary celebrations have added further publications, including the 2022 special issue of the *Journal of Mennonite Studies*. Much of the literature on MCC has been published by Canadian and American Mennonite publishing companies. See also doctoral dissertations by Jantzi (2000) and Welty (2010). Clearly, while MCC has rarely made it into development studies journals (one exception being Dicklitch and Rice 2004), it is only a "blind spot" (cf. Marshall 2001, 368) for certain sections of academia and/or the development industry. MCC has received extensive attention from Canadian and American Mennonite scholars.

111 In April 2012 it changed its name to *Mennonite World Review*, and then in September 2020 it merged with denominational magazine *The Mennonite* to become *Anabaptist World*.

112 R. Toews (1996, 52–3).

113 Schildt (2005).

114 Redekop (1993, 99).

115 Detweiler (2000); Wiebe (1976).

116 MTS Travel (n.d.).

117 J. Yoder (1989); Keahey et al. (2011); and Zwissler (2017).

118 Initially, Byler's work took place under the name Overseas Needlepoint and Crafts Project. In the 1970s it became known as the MCC Self Help Program and in the 1980s changed names again to SELFHELP Crafts of the World (J. Yoder 1989). The term "Ten Thousand Villages" is said to derive from a quote by Gandhi.

119 Urry (2006, 12).
120 Driedger and Kraybill (1994).
121 de León-Hartshorn et al. (2001); Marr (2001).
122 Graber Miller (1996); Bush (1998).
123 Shearer (2011).
124 Miller (2000, 8–19).
125 Marr (2003, 267).
126 Kreider (1970, 260).
127 Marr (2003, 17).
128 Kreider (1970, 245 and 253) describes MCC as a "generator of change" among North American Mennonites such that no other "institution or program of Mennonites approaches the MCC in the many ways it touches concretely the life of the home congregation." Oyer (1970, 212) suggests that it is difficult "to overestimate the significance" of MCC on sponsoring churches. Kraybill (1996, 23) points to the immense influence MCC has had on restructuring "the meaning and essence of Mennonite identity." Kraybill goes on to argue that it is as if MCC has "printed a new logo on the nametag of Mennonite identity" that states that "these are the people who serve the needs of others outside their tribal groups, who engage in active peacemaking, who witness to the international Kingdom of God, and who work in a collegial manner with other religious bodies around the world" (29).
129 For an extended discussion about MCC's canned meat see Fountain (2014).
130 The information on canned meat in this section is drawn from interviews with MCCers, supplemented by Jurgelski (2010); W. Yoder (2010); Suderman (n.d.); and the MCC website.
131 Kreider (1996, 7).
132 This information was provided on http://canning.mcc.org/canning/involved/.
133 I was part of a visiting group at the Ephrata Material Resource Centre in Lancaster County, Pennsylvania, when a staff member told us that this shift had been responsible for raising the cost of turkey in the US from forty-five cents to over one dollar a pound.
134 Fischer (2011) explores the contested and changing conceptualization of halal among the contemporary Malay Muslim diaspora and points to the increasing significance of halal practices during the twentieth century.
135 Jurgelski (2010).
136 W. Yoder (2010).
137 Ibid., 22 and 87.

138 This information was provided on http://canning.mcc.org/canning/recipe/.
139 W. Yoder (2010, 17).
140 Ibid., 67.
141 Ibid., 5.
142 This begins to break down in her own practice of giving and receiving, discussed towards the end of the book. Yoder is given an unexpected gift, which is said to exemplify the words of Jesus that: "It is more blessed to give than to receive." But Yoder adds that "the blessings flowed both ways!" (W. Yoder 2010, 85).
143 Ibid., vii and 32.
144 Ibid., 85-6.
145 Mennonite Central Committee (2007a). The second part, "Trees of Hope," which I do not discuss here, narrates the distribution of canned meat in Burundi as a part of a meat-for-work program for a reforestation project (Mennonite Central Committee 2007b).
146 Braun (2005). This regular column, written by Braun and Aiden Enns, seeks to "build on commonalities with 'orthodox' Mennonites, while also portraying new and unique expressions of Anabaptist faith" (Dyck 2005). The column's name is a parody of a former column in the same magazine called "Old Order Voice," which provided space to and for Old Order Mennonite voices. There is no discernible relationship between "New Order Voice" and the Indonesian regime of President Suharto.
147 Unruh's (1952) early history of MCC is entitled *In the Name of Christ*, although the motto's association with MCC pre-dated his usage. See also Epp Weaver (2020, 43–65).
148 W. Yoder (2010, 59).
149 The framing of the cans as conveying a "message" indicates that intent to evangelize may very well be present among at least some of those involved in the production process.
150 Given that the same equipment was used for processing pork, which is considered haram, or forbidden, by most Muslims, the meat does not meet orthodox halal or permissible food requirements. I do not know whether the lack of halal status was considered a problem among consumers of the meat or MCC's local partner in Iraq.
151 On the high levels of support for MCC within its constituency see especially Green and Krabill (2011).
152 Hilhorst (2003, 3–4).
153 Ibid., 5.

CHAPTER TWO

1 Loewen (1992).
2 cf. Appadurai (1988).
3 Feener (2013).
4 Rottenburg (2009, xxvi) frames the anthropology of development as focused on translation practices. His study examines "development experts as actors in interstitial spaces and on the boundary objects and traveling ideas of those actors."
5 Mosse (2005, 6–11). The focus on translation, however, is not new for the anthropology of development. The actor-oriented sociology of development, closely associated with Norman Long and the "Wageningen School" (Arce and Long 1992; Arce and Long 2000; Hilhorst 2003; Long 1989; Long 2001; Long and Long 1992), pioneered the study of translation by focusing on "interfaces" between different actors and the ambivalent mediators that are placed in between, and work across, these gaps. Anthropologists of the Association Euro-Africaine pour l'Anthropologie du Changement Social et du Développement (Euro-African Association for the Anthropology of Social Change and Development, APAD) have also usefully deployed translation as an analytical frame and have furnished numerous empirical studies of development *courtiers* and their influence on development flows, largely in Francophone Africa (Bierschenk et al. 2002; Neubert 1996; Olivier de Sardan 2005).
6 Lewis and Mosse (2006b); Mosse and Lewis (2006).
7 A notable exception is James Ferguson's (1994) study of the "anti-politics machine" in Lesotho, which, though sharing post-development concerns with discourses of development, also examines actual practices and interactions in great detail.
8 Bhabha (1994).
9 On this paradox see Cronin 2000 (100–1).
10 *Intercom* ran from January 1961 through to December 2005. It included articles, poems, stories, reports from the field, parables, cartoons, jokes, and formal announcements detailing shifts in organizational priorities. It operated as something of a transnational conversation among dispersed MCCers and therefore is an invaluable resource in offering a window into the pulse of the organization during this period. *Intercom* was distributed to both current MCCers and alumni.
11 The idea of active, interventionist translation is championed by Latour (1993, 78–82; see also Latour 1996; 1999; 2005). For Latour, every actor – and he includes all objects, human and non-human, within his

frame of reference – is a mediator capable of connecting dispersed and radically different objects across a world riddled with gaps. These mediators are also equally capable of failing to make these connections. Graham Harman (2009, 16) neatly summarizes Latour's approach: "No layer of the world is a transparent intermediary, since each is a medium: or in Latour's preferred term, a mediator. A mediator is not some sycophantic eunuch fanning its masters with palm-leaves, but always does new work of its own to shape the translation of forces from one point of reality to the next. Here as elsewhere, Latour's guiding maxim is to grant dignity even to the least grain of reality. Nothing is mere rubble to be used up or trampled by mightier actors. Nothing is a mere intermediary." Mosse (2005) deploys Latour's actor network theory in his study of transnational development. Chambon (2020) helpfully brings Latour's approach into conversation with the anthropology of Christianity in his study of the materiality of religion in China.

12 The point has been forcefully made by Asad (2003, 67–99).

13 Mahmood (2001; 2005).

14 For example, Wallace, Bornstein, and Chapman (2006), McNamara and Morse (2004), and Bebbington and Kothari (2006) all deploy the notion of "aid chain" in their analysis of development.

15 This included an informal paper that I shared among staff and volunteers in MCC Indonesia and that was distributed among some of MCC's staff in Akron and Winnipeg.

16 Eleven countries were directly affected by the tsunami, but because of its proximity to the epicentre of the earthquake North Sumatra in Indonesia was especially badly hit. For thorough overviews of the impact of the tsunami disaster see: Brusset and Evaluation Team (2009); Daly, Feener, and Reid (2012); Rofi et al. (2006); Telford and Cosgrave (2007); Telford et al. (2006); Clarke et al. (2010); and Silva (2010). On death-toll estimates see: Kenny et al. (2010, 4); Silva (2010, 8); Gaillard et al. (2008, 516); and Leitmann (2007, 144–5).

17 On the Aceh conflict see: Aspinall (2005; 2006; 2009); Aspinall and Crouch (2003); Bauman, Gazala, and Mengistu (2009); Daly, Feener, and Reid (2012); Drexler (2008); Kingsbury (2010); Miller (2009); Reid (2006); and Schulze (2004). Kingsbury (2010, 64) estimates that, during the height of the Military Operational Zone (*Daerah Operasi Militer*, DOM) period (1989–98) between 10,000 and 26,000 people were killed and up to 200,000 became refugees. See also Grayman, Good, and Good (2009) on conflict nightmares and trauma.

18 Brusset and Evaluation Team (2009, 83).

19 Hadiwinata (2003); Tsing (2005, 226).
20 Telford (2012, 30). Silva (2010, 33) proposes that a unique challenge with this relief operation was that there was "too much rather than too little money available." But this suggestion is mistaken. While in comparison to many other disaster responses the funding for the 2004 tsunami relief effort was extraordinary, it could also be pointed out – as an MCCer did to me – that the resources for reconstruction in Aceh were, at best, merely adequate and that those many other disasters across Asia and elsewhere were vastly, even grotesquely, under-resourced.
21 Shenk (2008).
22 Telford et al. (2006, 93).
23 For introductions to "Aidland," see Hindman and Fechter (2011) and Mosse (2011).
24 Olivier de Sardan (2005, 174).
25 Hilhorst (2003, 94).
26 The concern movement included some of the most prominent Mennonite scholars over the following three decades, including theologians John Howard Yoder, C. Norman Kraus, and John W. Miller, and sociologists Calvin Redekop and Paul Peachey. For more on the concern movement see Toews (1990; 1996, 232–6) and Redekop (1990).
27 And, for this reason, the "supply-driven" approach of the relief work in Aceh noted earlier was entirely against enshrined norms of program design and implementation.
28 MCC in-country leadership was known as "Country Representatives" (CRs) until 2007, when the name changed to "MCC Representatives" (MCC Reps).
29 IVEP was initiated by MCC in 1950 as the Agricultural Trainee Program, providing agricultural internships for European young men on Mennonite farms in North America. Over the following decades it underwent a series of changes until, in the 1970s, it morphed into the International Visitor Exchange Program. Later, the word "visitor" was switched with "volunteer" to reflect its current title. The first Indonesians to participate in the program joined in 1969. Participants were expected to be "committed to the Christian faith, single/unmarried, 18 to 30 years old, and able to speak English" as well as to have a "spirit of learning and service … [and] a desire to live a simple life" (Mennonite Central Committee n.d., 6–7). IVEP was often conceptualized in MCC Indonesia as an exchange program running in parallel to the Service and Learning Together (SALT) program, in which Canadian and American volunteers would undertake eleven months of service around the world.

30 This was apparent, for example, in the fact that, unlike the rest of the MCC staff in Aceh and across Indonesia, he was not invited to attend annual team meetings and retreats.

31 Secondment, the dominant mechanism through which expatriate MCCers worked in Indonesia by being "loaned" to other local organizations (see chapters 7 and 8), was also seen as being a kind of partnership that relied on Indonesian partners for its implementation.

32 On "partnership" within wider development discourse see: Brinkerhoff (2002); Cornwall (2007, 475); Cornwall and Brock (2005, 1047); Crawford (2003); Whaites (1999); and Alfini and Chambers (2007, 495).

33 Formal recognition as a *lembaga* or *yayasan* facilitated access to banking services and also provided the basis for negotiations with government agencies about access, movement, and operations.

34 Yoder (2008, 11).

35 Redfield (2013).

36 Interestingly, despite these traces of a peaceable theology, and despite MCC identifying itself as a peace organization, specific peace programs were not a major focus of MCC's activities. This is surprising given the clear needs stemming from the long history of violent conflict in Aceh. The major exception to this was MCC's financial support for around twenty Acehnese to attend the Mindanao Peacebuilding Institute (MPI) in mid-2008. MPI was founded in 2000 through the cooperative efforts of the Catholic Agency for Overseas Development (CAFOD), Catholic Relief Services (CRS), and MCC.

37 On Islamic history and identity in Aceh see especially Feener (2013) and Reid (2006).

38 In his classic anthropological study of Aceh in the 1960s, Siegel (1969) describes *meunasah* in a variety of ways. Men used these buildings "as a meeting place to discuss village problems and to pray together during the fasting month" (52). He also describes meunasah as places for training in chanting the Quran (150–4). Siegel glosses meunasah as both "buildings for religious purposes" (42) and a "dormitory and meeting place for men" (287). Feener's (2013, 61–6) study notes that *meunasah* are a "ubiquitous feature" of contemporary Acehnese villages, uses for Islamic religious education as well as social and political organization. See Fountain (2016, 178–9) for further discussion.

39 McGregor (2010, 742) also sites an example of an international NGO "portraying meunasah as the local equivalent of community centres."

40 Olivier de Sardan (2005, 173).

41 This strategy is proposed by Bebbington and Kothari (2006). My further research included interviews with MCC staff in Aceh, Central Java, Canada, and the US, as well as GenAssist staff in Indonesia. It did not include project "beneficiaries," CIDA personnel, or either of the consultants referred to in the narratives that follow.

42 See Salemink (2006, 103) for a discussion of mistranslation as enabling development interventions.

43 The final report for MCC's work in Aceh notes: "GenAssist is a partner that the Aceh office initially resisted using. While officially a local NGO, they were fully sponsored, supported and created by CRWRC North American office, an international NGO ... It was hard for us to see how supporting an organization like GenAssist provided a benefit that would be different than had MCC chosen to become operational itself ... We are currently very happy with our partnership with GenAssist, in all respects, but questions about our rationale for partnering with them still linger" (Yoder 2008, 16).

44 By June 2009 CIDA had helped fund the construction of 6,886 *rumah bantuan* in Aceh (CIDA 2009).

45 Hedman (2005; 2009).

46 Morrison (1998, 244–8). The Brundtland Commission (1987) report, *Our Common Future*, is widely regarded as playing a vital role in placing environmental issues and sustainability on the global political agenda.

47 "Continually changing priorities have also reflected sweeping global changes, altered ideological assumptions, shifts in political and commercial objectives, and efforts to make development assistance more saleable to sceptical taxpayers.... Like other donors, but with more alacrity than most, CIDA has associated itself with new fashions and policy thrusts" (Morrison 1998, 18–19).

48 Li (2007).

49 This teacher was familiar to MCC. New expatriate MCCers had begun taking Indonesian language classes with him since 2005. When I arrived in Indonesia, I also studied Indonesian with him. He was an outstanding cultural broker and language teacher.

50 Marr (2003, 205–6).

51 See Fountain (2012) for further discussion of these issues.

52 See Epp-Tiessen (2013).

53 Durie (1988, 101) notes a "wealth of dialect diversity" in Acehnese. Which dialect(s) the GenAssist staff used, however, I do not know.

54 Jed had heard, although had not been able to verify, that the project site had changed up to eight times before Ulee Tuy was finally confirmed.

55 The initial plan had been to build two hundred houses; however, GenAssist had been able to stretch the finances further than initially expected and so was able to build an extra twelve houses.

56 CIDA (2009).

57 This tripartite framing draws on Cronin (2000, 2): *intralingual* translation takes place within a single language, *interlingual* translation occurs between languages, and *intersemiotic* translation takes place between verbal and non-verbal sign systems.

58 Mosse and Lewis (2006, 16).

59 Hindman and Fechter (2011, 4). This observation parallels Venuti's (1995) claim that translators are often made to seem "invisible."

60 Bierschenk et al. (2002, 10).

61 The point about ignorance as inherent to development processes has been made by Quarles van Ufford (1993).

62 Geertz (1960a).

63 See Woodward (1989); Beatty (1999).

64 For example, the theme of Indonesian cultural brokerage was the focus of a Dutch conference in the early 1980s that explored colonial era go-betweens (Schutte and Sutherland 1982). In his analysis of the concept of "middlemen" in Indonesian history, Kuitenbrouwer (1982) rejects overly rigid approaches predicated on fully elaborated frameworks and instead proposes more inclusive and provisional studies that leave room for elucidation from empirical research. This approach assumes that the notion of broker is largely indeterminable. Kahin (1983, 136) critiques this overly elastic terminology. Scholarly literature on Indonesian brokers explores a diverse set of actors: Firman (2000, 15; 2004, 355) considers the role of property brokers (In. *calo tanah*) in facilitating land acquisition in Jakarta; Spaan (1994) and Lindquist (2012) analyze mediation in international migration; Visser (2008) addresses the roles of Indigenous governing elites in Papua under Dutch colonial rule; and Bosma and Raben (2008, xv) point to the important role that Indies-born Europeans, or Indische, played in Dutch Colonial Indies as "go-betweens, linking European and Asian aspects of the community."

65 Wolf (1956, 1,076).

66 Kuitenbrouwer (1982, 120).

67 Similarly, but specifically in the context of development programs, Heaton Shrestha (2006, 213) suggests that NGO workers in Nepal do not seek to bridge disjunctures but, rather, to keep distinct "the world of beneficiaries ... and the world of benefactors."

68 Another narrative from the Ulee Tuy housing project in Aceh provides a useful point of comparison. The advantage of partnership for MCC was apparent when it came to negotiating with the Aceh Transition Committee (Komite Peralihan Aceh, KPA) over contracts. KPA is a loose-knit group of former Free Aceh (Gerakan Aceh Merdeka, GAM) guerrillas who with "muscle and intimidation" (Aspinall 2007) pursue "rent" from reconstruction funds by monopolizing contracts for raw materials. According to the International Crisis Group (2009, 1) KPA extortion in Aceh during the reconstruction was "rampant." Avoiding KPA altogether was not a viable option. However, due to partnership, MCC did not have to. By devolving responsibility to its implementing partners, who in turn often devolved responsibility to other intermediaries, MCC buffered itself from facing unsavory decisions for collaboration between a peacebuilding NGO and an extortion racket.

69 EMEK is the mission organisation of Dutch, German, French, and Swiss Mennonites. It was organized soon after the Second World War.

70 On child sponsorship more generally see Bornstein (2001) and Kaell (2020).

71 Crous et al. (1987).

72 Bjork (2005).

73 Li (2007, 126).

74 Ibid.,132.

75 Olivier de Sardan (2005, 172).

76 Fassin (2012, 253) argues that humanitarianism "institutes a radically unequal order" between givers and receivers that is a "structural fact ... regardless of the motivations of actors." This relationship is "unavoidable, precisely because it is socially instituted, not the result of individual choices or conducts."

77 No MCCer ever framed their organization to me as a "funding agency." Yet the ability of MCCers to control funding flows meant that this label may be more applicable than they would have liked. Hilhorst (2003, 193) points out that "funding agencies" have almost completely "escaped ethnographic attention," and she calls for "the lifting of the veils on their representations, revealing the dynamics underneath, and looking at the practices of donor actors with a view to defining the meaning of their organizations and modes of legitimacy." She also suggests that funding agencies may "take on several roles or identities" (193). This multiplicity of identities reflects MCC's reality.

78 The phrase "transmission belts" is from Olivier de Sardan (2005, 167).

CHAPTER THREE

1 Van Biema (2003a).
2 The *Time* magazine "prospectus" for this story outlines three predetermined types of missionaries that reporters are asked to profile: "hard-core" or "gung-ho" evangelists, "those who provide serious aid but also evangelize," and those "who do only aid but are Christian organizations" (Rosenberg 2003).
3 Van Biema (2003b).
4 This was particularly as an earlier *Time* magazine article published in April 2003 had already addressed similar themes (McGeary 2003). Steve Weaver, a "Pennsylvania Mennonite," who worked for Christian World Service, is quoted in this earlier article as saying that "mixing proselytizing with humanitarian work is not appropriate at any time." MCC is itself identified as a "nonevangelical" agency whose leaders "forbid preaching."
5 Ron Mathies kindly gave me access to his personal file of correspondence on this issue on the basis that none of the authors would be identified in writing. I therefore do not use citations or indicate the position of the writer when quoting this material.
6 The question of what Edward Miller actually said was discussed extensively. What emerged is that Miller had three separate interviews with the reporter during which he engaged in wide-ranging discussion about diverse aspects of Christian humanitarianism, his own background and upbringing, and the work of MCC in war-torn Iraq. The few brief quotes cited in the insert were plucked from these interviews and deployed within a predefined script devoid of explanatory background and context. This script positioned MCC as the antithesis of a similarly caricatured American evangelicalism and fundamentalism with its macho aggressive evangelistic zeal and close association with a crusading Bush administration.
7 Schrag (2003).
8 Epp Weaver (2007, 13).
9 Hilhorst (2003, 106). See also: Bierschenk, Chauveau, and Olivier de Sardan (2002, 10); Mosse and Lewis (2006, 17); and Rottenburg (2009, xx).
10 There are currently three Indonesian Mennonite churches. In the 1970s, a splinter group under the leadership of Adi Sutanto, a charismatic GKMI pastor, separated to form a new church, Jemaat Kristen Indonesia (Christian Congregations of Indonesia, JKI). JKI is notable for its Pentecostal-style worship practices (Yoder 2006, 360–2). It was formally established as an independent church in 1985. This third Indonesian

Mennonite Church is active transnationally and has established congregations in the United States, the Netherlands, and Australia. It has historically been less closely associated with the work of MCC in Indonesia than have the other two churches.

11 Yoder (1990). Doopsgezinde Zendingsvereeniging changed its name to Doopsgezinde Zendingsraad in 1957. Doopsgezinde Zendingsraad is part of the inter-Mennonite European agency Europäisches Mennonitisches Evangelisationskomitee (EMEK).

12 Hoekema (1978); L.M. Yoder (2006, 28–31).

13 Russian Mennonite missionaries began evangelistic work in Sumatra in 1871 among ethnic Mandailing/Batak communities. After the devastation experienced by the Russian Mennonites during the 1920s and 1930s, the Russian Mennonite mission in the Dutch East Indies folded in the 1930s. The Mennonite congregations in Sumatra were subsequently incorporated within the larger Huria Kristen Batak Protestan denomination (Batak Christian Protestant Church, HKBP) (van den End and Weitjens 1999, 184). In the 1950s the Mennonite congregations separated out from HKBP to form Gereja Mennonite Mandailing (Mandailing Mennonite Church, GMM) (Bender and Yoder 2014). However, in 1976 the Mennonite congregations joined a newly formed regional church, Huria Kristen Batak Protestan Angkola (Angkola Batak Christian Protestant Church, HKBPA). Sigalingging (2016, 30–1) notes that when these Mennonite churches merged with the Lutheran HKBPA, they were given permission to maintain distinctive Mennonite practices in their church services. In 1950 Dutch Mennonites initiated a new mission in the Southwest of the Bird's Head region of Papua, which at the time was part of Dutch New Guinea. The mission planted churches among Inanwatan, Ayamaru, and Teminabuan communities (Timmer 2000, 13). In 1956 the Mennonite congregations were incorporated into what is now known as Gereja Kristen Injili di Tanah Papua (Evangelical Christian Church of Papua, GKI-Tanah Papua), although Mennonite missionaries remained active in the area for a few more years (Timmer 2000, 246–9).

14 Yoder (2017, 153).

15 Yoder (1989).

16 This strategy was developed under Pieter Jansz but was energetically pursued under the leadership of Jansz' son, Pieter Antonie Jansz, from 1881 (Hoekema, 2001; Yoder, 2017).

17 Zulkarnain (2019); Roth (2021, 97–8).

18 Yoder (2006, 43–8); Roth (2021, 107–13).

19 Yoder (2006, 49–54).

20 The group also used the Indonesian name Jemaat Kristen Mennonite Tionghoa, and, in the 1940s, it was known in Chinese as Tiong Hwa Kie Tok Kauw Hwee. See Hadianto (2008, 11); Roth (2021, 116).

21 Writing about this period, Yoder (2006, 142–3) discusses the dilemma faced by young Chinese Indonesian Mennonites who wanted to participate in the nationalist struggle and therefore "felt forced to lay aside their teaching of non-violence in order to participate actively in the struggle and unequivocally discredit accusations from Muslim groups that, being Christians (followers of the so-called 'Dutch religion'), they were surely supporters of Dutch colonial rule."

22 Dyck (1980b, 91–104); Reedy (1973, 41). In early 1947 Alan E. Kreider made a "preliminary study visit" to Indonesia in order to explore the possibility of MCC undertaking work in the newly emerging republic. Soon after, two MCC workers, Martin H. Schrag and William H. Yoder, were sent to Indonesia tasked with setting up the relief program. Orie O. Miller, MCC's executive secretary, visited in June 1947 to help organize the program.

23 Erb (1969, 164). Erb's sources for this are uncertain.

24 Yoder (2006, 200). As noted in chapter 1, while at this time numerous Canadian Mennonites were involved in MCC, it was formally an American Mennonite agency.

25 As Vickers (2005, 85–103) records, this region had been devastated by years of war and military rule.

26 Dyck (1980b, 94).

27 See also Redekop (1994, 76).

28 Yoder (2006, 258).

29 Yoder (2006, 201) narrates a meeting between GKMI leaders and Orie O. Miller in 1949 at which Miller refused to fund explicit evangelistic projects: "MCC identified itself not as a mission board but as a Christian relief and service organization." However, Yoder goes on to note that, while this division seemed clear to Mennonite churches, for "the churches in Indonesia it was strange and confusing" (202). More important, despite Miller's attempt to articulate clarity, this distinction tended to be thoroughly blurred in practice (202–3).

30 For discussions of various aspects of MCC's work with the Indonesian Mennonite churches see especially Yoder (2006) and Yoder (1998). Reedy (1973, 40–53) and Friesen (1995, 37–46) are also helpful on medical work.

31 Mennonite Central Committee Indonesia (1958).

32 Dyck (1980b, 99).

33 Ibid., 104.

34 None of the three Indonesian Mennonite Churches (GITJ, GKMI, and JKI) use translations of either "Mennonite" or "Anabaptist" in their titles. Nevertheless, all three are affiliated with Mennonite World Conference, the global umbrella body of Anabaptist church groups.

35 Reedy (1973, 38–40).

36 Shenk (1988, 110); Yoder (2006, 210).

37 Aritonang and Steenbrink (2008, 833). See also Titaley (2008, 80). For further background on the DGI see Rui (2018).

38 Yoder (2006, 194–6). The drive towards amalgamation in the DGI was only officially relinquished at a 1984 conference during which the name was changed from DGI to Persekutuan Gereja-Gereja di Indonesia (Fellowship of Churches in Indonesia, PGI). Ecumenical ties were still important, but the goal of uniformity of structure or liturgy was abandoned (Aritonang and Steenbrink 2008, 835; Titaley 2008, 84).

39 In discussing one such Protestant merger in Java during this period, Aritonang and Steenbrink (2008, 687) note that GITJ and GKMI were "a little more fortunate" because "as early as 1949, 1950 the North American Mennonite Central Committee (MCC) was able to send some personnel, and in 1953 Dutch and German mission workers, too, were welcome again" (emphasis in original). Yoder (2006, 194–6) also argues that the decision among GKMI leaders to remain independent was clearly influenced by the arrival of MCC in the Muria region in 1949, which "raised hopes for cooperation with the Mennonite churches of North America. This helped reduce the church's feelings of smallness and peculiarity."

40 Benedict Anderson's (1991) seminal study argues that the modern nation-state is an "imagined community." Just as nations are imagined, so too global denominational communities may be considered cultural artefacts.

41 During this early period MCC also carried out work in other Indonesian regions beyond Central Java, including: Tobelo, North Maluku (1957–66); Pakantan, North Sumatra (1971–75); and Kupang, West Timor (1955–67). These projects were all in partnership with various church-related agencies, although not all were directly connected with the Indonesian Mennonite churches.

42 Vickers (2005, 193).

43 Rich (1994, 34).

44 Guggenheim (2006, 119).

45 Lamoureux (2003, 78).

46 Tirtosudarmo (2001, 213).

47 Rich (1994, 34–8).

48 MCC initially formed a partnership with the Directorate General of Transmigration in the Department of Manpower and Transmigration. Following the formation of the independent Department of Transmigration in 1983, MCC's official relationship and sponsorship shifted to this new agency. Tirtosudarmo (2001, 205) notes other "migrations" of the office of resettlement through its checkered history. To be succinct, in this chapter the "Department of Transmigration" encompasses all these entities.

49 Cleary (1995).

50 "Pancasila" is a Sanskrit term meaning "five principles." It was declared the official ideology of the Indonesian state in the 1945 Constitution. However, the New Order state made use of the ideology in new and far-reaching ways. There is a vast literature on Pancasila in the New Order. See Morfit (1981), Hadiwinata (2003, 52–3), and Hadiz (2004) for useful introductions.

51 "NGO" can be translated into Indonesian in a number of ways; literally, as Organisasi Non-Pemerintah (ORNOP) or, according to the Indonesian state's preferred term, Lembaga Swadaya Masyarakat (LSM), meaning "Institution for People's Self-Reliance." Various other informal terms are also regularly used. For discussions on the terminology of naming Indonesian NGOs see Eldridge (1995, 12–16) and Hadiwinata (2003, 6–7).

52 The *asas tunggal* issue has been widely discussed in the literature on NGOs in Indonesia (Prawiranegara 1984; Mujiburrahman 2006, 149–53; Eldridge 1995, 45–51; Hefner 2000, 17; Abbas 2021, 144–6). Law no. 3/1985 required all political parties to make Pancasila their sole basis. A few months later, Law no. 8/1985 required the same for all social or mass organizations, ORMAS or peoples' organizations (In. *organisasi masyarakat*), which included voluntary, professional, and religious organizations (Intan 2006, 58). On New Order suppression of civil society in Indonesia see also: Collins (2007, 15–20); Eldridge (1989; 1996); Honna (2001); and Nyman (2006, 35–6; 2009).

53 Hefner (2000, 92). See also van Klinken and Barker (2009, 2) who argue that the New Order was plagued by "internal contradictions" and "competing groups."

54 For analysis of the New Order's technocratic approach to development see: Feener (2013, 263–7); Honna (2001); Li (2007, 61–95); McDougall (1979); and Schlegel (1979). Tsing (2005, 21) regards development as the "state religion" of the New Order.

55 Mennonite Central Committee (1985, 3–4).

56 See Glick (1985, 31) who identifies in-country leadership change as a key factor in the transformation of MCC Bolivia's program in the late 1960s. Epp Weaver and Weaver (1999, 54–5) also argue that the transition to a more proactive political stance within MCC Palestine in the mid-1970s was due to leadership change.

57 The locations and timing for each of these *transmigrasi* programs are: Way Abung II, North Lampung, Southern Sumatra (1975–83); Tulang Bawang, North Lampung, Southern Sumatra (1980–85); Rasau Jaya, West Kalimantan (1980–85); and Mayoa, Poso, Central Sulawesi (1985–91).

58 Bowman (1978).

59 This is reflected in their fulsome titles. For example: "Agricultural Research on Rasau Jaya Peat Soil: Report on MCC Agricultural Research Activities in Rasau Jaya, Kalbar" (Caldwell et al. 1986); "The Use of Credit in Integrated Rural Development: Report on the MCC Livestock Program in the Tulang Bawang and Rasau Jaya Second Stage Development Project with a Focus on Integrating Rural Credit and Pre-Cooperative Group Development" (Harder 1986); "Report on Activities of the Small Irrigation Improvement Project in the Mayoa Transmigration Site Implemented by Department of Transmigration and Mennonite Central Committee 1988–1989" (Mennonite Central Committee 1989); and "From Livestock Credit to Establishing Farmers' Cooperatives: The Changing Focus of MCC Indonesia" (Jurey 1984).

60 Li (2007).

61 On broader discourses of agricultural development see Bunch (1982) and Chambers (1983). Epp Weaver and Weaver (1999, 55) in their history of MCC in Palestine note that the Hillsboro Resolution, passed at the 1974 MCC Annual General Meeting in Kansas, called on MCC "to strengthen its rural development projects worldwide." This precipitated a decade of agriculturally focused development work by MCC Palestine. Baniaga and Liechty Glick (2005, 131–9) include a chapter on agriculture in their edited collection of documents on MCC in the Philippines. The chapter is particularly focused on the 1970s and 1980s. The chapter on MCC's work in Bangladesh by Kreider and Goossen (1988, 163–76) emphasizes how, in the early 1970s, "agricultural development was the kingpin on which MCC's broad strategy rested" (169). Between the 1960s and 1980s, the MCC newsletter *Intercom* features numerous articles by MCCers exploring dimensions of their rural development work, particularly around the time of the Hillsboro Resolution (see Mennonite Central Committee 1974). For example, Erb (1968) details how to construct a "forage chopper." Writing in 1970, Kehler (1970, 302) proposes a certain cultural affinity between

Mennonites and agricultural development: "Mennonites have been people of the soil for hundreds of years. It is quite understandable, therefore, that they would think rather quickly of using their expertise in this area to help struggling farmers in underdeveloped countries."

62 Hadiwinata (2003, 121) notes that Bimas "provided farmers with a package of services which included the provision of high yielding varieties (HYVs) seeds, operating credit, guidance from the PPLs (extension workers) stationed in each village, fertilizer and pesticides at subsidised rates." See also Tirtosudarmo (2001, 201) and Rieffel (1969).

63 The Working Agreement, signed by representatives of both MCC and the Department of Transmigration, stated that transmigration "is a good program and should be supported internationally because it reduces population pressure on Java and Bali; and more importantly, it brings substantially more land into production. This of course helps reduce the yearly shortfall of food production within Indonesia. The Mennonite Central Committee supports this program and wishes to participate in a modest way with the Government in the implementation thereof. MCC can make a positive contribution to the total effort because of its seasoned experience in rural community development on the international scene. Furthermore, MCC has had experience with transmigration program in other parts of the world" (Mennonite Central Committee and Directorate General of Transmigration 1980).

64 Harder (1985, 1–2).

65 Froese (1980).

66 Froese (1981).

67 Mennonite Central Committee (1979).

68 These personnel will look after the interests of the villagers even before their own. They learn the language throughly [*sic*]. They study the culture, and where possible and proper, even try to become a part of it. They make special efforts to get to know the villagers on an individual basis. He [*sic*] strives to be a good listener. He discusses the problems facing the villagers. He tries to help the villagers understand the many economic, political, and economic forces that shape their lives. From this kind of interchange, a 'participant observer' type survey can be carried out. The practioner [*sic*] does a survey of the village by becoming a participant in the village routine. This type of survey usually provides a much truer picture of the situation than the standard questionnaire surveys, even though it is often used to supplement the former. It is this kind of immersion into the village life that builds the dynamic partnership (Mennonite Central Committee 1979).

69 For example, in the final report for the Mayoa Transmigration Program in Sulawesi (Shires et al. 1991), MCC is referred to as: "an international relief and development agency supported by the Mennonite and Brethren in Christ churches of North America (USA and Canada) … MCC service is offered without any political, cultural, racial or religious strings attached. The main aim is to serve all with love."

70 Mujiburrahman (2006, 54–6; see also 57–104).

71 Mujiburrahman (2006, 81–91). The decrees were issued in August 1978 by the minister of religion. Decree no. 70 stipulated that "religious propagation is not allowed (1) to be directed to the people who have another religion; (2) to use money, clothes, medicine etc. as a means to convert people; (3) to be carried out by spreading pamphlets, books, bulletins and magazines to the houses of people who have another religion; (4) to be carried out by a door-to-door visit to the houses of people who have another religion." Decree no.77 indicates "that any form of aid (personnel and/or material) given by a foreign Government, organization or individual to a religious institution should be based on the agreement or recommendation of the Minister of Religion." Feener (2007, 99–100) notes that these decrees were preceded by a 1968 decree by President Suharto that "called for a toning down of Christian missionary activity in predominantly Muslim areas of the country."

72 In keeping with the pseudonymous designation I have used for interview material in this section, references to "Howard Miller" in the archival material likewise deploy the same pseudonym.

73 For further background, discussion, and analysis of MCC's work in West Kalimantan see: Fountain (2012); Fountain and Yoder (2018).

74 MCC News Service (1977).

75 Mennonite Central Committee (1985).

76 Shenk (1988, 106).

77 P. Toews (1996, 208). See also Glick (1985, 29) for discussion of MCC evangelism in Bolivia.

78 Roosa (2006).

79 Cribb (2001). See also Cribb (2002, 557–9); Cribb (2009).

80 Menchik (2014, 594). See also Menchik (2016).

81 Connolly (2009, 182).

82 On religion and the techno-politics of development see Scheer, Fountain, and Feener (2018), and, especially, Feener and Scheer's (2018) introductory chapter.

83 Mujiburrahman (2006, 81–91).

84 Ibid., 90.

85 Feener (2014, 4).
86 Mujiburrahman (2006, 81).
87 Aritonang and Steenbrink (2008, 521).
88 Aragon (2000).
89 Ibid., 275.
90 Ibid., 277 and 305.
91 Ibid., 279–80.
92 Ibid., 310. See also Connolly (2009) and Larsen (2018) for further discussion of the politics of Christianity in the interior regions of Indonesia.
93 cf. Hartch (2006).
94 Aragon (2000, 305).
95 Engelke (2009).
96 The relationship between mission and secularism is complex and contested. Larry Grubbs (2009) argues that American development workers in Africa in the 1960s were "secular missionaries." Mennonite missionary-turned-anthropologist Elmer Miller (1970) complicates this by arguing that Christian missionaries were influential agents of secularization around the world as they tended to seek scientific explanations for day-to-day experiences. Miller proposes, therefore, that Christian mission projects of evangelism were also secular missions. See Fountain (2015) for further discussion of development as proselytizing. See also Klassen (2011); Milbank (2006); Asad (2003); and Taylor (2007) on Christian entanglements in the history of secularity.
97 This said, David Froese's resignation, discussed above, also suggests that discourses and practices are not entirely separated either, at least for those who inhabit the tensions that inhere in the gaps between them.
98 Hovland (2008, 172).

CHAPTER FOUR

1 Nolt (2011).
2 Latour (1996, 85–6).
3 Mosse and Lewis (2006, 13).
4 On policy as enrolment strategy see Mosse (2004; 2005, 14–16).
5 See Mennonite Central Committee (1999). The "rusty nail" document replaced the previous mission statement known as the "purple egg," presumably also for the aesthetic associations.
6 Four-part a cappella is often emically regarded as definitively "Mennonite." However, such singing practices are more characteristic of some Mennonite groups than others.

7 Kasdorf (2009, 91).

8 Empahsis in original. Without understatement, Kasdorf (2009, 90–1) captures a dynamic I encountered during my fieldwork:

> For some time I've tried to capture in language what happens when traditional Mennonites sing in four parts, to describe that remarkable quality of passion and joy that makes heavy Anabaptist bodies almost levitate during congregational singing … Unlike imaginative writing, singing uniquely binds people in a shared task and creates an artistic and spiritual event that all can experience at once. Mennonites raised in traditional congregations learn early how to blend their voices in four-part harmony. On a Sunday morning, ordinary homemakers, farmers, and business folk sing with heart-rending clarity and passion. On Sunday evenings, Cambridge intellectuals gathered for worship at the tiny Mennonite fellowship in Sommerville, Massachusetts, sing the old hymns a cappella. At Ohio family reunions, several generations sing together for entire afternoons. As the last note of a hymn barely falls silent, someone calls out the number of the next. During my adolescence, my apparently assimilated Mennonite peers dragged hymnals along on bus trips and campouts so we could practice the most complicated, several-paged arrangements at the back of the hymnal – not unlike our Amish counterparts, whose primary social activity is the hymn sing.

9 Information was provided on http://mcc.org/serve.

10 The application of these three screens in hiring processes was uneven, as my conversations and interviews with expatriate MCCers about the recruitment process revealed. Some prospective MCCers were grilled closely about matters doctrinal and ecclesial, while others merely had informal chats consisting of nostalgic reminiscence of previous encounters with the organization. The MCC Reps in Indonesia had taken the initiative to make the hiring process symmetrical between expats and Indonesian staff. Some other MCC country programs in Asia did not use these screens and consequently hired staff from a range of religious backgrounds.

11 The final page of the "rusty nail" document is a list of references. These include "Historical/Theological" texts and "MCC Documents," primarily written by Mennonite authors. However, the relationship of these documents to MCC's work – whether they are normative or descriptive, binding or merely helpful – is unclear. The following is also included under the "Biblical" heading: "There are many texts which inspire the MCC mission. Some typical ones would include: Lev. 25, Deut. 5, Isa 58:6–8, 61:1–4,

Micah 6:6–8, Matt. 5–8, 25:31–46, Luke 4, 10:25–27, John 13:31–35, 15, Rom. 12–13, II Cor. 8–9, Gal. 5–6, Eph. 2:14–22, Phil. 2:1–11, Col. 3:12–17, Heb. 13:1–16, James, I John 3–4." What these texts *do* for MCC's mission is ambiguous and opaque.

12 For further discussion and analysis of these dynamics see Fountain (2017).

13 Brubacher (1991).

14 I draw on two archival sources for the material in this section. The first is Nancy Heisey's personal collection of documents, which she kindly granted me permission to peruse. The second is the official MCC files archived in Akron, Pennsylvania. Given the nature of the material, I have not used pseudonyms in this section for authors of the archived documents.

15 An article in another issue of *Intercom* published just prior to Brubacher's article discusses both documents (Rupley 1991). The mission statement in 1991 was only slightly modified in the 1999 "rusty nail" version. "Growing Edges" were areas that MCC binational affirmed as cross-cutting themes that deserved increased attention but were generally not regarded as obligatory. The growing edges for the period from 1991 to 1994 included increasing work in Islamic contexts, educational programs with North American churches, overseas conciliation work, expanding the visitor exchange programs, and exploring programs among Indigenous peoples in Latin America and pastoralists in Africa.

16 In a letter to Nancy Heisey, who authored the draft missiological statements discussed below, Brubacher (1992) wrote: "I would like the statement to be above all practical and useful as opposed to theoretical. I would like the final product to be a useful document for all workers within MCC. I see it primarily as an internal document, but if, at the end, there seems to be reason to share it more broadly, we can then make that decision ... [T]he document should help all of us understand our role in the world as a mission agency with the rather unique mandate not to plant churches (although to say that reflects a fairly narrow view of mission and of church)."

17 See *Research Survey Report on MCC Missiology Dialogue* by Foster and colleagues (1992).

18 The results were published in Heisey and Longacre's *Mennonite International Study Project* (1990).

19 Heisey (1993b).

20 See Fountain and Yoder (2022) for further analysis of this dynamic in connection with anniversary celebrations of MCC, including its centennial commemoration in 2021.

21 Heisey (1993a).

22 Heisey wrote: "While our work is very important, neither any task nor any particular end result is primary. Our love of God and right relationships with neighbors are the only end we need seek. God will make of that what is necessary for God's mission in the world."

23 Heisey (1993b).

24 Brubacher (1993).

25 Mosse (2005, 14).

26 Ibid., 21.

27 Ibid., 35.

28 The language of public and hidden transcripts is borrowed from Scott (1990).

29 Mosse (2005, 46).

30 Cornwall (2007, 472) poses a parallel argument in her analysis of development buzzwords. For Cornwall many of the most common terms in development "gain their purchase and power through their vague and euphemistic qualities, their capacity to embrace a multitude of possible meanings, and their normative resonance." In their analysis of the concept of "social capital" in the World Bank, Bebbington and colleagues (2006a) make the same case. While the term itself has had its fair share of both detractors and advocates, in their conclusion the authors argue that much of this has been overblown. By paying close attention to the practices and meanings of social capital within various parts of the (exceedingly complex) World Bank, they suggest that the term is inherently polyvocal. It is not that the concept of social capital is irrelevant to World Bank practices but that, in and of itself, it is not determinative. Instead, "the devil is in the details" (274). For those agitating for progressive change in the World Bank, social capital was relationally advantageous for coalition building. This work of "enrolling" others into a common project took place through "broadening and blurring the core ideas associated with the project, in order to make it intelligible, interesting, and motivating" (277). Here, therefore, development policy was seen as necessarily vague and flexible.

31 Mosse (2005, 230), emphasis in original.

32 Ibid, 14.

33 Liechty (1991).

34 Miller (1992).

35 The phrase "unity amidst diversity" was the title of an edited publication celebrating MCC's seventy-fifth anniversary (Kreider and Mathies 1996).

36 Kraybill (1996, 37).

37 The "table" metaphor is used in the title of the edited publication celebrating MCC's ninetieth anniversary (Epp Weaver 2011b). In his introduction, Epp Weaver (2011a) roots the notion of table in ideas of hosting, welcome, food, and meetings. He also directly evokes the table of "Eucharistic communion" and thereby locates MCC's work within a divine economy of "excessive grace" and "thanksgiving." Andrew Beatty's (1999) meditations on a rather different ritual meal, the Javanese *slamatan*, provides an interesting point of comparison. The *slamatan* has been an enduring fixture for the anthropology of religion since Clifford Geertz's (1960b) seminal study located this communal feast at the centre of Javanese ritual practices. Beatty proposes that "traditionalist" and "modernist" Muslims in East Java are willing to gather around the same ritual meal, despite vast theological differences, precisely because the meanings of the ritual are left indeterminate. Clouded in opaque metaphors and ambiguous explanations, the *slamatan* is both central and obstinately irresolute. Religious conflict is avoided and communal harmony is manifested precisely through a suppression of the need for shared and common understanding. Just as Beatty's heterogeneous Muslims practise togetherness through an absence of forthright communication, so too Mennonites of all types participate around the "table" of MCC by putting aside the need for a common theology.

38 Only a portion of the funds raised during the Leamington event went to MCC, with other local Christian organizations also receiving a share of the donations. Nevertheless, the Leamington event shared the same elements as did relief sales dedicated only to raising money for MCC.

39 Beck (2004, 188) notes the following in his illuminating analysis of the Michiana Relief Sale in Elkhart, Indiana: "What these people sense – and what the folklorist knows – is that the Mennonite Relief Sale is also a folk festival. It is an unselfconscious expressive performance by Mennonites of their ethnic identity. The relief sale, as festival, strengthens the Michiana Mennonite community as much as it relieves suffering in the wider world."

40 "About Us," Christian Aid Ministries website, https://christianaidministries.org/about/#what-we-do.

41 Nolt (2011, 147).

42 Ibid., 148.

43 Urbane Peachey (2022) provides a detailed historical survey of Peace Section.

44 Driedger and Kraybill (1994, 142–5).

45 For example, Paul Toews (1996, 329) describes an MCC Peace Section pamphlet entitled *The Draft Should Be Abolished*, published in May 1970, which argues that the special privileges that the historic peace churches obtained for conscientious objection and alternative service were inequitable and ought also to be reconsidered. This pamphlet served as a radical critique not only of the American military complex but also of Mennonite traditions of peacemaking, which, since the Second World War, had sought special exemption for their own members while avoiding direct confrontation with the US government.

46 Driedger and Kraybill (1994, 142–5).

47 The phrase is Miller's (2000, 6).

48 Dyck and Dyck (1991, 364–82). An earlier paper by Peter Dyck (1970) also examines these issues.

49 Kraus (1994); Classen (2003).

50 Lind (n.d.).

51 Including papers by Peter Dyck (n.d.; 1968; 1979), a paper by Lind (1988), and an unpublished monograph by Lawrence Yoder.

52 G.W. Schlabach (1991). At the time of writing Schlabach was a member of Kern Road Mennonite Church in South Bend, Indiana. In 2004 Schlabach converted to Roman Catholicism and now regards himself as a "Mennonite Catholic" (Schlabach 2007).

53 G.W. Schlabach (1991, 83). Mirroring Edward Miller's comments cited in chapter 3, and perhaps also presaging his conversion to Roman Catholicism, Schlabach states that Christians from the west "have at least as much to learn from the churches of the South as they have to give" (95).

54 Schlabach (2001, 41).

55 Ibid., 42.

56 Schlabach's argument reflects a recurring theme among Mennonite writers. For Peter Dyck (1970, 262), although Mennonites have long lacked a clear systematized theology of service, this absence was largely seen as a "semantic problem" because Mennonites have a long tradition of addressing their "philosophy of service." It is not clear from Dyck's discussion what, exactly, he thinks is the difference between philosophy and theology. Robert Friedmann (1990, 4) proposes that Mennonites have historically lacked a systematic theology "comparable to … the Reformers of the sixteenth century" such that analysis of Mennonite theological thought must be primarily concerned with an "implied" rather than an "explicit system of theology." Although, as we have seen, both CAM and

Peace Section clearly did not consider implicit theological articulation as sufficient for their purposes.

57 Three questions were used to guide the consultations: "What is the task that God is calling MCC to in the 21st century (our purpose)? To whom is MCC accountable (who is the 'keeper of the MCC soul')? What is the appropriate structure for ensuring that the values and principles held by MCC are effectively expressed at every level and drive exemplary programming?"

58 Terichow (2009).

59 Despite generally being regarded as non-credal, Mennonites have been prodigious producers of statements of faith over the centuries, but these have tended to be at the level of churches or conferences. See Fountain (2017) for further discussion of Mennonite approaches to credal articulation.

60 Walker (2011).

61 This process was concluded in March 2012, when the binational MCC organization was officially dissolved and MCC Canada and MCC US were commissioned to jointly carry out MCC's international programs.

62 This makes the fifty-year story of Mennonite Scholarship Commission discussed in chapter 2 even more exceptional.

63 Green and Krabill (2011).

64 Grace et al (1995, 384).

65 This is a reworking of Mosse's (2004) question: "Is good policy unimplementable?"

CHAPTER FIVE

1 The phrase was coined by Bernard Lewis (1990) and was popularized by Samuel Huntington (1993; 1997). Both scholars drew upon and reinterpreted a longer tradition of civilizational thinking (Dabashi 2001). Abbas (2021, 39–44) helpfully shows that civilizational framings are not the exclusive prerogative of Western geopolitical imaginations.

2 The literature on this topic is vast. For examples of discourse analysis of media coverage of Islam after 9/11 see especially Ibrahim (2010); Jackson (2010); and Watt (2008).

3 Leverett and Leverett (2010).

4 Mahmood (2005, 189). Yet, perhaps ironically, at the same time as it chastised the failures of insufficiently privatized Islam, the Bush administration actively encouraged new forms of Christian religion in the American public sphere. The Bush administration coincided and helped catalyze seismic shifts in the entanglements between religion, market, and

the state. This included emergent forms of "Christian capitalism" (Moreton 2009) and new mechanisms for the provision of social services and disaster relief facilitated under the rubric of "faith-based initiatives." See Feener and Fountain (2018, 4). For further analysis of the faith-based initiative in the US see: Black et al. (2004); Formicola et al. (2003); and Hackworth (2012).

5 Dula and Epp Weaver (2007).

6 See Herr and Zimmerman Herr (2007), who identify building bridges as "a common metaphor for peacemaking."

7 Tsing (2005, 4–9).

8 Ibid., 267.

9 Hope, in Miyazaki's (2006) framing, is a "prospective momentum."

10 The idea of MCC as a "peace agency" has been an important and long-standing historical framing (Lapp 1970).

11 Epp-Tiessen (2009) uses precisely this language to frame peace as the "essence" of MCC.

12 Koop (2016). As Koop examines in the writings of Wilhelm Mannhardt, an eighteenth-century Prussian Mennonite, this stance is not without historical and contemporary contestation, a point I examine below.

13 Wiebe (1962, 11–12).

14 Merry (2000, 216–17). Merry goes on to suggest that Mennonite interest in peace is founded "on a spiritual commitment to nonviolent strategies," which differs significantly from secular practices and stands in sharp opposition to "characteristic American modes of intervention based on mastery and accomplishment."

15 Driedger and Kraybill (1994, 45–58).

16 Bender (1944).

17 Driedger and Kraybill (1994, 136–9). These "change agents" included church leaders and activists who mediated innovations with other Mennonites. Driedger and Kraybill also discuss "ideological brokers" – a term that encompasses theologians, scholars, and community elders – who negotiated between traditional convictions and new social realities in instituting peace reforms (42–5).

18 Dridger and Kraybill (1994, 13).

19 Kniss (1997, 13).

20 Ibid., 189–91.

21 Ibid., 6.

22 Ibid., 65.

23 Drawing on Adorno, Michael Jackson (2002, 115) proposes that every form of identity thinking is "insidious" because it reifies, simplifies, and

generalizes and thereby inhibits synthesis or resolution. However, in keeping with Tsing's discussion of the ambivalence of friction, I argue that identity formation can also be a profoundly creative and enabling process. While reification is certainly possible, identification remains ambivalent. In the friction of relational encounters, communal identities can both produce divisions and dissolve them. Furthermore, rather than positing an abstract "identity thinking" it is necessary to explore the kinds of communities which collective identities inspire.

24 Sanneh (2009, 262).

25 The other organizations involved were American Friends Service Committee, the Quaker United Nations Office, Religions for Peace, and the Commission of the Churches on International Affairs of the World Council of Churches, in consultation with the Permanent Mission of the Islamic Republic of Iran to the United Nations.

26 The previous interfaith dialogues with President Ahmadinejad took place in September 2006, February 2007, and September 2007.

27 The contributors to Cynthia Sampson and John Paul Lederach's (2000) edited volume *From the Ground Up: Mennonite Contributions to International Peacemaking* return to this theme repeatedly. For example, in her chapter the anthropologist Sally Engle Merry (2000, 203–4) recounts the response she received when she tried to draw commonalities between her background as a Quaker and that of her Mennonite peace workers: "No, everyone told me quickly, Quakers do not operate quite the same as Mennonites. Quakers sometimes negotiate with the powerful, the people on the top, the key leaders, as well as working with grassroots groups. We primarily emphasize the grassroots." Merry continues by noting that "a fundamental part of Mennonite practice is focusing on grassroots and midlevel leaders and activities." The propensity of Mennonites to work at the "village level" is also noted by Mennonite sociologists Richard Yoder, Calvin Redekop and Vernon Jantzi (2004, 274), who note that "the largest share of Anabaptist resources (people and money) work at the grassroots level." Mennonite sociologist and peace activist John Paul Lederach repeatedly returns to the theme of relationships in his writings on peace. In *Preparing for Peace* Lederach (1995, 96) describes conflict as a "relational journey," and he promotes an "elicitive" model of peace pedagogy premised on "relationship building" with the end goal being the cultivation of "networks and linkages" (117–18). In *Building Peace* Lederach (1997, 26) proposes that relationships are "the basis of

both ... conflict and its long-term solution." *The Journey Toward Reconciliation* places "movement into relationship" at the centre of his "mission methodology" (Lederach 1999, 164). *The Little Book of Conflict Transformation* similarly posits relationships as "the heart of transformational processes," and Lederach (2003, 17) argues that it is better conceptualized as "a continuously evolving and developing quality of relationships" (20–1). Finally, in *The Moral Imagination*, Lederach (2005, 34) claims that relationships are central to "both the context in which cycles of violence happen and the generative energy from which transcendence of those same cycles burst forth."

28 Lefranc (2008, 47–8).

29 Graber Miller (1996).

30 Ibid., 51.

31 For descriptions and analysis of these interfaith theological conferences see particularly: Benner (2009); Bergen (2009); Hange (2007); Pierce (2007); and Reimer (2003).

32 Martin (2007, 2).

33 Rhodes (2007, 33).

34 Mennonite Central Committee Staff (2008).

35 Finger (2008).

36 Wall Street Journal Editor (2007).

37 MacDonald (2008).

38 Ibid.

39 Land (2008).

40 Dyck (2008).

41 Muir and Rogalsky (2007).

42 Tourage (2009). Hajj Muhammad Legenhausen (2007) also points out that, in tandem to the vilification of the dialogues by some North American groups, so too some Iranian Muslims have seen the dialogues as distasteful, if not thoroughly mistaken.

43 An article in *Maclean's*, discussing the 2007 Muslim-Mennonite theological conference in Ontario, quotes MCCer Rick Cober Bauman as saying: "This comes very much out of Mennonite Christian beliefs. We're people who believe that loving the 'enemy' is a real command ... Peace is built by people talking." To which the author adds: "So, it seems, is conflict" (Gatehouse 2007).

44 Pierson Lester (2007); see also Byler (2007).

45 Klassen and Byler (2008a; 2008b); Mennonite Central Committee (2008a; 2008b).

46 I do not recall ever seeing the name Mary Klassen written down. Therefore, the spelling of "Klassen" is my own. Other possible renderings of the same Mennonite family name include: Claassen, Claasen, Classen, Claussen, Klaassen, and Klaeszen (cf. Reimer 1953).

47 The communal violence surrounding the *reformasi* has spawned numerous important studies. See especially: Bertrand (2004); Coppel (2006); Davidson (2009); Duncan (2013); Hasan (2006); Hedman (2008); van Klinken (2007); McRae (2013); Purdey (2006); Reid (2006); Sidel (2006); Tajima (2014); and Wilson (2005; 2008).

48 Fealy (2004). The case of growing hostility and violence directed against Ahmadiyah is particularly relevant (Crouch 2009; Hicks 2018; Nurhayati 2020).

49 The peace partnership at the centre of this narrative is discussed in the opening ethnographic vignette in the introduction. The narrative told in this section is drawn from numerous interviews conducted during my research with the key MCCers and members of the other organizations involved.

50 "Pasukan Islam" is a pseudonym.

51 Wildan (2013) provides a comprehensive overview of radical Muslim groups in Solo during the post-Suharto period.

52 "Sweepings" were acts of vigilante surveillance and coercion undertaken by hardline Islamic groups in Indonesia in the early 2000s. They were often directed against perceived foreign interests and those activities deemed immoral (e.g., brothels, restaurants open during the daytime during the fasting month of Ramadan, etc.). They relied upon the threat, and sometimes also the active practice, of violence. See International Crisis Group (2001).

53 On Laskar Jihad see Hasan (2006).

54 Ricklefs's (2012, 416) study of Islamization in Java helpfully locates the rise of Islamist groups following the fall of the New Order within a broader historical context stretching back to the 1930s. He argues that Solo was a conducive place for Islamic radicalism, "with a history since the 1970s of Islamic activism by several organisations, a society polarized on Christian-Muslim lines, and a long and ever-permutating list of vigilante groups prepared to threaten or commit mayhem."

55 Purdey (2006, 124–40).

56 "Adem Ayem" is also Javanese for "tranquility."

57 Hefner (2000); Feener (2007); and Bush (2009).

58 Jantzi (2007, 20–1). This chapter was included in *Borders and Bridges: Mennonite Witness in a Religiously Diverse World*, edited by Peter Dula and Alain Epp Weaver, which brought together reflections on MCC's

inter-faith peacebuilding work around the world in response to the "key initiative" introduced in 2006.

59 Jantzi (2007, 20–1).

60 Ibid., 29–30.

61 Hasan (2006, 203–13) argues that the consolidation of power by national political elites, particularly under the presidency of Megawati Sukarnoputri (2001–04), accounts in large part for the closure of Laskar Jihad in 2002. Ricklefs (2012, 424–5) provides a regional frame, noting that the decline of violence in Solo was, in significant part, due to the election of future president Joko Widodo ("Jokowi") as the city's mayor (2005–12) who "brought a refreshing level of competence and transparency to the local government," and the appointment of Yotje Mende as the local police chief (2006–09), who took a strong stance against "sweeping" operations. Ricklefs also notes that police increasingly enacted "most of what the extremists demanded, shutting down illegal gambling joints, publicly destroying bottles of alcohol, arresting prostitutes and shaming courting couples discovered in such places."

62 See chapter 2 for an extended discussion of the model of partnership within MCC Indonesia.

63 I was told by numerous MCCers in Indonesia and elsewhere that they would never consider working with funding from USAID as it was seen as tainted by association with American imperialism and militarism. While MCC did receive funding from the Canadian government during the period of my fieldwork, there was significant tension in the organization over this funding arrangement. Attempts to access USAID funding had been the cause of early termination for an MCCer who had worked in Indonesia in the 1970s (Yoder 2006, 343). In 1976 an American MCCer was assigned to leadership in the Muria Cooperative Economic Development Foundation (Yayasan Kerjasama Ekonomi Muria, YAKEM), a cooperative agency formed by Mennonite synods and MCC. This MCCer worked on agricultural development projects that relied on expensive equipment inputs and to help finance these he applied to USAID for funding. Yoder writes: "Regrettably, because of what were considered administrative shortcomings and disregard for MCC's policy of not using USAID funding for overseas projects, the new staff head, who had been on the job for just nine months, was recalled" (ibid.).

64 See, for example, L. Bornstein (2006); Chernela (2005); Harris (2008); Michael (2004); and Wallace, Bornstein, and Chapman (2006).

65 One of the few occasions in which I heard an explicit critique levelled at MCC from a partner organization was decidedly not private. At the

Annual Team Meeting for MCC Indonesia in October 2007, an Indonesian Mennonite pastor from Gereja Kristen Muria Indonesia (GKMI) presented a talk on Indonesian Anabaptism. During the question and answer session at the end of his talk, this pastor told the group that historically MCC's "helping" had been both a "blessing and a curse" for the Indonesian Mennonite churches. MCC had helped with many good things, but it had also perpetuated a dynamic of "dependency" among members of Gereja Injili di Tanah Jawa (GITJ). Somewhat irreverently, given his role as a GKMI pastor and the presence of GITJ Mennonites at the meeting, he told a joke in which GITJ prayers began: "Our Father in heaven, *and* in America, *and* in the Netherlands." The "blessings" of MCC had also been the cause of dependency "curse."

66 According to Lash (1996, 42) one possible summary of the Christian gospel is that "we have been made capable of friendship." This formula doesn't limit the capacity to engage in amicable and caring relationships to any one group; instead, the "we" is unrestricted and "refers to everyone." Lash's framing is passive so as to locate friendship as gift or grace. It is also a capacity that is not always actualized but that remains a potent potentiality.

67 On the complexities and pluralities of Islamic identity in Java see: Beatty (1999); Geertz (1960b); Hefner (2000); Siegel (1993); and Woodward (1989).

68 See Tsing's (2005, 88) discussion of the universal claims of both God and nature.

69 Keane (2007, 42-4). See also Badiou (2003), who argues that Saint Paul was the founder of universalism.

70 In Aceh, MCC's Indonesian staff members often faced careful interrogation by potential Muslim partners about their motivation and goals. Wisnu, a Javanese staff member who worked with MCC in Aceh, told me that the saying *di balik batu, pasti ada udang* (In. underneath the stone there is surely a shrimp) encapsulated the suspicion that was often directed towards MCC as a Christian organization.

71 See Benthall (2007; 2009); MacFarquhar (2007); Macrae and Harmer (2009); Juul Petersen (2011); Pincus (2007); and Zharkevich (2010). The 2010 *Humanitarian Law Project v. Holder* decision by the US Supreme Court further exacerbated the climate of anxiety among American peacebuilding and humanitarian organizations given the extraordinarily broad definition the court used for what constituted "material support." On this decision and its implications for peacebuilding and humanitarianism see: Freedman (2010); Gross (2011); Margulies (2011); McKee (2010); Shanor (2011); and Zerwas (2010).

72 North American Mennonites frequently suggested to me that the characteristic mode of Swiss-German Mennonite politics was "passive aggressive" – a term drawn from pop psychology that was used to describe a tendency for opaque and subtle forms of interpersonal conflict rather than confrontational and direct styles. One former MCCer talked about this in terms of "soft authoritarianism," in which a kind of gentle coercion is deployed to achieve objectives. There are clear parallels between this dynamic and the discussion in chapter 2 of tensions within ethnic Mennonite society between democratic, congregational inclinations, and the authority of a bishop or centralized conference (see also Nolt 2004). It was also pointed out to me that Dutch Russian Mennonites did not suffer from similar inclinations of averting direct confrontation.

CHAPTER SIX

1 Miller (1995, 47).

2 That Miller specifically notes that the quality of his relationships with the Toba declined *after* he became an anthropologist is testimony both to the ways in which Mennonite models of service privileged relationality and an indictment of the disciplinary mechanisms (as inculcated into Miller in graduate school at the University of Pittsburgh) operating within anthropology that relegated the Toba to being seen primarily as a source of "data": "While associated with the Mennonite mission from 1959 to 1963, the Toba determined a role for me as religious savant and instructor that was gratifying, although not always easy to fill. It was a role they clearly valued highly … [My failures in living up to Toba expectations as a missionary] clearly paled in comparison to my limitations as an ethnographer. The point is that the Toba simply saw no central purpose or value in anthropology; it fit no cultural category. No logical role for ethnographic research had been established that made sense. On the contrary, it carried negative tones since the investigator 'took away' thoughts, ideas, knowledge, photographs, recordings, but gave nothing of significant value in return. Not only was anthropology irrelevant, it was distrusted" (Miller 1995, 118).

3 This general pattern has been analyzed by Sally Engle Merry (2000, 216), who argues that Mennonite models of peacebuilding involve "a long investment of time, careful listening, being inside and outside at the same time, understanding the situation but not taking charge, taking a non-directive stance but walking with or being there and working with a profound spirituality and sense of witnessing for God, which diminishes the need for immediate outcomes."

4 Keane (2007, 31).
5 Graber Miller (1996, 9).
6 Yoder (2003, 168–80); Epp Weaver (2008, 25–40). Both Yoder and Epp Weaver served with MCC. Each place an emphasis on "exile" as the place where Christians learn to live lightly and non-violently in a land that is not their own.
7 For discussion of each see: Kilby (2006); Cooke and Kothari (2001); Lewis (1998); and Morse and McNamara (2006).
8 Lister (2004), cited in Hearn (2007, 1097).
9 Smith (1989).
10 McNaughton (2006).
11 These terms are used by Erb (2000) and Selwyn (2000), respectively, in their anthropological studies of tourism relationships.
12 Cf. van Gennep (1960); Turner (1979).
13 At the time of this research MCC "binational" offices were located primarily in Akron, PA. This entity was dissolved in 2012 and, instead, MCC Canada and MCC US were jointly tasked with administering MCC's international program.
14 Erb (1969, 162).
15 These comments were followed by a further question: "Do our partners out there also own us? If they do, can they tell us what to do?" Ensuring that partners had a full voice in MCC was considered a "risk" because "What if they tell us something we don't want to hear?" Nevertheless, giving voice to "global partners" was considered important and was being addressed at that time through the organization-wide New Wines/New Wineskins appreciative inquiry process that had recently been initiated. Here a tension is apparent between seeking to engage both partners in the field and constituents at home as an intermediary or a translator between them.
16 The handout was an article by McKnight (1989).
17 Foucault (1978, 61).
18 Although it was considered possible for MCC's local Indonesian staff to hold senior leadership positions in another country, there is a long-standing hesitancy in MCC to appoint local staff to voluntary positions of leadership within their home country. While not a written policy, this approach was expressed to me on a number of occasions by senior MCC leaders.
19 The SALT program was initiated in 1977. SALT participants are between eighteen and twenty-seven years old, single, and have no dependents. They join MCC for an eleven-month period of international voluntary work.

SALTers contribute to the costs of their international service, advertised in 2011–12 at US$4,600 or CA$4,800 (http://salt.mcc.org/). The SALT program was often described by expatriate and local MCC staff in Indonesia as being an "exchange" (In. *pertukaran*) in relation to the International Visitor Exchange Program (IVEP), which involved young Indonesians of roughly the same age spending a parallel eleven months in North America (see chapter 2 for further background to IVEP). However, it was also generally understood that the two programs were not exact equivalents. Traditionally, SALT had been designed to facilitate "service" opportunities by North Americans to other parts of the world, whereas IVEP was designed to send young adults from countries on the receiving end of MCC's service to North America for their "training." Much has been done to attempt to achieve greater equivalency between the two programs through shared discourses of volunteerism and service.

20 Brewster and Brewster (1980). For introductions to SIL as a linguistic, missionary, and Bible translation organization, and its relationship with Wycliffe Bible Translators see Hartch (2006) and Svelmoe (2007).

21 Fechter (2007).

22 Ibid., 154–5.

23 Ibid., 43.

24 Ibid., 150-4.

25 The paradox I highlight here runs parallel to the case of child sponsorship practices in World Vision Zimbabwe as discussed by Erica Bornstein (2001). Bornstein argues that "evangelical narratives of child sponsorship simultaneously transcend difference and exacerbate it" (595). For while child sponsorship is premised on ideas of transnational Christian unity and manifests a Christian theology of "transcendent love for a stranger" (598), given that the process of child sponsorship rests on the inequitable political economy of donors living in some countries and recipients living in others, it also inscribes differences such that "inequalities are constituted through child sponsorship" (612). See also Bornstein (2005).

26 A number of attempts were initiated during my fieldwork to seek to displace English as the primary language for staff meetings in Central Java. Each of these was unsuccessful and English remained the language of choice. The Banda Aceh MCC office, however, did operate primarily in Bahasa Indonesia at the insistence of Willis Bender, who wanted the practice and felt strongly that the office should operate in the nation's national language. Nevertheless, all MCC staff members in that office were also fluent in English, and informal conversations would frequently switch between languages.

27 This was also acknowledged by Anna and Jake in their introduction to the local staff orientation. Although Anna and Jake had been in Indonesia since 2001 they had only hired their first local staff member in 2005, and this had taken place during the frenetic and urgent activity of establishing MCC Indonesia's tsunami response in Aceh. The two new staff members only joined MCC in Central Java in early 2007, after Iris and I had arrived.

28 The Second Iraq War began with the US invasion of Iraq in March 2003 and was still very much an active conflict throughout 2007. Formal US withdrawal only took place in December 2011, three years after the election of Barrack Obama as US president.

29 Anna and Jake were more reserved in their critiques of the Canadian government, though they clearly did not believe that the Canadian government was more benign than their own. They noted on a number of occasions that it seemed peculiar that Canadian MCCers were often more willing to embrace Canadian nationalism – such as through the symbolism of the national anthem or prominent display of a maple leaf motif – than their American MCC colleagues were to embrace American nationalism.

30 Similarly, in the orientation for service workers discussed above, Anna and Jake told the orientees that partnership was one way that MCC sought to avoid a "takeover" of the agendas and work of local Indonesian organizations. It was suggested that "it is important to keep our identities separate" but also to "work together." Partnership was the process that enabled these tensions to be held together.

31 This partnership model contrasts with various other models that NGOs have employed. For example, deploying a biblical metaphor, World Vision has imagined itself as a global "body" of many parts (Whaites, 1999). Accordingly, in each country in which World Vision works it operates as a *local* organization such that, for example, Bornstein's (2005) ethnography of World Vision in Zimbabwe was of a Zimbabwean organization. Only one expatriate was employed on the organization's staff.

32 MCC's general policy was that staff members serving in their own country of citizenship should be salaried rather than voluntary. The main exception to this was that some Americans and Canadians served as volunteers in their countries of citizenship.

33 This expatriate-local split is also reflected in the books published about different MCC country programs, in which a "roll call" of the names of MCCers who served in the country is frequently listed in the appendices. Rarely is a complete list of local staff included among these names (see Baniaga and Glick 2005; Epp Weaver and Weaver 1999; Yoder 1998). A

part of the reason for this is that MCC's Department of Human Resources does not keep detailed records of local staff hires, whereas the files of expatriate workers are stored in the centralized archives. This makes locating the full names and details of local staff a much more difficult task for North American-based authors and researchers.

34 Acehnese visions of "Javanese invaders" date back to the Dutch Colonial era and the early years of Indonesian independence. See chapters in Reid (2006) for a nuanced analysis of the relationship between Acehnese and the Indonesian state.

35 The sense that non-Acehnese Indonesian staff felt like "outsiders" was shared by the staff of other NGOs (Hellman and Forell 2015, 61).

36 See Fountain (2011).

37 Likewise, in the 1970s and 1980s, MCC in Palestine also assumed a highly political stance, including country representative Paul Quiring writing journal articles about "Israeli theft of private Palestinian land" and providing "high-profile testimony" to the US Congress, actions that led to his being denied a new visa by the Israeli authorities (Epp Weaver and Weaver 1999, 84–7).

38 Hilhorst (2003, 51).

39 P. Toews (1996, 197).

CHAPTER SEVEN

1 Weaver is quoted in Shirlee Kohler Yoder's (1998, 5) fiftieth anniversary collection of stories about MCC Indonesia. To this, Yoder adds: "Probably every MCCer to Indonesia would affirm that. But we might also add: 'We never knew for sure what we would be doing until we got here nor could we know how we might be transformed by living in Indonesia!'"

2 On the Canadian Mennonite experience of negotiating with the state over exemption from military service see Klippenstein (1998); Marr (2003, 47–55); and Regehr (1996, 3:35–59). On the American experience see Bush (1998, 69–72); P. Toews (1996, 129–53); and Unruh (1952, 230–73).

3 Charles (2002, 105) notes that as high as 54 percent of US Mennonite and 38 percent of Canadian Mennonite young men served in the military as either combatants or non-combatants during the Second World War. Also citing the US figure, P. Toews (1996, 173) notes that "no doubt due to a Mennonite ideological bias" the story of those who served in the military "remains marginal to Mennonite memory."

4 See Bush (1998, 78–9); P. Toews (1996, 157). The second phrase references the Sermon on the Mount, in which Jesus commands his disciples: "if anyone forces you to go one mile, go also the second mile" (Mathew 5:41).
5 Hein (1998, 102 and 108).
6 Ibid., 111–12.
7 Bush (1998, 79 and 75). These innovations drew on narratives with long histories in Mennonite communities. For example, in his chronicle of MCC's early activities, Unruh (1952, 9) locates the North American Mennonite impulse for embodied service in the experiences of the sixteenth century Anabaptists of the radical reformation and, ultimately, also to the authority of Christian Scripture. This theological and historical legitimation of practices of service was an important element in justifying the significant reconfigurations being implemented in and through MCC.
8 P. Toews (1996, 141).
9 Van Braght (2002 [1660], 741–2). The *Martyrs Mirror* was introduced in chapter 1. Weaver-Zercher (2016, x) argues that the martyrology became a "measure of Christian faithfulness" among Mennonites who looked to martyrs as "exemplars of spiritual resolve" and as emblems of "authentic faith."
10 Fassin (2012, 209–15) notes that the term "martyr" means "witness."
11 Weaver-Zercher (2016, 264–91).
12 The decline has continued since that time, including as a consequence of Covid-19 disruptions to international travel since early 2020.
13 Kraybill (1996, 37–8).
14 Burkholder (2010, 373–94) notes the etymology of liturgy within the koine Greek term "leitourgia," which he suggests can be translated into "worship," "ministry," "public work," and "service." Burkholder's reflections on the liturgy of service emerged following a "provocative encounter" with Amos Orley Swartzentruber, a former Mennonite missionary turned Episcopal priest. Swartzentruber tells Burkholder that Mennonites are "doomed to extinction" because the Mennonite church lacks a central sacramental focus. With the irretrievable loss of traditional, separated rural communities, and lacking the ritual centre of high church liturgy, Swartzentruber tells Burkholder that "Mennonites have only sermons, four-part singing, and service projects." Burkholder's response is to freight the idea of service with sufficient weight so that it can furnish a sacred core for Mennonites.
15 Cronin (2000, 134).

16 For helpful analysis of the roles of fieldwork within anthropology see: Borneman and Hammoudi (2009); Coleman and Collins (2006b); Gupta and Ferguson (1997); and Rabinow (2007).

17 Cf. Turner (1979).

18 Peirano (1998, 105) points out that, for most of the history of the discipline of anthropology, the idea of an anthropology at home was "a paradox and a contradiction of terms."

19 The olfactory repugnance of durian for Western nostrils has a substantial history (Montanari 2011).

20 Jackson (2009, 232). See also Jackson (2002, 262).

21 Jackson (2009, 105–6). The intersubjective reworking of the self involves crossing "the dark sea that lies between the known and the unknown, embarking on journeys in which we hazard all that we are and from which we return transformed."

22 The orientation sessions ran a shortened version of the usual Damascus Road anti-racism training. This program was considered controversial among some MCCers and the Mennonite constituency. A number of people expressed concerns to me, indicating that the main point of contention was the pedagogical strategies rather than the goal of countering racism.

23 Fechter (2007, 73).

24 "Landa" is a truncated rendition of "Belanda" (Holland). Along with the Indonesian term "bule," it conveys ideas of whiteness, foreignness, and wealth (Heryanto 1999).

25 YAMEN! was launched in 2008 and, like SALT and IVEP, involved an eleven-month term of service for young adults. Whereas the other two programs centred on North America as either origin or host, YAMEN! was designed as a South-South exchange involving countries other than Canada or the US.

26 Siegel (1993, 118–25). "Foreigners are seen as incapable of speaking Javanese or Indonesian, and thus in a sense as incapable of language altogether. They are therefore without the first notion of proper behavior, and for that reason, they are fit objects of contempt. They are also, however, seen to be extremely attractive. Foreign women are thought to be without morals and thus appropriate sexual objects, whereas both men and women are assumed to be wealthy. As they pass on the street, male students, usually high-school students, shout 'hello,' 'hallo mister,' or for some reason, 'hallo, Mac,' behavior that would be quite impolite to anyone in Javanese society. Foreign women particularly are targets. If they are alone, such women are likely to be treated to sexual gestures."

27 This emphasis on doing theology within the context of community is a prominent feature of the Mennonite theological tradition. Robert Friedmann (1990, 7) summarizes this communal hermeneutic in these terms: "The church … and the brotherhood are with the Anabaptists one and the same, both a sacred and a secular body without separation of these two functions. No one can ever reach God except together with his brother."

28 As noted in chapter 5, one of the three "screens" for MCC expatriate volunteers was that they would "exhibit a commitment to personal Christian faith." A certain leniency, however, was sometimes applied to young Mennonites, perhaps in the hope that the experience would enhance their faith and allow an opportunity to embrace a theology of service.

29 Mosse (2005, 18). Van den Berg and Quarles van Ufford (2005, 202) also argue that development practices "emerge from a confrontation with various kinds of disjuncture."

30 There are three "MCC Cookbooks": Longacre's (1976) *More-with-Less Cookbook*, Schlabach's (1991) *Extending the Table*, and Lind and Hockman-Wert's (2005) *Simply in Season*. For good introductions to the themes of the cookbooks see Bailey-Dick (2005) and Berry (2011).

31 Heaton Shrestha (2006, 206).

32 This is sometimes suggested in actor-oriented sociology, such as Norman Long and Ann Long's (1992) "battlefields of knowledge," or in the language of "interfaces" between contrasting "worlds of knowledge" (Long 2001, 89). Rossi (2006, 28–9) critiques Long's tendency to compartmentalize "aid givers" and "aid receivers" into entirely different categories, arguing that this rigid boundedness rarely exists in practice.

33 This reference to Japan was in response to a story I had shared about my visit to the MCC Material Resources Center in Ephrata, Lancaster County, along with Iris, my wife. I had been asked to talk with a group of Amish volunteers who had spent the day assembling relief buckets. After the talk Iris had a conversation with someone who wanted to know where she was from. She had explained that she was from Malaysia, which had elicited a question about whether that was near Japan.

34 Cronin (2006, 70).

35 Constable (1999, 223–5).

36 Bush (1998, 79).

CONCLUSION

1 On the limitations of "mapping" exercises on religion and NGOs see Fountain and Feener (2017). Latour (2010, 99–124) holds the commandment "thou shalt not freeze frame" as a sacred scholarly obligation.
2 See Fountain and Yoder (2022) for further discussion of these dynamics.
3 See Durantaye (2012, 50), who cites the phrase to describe Giorgio Agamben's philological method of enquiry.

References

Abbas, Megan Brankley. 2021. *Whose Islam? The Western University and Modern Islamic Thought in Indonesia*. Stanford, CA: Stanford University Press.

Abruzzo, Margaret. 2011. *Polemical Pain: Slavery, Cruelty, and the Rise of Humanitarianism*. Baltimore, MD: Johns Hopkins University Press.

Adams, Vincanne. 2013. *Markets of Sorrow, Labors of Faith: New Orleans in the Wake of Katrina*. Durham, NC: Duke University Press.

Ager, Alastair, and Joey Ager. 2011. "Faith and the Discourse of Secular Humanitarianism." *Journal of Refugee Studies* 24, no. 3: 456–72.

Alfini, Naomi, and Robert Chambers. 2007. "Words Count: Taking a Count of the Changing Language of British Aid." *Development in Practice* 17, no. 4: 492–504.

Ali, Muhamad. 2010. "They Are Not All Alike: Indonesian Muslim Intellectual's Perception of Judaism and Jews." *Indonesia and the Malay World* 38, no. 112: 329–47.

Ammerman, Nancy T. 2014. "Finding Religion in Everyday Life." *Sociology of Religion* 75, no. 2: 189–207.

– 2020. "Rethinking Religion: Toward a Practice Approach." *American Journal of Sociology* 126, no. 1: 6–51.

Anderson, Benedict. 1991. *Imagined Communities: Reflections on the Origin and Spread of Nationalism*. London: Verso.

Appadurai, Arjun. 1988. "Introduction: Commodities and the Politics of Value." In *The Social Life of Things: Commodities in Cultural Perspective*, ed. Arjun Appadurai, 3–63. Cambridge: Cambridge University Press.

Aragon, Lorraine. 2000. *Fields of the Lord: Animism, Christian Minorities, and State Development in Indonesia*. Honolulu: University of Hawai'i Press.

Arce, Alberto, and Norman Long. 1992. "The Dynamics of Knowledge: Interfaces between Bureaucrats and Peasants." In *Battlefields of Knowledge:*

The Interlocking of Theory and Practice in Social Research and Development, ed. Norman Long and Ann Long, 211–46. London: Routledge.
– 2000. *Anthropology, Development and Modernities: Exploring Discourses, Counter-Tendencies and Violence*. London: Routledge.
Aritonang, Jan, and Karel Steenbrink, eds. 2008. *A History of Christianity in Indonesia*. Leiden: Brill.
Asad, Talal. 1983. "Anthropological Conceptions of Religion: Reflections on Geertz." *Man* 18, no. 2: 237–59.
– 1993. *Genealogies of Religion: Discipline and Reasons of Power in Christianity and Islam*. Baltimore: Johns Hopkins University Press.
– 2003. *Formations of the Secular: Christianity, Islam, Modernity*. Stanford, CA: Stanford University Press.
– 2009. "The Idea of an Anthropology of Islam." *Qui Parle* 17, no. 2: 1–30.
Aspinall, Edward. 2005. *The Helsinki Agreement: A More Promising Basis for Peace in Aceh?* Washington: East-West Center.
– 2006. "Aceh: Elections and the Possibility of Peace." *APSNet Policy Forum*. https://nautilus.org/apsnet/0637a-aspinall-html/.
– 2007. "Guerillas in Power." *Inside Indonesia* 90. https://www.insideindonesia.org/guerillas-in-power.
– 2009. *Islam and Nation*. Stanford, CA: Stanford University Press.
Aspinall, Edward, and Harold Crouch. 2003. *The Aceh Peace Process: Why It Failed*. Washington: East-West Center.
Atia, Mona. 2013. *Building a House in Heaven: Pious Neoliberalism and Islamic Charity in Egypt*. Minneapolis: University of Minnesota Press.
Aunger, Robert. 1995. "On Ethnography: Storytelling or Science?" *Current Anthropology* 36, no. 1: 97–114.
Badiou, Alain. 2003. *Saint Paul: The Foundation of Universalism*. Stanford, CA: Stanford University Press.
Bailey-Dick, Matthew. 2005. "The Kitchenhood of All Believers: A Journey into the Discourse of Mennonite Cookbooks." *Mennonite Quarterly Review* 79, no. 22: 153–78.
Baniaga, Benjamin, and Helen Liechty Glick. 2005. *Where Will They Sit? The Life and Work of Mennonite Central Committee in the Philippines*. Davao City: Mennonite Central Committee Philippines.
Banner, Michael. 2014. *The Ethics of Everyday Life: Moral Theology, Social Anthropology, and the Imagination of the Human*. Oxford: Oxford University Press.
Barnes, Amy, and Garrett Wallace Brown. 2011. "The Idea of Partnership within the Millennium Development Goals: Context, Instrumentality and the Normative Demands of Partnership." *Third World Quarterly* 32, no. 1: 165–80.

Barnett, Michael. 2011. *Empire of Humanity: A History of Humanitarianism.* Ithaca, NY: Cornell University Press.

Bauman, Peter, Mengistu Ayalew, and Gazala Paul. 2009. "Beyond Disaster: A Comparative Analysis of Tsunami Interventions in Sri Lanka and Indonesia/Aceh." *Journal of Peacebuilding and Development* 3, no. 3: 6–21.

Beatty, Andrew. 1999. *Varieties of Javanese Religion: An Anthropological Account.* Cambridge: Cambridge University Press.

Bebbington, Anthony, Scott Guggenheim, and Michael Woolcock. 2006a. "Concepts: Their Contexts and Their Consequences." In *The Search for Empowerment: Social Capital as Idea and Practice at the World Bank*, ed. Anthony Bebbington, Michael Woolcock, Scott Guggenheim, and Elizabeth Olson, 261–87. Bloomfield, CT: Kumarian Press.

– 2006b. "The Ideas-Practice Nexus in International Development Organizations: Social Capital at the World Bank." In *The Search for Empowerment: Social Capital as Idea and Practice at the World Bank*, ed. Anthony Bebbington, Michael Woolcock, Scott Guggenheim, and Elizabeth Olson, 1– 27. Bloomfield, CT: Kumarian Press.

Bebbington, Anthony, Sam Hickey, and Diana Mitlin. 2008. "Introduction: Can NGOs Make a Difference? The Challenge of Development Alternatives." In *Can NGOs Make a Difference? The Challenge of Development Alternatives*, ed. Anthony Bebbington, Sam Hickey, and Diana Mitlin, 3–37. London: Zed.

Bebbington, Anthony, and Uma Kothari. 2006. "Transnational Development Networks." *Environment and Planning A* 38, no. 5: 849–66.

Beck, Ervin. 2004. *MennoFolk: Mennonite and Amish Folk Traditions.* Scottdale, PA: Herald Press.

Bender, Harold S. 1944. "The Anabaptist Vision." *Church History* 13, no. 1: 3–24.

Bender, Harold S., and Lawrence M. Yoder. 2014. "Indonesia." *Global Anabaptist Mennonite Encyclopedia Online.* https://gameo.org/index.php?title=Indonesia.

Bender, Urie A. 1969. *Soldiers of Compassion*, Scottdale, PA: Herald Press.

Benner, Dick. 2009. "Redemption through Suffering." *Canadian Mennonite* 13, no. 20: 2.

Benthall, Jonathan. 1993. *Disasters, Relief and the Media.* London: I.B. Tauris.

– 2007. "The Overreaction against Islamic Charities." *ISIM Review* 20: 6–7.

– 2009. "Humanitarianism, Islam and 11 September." *HPG Policy Briefs* 11. London: Overseas Development Institute. https://cdn.odi.org/media/documents/351.pdf.

Benthall, Jonathan, and Jérôme Bellion-Jourdan. 2008. *The Charitable Crescent: Politics of Aid in the Muslim World.* London: I.B. Tauris.

Bergen, Jeremy. 2009. "Justice at the Expense of Peace? Peace at the Expense of Justice?" *Canadian Mennonite* 13, no. 15: 22.

Berry, Malinda Elizabeth. 2011 "The Gifts of an Extended Theological Table: MCC's World Community Cookbooks as Organic Theology." In *A Table of Sharing: Mennonite Central Committee and the Expanding Networks of Mennonite Identity*, ed. Alain Epp Weaver, 284–309. Telford, PA: Cascadia.

Bertrand, Jacques. 2004. *Nationalism and Ethnic Conflict in Indonesia*. New York: Cambridge University Press.

Bhabha, Homi K. 1994. *The Location of Culture*. London: Routledge.

Bierschenk, Thomas, Jean-Pierre Chauveau, and Jean-Pierre Olivier de Sardan. 2002. *Local Development Brokers in Africa: The Rise of a New Social Category*. Mainz, DE: Institut für Ethnologie und Afrikastudien, Johannes Gutenberg-Universität.

Bjork, Christopher. 2005. *Indonesian Education: Teachers, Schools, and Central Bureaucracy*. New York: Routledge.

Black, Amy, Douglas Koopman, and David Ryden. 2004. *Of Little Faith: The Politics of George W. Bush's Faith-Based Initiatives*. Washington, DC: Georgetown University Press.

Bolotta, Giuseppe, Philip Fountain, and R. Michael Feener. 2020. "Transcendence, Sacrifice, and Aspiration: The Political Theology of Development in Asia." In *Political Theologies and Development in Asia: Transcendence, Sacrifice and Aspiration*, ed. Giuseppe Bolotta, Philip Fountain, and R. Michael Feener, 1–17. Manchester: Manchester University Press.

Borneman, John, and Abdellah Hammoudi. 2009. "The Fieldwork Encounter, Experience, and the Making of Truth: An Introduction." In *Being There: The Fieldwork Encounter and the Making of Truth*, ed. John Borneman and Abdellah Hammoudi, 1–24. Berkeley: University of California Press.

Bornstein, Erica. 2001. "Child Sponsorship, Evangelism, and Belonging in the Work of World Vision Zimbabwe." *American Ethnologist* 28, no. 3: 595–622.

– 2005. *The Spirit of Development: Protestant NGOs, Morality, and Economics in Zimbabwe*. Stanford: Stanford University Press.

– 2013. *Disquieting Gifts: Humanitarianism in New Delhi*. Stanford: Stanford University Press.

Bornstein, Lisa. 2006. "Systems of Accountability, Webs of Deceit? Monitoring and Evaluation in South African NGOs." *Development* 49, no. 2: 52–61.

Bosma, Ulbe, and Remco Raben. 2008. *Being "Dutch" in the Indies: A History of Creolisation and Empire, 1500–1920*. Trans. Wendie Shaffer. Singapore: NUS Press.

Bowman, John, 1978. "MCC Development Program, Way Abung II North Lampung, Indonesia." Mennonite Central Committee Indonesia. MCC Archives (Akron, PA).

Brady, Ivan. 2004. "In Defense of the Sensual: Meaning Construction in Ethnography and Poetics." *Qualitative Inquiry* 10, no. 4: 622–44.

Braun, Will. 2005. "Buckets, Blankets and the WTO." *Canadian Mennonite* 9, no. 24: 14.

Bretherton, Luke. 2012. "Coming to Judgment: Methodological Reflections on the Relationship between Ecclesiology, Ethnography and Political Theory." *Modern Theology* 28, no. 2: 167–96.

Brewster, E. Thomas, and Elizabeth S. Brewster. 1980. *Bonding and the Missionary Task: Establishing a Sense of Belonging*. Dallas, TX: Summer Institute of Linguistics.

Brinkerhoff, Jennifer M. 2002. "Government-Nonprofit Partnership: A Defining Framework." *Public Administration and Development* 22, no. 1: 19–30.

Brubacher, Ray. 1991. "A Missiology for MCC." *Intercom* 35, no. 9: 8.

– 1992. "A Missiology for MCC." Letter to Nancy Heisey, 28 Febrary 1992. MCC Archives (Akron, PA).

– 1993. "Missiology Statement." Letter to Ed Martin and Ed Metzler, 14 April 1993. MCC Archives (Akron, PA).

Brundtland, Gro H., and World Commission on Environment and Development. 1987. *World Commission on Environment and Development: Our Common Future*. Oxford: Oxford University Press.

Bruner, Edward. 1997. "Ethnography as Narrative." In *Memory, Identity, Community: The Idea of Narrative in the Human Sciences*, ed. Lewis Hinchman and Sandra Hinchman, 264–80. Albany: State University of New York Press.

Brusset, Emery, and Evaluation Team. 2009. *A Ripple in Development? Long Term Perspectives on the Response to the Indian Ocean Tsunami 2004: A Joint Follow-Up Evaluation of the Links between Relief, Rehabilitation and Development (LRRD)*. Stockholm: SIDA.

Bunch, Roland. 1982. *Two Ears of Corn: A Guide to People-Centered Agricultural Improvement*. Oklahoma City: World Neighbors.

Burhanuddin, Muhtadi. 2007. "The Conspiracy of Jews: The Quest for Anti-Semitism in *Media Dakwah*." *Graduate Journal of Asia-Pacific Studies* 5, no. 2: 53–76.

Burkholder, John Richard. 2010. "Leitourgia: Beyond Altar and Sacrifice – How Then Shall We Worship/Serve God?" In *Prophetic Peacemaking: Selected Writings of J.R. Burkholder*, ed. Keith Graber Miller, 373–94. Scottdale, PA: Herald Press.

Burridge, Kate. 1997. "'Separate and Peculiar': The Survival of Pennsylvania 'Dutch' in Ontario." In *Canada-Australia: Towards a Second Century of Partnership*, ed. Kate Burridge, Lois Foster, and Gerry Turcotte, 247–66. Ottawa: Carleton University Press and the International Council of Canadian Studies.

– "A Separate and Peculiar People: Fieldwork and the Pennsylvania Germans." *Language Typology and Universals* 60, no. 1: 32–41.

Bush, Perry. 1998. *Two Kingdoms, Two Loyalties: Mennonite Pacifism in Modern America*. Baltimore, MD: Johns Hopkins University Press.

Bush, Robin, 2009. *Nahdlatul Ulama and the Struggle for Power within Islam and Politics in Indonesia*. Singapore: Institute of Southeast Asian Studies.

Byler, J. Daryl. 2007. "A New Narrative?" *Peace Office Newsletter* 37, no. 3: 7–8.

Caldwell, Melissa. 2017. *Living Faithfully in an Unjust World: Compassionate Care in Russia*. Los Angeles: University of California Press.

Caldwell, Stephen, Brian Wiebe, Cresenciana Jurey, and Dwight Jurey, 1986. "Agricultural Research on Rasau Jaya Peat Soil: Report on MCC Agricultural Research Activities in Rasau Jaya, Kalbar, 1982–1985." Mennonite Central Committee Indonesia. MCC Archives (Akron, PA).

Canadian International Development Agency (CIDA). 2009. "Building Houses – and Hope – in Aceh." *Canadian International Development Agency*. Available at: http://w3.acdi-cida.gc.ca/acdi-cida/acdi-cida.nsf/eng/ANN-515152120-QPV. Viewed April 2011.

Cannell, Fenella, 2006a. "The Anthropology of Christianity." In *The Anthropology of Christianity*, ed. Fenella Cannell, 1–50. Durham, NC: Duke University Press.

– 2006b. *The Anthropology of Christianity*. Durham, NC: Duke University Press.

Cavanaugh, William. 2009. *The Myth of Religious Violence: Secular Ideology and the Roots of Modern Conflict*. Oxford: Oxford University Press.

Chambers, Robert. 1983. *Rural Development: Putting the Last First*. London: Longman.

Chambon, Michel. 2020. *Making Christ Present in China: Actor-Network Theory and the Anthropology of Christianity*. Cham: Palgrave Macmillan.

Charles, J. Robert. 2002. "The Varieties of Mennonite Peacemaking: A Review Essay." *Mennonite Quarterly Review* 76, no. 1: 105–19.

Chernela, Janet. 2005. "The Politics of Mediation: Local-Global Interactions in the Central Amazon of Brazil." *American Anthropologist* 107, no. 4: 620–31.

Chua, Liana. 2012. "Conversion, Continuity, and Moral Dilemmas among Christian Bidayuhs in Malaysian Borneo." *American Ethnologist* 39, no. 3: 511–26.

Clarke, Gerald. 2006. "Faith Matters: Faith-Based Organizations, Civil Society and International Development." *Journal of International Development* 18, no. 6: 835–48.

Clarke, Gerald, and Mark Jennings, eds., 2008a. *Development, Civil Society and Faith-Based Organizations: Bridging the Sacred and the Secular*. Hampshire: Palgrave Macmillan.

– 2008b. "Introduction." In *Development, Civil Society and Faith-Based Organizations: Bridging the Sacred and the Secular*, ed. Gerald Clarke and Mark Jennings, 1–16. Hampshire: Palgrave Macmillan.

Clarke, Matthew, Ismet Fanany, and Sue Kenny, eds. 2010. *Post-Disaster Reconstruction: Lessons from Aceh*. London: Earthscan.

Classen, Susan. 2003. *A Spirituality of Service: Freely Give, Freely Receive*. Akron, PA: Mennonite Central Committee.

Cleary, Seamus. 1995. "In Whose Interest? NGO Advocacy Campaigns and the Poorest: An Exploration of Two Indonesian Examples." *International Relations* 12, no. 5: 9–35.

Clifford, James. 1997. *Routes: Travel and Translation in the Late Twentieth Century*. Cambridge, MA: Harvard University Press.

Coates, Ruth. 1999. *Christianity in Bakhtin: God and the Exiled Author*. Cambridge: Cambridge University Press.

Coleman, Simon, and Peter Collins. 2006a. "Introduction: 'Being … Where?' Performing Fields on Shifting Grounds." In *Locating the Field: Space, Place and Context in Anthropology*, ed. Simon Coleman and Peter Collins, 1–21. Oxford: Berg.

– eds. 2006b. *Locating the Field: Space, Place and Context in Anthropology*. Oxford: Berg.

Collins, Elizabeth. 2007. *Indonesia Betrayed: How Development Fails*. Honolulu: University of Hawai'i Press.

Connolly, Jennifer. 2009. "Christian Conversion and Ethnic Identity in East Kalimantan." In *Casting Faiths: Imperialism and the Transformation of Religion in East and Southeast Asia*, ed. Thomas David DuBois, 175–89. London: Palgrave Macmillan.

Constable, Nicole. 1999. "At Home But Not at Home: Filipina Narratives of Ambivalent Returns." *Cultural Anthropology* 14, no. 2: 203–28.

Cooke, Bill, and Uma Kothari. 2001. *Participation: The New Tyranny?* London: Zed Books.

Coppel, Charles A., ed. 2006. *Violent Conflicts in Indonesia: Analysis, Representation, Resolution*. New York: Routledge.

Cornwall, Andrea, 2007. "Buzzwords and Fuzzwords: Deconstructing Development Discourse." *Development in Practice* 17, no. 4: 471–84.

Cornwall, Andrea, and Karen Brock. 2005. "What Do Buzzwords Do for Development Policy? A Critical Look at 'Participation,' 'Empowerment' and 'Poverty Reduction.'" *Third World Quarterly* 26, no. 7: 1043–60.
Crawford, Gordon. 2003. "Partnership or Power? Deconstructing the 'Partnership for Governance Reform' in Indonesia." *Third World Quarterly* 24, no. 1: 139–59.
Cribb, Robert. 2001. "How Many Deaths? Problems in the Statistics of Massacre in Indonesia (1965–1966) and East Timor (1975–1980)." In *Violence in Indonesia*, ed. Ingrid Wessel and Georgia Wimhöfer, 82–98. Hamburg: Abera Verlag Markus Voss.
– 2002. "Unresolved Problems in the Indonesian Killings of 1965–1966." *Asian Survey* 42, no. 4: 550–63.
– 2009. "The Indonesian Massacres." In *Century of Genocide: Critical Essays and Eyewitness Accounts*, ed. Samuel Totten and William S. Parsons, 193–217. New York: Routledge.
Cronin, Michael. 2000. *Across the Lines: Travel, Language, Translation*. Cork: Cork University Press.
– 2003. *Translation and Globalization*. Abingdon, Oxon: Routledge.
– 2006. *Translation and Identity*. Abingdon, Oxon: Routledge.
Crouch, Melissa. 2009. "Indonesia, Militant Islam and Ahmadiyah: Origins and Implications." ARC Federation Fellowship, 'Islam, Shariah and Governance' Background Paper Series No. 4. https://ssrn.com/abstract=1551645.
Crous, Ernst, Nanne van der Zijpp, and Lawrence M. Yoder. 1987. "Pati (Indonesia)." *Global Anabaptist Mennonite Encyclopedia Online*. http://www.gameo.org/encyclopedia/contents/P3843.html.
Cullather, Nick. 2013. *The Hungry World: America's Cold War Battle against Poverty in Asia*. Cambridge, MA: Harvard University Press.
Curtis, Heather D. 2018. *Holy Humanitarians: American Evangelicals and Global Aid*. Cambridge, MA: Harvard University Press.
Dabashi, Hamid. 2001. "For the Last Time: Civilizations." *International Sociology* 16, no. 3: 361–68.
Daly, Patrick, R. Michael Feener, and Anthony Reid, eds. 2012. *From the Ground Up: Perspectives on Post-Tsunami and Post-Conflict Aceh*. Singapore: Institute of Southeast Asian Studies.
da Silva, Jo. 2010. *Lessons from Aceh: Key Considerations in Post-Disaster Reconstruction*. Warwickshire: Practical Action.
Davies, Thomas. 2013. *NGOs: A New History of Transnational Civil Society*. London: Hurst.
Davidson, Jamie S. 2009. *From Rebellion to Riots: Collective Violence on Indonesian Borneo*. Singapore: NUS Press.

Davidson, Joanna. 2016. *Sacred Rice: An Ethnography of Identity, Environment, and Development in Rural West Africa*. Oxford: Oxford University Press.

de León-Hartshorn, Iris, Tobin Miller Shearer, and Regina Shands Stoltzfus. 2001. *Set Free: A Journey toward Solidarity against Racism*. Scottdale, PA: Herald Press.

Deneulin, Séverine, and Carole Rakodi. 2011. "Revisiting Religion: Development Studies Thirty Years On." *World Development* 39, no. 1: 45–54.

Deneulin, Séverine, with Masooda Bano. 2009. *Religion in Development: Rewriting the Secular Script*. London: Zed Books.

Deppermann, Klaus, Werner Packull, and James Stayer. 1975. "From Monogenesis to Polygenesis: The Historical Discussion of Anabaptist Origins." *Mennonite Quarterly Review* 49, no. 2: 83–121.

Detweiler, Lowell. 2000. *The Hammer Rings Hope: Photos and Stories from Fifty Years of Mennonite Disaster Service*. Scottdale, PA: Herald Press.

Dicklitch, Susan, and Heather Rice. 2004. "The Mennonite Central Committee (MCC) and Faith-Based NGO Aid to Africa." *Development in Practice* 14, no. 5: 660–72.

Dilley, Roy M. 2002. "The Problem of Context in Social and Cultural Anthropology." *Language and Communication* 22, no. 4: 437–56.

Dixon, C. Scott. 2017. "The Radicals." In *The Oxford Handbook of the Protestant Reformations*, ed. Ulinka Rublack, 190–213. Oxford: Oxford University Press.

Drexler, Elizabeth F. 2008. *Aceh, Indonesia: Securing the Insecure State*. Philadelphia: University of Pennsylvania Press.

Driedger, Leo, and Donald Kraybill. 1994. *Mennonite Peacemaking: From Quietism to Activism*. Scottdale, PA/Waterloo, ON: Herald Press.

Dubuisson, Daniel. 2003. *The Western Construction of Religion: Myths, Knowledge, and Ideology*. Baltimore, MD: Johns Hopkins University Press.

Dueck, Al. 2002. "Babel, Esperanto, Shibboleths, and Pentecost: Can We Talk?" *Journal of Psychology and Christianity* 21, no. 1: 72–80.

Dula, Peter, and Alain Epp Weaver. eds. 2007. *Borders and Bridges: Mennonite Witness in a Religiously Diverse World*. Telford, PA: Cascadia.

Duncan, Christopher R. 2013. *Violence and Vengeance: Religious Conflict and Its Aftermath in Eastern Indonesia*. Ithaca, NY: Cornell University Press.

Durantaye, Leland de la. 2012. "Afterword: On Method, the Messiah, Anarchy and Theocracy." In *The Church and the Kingdom*, by Giorgio Agamben, 48–59. Trans. Leland de la Durantaye. London: Seagull Books.

Durie, Mark. 1988. "The So-Called Passive of Acehnese." *Language* 64, no. 1: 104–13.

Dyck, Bruno. 2003. "Exploring Congregational Clans: Playing the 'Mennonite Game' in Winnipeg." *Journal of Mennonite Studies* 21: 137–54.
Dyck, Cornelius J., ed. 1980a. *From the Files of* MCC. Scottdale, PA: Herald Press.
– ed. 1980b. *Responding to Worldwide Needs*. Scottdale, PA: Herald Press.
– ed. 1980c. *Witness and Service in North America*. Scottdale, PA: Herald Press.
– ed. 1981. *Something Meaningful for God: The Stories of Some who Served with* MCC. Scottdale, PA: Herald Press.
Dyck, Dan. 2008. "Christians Insulting Christians Unhelpful." *Mennonite Church Canada*. http://www.mennonitechurch.ca/news/releases/2008/10/Release01.htm. Viewed April 2011.
Dyck, Peter J. 1968. "When Is Service Christian?" MCC *News Service Bulletin*, 24 May 1968.
– 1970. "A Theology of Service." *Mennonite Quarterly Review* 44, no. 3: 262–80.
– 1979. "The Earth Is the Lord's." In MCC *Annual Meeting 1979*. Reedley, CA: Mennonite Central Committee.
– n.d. *The Church as Servant*. Unpublished paper. Akron, PA: Mennonite Central Committee.
Dyck, Peter J., and Elfrieda Dyck. 1991. *Up from the Rubble*. Scottdale, PA: Herald Press.
Dyck, Tim Miller. 2005. "New Column." *Canadian Mennonite* 9, no. 8: 2.
Eby, Omar. 1972. *How Full the River*. Scottdale, PA: Herald Press.
Ekbladh, David. 2011. *The Great American Mission: Modernization and the Construction of an American World Order*. Princeton, NJ: Princeton University Press.
Eldridge, Philip. 1989. *NGOs in Indonesia: Popular Movement or Arm of Government?* Clayton: Monash University.
– 1995. *Non-Government Organizations and Democratic Participation in Indonesia*. New York: Oxford University Press.
– 1996. "Development, Democracy and Non-Government Organizations in Indonesia." *Asian Journal of Political Science* 4, no. 1: 17–35.
Elisha, Omri. 2011. *Moral Ambition: Mobilization and Social Outreach in Evangelical Megachurches*. Berkeley: University of California Press.
Engelke, Matthew. 2002. "The Problem of Belief: Evans-Pritchard and Victor Turner on 'The Inner Life.'" *Anthropology Today* 18, no. 6: 3–8.
– 2009. "Strategic Secularism: Bible Advocacy in England." *Social Analysis* 53, no. 1: 39–54.
Epp, Esther Ruth. 1980. "The Origins of Mennonite Central Committee (Canada)." MA thesis, University of Manitoba.

Epp, Frank H. 1974. *Mennonites in Canada, 1786–1920: The History of a Separate People*. Toronto: Macmillan of Canada.

– 1982. *Mennonites in Canada, 1920–1940: A People's Struggle for Survival*. Scottdale, PA/Waterloo, ON: Herald Press.

– ed. 1983. *Partners in Service: The Story of the Mennonite Central Committee Canada 1963–1982*. Winnipeg: Mennonite Central Committee Canada.

Epp Weaver, Alain. 2006. "A Missiological Shift? Reflections on the Introduction of Results-Based Management within Mennonite Central Committee." *Mission Focus* 14: 28–42.

– 2007. "Introduction: Meeting Jesus in the Borderlands." In *Borders and Bridges: Mennonite Witness in a Religiously Diverse World*, ed. Peter Dula and Alain Epp Weaver, 11–14. Telford, PA: Cascadia.

– 2008. *States of Exile: Visions of Diaspora, Witness, and Return*. Scottdale, PA and Waterloo, ON: Herald Press.

– 2011a. "Introduction: A Table of Sharing." In *A Table of Sharing: Mennonite Central Committee and the Expanding Networks of Mennonite Identity*, ed. Alain Epp Weaver, 14–18. Telford, PA: Cascadia.

– ed. 2011b. *A Table of Sharing: Mennonite Central Committee and the Expanding Networks of Mennonite Identity*. Telford, PA: Cascadia.

– 2020. *Service and the Ministry of Reconciliation: A Missiological History of Mennonite Central Committee*. North Newton, KS: Bethel College.

Epp Weaver, Alain, and Sonia K. Weaver. 1999. *Salt and Sign: Mennonite Central Committee in Palestine, 1949–1999*. Akron, PA: Mennonite Central Committee.

Epp-Tiessen, Esther. 2009. *Pursuing Peace: The Essence of Mennonite Central Committee*. Winnipeg: Mennonite Central Committee Canada.

– 2011. "New Wine for New Wineskins: MCC and the Formation of MCC Canada." In *A Table of Sharing: Mennonite Central Committee and the Expanding Networks of Mennonite Identity*, ed. Alain Epp Weaver, 41–65. Telford, PA: Cascadia.

– 2013. *Mennonite Central Committee in Canada: A History*. Winnipeg: CMU Press.

Erb, K., 1968. "Using What's at Hand ... To Make a Forage Chopper." *Intercom* 8, no. 5: 1.

Erb, Maribeth. 2000. "Understanding Tourists: Interpretations from Indonesia." *Annals of Tourism Research* 27, no. 3: 709–36.

Erb, Paul. 1969. *Orie O. Miller: The Story of a Man and an Era*. Scottdale, PA: Herald Press.

Eriksen, Thomas Hylland. 2006. *Engaging Anthropology: The Case for a Public Presence*. Oxford: Berg.

Escobar, Arturo. 1995. *Encountering Development: The Making and Unmaking of the Third World*. Princeton, NJ: Princeton University Press.

Estes, Steven R. 1989. *Love in Action: The Story of Thirty Illinois Mennonite Relief Sales*. Henry: Illinois Mennonite Relief Sale Association.

Esteva, Gustavo. 1992. "Development." In *The Development Dictionary: A Guide to Knowledge as Power*, ed. Wolfgang Sachs, 6–25. London: Zed Books.

Fassin, Didier, 2010. "*Noli Me Tangere*: The Moral Untouchability of Humanitarianism." In *Forces of Compassion: Humanitarianism Between Ethics and Politics*, ed. Erica Bornstein and Peter Redfield, 35–52. Santa Fe, NM: SAR Press.

– 2012. *Humanitarian Reason: A Moral History of the Present*. Berkeley: University of California Press.

Fealy, Greg. 2004. "Islamic Radicalism in Indonesia: The Faltering Revival?" *Southeast Asian Affairs*, pp. 104–22.

Fearon, James, 2008. "The Rise of Emergency Relief Aid." In *Humanitarianism in Question: Politics, Power, Ethics*, ed. Michael Barnett and Thomas G. Weiss, 49–72. Ithaca, NY: Cornell University Press.

Feener, R. Michael. 2007. *Muslim Legal Thought in Modern Indonesia*. Cambridge: Cambridge University Press.

– 2013. *Shari'a and Social Engineering: The Implementation of Islamic Law in Contemporary Aceh, Indonesia*. Oxford: Oxford University Press.

Feener, R. Michael, and Philip Fountain. 2018. "Religion in the Age of Development." *Religions* 9, no. 12, 382: 1–23.

Feener, R. Michael, and Catherine Scheer. 2018. "Development's Missions." In *The Mission of Development: Religion and Techno-Politics in Asia*, ed. Catherine Scheer, Philip Fountain, and R. Michael Feener, 1–27. Leiden: Brill.

Fechter, Anne-Meike. 2007. *Transnational Lives: Expatriates in Indonesia*. London: Ashgate.

Ferguson, James. 1994. *The Anti-Politics Machine: "Development," Depoliticization, and Bureaucratic Power in Lesotho*. Minneapolis: University of Minnesota Press.

Fiddian-Qasmiyeh, Elena. 2014. *The Ideal Refugees: Gender, Islam, and the Sahrawi Politics of Survival*. Syracuse, NY: Syracuse University Press.

Finger, Thomas. 2008. "Demonization and Dialogue." *Anabaptist-Mennonite Scholars Network Newsletter* 11, no. 2: 9–11.

Firman, Tommy. 2000. "Rural to Urban Land Conversion in Indonesia during Boom and Bust Periods." *Land Use Policy* 17, no. 1: 13–20.

– 2004. "New Town Development in Jakarta Metropolitan Region: A Perspective of Spatial Segregation." *Habitat International* 28, no. 3: 349–68.

Fischer, Johan. 2011. *The Halal Frontier: Muslim Consumers in a Globalized Market*. New York: Palgrave Macmillan.

Fisher, William F. 1997. "Doing Good? The Politics and Antipolitics of NGO Politics." *Annual Review of Anthropology* 26: 439–64.

Fitzgerald, Timothy. 2003. *The Ideology of Religious Studies*. New York: Oxford University Press.

– ed. 2007. *Religion and the Secular: Historical and Colonial Formations*. London: Equinox.

– 2011. *Religion and Politics in International Relations: The Modern Myth*. London: Continuum.

Flueckiger, Joyce Burkhalter. 2006. *In Amma's Healing Room: Gender and Vernacular Islam in South India*. Bloomington and Indianapolis: Indiana University Press.

– 2015. *Everyday Hinduism*. West Sussex: Wiley Blackwell.

Foster, Greg, Scott Coats, Kevin Stout, and Chandran Williams. 1992. *Research Survey Report on MCC Missiology Dialogue*. Philadelphia, PA, Eastern College. MCC Archives (Akron, PA).

Formicola, Jo-Renee, Mary Segers, and Paul Weber. 2003. *Faith-Based Initiatives and the Bush Administration: The Good, the Bad, and the Ugly*. Lanham, MD: Rowman and Littlefield.

Foucault, Michel. 1978. *The History of Sexuality: An Introduction*. New York: Pantheon.

Fountain, Philip. 2011. "Orienting Guesthood in the Mennonite Central Committee, Indonesia." In *Inside the Everyday Lives of Development Workers: The Challenges and Futures of Aidland*, edited by Anne-Meike Fechter and Heather Hindman, 83–106. Bloomfield, CT: Kumarian.

– 2012. "Blurring Mission and Development in the Mennonite Central Committee." In *Mission and Development: God's Work or Good Work*, edited by Matthew Clarke, 143–166. London, Continuum.

– 2013a. "The Myth of Religious NGOs: Development Studies and the Return of Religion." *International Development Policy: Religion and Development* 4: 9–30.

– 2013b. "The Perils of Fieldwork." *Manusia dan Masyarakat: New Series* 24: 21–45.

– 2013c. "Toward a Post-Secular Anthropology." *Australian Journal of Anthropology* 24, no. 3: 310–28.

– 2014. "Development Things: A Case of Canned Meat." *Sites: New Series* 11, no. 1: 39–73.

– 2015. "Proselytising Development." In *The Routledge Handbook of Religions and Global Development*, ed. Emma Tomalin, 80–97. London: Routledge.

– 2016. "Mennonite Disaster Relief and the Interfaith Encounter in Aceh, Indonesia." *Asian Ethnology* 75, no. 1: 163–90.

– 2017. "Creedal Monologism and Theological Articulation in the Mennonite Central Committee." In *The Monologic Imagination*, ed. Matt Tomlinson and Julian Millie, 203–30. Oxford: Oxford University Press.

– 2020. "Mennonites and Anthropology: An Introduction." *Journal of Mennonite Studies* 38: 11–22.

Fountain, Philip, Robin Bush, and R. Michael Feener. 2015a. "Religion and the Politics of Development." In *Religion and the Politics of Development*, ed. Philip Fountain, Robin Bush, and R. Michael Feener, 11–34. Hampshire: Palgrave.

– 2015b. "Religious Actors in Disaster Relief: An Introduction." *International Journal of Mass Emergencies and Disasters* 33, no. 2: 1–16.

Fountain, Philip, and R. Michael Feener. 2017. "Navigating a World of Religious NGOs: Ethnography, Abstraction, and Views of the Horizon." *Geography Compass* 11, no. 10: e12328.

Fountain, Philip, and Sin Wen Lau. 2013. "Anthropological Theologies: Engagements and Encounters." *Australian Journal of Anthropology* 24, no. 3: 227–34.

Fountain, Philip, and Levi McLaughlin. 2016. "Salvage and Salvation: An Introduction." *Asian Ethnology* 75, no. 1: 1–28.

Fountain, Philip, and Marie Juul Petersen. 2018. "NGOs and Religion: Instrumentalisation and its Discontents." In *Handbook of Research on NGOs*, ed. Aynsley Kellow and Hannah Murphy-Gregory, 404–32. Cheltenham: Edward Elgar.

Fountain, Philip, and Laura Meitzner Yoder. 2018. "Quietist Techno-Politics: Agricultural Development and Mennonite Mission in Indonesia." In *The Mission of Development: Religion and Techno-Politics in Asia*, ed. Catherine Scheer, Philip Fountain, and R. Michael Feener, 214–42. Leiden: Brill.

– 2022. "Celebration, Critique, and Belonging: Commemorating the Mennonite Central Committee." *Journal of Mennonite Studies* 40, no. 1, 11–32.

Freedman, Michael G. 2010. "Prosecuting Terrorism: The Material Support Statute and Muslim Charities." *Hastings Constitutional Law Quarterly* 38, no. 4: 1113–47.

Friedmann, Robert. 1990. "Anabaptist Theology." *Mennonite Historical Bulletin* 51, no. 2: 4–7.

Friesen, Herb. 1995. *A Reluctant Surgeon: Reflections of a Farm Boy Turned Ophthalmologist*. Islamabad: Author.

Friesen, Leonard G. 2018. "Introduction." In *Minority Report: Mennonite Identities in Imperial Russia and Soviet Ukraine Reconsidered, 1789–1945*, ed. Leonard G. Friesen, 3–22. Toronto: University of Toronto Press.

Froese, D.C. 1980. "MCC Quarterly Report: May – June – July 1980: Transmigration Program – Indonesia." Mennonite Central Committee Indonesia. MCC Archives (Akron, PA).

– 1981. "Froese Termination of Service and Departure Plans." Mennonite Central Committee Indonesia. MCC Archives (Akron, PA).

Furani, Khaled. 2019. *Redeeming Anthropology: A Theological Critique of a Modern Science*. Oxford: Oxford University Press.

Gaillard, Jean-Christophe, Elsa Clavé, and Ilan Kelman. 2008. "Wave of Peace? Tsunami Disaster Diplomacy in Aceh, Indonesia." *Geoforum* 39, no. 1: 511–26.

Gatehouse, Jonathon. 2007. "You've Been Talking to Who?" *Maclean's*, 21 May, 20.

Geertz, Clifford, 1960a. "The Javanese Kijaji: The Changing Role of a Cultural Broker." *Comparative Studies in Society and History* 2, no. 2: 228–49.

– 1960b. *The Religion of Java*, Chicago: University of Chicago Press.

– 1973. *The Interpretation of Cultures*. New York: Basic Books.

Gingerich, Ray, and Earl Zimmerman, eds. 2006. *Telling Our Stories: Personal Accounts of Engagement with Scripture*. Telford, PA: Cascadia.

Glick, Helen Liechty. 1985. *Spiritsong: Mennonite Central Committees' 25 years in Bolivia*. Akron, PA: Mennonite Central Committee.

Goossen, Benjamin. 2016. "From Aryanism to Anabaptism: Nazi Race Science and the Language of Mennonite Ethnicity." *Mennonite Quarterly Review* 90, no. 2: 135–63.

– 2017. *Chosen Nation: Mennonites and Germany in a Global Era*. Princeton, NJ: Princeton University Press.

– 2018. "A Small World Power: How the Nazi Regime Viewed Mennonites." *Mennonite Quarterly Review* 92, no. 2: 173–206.

Goossen, Rachel Waltner. 1997. *Women against the Good War: Conscientious Objection and Gender on the American Home Front, 1941–1947*. Chapel Hill: University of North Carolina Press.

– 2015. "'Defanging the Beast': Mennonite Responses to John Howard Yoder's Sexual Abuse." *Mennonite Quarterly Review* 89, no. 1: 7–80.

Graber Miller, Keith. 1996. *Wise as Serpents, Innocent as Doves: American Mennonites Engage Washington*. Knoxville: University of Tennessee Press.

Grace, Kristen A., D. Merril Ewert, and Paul R. Eberts. 1995. "MCCers and Evangelicals: Perspectives of Development." *Conrad Grebel Review* 13, no. 3: 365–89.

Graeber, David. 2009. *Direct Action: An Ethnography*. Oakland, CA: AK Press.

Grayman, Jesse Hession, Mary-Jo Delvecchio Good, and Byron J. Good. 2009. "Conflict Nightmares and Trauma in Aceh." *Culture, Medicine, and Psychiatry* 33, no. 2: 290–312.

Green, Maia. 2009. "Doing Development and Writing Culture." *Anthropological Theory* 9, no. 4: 395–417.

Green, Stanley W., and James R. Krabill. 2011. "The Missiology of MCC: A Framework for Assessing Multiple Voices within the MCC Family." In *A Table of Sharing: Mennonite Central Committee and the Expanding Networks of Mennonite Identity*, ed. Alain Epp Weaver, 192–212. Telford, PA: Cascadia.

Gregory, Brad S. 1999. *Salvation at Stake: Christian Martyrdom in Early Modern Europe*. Cambridge, MA: Harvard University Press.

Gross, Joshua. 2011. "Proscription Problems: The Practical Implications of Terrorist Lists on Diplomacy and Peacebuilding in Nepal." *Praxis* 26: 38–59.

Grubbs, Larry, 2009. *Secular Missionaries: Americans and African Development in the 1960s*. Amherst: University of Massachusetts Press.

Guenther, Bruce L. 2011. "Evangelicalism in Mennonite Historiography: The Decline of Anabaptism or a Path towards Dynamic Ecumenism?" *Journal of Mennonite Studies* 24: 35–53.

Guggenheim, Scott. 2006. "Crises and Contradictions: Understanding the Origins of a Community Development Project in Indonesia." In *The Search for Empowerment: Social Capital as Idea and Practice at the World Bank*, ed. Anthony Bebbington, Michael Woolcock, Scott Guggenheim, and Elizabeth Olson, 111–44. Bloomfield, CT: Kumarian Press.

Gupta, Akhil. 1995. "Blurred Boundaries: The Discourse of Corruption, the Culture of Politics, and the Imagined State." *American Ethnologist* 22, no. 2: 375–402.

– 2012. *Red Tape: Bureaucracy, Structural Violence, and Poverty in India*. Durham, NC: Duke University Press.

Gupta, Akhil, and James Ferguson, eds. 1997a. *Anthropological Locations: Boundaries and Grounds of a Field Science*. Berkeley: University of California Press.

– 1997b. "Discipline and Practice: 'The Field' as Site, Method, and Location in Anthropology." In *Anthropological Locations: Boundaries and Grounds of a Field Science*, ed. Akhil Gupta and James Ferguson, 1–46. Berkeley: University of California Press.

Gustafson-Zook, Les. 2007. "Penny Power Song." Akron, PA: MCC. http://pennypower.org/resources/pennysong/PennyPower_G_Zook.pdf.

Gusterson, Hugh. 1997. "Studying Up Revisited." *PoLAR: Political and Legal Anthropology Review* 20, no. 1: 114–19.

Hackworth, Jason. 2012. *Faith Based: Religious Neoliberalism and the Politics of Welfare in the United States*. Athens: University of Georgia Press.

Hadianto, Gunawan Susanto. 2008. "Sejarah Pembentukan Gereja-Gereja Tionghoa di Jawa Ditinjau Dari Sudut Pandang Misiologi." *Jurnal Amanat Agung* 4, no. 2: 199–225.

Hadiwinata, Bob S. 2003. *The Politics of NGOs in Indonesia: Development Democracy and Managing a Movement*. London: RoutledgeCurzon.

Hadiz, Vedi R. 2004. "The Failure of State Ideology in Indonesia: The Rise and Demise of *Pancasila*." In *Communitarian Politics in Asia*, ed. Chua Beng Huat, 148–61. London: RoutledgeCurzon.

Hall, Sarah Marie. 2009. "'Private Life' and 'Work Life': Difficulties and Dilemmas When Making and Maintaining Friendships with Ethnographic Participants." *Area* 41, no. 3: 263–72.

Hange, Roy. 2007. "A Dialogue of Civilizations: The Encounter of Iranian Shi'ites and North American Mennonites." In *Borders and Bridges: Mennonite Witness in a Religiously Diverse World*, ed. Peter Dula and Alain Epp Weaver, 105–16. Telford, PA: Cascadia.

Hann, Chris, and Hermann Goltz. 2010. "Introduction: The Other Christianity?" In *Eastern Christians in Anthropological Perspective*, ed. Chris Hann and Hermann Goltz, 1–29. Los Angeles and San Francisco: University of California Press.

Hannerz, Ulf. 2003. "Being There … and There … and There! Reflections on Multi-Site Ethnography." *Ethnography* 4, no. 2: 201–16.

– 2004. *Foreign News: Exploring the World of Foreign Correspondents*. Chicago: University of Chicago Press.

– 2006. "Studying Down, Up, Sideways, Through, Backwards, Forwards, Away and at Home: Reflections on the Field Worries of an Expansive Discipline." In *Locating the Field: Space, Place and Context in Anthropology*, ed. Simon Coleman and Peter Collins, 23–41. Oxford: Berg.

Harder, Alan. 1985. "Mennonite Central Committee (Indonesia) Transmigration Program Plan FY 1986." Mennonite Central Committee Indonesia. MCC Archives (Akron, PA).

– 1986. "The Use of Credit in Integrated Rural Development: Report on the MCC Livestock Program in the Tulang Bawang and Rasau Jaya Second Stage Development Project with a Focus on Integrating Rural Credit and Pre-Cooperative Group Development." Mennonite Central Committee Indonesia. MCC Archives (Akron, PA).

Harding, Susan. 1991. "Representing Fundamentalism: The Problem of the Repugnant Cultural Other." *Social Research* 58, no. 2: 373–93.

Harman, Graham, 2009. *Prince of Networks: Bruno Latour and Metaphysics*. Melbourne: Re-Press.

Harris, Vandra. 2005. "The Development Contact Zone: Practitioner Perspectives on Culture, Power and Participation in Cambodia and the Philippines." PhD diss., Flinders University (Adelaide).

– 2008. "Mediators or Partners? Practitioner Perspectives on Partnership." *Development in Practice* 18, no. 6: 701–12.

Hartch, Todd. 2006. *Missionaries of the State: The Summer Institute of Linguistics, State Formation, and Indigenous Mexico, 1935–1985*. Tuscaloosa: University of Alabama Press.

Hartzler, Ken. 2011. "Inflows and Outflows." *Sounding Board: A Newsletter of the North American Mennonite Relief Sale Board* (January): 3.

Hasan, Noorhaidi. 2006. *Laskar Jihad: Islam, Militancy, and the Quest for Identity in Post-New Order Indonesia*, Ithaca, NY: Cornell University Press.

Haynes, Jeffrey. 2007. *Religion and Development: Conflict or Cooperation?* Houndmills: Palgrave Macmillan.

Hearn, Julie. 2007. "African NGOs: The New Compradors?" *Development and Change* 38, no. 6: 1095–1110.

Heaton Shrestha, Celayne. 2006. "'They Can't Mix Like We Can': Bracketing Differences and the Professionalization of NGOs in Nepal." In *Development Brokers and Translators: The Ethnography of Aid and Agencies*, ed. David Lewis and David Mosse, 195–216. Bloomfield, CT: Kumarian Press.

Hedman, Eva-Lotta E. 2005. "Back to the Barracks: Relokasi Pengungsi in Post-Tsunami Aceh." *Indonesia* 80: 1–19.

– ed. 2008. *Conflict, Violence, and Displacement in Indonesia*. Ithaca, NY: Cornell Southeast Asia Program Publications.

– 2009. "Deconstructing Reconstruction in Post-Tsunami Aceh: Governmentality, Displacement and Politics." *Oxford Development Studies* 37, no. 1: 63–76.

Hefferan, Tara. 2007. *Twinning Faith and Development: Catholic Parish Partnering in the US and Haiti*. Bloomfield, CT: Kumarian Press.

Hefferan, Tara, and Tim Fogarty. 2010. "The Anthropology of Faith and Development: An Introduction." *NAPA Bulletin* 33, no. 1: 1–11.

Hefner, Robert W. 2000. *Civil Islam: Muslims and Democratization in Indonesia*. Princeton, NJ: Princeton University Press.

Hein, Marvin. 1998. *A Community Is Born: The Story of the Birth, Growth, Death and Legacy of Civilian Public Service Camp #138-1, Lincoln, Nebraska 1944–1947*. Self-published.

Heisey, M.J., 2003. *Peace and Persistence: Tracing the Brethren in Christ Peace Witness through Three Generations*. Kent, OH: Kent State University Press.

Heisey, Nancy. 1995. "Brethren in Christ Participation in Mennonite Central Committee; Integral Part or Burden?" *Brethren in Christ History and Life* 18, no. 2: 177–227.

– 1993a. “MCC Missiology Statement: Draft 4.” MCC Archives (Akron, PA).
– 1993b. Missiology. Letter to John Lapp, 1 February 1993. MCC Archives (Akron, PA).
– 1996. “Race, Ethnicity, and Gender in MCC Work.” In *Unity Amidst Diversity: Mennonite Central Committee at 75*, ed. Robert S. Kreider and Ronald J. R. Mathies, 55–67. Akron, PA: Mennonite Central Committee.
– 2006. “Pilgrimage, Place, and People: A History of the Locations of Mennonite World Conference Assemblies, 1925–2003.” *Church History* 75, no. 4: 849–79.
Heisey, Nancy, and Paul Longacre. 1990. *Final Report: Mennonite International Study Project*. Elkhart, IN: Mennonite Board of Missions.
Hellman, Jörgen, and Sara Forell. 2015. “Who Is Rebuilding Aceh? Tensions between Groups of Staff in an NGO.” *Development in Practice* 25, no. 1: 58–70.
Herr, Bob, and Judy Zimmerman Herr. 2007. “Appendix: Interfaith Bridge Building – MCC International Program Department ‘Key Initiative,’ 2006–2010.” In *Borders and Bridges: Mennonite Witness in a Religiously Diverse World*, ed. Peter Dula and Alain Epp Weaver, 171–6. Telford, PA: Cascadia.
Hershberger, Guy F., ed. 1957. *The Recovery of the Anabaptist Vision*. Scottdale, PA: Mennonite Publishing House.
– 1970. “Historical Background to the Formation of the Mennonite Central Committee.” *Mennonite Quarterly Review* 44, no. 3: 213–44.
Heryanto, Ariel. 1999. “The Years of Living Luxuriously: Identity Politics of Indonesia’s New Rich.” In *Culture and Privilege in Capitalist Asia*, ed. Michael Pinches, 160–88. London: Routledge.
Hicks, Jacqueline. 2018. “Heresy and Authority: Understanding the Turn against Ahmadiyah in Indonesia.” *South East Asia Research* 22, no. 3: 321–39.
Hiebert, Peter Cornelius, and Orie O. Miller. 1929. *Feeding the Hungry: Russia Famine 1919–1925: American Mennonite Relief Operations under the Auspices of Mennonite Central Committee*. Scottdale, PA: Mennonite Central Committee.
Hilhorst, Dorothea. 2003. *The Real World of NGOs: Discourses, Diversity and Development*. London: Zed Books.
Hindman, Heather, and Anne-Meike Fechter. 2011. “Introduction.” In *Inside the Everyday Lives of Development Workers: The Challenges and Futures of Aidland*, ed. Anne-Meike Fechter and Heather Hindman, 1–20. Bloomfield, CT: Kumarian Press.
Hoekema, Alle. 1978. “Pieter Jansz (1820–1904) First Mennonite Missionary to Java.” *Mennonite Quarterly Review* 52: 58–76.
– 2001. *Dutch Mennonite Mission in Indonesia: Historical Essays*. Elkhart, IN: Institute of Mennonite Studies.

Honna, Jun. 2001. "Military Ideology in Response to Democratic Pressure during the Late Suharto Era: Political and Institutional Contexts." In *Violence and the State in Suharto's Indonesia*, ed. Benedict R.O. Anderson, 54–89. Ithaca, NY: SEAP Publications.

Hopgood, Stephen. 2006. *Keepers of the Flame: Understanding Amnesty International*. Ithaca, NY: Cornell University Press.

– 2013. *The Endtimes of Human Rights*. Ithaca, NY: Cornell University Press.

Horst, Irvin B. 1950. *A Ministry of Goodwill*. Akron, PA: Mennonite Central Committee.

Hostetter, C. Nelson., E. Morris Sider, and Samuel Steiner. 2018. "Brethren in Christ Church." *Global Anabaptist Mennonite Encyclopedia Online*. https://gameo.org/index.php?title=Brethren_in_Christ_Church.

Hovland, Ingie. 2008. "Who's Afraid of Religion? Tensions between 'Mission' and 'Development' in the Norwegian Mission Society." In *Development, Civil Society and Faith-Based Organizations: Bridging the Sacred and the Secular*, ed. Gerard Clarke and Michael Jennings, 171–86. Houndmills: Palgrave Macmillan.

Huang, C. Julia. 2009. *Charisma and Compassion: Cheng Yen and the Buddhist Tzu Chi Movement*. Cambridge, MA: Harvard University Press.

Hull, Matthew. 2012. *Government of Paper: The Materiality of Bureaucracy in Urban Pakistan*. Berkeley: University of California Press.

Huntington, Samuel P. 1993. "The Clash of Civilizations." *Foreign Affairs* 72, no. 3: 22–49.

– 1997. *The Clash of Civilizations and the Remaking of World Order*. New York: Touchstone.

Ibrahim, Dina. 2010."The Framing of Islam on Network News Following the September 11th Attacks." *International Communication Gazette* 72, no. 1: 111–25.

Immerwahr, Daniel. 2015. *Thinking Small: The United States and the Lure of Community Development*. Cambridge, MA: Harvard University Press.

Intan, Benyamin F. 2006. *"Public Religion" and the Pancasila-Based State of Indonesia: An Ethical and Sociological Analysis*. New York: Peter Lang.

International Crisis Group. 2001. *Indonesia: Violence and Radical Muslims*, Jakarta/Brussels: International Crisis Group, 10 October. https://www.crisisgroup.org/asia/south-east-asia/indonesia/indonesia-violence-and-radical-muslims.

– 2009. *Indonesia: Deep Distrust in Aceh as Elections Approach*. Jakarta/Brussels: International Crisis Group, 23 March. https://www.crisisgroup.org/asia/south-east-asia/indonesia/indonesia-deep-distrust-aceh-elections-approach.

Jackson, Liz. 2010. "Images of Islam in US Media and Their Educational Implications." *Educational Studies* 46, no. 1: 3–24.

Jackson, Michael. 1995. *At Home in the World*. Durham, NC: Duke University Press.

– 1998. *Minima Ethnographica: Intersubjectivity and the Anthropological Project*. Chicago: University of Chicago Press.

– 2002. *The Politics of Storytelling: Violence, Transgression and Intersubjecitivty*. Copenhagen: Museum Tusculanum Press.

Jamison, Matthew. 2011. "Humanitarian Intervention since 1990 and 'Liberal Interventionism.'" In *Humanitarian Intervention: A History*, ed. Brendan Simms and D.J.B. Trim, 365–80. Cambridge: Cambridge University Press.

Jantzen, Mark, and John Thiesen, eds. 2020. *European Mennonites and the Holocaust*. Toronto: University of Toronto Press.

Jantzi, Jeanne Z. 2007. "Indonesia: Living in the Mystery." In *Borders and Bridges: Mennonite Witness in a Religiously Diverse World*, ed. Peter Dula and Alain Epp Weaver, 17–30. Telford, PA: Cascadia.

Jantzi, Terrence Lee. 2000. "Local Program Theories and Social Capital: A Case Study of a Non-Governmental Organization in Eastern Bolivia." PhD diss., Cornell University.

Jones, Ben, and Marie Juul Petersen. 2011. "Instrumental, Narrow, Normative? Reviewing Recent Work on Religion and Development." *Third World Quarterly* 32, no. 7: 1291–306.

Juhnke, James C. 1989. *Vision, Doctrine, War: Mennonite Identity and Organization in America, 1890–1930*. Scottdale, PA: Herald Press.

– 1996. "War and the Mennonite Agenda in the 20th Century." In *Unity Amidst Diversity: Mennonite Central Committee at 75*, ed. Robert Kreider and Ronald J.R. Mathies, 11–18. Akron, PA: Mennonite Central Committee.

– 2011. "Turning Points, Broken Ice, and Glaubensgenossen: What Happened at Prairie Street on July 27–28, 1920?" In *A Table of Sharing: Mennonite Central Committee and the Expanding Networks of Mennonite Identity*, ed. Alain Epp Weaver, 66–83. Telford, PA: Cascadia.

Juul Petersen, Marie. 2011. "Islamizing Aid: Transnational Muslim NGOs After 9.11." *VOLUNTAS: International Journal of Voluntary and Nonprofit Organizations* 23, no. 1: 126–55.

– 2016. *For Humanity or for the Umma? Aid and Islam in Transnational Muslim NGOs*. London: Hurst.

Jurey, D. 1984. "From Livestock Credit to Establishing Farmers' Cooperatives: The Changing Focus of MCC Indonesia." Mennonite Central Committee Indonesia. MCC Archives (Akron, PA).

Jurgelski, Susan. 2010. "Mennonite Central Committee Goes Mobile with Meat: Helping Feed the Hungry Worldwide." *LancasterOnline.com*. Available at: https://lancasteronline.com/features/mennonite-central-committee-goes-mobile-with-meat/article_7878b41e-4a79-5ce8-9d98-072983869683.html.

Kaell, Hillary. 2020. *Christian Globalism at Home: Child Sponsorship in the United States*. Princeton, NJ: Princeton University Press.

Kahin, Audrey R. 1983. "Brokers and Middlemen in Indonesian History: A Review." *Indonesia* 36: 135–42.

Kahn, Joel S. 2011. "Understanding: Between Belief and Unbelief." *Australian Journal of Anthropology* 22, no. 1: 76–88.

Kanagy, Conrad. 2007. *Road Signs for the Journey: A Profile of Mennonite Church USA*. Scottdale, PA: Herald Press.

Kasdorf, Julia S. 2009. *The Body and the Book: Writing from a Mennonite Life*. University Park: Pennsylvania State University Press.

Kauffman, J. Howard, and Leo Driedger. 1991. *The Mennonite Mosaic: Identity and Modernization*. Scottdale, PA: Herald Press.

Keahey, Jennifer, Mary A. Littrell, and Douglas Murray. 2011. "Business with a Mission: The Ongoing Role of Ten Thousand Villages within the Fair Trade Movement." In *A Table of Sharing: Mennonite Central Committee and the Expanding Networks of Mennonite Identity*, ed. Alain Epp Weaver, 265–83. Telford, PA: Cascadia.

Keane, Webb. 2007. *Christian Moderns: Freedom and Fetish in the Mission Encounter*. Berkeley: University of California Press.

Kehler, Larry. 1970. "The Many Activities of the Mennonite Central Committee." *Mennonite Quarterly Review* 44, no. 3: 298–315.

Keim, Albert N. 1998. *Harold S. Bender, 1897–1962*. Scottdale, PA: Herald Press.

Kenny, Sue, Matthew Clarke, Ismet Fanany, and Damien Kingsbury. 2010. "Deconstructing Aceh's Reconstruction." In *Post-Disaster Reconstruction: Lessons from Aceh*, ed. Matthew Clarke, Ismet Fanany, and Sue Kenny, 3–27. London: Earthscan.

Kilby, Patrick. 2006. "Accountability for Empowerment: Dilemmas Facing Non-Governmental Organizations." *World Development* 34, no. 6: 951–63.

King, Sidney. 2001. "In the Footsteps of Clayton Kratz." In *Gathering at the Hearth: Stories Mennonites Tell*, ed. John E. Sharp, 212–13. Scottdale, PA: Herald Press.

Kingsbury, Damien, 2010. "Political Reconstruction in Aceh." In *Post-Disaster Reconstruction: Lessons from Aceh*, ed. Matthew Clarke, Ismet Fanany, and Sue Kenny, 61–78. London: Earthscan.

Klassen, Arli, and Daryl Byler. 2008a. "MCC Dialogue Toward Peace with Iran." *Mennonite Central Committee*. 30 September. http://mcc.org/news/news/article.html?id=396. Viewed April 2011.

– 2008b. "MCC: Called to Talk with the 'Enemy.'" *Mennonite Weekly Review* 86, no. 37: 6.

Klassen, Pamela. 2011. *Spirits of Protestantism: Medicine, Healing, and Liberal Christianity*. Berkeley: University of California Press.

Klets, Viktor. 2018. "Caught between Two Poles: Ukrainian Mennonites and the Trauma of the Second World War." In *Minority Report: Mennonite Identities in Imperial Russia and Soviet Ukraine Reconsidered, 1789–1945*, ed. Leonard Friesen, 187–317. Toronto: University of Toronto Press.

Klippenstein, Lawrence. 1998. "Canadian Mennonite Service in World War II." In *Alternative Service for Peace in Canada during World War II, 1941–1946*, ed. A.J. Klassen, 2–9. Abbotsford, BC: Mennonite Central Committee (BC) Seniors for Peace.

Kniss, Fred. 1997. *Disquiet in the Land: Cultural Conflict in American Mennonite Communities*. New Brunswick, NJ: Rutgers University Press.

Koop, Karl. 2014. "Anabaptist and Mennonite Identity: Permeable Boundaries and Expanding Definitions." *Religion Compass* 8, no. 6: 199–207.

– 2016. "A Complication for the Mennonite Peace Tradition: Wilhelm Mannhardt's Defense of Military Service." *Conrad Grebel Review* 34, no. 1: 28–48.

Korten, David C. 1990. *Getting to the 21st Century: Voluntary Action and the Global Agenda*. West Hartford, CT: Kumarian Press.

Kraus, C. Norman. 1994. *A Theological Basis for Intervention Ministries*. Akron, PA: Mennonite Central Committee.

Kraybill, Donald B. 1996. "From Enclave to Engagement: MCC and the Transformation of Mennonite Identity." In *Unity Amidst Diversity: Mennonite Central Committee at 75*, ed. Robert S. Kreider and Ronald J. R. Mathies, 19–42. Akron, PA: Mennonite Central Committee.

Kraybill, Mary Jean. 2003. "Reflections on Growing up Mennonite in Lancaster County." *Mennonite Quarterly Review* 77, no. 2: 217–34.

Kreider, Robert S. 1970. "The Impact of MCC service on American Mennonites." *Mennonite Quarterly Review* 44, no. 3: 245–61.

– 1996. "The Multiple Visions of MCC's 75 Years." In *Unity Amidst Diversity: Mennonite Central Committee at 75*, ed. Robert S. Kreider and Ronald J. R. Mathies, 1–10. Akron, PA: Mennonite Central Committee.

Kreider, Robert S., and Rachel Waltner Goossen. 1988. *Hungry, Thirsty, a Stranger: The MCC Experience*. Scottdale, PA: Herald Press.

Kreider, Robert S., and Ronald J.R. Mathies, eds. 1996. *Unity Amidst Diversity: Mennonite Central Committee at 75*. Akron, PA: Mennonite Central Committee.

Kuitenbrouwer, Maarten. 1982. "The Concept of Middleman and the Study of Indonesian History." In *Papers of the Dutch-Indonesian Historical Conference Held at Lage Vuursche, the Netherlands, 23–27 June 1980*, ed. Gerrit Schutte and Heather Sutherland, 98–128. Leiden and Jakarta: Bureau of Indonesian Studies.

Kusenbach, Margarethe. 2003. "Street Phenomenology". *Ethnography* 4, no. 3: 455–85.

Lamoureux, Florence. 2003. *Indonesia: A Global Studies Handbook*. Santa Barbara, CA: ABC-CLIO.

Land, Richard. 2008. "Let It Be Recorded: We Are Not Silent!" *The Ethics and Religious Liberty Commission of the Southern Baptist Convention*. http://erlc.com/article/let-it-be-recorded-we-are-not-silent/. Viewed April 2011.

Lapp, John A. 1970. "The Peace Mission of the Mennonite Central Committee." *Mennonite Quarterly Review* 44, no. 3: 281–97.

Larsen, Erica M. 2018. "Developing Faith and Character to Develop the Nation: Perspectives from an Elite Indonesian Catholic School." In *The Mission of Development: Religion and Techno-Politics in Asia*, ed. Catherine Scheer, Philip Fountain, and R. Michael Feener, 165–89. Leiden: Brill.

Lash, Nicholas. 1996. *The Beginning and the End of "Religion."* Cambridge: Cambridge University Press.

Latour, Bruno. 1993. *We Have Never Been Modern*. Cambridge, MA: Harvard University Press.

– 1996. *Aramis, or, The Love of Technology*. Cambridge, MA: Harvard University Press.

– 1999. *Pandora's Hope: Essays on the Reality of Science Studies*. Cambridge, MA: Harvard University Press.

– 2005. *Reassembling the Social: An Introduction to Actor-Network-Theory*. Oxford: Oxford University Press.

– 2010. *On the Modern Cult of the Factish Gods*. Durham, NC: Duke University Press.

Lederach, John Paul. 1995. *Preparing for Peace: Conflict Transformation Across Cultures*. Syracuse, NY: Syracuse University Press.

– 1997. *Building Peace: Sustainable Reconciliation in Divided Societies*. Washington, DC: United States Institute of Peace.

– 1999. *The Journey toward Reconciliation*. Scottdale, PA/Waterloo, ON: Herald Press.

– 2003. *The Little Book of Conflict Transformation.* Intercourse, PA: Good Books.

– 2005. *The Moral Imagination: The Art and Soul of Building Peace.* New York: Oxford University Press.

Lefranc, Sandrine. 2008. "Des Pacificateurs Inspirés: Notes sur des Groupes Anabaptistes et Evangeliques Americains." *Terrain* 51: 42–9.

Legenhausen, Hajj Muhammad. 2007. "Christians Talking with Muslims: An American Muslim's Perspective." *Peace Office Newsletter* 37, no. 3: 11–12.

Lehman, Celia. 1998. *History of the Ohio Mennonite Relief Sale.* Sugarcreek, OH: Carlisle Printing.

Leitmann, Josef. 2007. "Cities and Calamities: Learning from Post-Disaster Response in Indonesia." *Journal of Urban Health* 84, no. S1: 144–53.

Lemons, J. Derrick, ed. 2018. *Theologically Engaged Anthropology.* Oxford: Oxford University Press.

Lesher, Emerson L. 1985. *The Muppie Manual: The Mennonite Urban Professional's Handbook for Humility and Success.* Intercourse, PA: Good Books.

Leverett, Flynt, and Hillary Mann Leverett. 2010. "The United States, Iran and the Middle East's New 'Cold War.'" *International Spectator: Italian Journal of International Affairs* 45, no. 1: 75–87.

Lewis, Bernard. 1990. "The Roots of Muslim Rage." *Atlantic Monthly* 266, no. 3: 47–60.

Lewis, David. 1998. "Development NGOs and the Challenge of Partnership: Changing Relations between North and South." *Social Policy and Administration* 32, no. 5: 501–12.

– 2005. "Individuals, Organizations and Public Action: Trajectories of the Non-Governmental in Development Studies." In *A Radical History of Development Studies*, ed. Uma Kothari, 200–22. London: Zed Books.

Lewis, David, and Nazneen Kanji. 2009. *Non-Governmental Organizations and Development.* London: Routledge.

Lewis, David, and David Mosse, eds. 2006a. *Development Brokers and Translators: The Ethnography of Aid and Agencies.* Bloomfield, CT: Kumarian Press.

– 2006b. "Encountering Order and Disjuncture: Contemporary Anthropological Perspectives on the Organization of Development." *Oxford Development Studies* 34, no. 1: 1–13.

Li, Tania M. 2007. *The Will to Improve: Governmentality, Development, and the Practice of Politics.* Durham, NC: Duke University Press.

Liechty, Joseph. 1991. Letter to Ray Brubacher, 29 November 1991. MCC Archives (Akron, PA).

Lind, Mary Beth, and Cathleen Hockman-Wert. 2005. *Simply in Season: Recipes That Celebrate Fresh, Local Foods in the Spirit of More-with-Less*. Scottdale, PA/Waterloo, ON: Herald Press.

Lind, Timothy. 1988. *Service and Servanthood*. Akron, PA: Mennonite Central Committee.

– n.d. *Biblical Obedience and Development*. Akron, PA: Mennonite Central Committee.

Lindquist, Johan. 2012. "The Elementary School Teacher, the Thug and His Grandmother: Informal Brokers and Transnational Migration from Indonesia." *Pacific Affairs* 85, no. 1: 69–89.

Loewen, Bill. 1992. "The MCC Quilt." *Intercom* 36, no. 1: 4.

Loewen, Royden. 2008. "The Poetics of Peoplehood: Ethnicity and Religion among Canada's Mennonites." In *Christianity and Ethnicity in Canada*, ed. Paul Bramadat and David Seljak, 330–64. Toronto: University of Toronto Press.

Long, Norman, ed. 1989. *Encounters at the Interface: A Perspective on Social Discontinuities in Rural Development*. Wageningen: Agricultural University Wageningen.

Long, Norman. 2001. *Development Sociology: Actor Perspectives*. London: Routledge.

Long, Norman, and Ann Long, eds. 1992. *Battlefields of Knowledge: The Interlocking of Theory and Practice in Social Research and Development*. London: Routledge.

Longacre, Doris J. 1976. *More-with-Less Cookbook*. Scottdale, PA: Herald Press.

– 1980. *Living More with Less*. Scottdale, PA: Herald Press.

Lukens-Bull, Ronald A., and Mark R. Woodward. 2011. "Goliath and David in Gaza: Indonesian Myth-Building and Conflict as a Cultural System." *Contemporary Islam* 5, no. 1: 1–17.

MacDonald, G. Jeffrey. 2008. "Pacifist Churches under Fire for Ahmadinejad Dinner." *National Catholic Reporter*, 19 September. https://www.ncronline.org/news/pacifist-churches-under-fire-ahmadinejad-dinner.

MacFarquhar, Neil. 2007. "As Muslim Group Goes on Trial, Other Charities Watch Warily." *New York Times*, 17 July. http://www.nytimes.com/2007/07/17/us/17charity.html?_r=1.

MacIntyre, Alasdair. 1988. *Whose Justice? Which Rationality?* Notre Dame, IN: University of Notre Dame Press.

MacMaster, Richard K. 1985. *Land, Piety, Peoplehood: The Establishment of Mennonite Communities in America, 1683–1790*. Scottdale, PA: Herald Press.

Macrae, Joanna, and Adele Harmer, eds. 2009. *Humanitarian Action and the "Global War on Terror": A Review of Trends and Issues*. London: Overseas Development Institute.

Mahmood, Saba. 2001. "Feminist Theory, Embodiment, and the Docile Agent: Some Reflections on the Egyptian Islamic Revival." *Cultural Anthropology* 16, no. 2: 202–36.

– 2005. *Politics of Piety: The Islamic Revival and the Feminist Subject*. Princeton, NJ: Princeton University Press.

Malkki, Liisa. 2015. *The Need to Help: The Domestic Arts of International Humanitarianism*. Durham, NC: Duke University Press.

Marcus, George E. 1995. "Ethnography in/of the World System: The Emergence of Multi-Sited Ethnography." *Annual Review of Anthropology* 24: 95–117.

– 1999. "What Is at Stake – and Is Not – in the Idea and Practice of Multi-Sited Ethnography." *Canberra Anthropology* 22, no. 2: 6–14.

Margulies, Peter. 2011. "Accountable Altruism: The Impact of the Federal Material Support Statute on Humanitarian Aid." *Suffolk Transnational Law Review* 34, no. 539: 1–19.

Markowitz, Lisa. 2001. "Finding the Field: Notes on the Ethnography of NGOs." *Human Organization* 60, no. 1: 40–6.

Marr, Lucille. 2001. "Breaking down Barriers: MCC Ontario and Ontario Native Communities, 1967–1999." *Journal of Mennonite Studies* 19, no. 1: 78–91.

– 2003. *The Transforming Power of a Century: Mennonite Central Committee and Its Evolution in Ontario*. Kitchener, ON: Pandora Press.

– 2005. "The History of Mennonite Central Committee: Developing a Genre." *Journal of Mennonite Studies* 23: 47–58.

Marshall, Katherine. 2001. "Development and Religion: A Different Lens on Development Debates." *Peabody Journal of Education* 76, nos 3 and 4: 339–75.

Marshall, Katherine, and Lucy Keough. 2004. *Mind, Heart, and Soul: In the Fight against Poverty*. Washington, DC: World Bank.

Marshall, Katherine, and Marisa Van Saanen. 2007. *Development and Faith: Where Mind, Heart, and Soul Work Together*. Washington, DC: World Bank.

Martin, Ed. 2007. "Introduction: Iran – Visits and Dialogue." *Peace Office Newsletter* 37, no. 3: 1–2.

Martin, Earl S. 1978. *Reaching the Other Side: The Journal of an American who Stayed to Witness Vietnam's Postwar Transition*. New York: Crown.

Mathies, Ronald J.R. 1996. "Service as (Trans)formation: MCC as Educational

Institution." In *Unity Amidst Diversity: Mennonite Central Committee at 75*, ed. Robert S. Kreider and Ronald J.R. Mathies, 69–81. Akron, PA: Mennonite Central Committee.

McCutcheon, Russell T. 1997. *Manufacturing Religion: The Discourse on Sui Generis Religion and the Politics of Nostalgia.* New York: Oxford University Press.

McDougall, John James. 1979. "The Technocrat's Ideology of Modernity." In *What Is Modern Indonesian Culture?*, ed. Gloria Davis, 156–84. Athens: Ohio University Center for International Studies.

McGeary, Johanna. 2003. "Christian Aid:To Preach or Not to Preach." *Time* 161, no. 16. https://content.time.com/time/subscriber/article/0,33009,1004671,00.html.

McGregor, Andrew. 2010. "Geographies of Religion and Development: Rebuilding Sacred Spaces in Aceh, Indonesia, after the Tsunami." *Environment and Planning A* 42, no. 3: 729–46.

McKee, Erin. 2010. "Arrested Are the Peacemakers: The Impact of *Holder v. Humanitarian Law Project* on Conflict Resolution Activists." *Unrest Magazine*. http://www.unrestmag.com/arrested-are-the-peacemakers-the-impact-of-holder-v-humanitarian-law-project-on-conflict-resolution-activists/.

McKnight, John. 1989. "Why 'Servanthood' Is Bad." *The Other Side* 25, no. 1: 38–40.

McNamara, Nora, and Stephen Morse. 2004. "Voices from the Aid 'Chain': The Personal Dynamics of Care." *Social and Cultural Geography* 5, no. 2: 253–70.

McNaughton, Darlene. 2006. "The 'Host' as Uninvited 'Guest': Hospitality, Violence and Tourism." *Annals of Tourism Research* 33, no. 3: 645–65.

McRae, Dave. 2013. *A Few Poorly Organized Men: Interreligious Violence in Poso, Indonesia*. Leiden: Brill.

Menchik, Jeremy. 2014. "Productive Intolerance: Godly Nationalism in Indonesia." *Comparative Studies in Society and History* 56, no. 3: 591–621.

– 2016. *Islam and Democracy in Indonesia: Tolerance without Liberalism*. Cambridge: Cambridge University Press.

MCC News Service. 1977. "Partnership in Obedience Characterizes Kalimantan Team." 19 August. MCC Archives (Akron, PA).

Mennonite Central Committee. 1974. "Hillsboro Hosts Annual Meeting." *Intercom* 14 (2): 1.

– 1979. "Background Paper on MCC's Philosophy of Development." MCC Archives (Akron, PA).

– 1985. *MCC in Indonesia – A Program Overview 1947–1985*. Mennonite Central Committee Indonesia. MCC Archives (Akron, PA).
– 1989. "Report on Activities of the Small Irrigation Improvement Project in the Mayoa Transmigration Site Implemented by Department of Transmigration and Mennonite Central Committee 1988–1989." Mennonite Central Committee Indonesia. MCC Archives (Akron, PA).
– 1999. *Principles That Guide Our Mission*. Akron, PA: Mennonite Central Committee.
– 2007a. *Taming Hunger*. Part 1: *Manna from Heaven*. Akron, PA: Mennonite Central Committee.
– 2007b. *Taming Hunger*. Part 2: *Trees of Hope*. Akron, PA: Mennonite Central Committee.
– 2008a. "MCC Defends Its Role in Meeting." *Mennonite Weekly Review* 86 (37): 2.
– 2008b. "Religious Dialogue Draws Fire." *Mennonite Weekly Review* 86 (37): 1–2.
– 2009. *Caring in the name of Christ: 2008/2009 Mennonite Central Committee Annual Report*. Akron, PA: Mennonite Central Committee.
– n.d. *IVEP Manual for Participants*. Akron, PA: Mennonite Central Committee. MCC Archives (Akron, PA).
Mennonite Central Committee and Directorate General of Transmigration. 1980. *Working Agreement between the Directorate General of Transmigration and Mennonite Central Committee (MCC)*. Jakarta.
Mennonite Central Committee Indonesia. 1958. "Annual Report and Program Plans – MCC Indonesia." Mennonite Central Committee Indonesia. MCC Archives (Akron, PA).
– 1975. "Annual Report and Program Plans – MCC Indonesia." Mennonite Central #Committee Indonesia. MCC Archives (Akron, PA).
– 1976. "Annual Report and Program Plans – MCC Indonesia." Mennonite Central Committee Indonesia. MCC Archives (Akron, PA).
– 1977. "Annual Report and Program Plans – MCC Indonesia." Mennonite Central Committee Indonesia. MCC Archives (Akron, PA).
Mennonite Central Committee Staff. 2008. "MCC-Sponsored Dialogue to Include Iranian President among Religious, Political Leaders." *Mennonite Weekly Review*. http://www.mennoweekly.org/2008/10/6/mcc-answers-questions-about-meeting-iranian-presid/.
Merry, Sally Engle. 2000. "Mennonite Peacebuilding and Conflict Transformation: A Cultural Analysis." In *From the Ground Up: Mennonite Contributions to International Peacebuilding*, ed. Cynthia Sampson and John Paul Lederach, 203–17. Oxford: Oxford University Press.

Michael, Sarah. 2004. *Undermining Development: The Absence of Power among Local NGOs in Africa*. Oxford: James Currey Publishers.

Milbank, John. 2006. *Theology and Social Theory: Beyond Secular Reason*, 2nd ed. Malden, MA: Wiley-Blackwell.

Miller, Elmer S. 1970. "The Christian Missionary, Agent of Secularization." *Anthropological Quarterly* 43, no. 1: 14–22.

– 1995. *Nurturing Doubt: From Mennonite Missionary to Anthropologist in the Argentine Chaco*. Urbana: University of Illinois Press.

Miller, Harold. 1992. "'Mission' Statements." Letter to Ray Brubacher, 26 May 1992. MCC Archives (Akron, PA).

– 2015. *Encounters in Africa*. Nairobi: Manqa Books.

Miller, Joseph S. 2000. "A History of the Mennonite Conciliation Service, International Conciliation Service, and Christian Peacemaker Teams." In *From the Ground Up: Mennonite Contributions to International Peacebuilding*, ed. Cynthia Sampson and John Paul Lederach, 3–29. Oxford: Oxford University Press.

Miller, Michelle A. 2009. *Rebellion and Reform in Indonesia: Jakarta's Security and Autonomy Policies in Aceh*. London: Routledge.

Miyazaki, Hirokazu. 2006. *The Method of Hope: Anthropology, Philosophy, and Fijian Knowledge*. Stanford, CA: Stanford University Press.

Montanari, Andrea. 2011. "The Stinky King – A Social and Cultural History of the Durian." MA thesis, National University of Singapore.

Moreton, Bethany. 2009. *To Serve God and Wal-Mart: The Making of Christian Free Enterprise*. Cambridge, MA: Harvard University Press.

Morfit, Michael. 1981."Pancasila: The Indonesian State Ideology According to the New Order Government." *Asian Survey* 21, no. 8: 838–51.

Morrison, David R. 1998. *Aid and Ebb Tide: A History of CIDA and Canadian Development Assistance*. Waterloo, ON: Wilfrid Laurier University Press.

Morse, Stephen, and Nora McNamara. 2006. "Analysing Institutional Partnerships in Development: A Contract Between Equals or a Loaded Process?" *Progress in Development Studies* 6, no. 4: 321–36.

Mosse, David. 2004. "Is Good Policy Unimplementable? Reflections on the Ethnography of Aid Policy and Practice." *Development and Change* 35, no. 4: 639–71.

– 2005. *Cultivating Development: An Ethnography of Aid Policy and Practice*. London: Pluto Press.

– 2011. "Introduction: The Anthropology of Expertise and Professionals in International Development." In *Adventures in Aidland: The Anthropology of Professionals in International Development*, ed. David Mosse, 1–32. New York: Berghahn Books.

Mosse, David, and David Lewis. 2006. "Theoretical Approaches to Brokerage and Translation in Development." In *Development Brokers and Translators: The Ethnography of Aid and Agencies*, ed. David Lewis and David Mosse, 1–26. Bloomfield, CT: Kumarian Press.

MTS Travel. n.d. "Our Story – MTS TRAVEL Corporate History, Part 1." http://www.mtstravel.com/about/index.html.

Muir, Ross W., and Dave Rogalsky. 2007. "Protest to Mennonite-Muslim Dialogue Covered Widely." *Canadian Mennonite* 11, no. 13: 32–3.

Mujiburrahman. 2006. *Feeling Threatened: Muslim-Christian Relations in Indonesia's New Order.* Amsterdam: Amsterdam University Press.

Nader, Laura. 1972. "Up the Anthropologist: Perspectives Gained from Studying Up." In *Reinventing Anthropology*, ed. Dell Hymes, 284–311. New York: Pantheon.

Neubert, Dieter. 1996. "The Role of Local Brokers in the Development System: Experiences with 'Self-Help Projects' in East Africa." *Bulletin de l'APAD* 11: 1–13.

Ngo, May. 2018. *Between Humanitarianism and Evangelism in Faith-Based Organisations: A Case from the African Migration Route.* London: Routledge.

Nolt, Steve. 1999. "A Two-Kingdom People in a World of Multiple Identities: Religion, Ethnicity and American Mennonites." *Mennonite Quarterly Review* 73, no. 3: 485–502.

– 2004. "From Bishops to Bureaucracy: Observations on the Migration of Authority." *Vision: A Journal for Church and Theology* 5: 14–24.

– 2011. "MCC's Relationship with 'Plain' Anabaptists in Historical Perspective." In *A Table of Sharing: Mennonite Central Committee and the Expanding Networks of Mennonite Identity*, ed. Alain Epp Weaver, 135–66. Telford, PA: Cascadia.

Nurhayati, Sitti Sani. 2020. "Contested Identities: Tuan Guru and Ahmadiyah in the Redrawing of Post-1998 Sasak–Muslim Boundary Lines in Lombok." PhD diss., Victoria University of Wellington.

Nyman, Mikaela. 2006. *Democratising Indonesia: The Challenges of Civil Society in the Era of Reformasi.* Copenhagen: NIAS Press.

– 2009. "Civil Society and the Challenges of the Post-Suharto Era." In *Democratization in #Post-Suharto Indonesia*, ed. Marco Bünte and Andreas Ufen, 251–75. London: Routledge.

O'Neill, Kevin L. 2010. *City of God: Christian Citizenship in Postwar Guatemala*. Berkeley: University of California Press.

Occhipinti, Laurie A. 2005. *Acting on Faith: Religious Development Organizations in Northwestern Argentina.* Lanham: Lexington Books.

Olivier de Sardan, Jean-Pierre. 2005. *Anthropology and Development: Understanding Contemporary Social Change.* London: Zed Books.

Ortner, Sherry B. 1995. "Resistance and the Problem of Ethnographic Refusal." *Comparative Studies in Society and History* 37, no. 1: 173–93.

Osa, Yukie. 2013. "The Growing Role of NGOs in Disaster Relief and Humanitarian Assistance in East Asia." In *A Growing Force: Civil Society's Role in Asian Regional Security*, ed. Rizal Sukma and James Gannon, 66–89. Tokyo: Japan Centre for International Exchange.

Oyer, John S. 1970. "Editorial Introduction to MCC Anniversary Issue." *Mennonite Quarterly Review* 44, no. 3: 212.

Packull, Werner. 2008. *Mysticism and the Early South German-Austrian Anabaptist Movement, 1525–1531*. Eugene, OR: Wipf and Stock.

Patzwald, Gari-Anne, and William Kostlevy. 2005. "From Mutual Aid to Global Action." *Christianity Today* 49. https://www.christianitytoday.com/history/issues/issue-84/from-mutual-aid-to-global-action.html.

Peachey, Paul. 1954. *Die Soziale Herkunft der Schweizer Täufer in der Reformationszeit: Eine Religionssoziologische Untersuchung*. Karlsruhe: Heinrich Schneider.

Peachey, Urbane. 2022. *Making Wars Cease: A Survey of MCC Peace Section, 1940–1990*. Morgantown, PA: Masthof Press.

Peirano, Mariza. 1998. "When Anthropology Is at Home: The Different Contexts of a Single Discipline." *Annual Review of Anthropology* 27: 105–28.

Phelps, Elizabeth. 2015. "Sequestered Inclusion: Social Service Discourses and New Latino Diaspora Youth in the Shenandoah Valley." PhD diss., Cornell University.

– 2020. "Transnational Labour and Social Justice Peacemakers: Advocating for Multiculturalism in Virginia." *Journal of Mennonite Studies* 38: 155–71.

Phillips, Brenda D. 2014. *Mennonite Disaster Service: Building a Therapeutic Community after the Gulf Coast Storms*. Lanham, MD: Lexington Books.

Pierce, Matthew. 2007. "Making Friends in Iran: Lessons Learned from the Mennonites." Boston College: eScholarship at Boston College. https://dlib.bc.edu/islandora/object/bc-ir%3A102755/datastream/PDF/view.

Pierson Lester, Marla. 2007. "Iran Delegation Members Reflect on the Fruit of Years of Work." Mennonite Central Committee. http://mcc.org/news/news/article.html?id=149. Viewed April 2011.

Pincus, Walter. 2007. "Foreign Aid Groups Face Terror Screens." *Washington Post*, 23 August. https://www.washingtonpost.com/wp-dyn/content/article/2007/08/22/AR2007082202847.html?sub=AR.

Pollock, Sheldon. 2000. "Cosmopolitan and Vernacular in History." *Public Culture* 12, no. 3: 591–625.

Pratt, Mary Louise. 1991. "Arts of the Contact Zone." *Profession* 91: 33–40.

Prawiranegara, Sjafruddin. 1984. "Pancasila as the Sole Foundation." *Indonesia* 38: 74–83.

Prieb, Wesley J. 1990. *Peter C. Hiebert: He Gave Them Bread*. Hillsboro, KS: Center for Mennonite Brethren Studies.

Purdey, Jemma. 2006. *Anti-Chinese Violence in Indonesia, 1996–99*. Honolulu: University of Hawai'i Press.

Quarles van Ufford, Philip. 1993. "Knowledge and Ignorance in the Practices of Development Policy." In *An Anthropological Critique of Development: The Growth of Ignorance*, ed. Mark Hobart, 135–60. London: Routledge.

Quarles van Ufford, Philip, and Matthew Schoffelleers, eds. 1988. *Religion and Development: Towards an Integrated Approach*. Amsterdam: Free University Press.

Quarles van Ufford, Philip, Ananta Kumar Giri, and David Mosse. 2003. "Interventions in Development: Towards a New Moral Understanding of our Experiences and an Agenda for the Future." In *A Moral Critique of Development: In Search of Global Responsibilities*, ed. Philip Quarles van Ufford and Ananta Kumar Giri, 3–40. London: Routledge.

Rabinow, Paul. 2007. *Reflections on Fieldwork in Morocco*. Berkeley: University of California Press.

Reck, Gregory G. 1983. "Narrative Anthropology." *Anthropology and Humanism Quarterly* 8, no. 1: 8–12.

Redekop, Calvin. 1980. *Strangers Become Neighbors: Mennonite and Indigenous Relations in the Paraguayan Chaco*. Scottdale, PA/Waterloo, ON: Herald Press.

– 1989. *Mennonite Society*. Baltimore, MD: Johns Hopkins University Press.

– 1990. "Concern Reflections: Calvin Redekop." *Conrad Grebel Review* 8, no. 2: 165–76.

– 1993. "The Mennonite Central Committee Story: A Review Essay." *Mennonite Quarterly Review* 67, no. 2: 84–103.

– 2001. *The Pax Story: Service in the Name of Christ, 1951–1976*. Telford, PA: Pandora Press.

Redekop, John H. 1994. "The Politics of the Mennonite Central Committee." *Direction Journal* 23, no. 2: 63–76.

– 1996. "The Roots of Nazi Support among Mennonites, 1930 to 1939: A Case Study Based on a Major Mennonite Paper." *Journal of Mennonite Studies* 14: 81–95.

Redfield, Peter. 2013. *Life in Crisis: The Ethical Journey of Doctors Without Borders*. Berkeley: University of California Press.

Reedy, Janet Umble. 1973. "A History of the Mennonite Medical Work in the Muria Mountain Area of Java, Indonesia 1894–1971." *Mennonite Quarterly Review* 47, no. 1: 31–53.

Rees, John A. 2011. *Religion in International Politics and Development: The World Bank and Faith Institutions*. Cheltenham: Edward Elgar.

Regehr, T.D. 1991. "Anatomy of a Mennonite Miracle: The Berlin Rescue of 30–31 January 1947." *Journal of Mennonite Studies* 9, no. 1: 11–33.

– 1996. *Mennonites in Canada, 1939–1970: A People Transformed.* Toronto: University of Toronto Press.

Reid, Anthony, ed. 2006. *Verandah of Violence: The Background to the Aceh Problem.* Singapore: NUS Press.

Reid, Anthony. 2010. "Jewish-Conspiracy Theories in Southeast Asia: Are Chinese the Target?" *Indonesia and the Malay World* 38, no. 112: 373–85.

Reimer, A. James. 2003. "Forward: Shi'i Muslims and Mennonite Christians in Dialogue – Two Religious Minority Groups Face the Challenges of Modernity." *Conrad Grebel Review* 21, no. 3: 3–13.

Reimer, Gustav. 1953. "Claassen (Claasen, Classen, Claesz, Claussen, Klaassen, Klassen, Klaeszen) Family." *Global Anabaptist Mennonite Encyclopedia Online.* https://gameo.org/index.php?title=Claassen_(Claasen,_Classen,_Claesz,_Claussen,_Klaassen,_Klassen,_Klaeszen)_family.

Reimer, Margaret Loewen. 2008. *One Quilt, Many Pieces: A Guide to Mennonite Groups in Canada.* Scottdale, PA: Herald Press.

Reimer, William, and Bruce N. Guenther. 2011. "Relationships, Rights, and 'Relief': Ninety Years of MCC's Integrated Response to Humanitarian Crises." In *A Table of Sharing: Mennonite Central Committee and the Expanding Networks of Mennonite Identity*, ed. Alain Epp Weaver, 353–74. Telford, PA: Cascadia.

Rhodes, Richard. 2007. "From High Hopes to Frustration: Former MCC Executive Director Urges 'On the Edge' Leadership." *Canadian Mennonite* 11, no. 15: 33.

Rich, Bruce. 1994. *Mortgaging the Earth: The World Bank, Environmental Impoverishment and the Crisis of Development.* Boston, MA: Earthscan.

Ricklefs, Merle C. 2012. *Islamisation and Its Opponents in Java: A Political, Social, Cultural and Religious History, c.1930 to Present.* Singapore: NUS Press.

Rieffel, Alexis. 1969. "The BIMAS Program for Self-Sufficiency in Rice Production." *Indonesia* 8: 103–33.

Riles, Annelise. 2000. *The Network Inside Out.* Ann Arbor: University of Michigan Press.

Rist, Gilbert. 2009. *The History of Development: From Western Origins to Global Faith.* New Delhi: Academic Foundation.

Robbins, Joel. 2003. "On the Paradoxes of Global Pentecostalism and the Perils of Continuity Thinking." *Religion* 33, no. 3: 221–31.

– 2004. *Becoming Sinners: Christianity and Moral Torment in a Papua New Guinea Society.* Berkeley: University of California Press.

– 2006. "Anthropology and Theology: An Awkward Relationship?" *Anthropological Quarterly* 79, no. 2: 285–94.
– 2007a "Between Reproduction and Freedom: Morality, Value, and Radical Cultural Change." *Ethnos* 72, no. 3: 293–314.
– 2007b "Continuity Thinking and the Problem of Christian Culture: Belief, Time, and the Anthropology of Christianity." *Current Anthropology* 48, no. 1: 5–17.
– 2013. "Beyond the Suffering Subject: Toward an Anthropology of the Good." *Journal of the Royal Anthropological Institute* 19, no. 3: 447–62.
– 2020. *Theology and the Anthropology of Christian Life*. Oxford: Oxford University Press.
Robbins, Joel, and Matthew Engelke. 2010. "Introduction." *South Atlantic Quarterly* 109, no. 4: 623–31.
Roberts, Laura Schmidt. 2021. "Addressing Sexual Violence in Mennonite Communities: The Case of John Howard Yoder." *Buddhist-Christian Studies* 41: 87–94.
Rofi, Abdur, Shannon Doocy, and Courtland Robinson. 2006. "Tsunami Mortality and Displacement in Aceh Province, Indonesia." *Disasters* 30, no. 3: 340–50.
Roosa, John. 2006. *Pretext for Mass Murder: The September 30th Movement and Suharto's Coup D'état in Indonesia.* Madison: University of Wisconsin Press.
Rosenberg, J.C. 2003. "*Time Magazine* Tackles 'Radical' Christian Evangelists in Muslim Nations." *Newsmax.com.* http://archive.newsmax.com/archives/articles/2003/4/21/151852.shtml.
Rossi, Benedetta. 2006. "Aid Policies and Recipient Strategies in Niger: Why Donors and Recipients Should Not Be Compartmentalized into Separate 'Worlds of Knowledge.'" In *Development Brokers and Translators: The Ethnography of Aid and Agencies*, ed. David Lewis and David Mosse, 27–49. Bloomfield, CT: Kumarian Press.
Roth, John D. 2002. "Recent Currents in the Historiography of the Radical Reformation." *Church History* 71, no. 3: 523–35.
– 2013. "The Complex Legacy of the *Martyrs Mirror* among Mennonites in North America." *Mennonite Quarterly Review* 87: 277–316.
– 2017. "How to Commemorate a Division? Reflections on the 500th Anniversary of the Lutheran Reformation and its Relevance for the Global Anabaptist-Mennonite Church Today." *Mennonite Quarterly Review* 91: 5–35.
– 2021. *A Cloud of Witnesses: Celebrating Indonesian Mennonites*. Scottdale, PA: Herald Press.
Rothman, E. Natalie. 2011. *Brokering Empire: Trans-Imperial Subjects between Venice and Istanbul*. Ithaca, NY: Cornell University Press.

Rottenburg, Richard. 2009. *Far-Fetched Facts: A Parable of Development Aid*. Cambridge, MA: MIT Press.

Rudnyckyj, Daromir. 2010. *Spiritual Economies: Islam, Globalization, and the Afterlife of Development*. Cornell, NY: Cornell University Press.

Rui, Noëmi. 2018. "The New Missionaries of Development: The Indonesian Council of Churches and Village Development Projects, 1971–1982." In *The Mission of Development: Religion and Techno-Politics in Asia*, ed. Catherine Scheer, Philip Fountain, and R. Michael Feener, 107–34. Leiden: Brill.

Rupley, Melody. 1991. "Do We Practice What We Preach?" *Intercom* 35, no. 7: 7.

Sachs, Wolfgang, ed. 1992. *The Development Dictionary: A Guide to Knowledge as Power*. London: Zed Books.

Salemink, Oscar. 2006. "Translating, Interpreting, and Practicing Civil Society in Vietnam: A Tale of Calculated Misunderstandings." In *Development Brokers and Translators: The Ethnography of Aid and Agencies*, ed. David Lewis and David Mosse, 101–26. Bloomfield, CT: Kumarian Press.

Sampson, Cynthia, and John Paul Lederach, eds. 2000. *From the Ground Up: Mennonite Contributions to International Peacebuilding*. Oxford: Oxford University Press.

Sanneh, Lamin O. 2009. *Translating the Message: The Missionary Impact on Culture*, 2nd ed. Maryknoll, NY: Orbis Books.

Sawatsky, Rodney. 1978. "Domesticated Sectarianism: Mennonites in the US and Canada in Comparative Perspective." *Canadian Journal of Sociology/ Cahiers canadiens de sociologie* 3, no. 2: 233–44.

– 1991. "Mennonite Ethnicity: Medium, Message and Mission." *Journal of Mennonite Studies* 9, no. 1: 113–21.

Scharen, Christian B. 2005. "'Judicious Narratives,' or Ethnography as Ecclesiology." *Scottish Journal of Theology* 58, no. 2: 125–42.

Scharen, Cristian B., ed. 2012. *Explorations in Ecclesiology and Ethnography*. Grand Rapids, MI: Eerdmans.

Scheer, Catherine, Philip Fountain, and R. Michael Feener, eds. 2018. *The Mission of Development: Religion and Techno-Politics in Asia*. Leiden: Brill.

Scherz, China. 2014. *Having People, Having Heart: Charity, Sustainable Development, and Problems of Dependence in Central Uganda*. Chicago: University of Chicago Press.

Schildt, L. 2005. "Facilitating a Federation: A Look at Mennonite Central Committee Binational's Structure, Culture and Leadership in a Changing Environment." Unpublished paper, Eastern Mennonite University, Conflict Transformation Program, MCC Archives (Akron, PA).

Schlabach, Gerald W. 1991. *To Bless All Peoples: Serving with Abraham and Jesus*. Scottdale, PA: Herald Press.

– 2001. "In the Belly of a Paradox: Reflections on the Dubious Service of Reflecting on Service." *Conrad Grebel Review* 19, no. 3: 41–53.

– 2007. "You Converted to What? One Mennonite's Journey." *Commonweal* 134, no. 11: 14–17.

Schlabach, Joetta Handrich. 1991. *Extending the Table: A World Community Cookbook*. Scottdale, PA: Herald Press.

Schlegel, Stuart A. 1979. "Technocrats in a Muslim Society: Symbolic Community in Aceh." In *What Is Modern Indonesian Culture?*, ed. Gloria Davis, 232–48. Athens: Ohio University Center for International Studies.

Schrag, Jim. 2003. "Wider View: Material Aid Part of the Gospel." *Third Way Café*. http://www.thirdway.com/wv/?Page=2666|Material+aid+part+of+gospel. Viewed April 2011.

Schulze, Kirsten E. 2004. *The Free Ache Movement (GAM): Anatomy of a Separatist Organization*. Washington, DC: East-West Center Washington.

Schutte, Gerrit, and Heather Sutherland, eds. 1982. *Papers of the Dutch-Indonesian Historical Conference Held at Lage Vuursche, the Netherlands, 23–27 June 1980*. Leiden and Jakarta: Bureau of Indonesian Studies.

Scott, James C. 1990. *Domination and the Arts of Resistance: Hidden Transcripts*. New Haven: Yale University Press.

Selinger, Leah. 2004. "The Forgotten Factor: The Uneasy Relationship between Religion and Development." *Social Compass* 51, no. 4: 523–43.

Selwyn, Tom. 2000. "An Anthropology of Hospitality." In *In Search of Hospitality: Theoretical Perspectives and Debates*, ed. Conrad Lashley and Alison Morrison, 18–36. Oxford and Woburn, MA: Butterworth Heinemann.

Shanor, Amanda. 2011. "Beyond Humanitarian Law Project: Promoting Human Rights in a Post-9/11 World." *Suffolk Transnational Law Review* 34, no. 3: 1–20.

Sharp, John S. 2015. *My Calling to Fulfill: The Orie O. Miller Story*. Scottdale, PA: Herald Press.

Shaw, Amy. 2009. *Crisis of Conscience: Conscientious Objection in Canada during the First World War*. Vancouver: UBC Press.

Shearer, Tobin Miller. 2011. "Whitening Conflicts: White Racial Identity Formation within Mennonite Central Committee, 1960–1985." In *A Table of Sharing: Mennonite Central Committee and the Expanding Networks of Mennonite Identity*, ed. Alain Epp Weaver, 215–38. Telford, PA: Cascadia.

Shenk, Stanley C. 1988. *Mission in Asia*. Goshen College, IN: Pinchpenny Press.

Shenk, Tim. 2008. "MCC Completes Indonesia Tsunami Response." *Mennonite Central Committee*. http://mcc.org/stories/news/mcc-completes-indonesia-tsunami-response. Viewed April 2011.

Shires, Paul, Soeyadi, and D. Soesanto. 1991. "Final Report: Mayoa Transmigration Project: A Cooperative Report of MCC (Mennonite Central Committee) and the Department of Transmigration." Mennonite Central Committee Indonesia. MCC Archives (Akron, PA).

Showalter, Shirley. 2001. "Shirley Showalter, President." *Journal of College and Character Presidents' Diaries* 23. http://journals.naspa.org/jcc_presidents_diaries/23/. Viewed April 2011.

Sidel, John T. 2006. *Riots, Pogroms, Jihad: Religious Violence in Indonesia.* Ithaca, NY: Cornell University Press.

Sider, E. Morris. 1982. *The Messenger of Grace: A Biography of C.N. Hostetter, Jr.* Nappanee, IN: Evangel Press.

Siegel, James T. 1969. *The Rope of God.* Ann Arbor: University of Michigan Press.

– 1993. *Solo in the New Order: Language and Hierarchy in an Indonesian City.* Princeton, NJ: Princeton University Press.

Sigalingging, Daniel Jonathan Tito. 2016. "Sejarah Gereja Kristen Protestan Angkola Di Tapanuli Selatan, 1988-2000." Undergraduate thesis, Universitas Sumatera Utara.

Smith, James Howard. 2008. *Bewitching Development: Witchcraft and the Reinvention of Development in Neoliberal Kenya.* Chicago: University of Chicago Press.

Smith, Jonathan Z. 2004. *Relating Religion: Essays in the Study of Religion.* Chicago: University of Chicago Press.

Smith, Valene L. 1989. *Hosts and Guests: The Anthropology of Tourism.* Philadelphia: University of Pennsylvania Press.

Smucker, Barbara C. 2006. *Henry's Red Sea.* Scottdale, PA/Waterloo, ON: Herald Press.

Spaan, Ernst. 1994. "Taikongs and Calos: The Role of Middlemen and Brokers in Javanese International Migration." *International Migration Review* 28, no. 1: 93–113.

Stamatov, Peter. 2013. *The Origins of Global Humanitarianism: Religion, Empires, and Advocacy.* Cambridge: Cambridge University Press.

Steiner, Sam. 2003. "The City and the Formation of 'Mennonite Church Eastern Canada.'" *Journal of Mennonite Studies* 21: 155–73.

Stoller, Paul. "Imaging Knowledge: Visual Anthropology, Storytelling and the Slow Path Toward Wisdom." *kritisk etnografi – Swedish Journal of Anthropology* 3, no. 1: 11-20.

Suderman, K. n.d. "Supplementing Food Needs – One Can at a Time." *Mennonite Central Committee.* http://canning.mcc.org/canning/stories/food_needs.html.

Supangkat, Eddy. 2007. *Salatiga: Sketsa Kota Lama.* Salatiga: Griya Media.

Svelmoe, William. 2007. "William Cameron Townsend and Missionary Linguistics." In *Anthropology's Debt to Missionaries*, ed. Leonard Plotnicov, Paula Brown, and Vinson Sutlive, 62–85. Ethnology Monographs. Pittsburgh: University of Pittsburgh Press.

Tajima, Yuhki. 2014. *The Institutional Origins of Communal Violence: Indonesia's Transition from Authoritarian Rule*. New York: Cambridge University Press.

Taylor, Charles. 2007. *A Secular Age*. Cambridge, MA: Harvard University Press.

Telford, John. 2012. "Disaster Recovery: An International Humanitarian Challenge?" In *From the Ground Up: Perspectives on Post-Tsunami and Post-Conflict Aceh*, ed. Patrick Daly, R. Michael Feener, and Anthony S. Reid, 25–39. Singapore: Institute of Southeast Asian Studies.

Telford, John, and John Cosgrave. 2007. "The International Humanitarian System and the 2004 Indian Ocean Earthquake and Tsunamis." *Disasters* 31, no. 1: 1–28.

Telford, John, John Cosgrave, and Rachel Houghton. 2006. *Joint Evaluation of the International Response to the Indian Ocean Tsunami: Synthesis Report*. London: Tsunami Evaluation Coalition.

Ter Haar, Gerrie, ed. 2011. *Religion and Development: Ways of Transforming the World*. London: Hurst and Company.

Terichow, Gladys. 2009. "New Wine: Shared Statements a Major Step as MCC Reshapes Its Future." *Mennonite Central Committee*. http://mcc.org/stories/news/sharedd-statements-major-step-mcc-reshapes-its-future. Viewed April 2011.

Thiesen, John D. 1999. *Mennonite and Nazi? Attitudes smong Mennonite Colonists in Latin America, 1933–1945*. Kitchener, Scottsdale, and Waterloo: Pandora Press and Herald Press.

Thornton, Robert. 1983. "Narrative Ethnography in Africa, 1850–1920: The Creation and Capture of an Appropriate Domain for Anthropology." *Man* 18, no. 3: 502–20.

Timmer, Jaap. 2000. "Living with Intricate Futures: Order and Confusion in Imyan Worlds, Irian Jaya, Indonesia." PhD diss., University of Nijmegen.

Tirtosudarmo, Riwanto. 2001. "Demography and Security: Transmigration Policy in Indonesia." In *Demography and National Security*, ed. Myron Weiner and Sharon S. Russell, 199–227. New York: Berghahn Books.

Titaley, John A. 2008. "From Abandonment to Blessing: The Theological Presence of Christianity in Indonesia." In *Christian Theology in Asia*, ed. Sebastian C.H. Kim, 71–88. Cambridge: Cambridge University Press.

Toews, Paul. 1990. "The Concern Movement: Its Origins and Early History." *Conrad Grebel Review* 8, no. 2: 109–26.

– 1996. *Mennonites in American Society, 1930–1970: Modernity and the Persistence of Religious Community*. Scottdale, PA: Herald Press.

– 2006. "Clayton Kratz: Went to Russia 1920." *Mennonite Brethren Historical Commission* 35. https://mbhistory.org/profiles/kratz/.

Toews, Reg. 1996. "The Organizational Conundrums of MCC." In *Unity Amidst Diversity: Mennonite Central Committee at 75*, ed. Robert S. Kreider and Ronald J.R. Mathies, 43–53. Akron, PA: Mennonite Central Committee.

Tomlinson, Matt. 2017. "Introduction: Imagining the Monologic." In *The Monologic Imagination*, ed. Matt Tomlinson and Julian Millie, 1–18. Oxford: Oxford University Press.

Tourage, Mahdi. 2009. "Fetishizing Dialogue and Commodifying Peacemaking." *American Journal of Islamic Social Science* 26, no. 1: 136–52.

Tse, Justin K.H. 2014. "Grounded Theologies: 'Religion' and the 'Secular' in Human Geography." *Progress in Human Geography* 38, no. 2: 201–20.

– 2015. "Under the Umbrella: Grounded Christian Theologies and Democratic Working Alliances in Hong Kong." *Review of Religion and Chinese Society* 2, no. 1: 109–42.

Tsing, Anna. 1993. *In the Realm of the Diamond Queen: Marginality in an Out-of-the-Way Place*. Princeton, NJ: Princeton University Press.

– 2005. *Friction: An Ethnography of Global Connection*. Princeton, NJ: Princeton University Press.

Turner, Victor. 1979. "Betwixt and Between: The Liminal Period in Rites de Passage." In *Reader in Comparative Religion: An Anthropological Approach*, ed. William Lessa and Evon Vogt, 234–43. New York: Harper and Row.

Tusan, Michelle. 2012. *Smyrna's Ashes: Humanitarianism, Genocide, and the Birth of the Middle East*. Berkeley: University of California Press.

Tvedt, Terje. 2006. "Understanding the History of the International Aid System and the Development Research Tradition: The Case of the Disappearing Religious NGOs." *Forum for Development Studies* 33, no. 2: 341–66.

Ulin, Robert C. 1994. "The Anthropologist and the Historian as Storytellers." *Dialectical Anthropology* 19, no. 4: 389–400.

Umble, Diane Zimmerman, and David Weaver-Zercher. 2008. *The Amish and the Media*. Baltimore, MD: Johns Hopkins University Press.

Unruh, John D. 1952. *In the Name of Christ: A History of the Mennonite Central Committee*. Scottdale, PA: Herald Press.

Urry, James. 1983. "Who Are the Mennonites?" *European Journal of Sociology* 24, no. 2: 241–62.

– 2006. *Mennonites, Politics, and Peoplehood: Europe – Russia – Canada: 1925 to 1980*. Winnipeg: University of Manitoba Press.

Van Biema, David. 2003a. "Missionaries Under Cover." *Time* 161, no. 26: 36–44.

– 2003b. "Religion: Keeping the Faith without Preaching It." *Time* 161, no. 26: 40–1.

Van Braght, Thieleman J. 2002 [1664]. *The Bloody Theater or Martyrs Mirror of the Defenseless Christians: Who Baptized Only Upon Confession of Faith, and Who Suffered and Died for the Testimony of Jesus, Their Saviour, From the Time of Christ to the Year A.D. 1660*. Scottdale, PA: Herald Press.

van Bruinessen, Martin. 2013. *Rakyat Kecil, Islam dan Politik*. Yogyakarta: Gading.

Van den Berg, Rob, and Philip Quarles van Ufford. 2005. "Disjuncture and Marginality – Towards a New Approach to Development Practice." In *The Aid Effect: Giving and Governing in International Development*, edited by David Mosse and David Lewis, 196–212. London and Ann Arbor, MI: Pluto Press.

van den End, Th., and J. Weitjens. 1999. *Ragi Carita: Sejarah Gereja Di Indonesia 1860an – Sekarang*, 3rd ed. Jakarta: BPK Gunung Mulia.

Van der Veer, Peter. 2001. *Imperial Encounters: Religion and Modernity in India and Britain*. Princeton, NJ: Princeton University Press.

van Doorn, Jacobus J.A. 1982. "A Divided Society: Segmentation and Mediation in Late-Colonial Indonesia." In *Papers of the Dutch-Indonesian Historical Conference Held at Lage Vuursche, the Netherlands, 23-27 June 1980*, ed. Gerrit Schutte and Heather Sutherland, 128–71. Leiden and Jakarta: Bureau of Indonesian Studies.

van Gennep, Arnold. 1960. *The Rites of Passage*. Trans. M.B. Vizedom and G.L. Caffee. Chicago: University of Chicago Press.

van Klinken, Gerry. 2007. *Communal Violence and Democratization in Indonesia: Small Town Wars*. New York: Routledge.

van Klinken, Gerry, and Joshua Barker. 2009. "Introduction: State in Society in Indonesia." In *State of Authority: The State in Society in Indonesia*, ed. Gerry van Klinken and Joshua Barker, 1–16. Ithaca, NY: SEAP Publications.

Venuti, Lawrence. 1995. *The Translator's Invisibility: A History of Translation*. London: Routledge.

Ver Beek, Kurt A. 2000. "Spirituality: A Development Taboo." *Development in Practice* 10, no. 1: 31–43.

Vickers, Adrian. 2005. *A History of Modern Indonesia*. Cambridge: Cambridge University Press.

Visser, Leontine E. 2008. "The Papuan Civil Servant as Development Broker: Governing New Guinea Between 1950 and 1962." In *Papers Presented at the Seminar on the Act of Free Choice*, 13–21. The Hague: Institute of Netherlands History.

Walker, C.Z. 2011. "Church Summit Points Way Ahead for MCC." *Mennonite Central Committee*. http://mcc.org/stories/news/church-summit-points-way-ahead-mcc. Viewed April 2011.

Wall Street Journal Editor. 2007. "Fallout Continues From Ahmadinejad's NY Trip." *Wall Street Journal*, 26 September. https://www.wsj.com/articles/BL-WB-3195.

Wallace, Tina, Lisa Bornstein, and Jennifer Chapman. 2006. *The Aid Chain: Commitment and Coercion in Development NGOs*. Warwickshire: ITDG.

Watenpaugh, Keith David. 2015. *Bread from Stones: The Middle East and the Making of Modern Humanitarianism*. Los Angeles: University of California Press.

Watson, Nicholas. 1995. "Censorship and Cultural Change in Late-Medieval England: Vernacular Theology, the Oxford Translation Debate, and Arundel's Constitutions of 1409." *Speculum* 70, no. 4: 822–64.

Watt, Diane. 2008. "Challenging Islamophobia Through Visual Media Studies: Inquiring into a Photograph of Muslim Women on the Cover of Canada's National News Magazine." *Simile: Studies in Media and Information Literacy Education* 8, no. 2: 1–14.

Watts, Michael. 2001. "Development Ethnographies." *Ethnography* 2, no. 2: 283–300.

Weaver-Zercher, David. 2001. *The Amish in the American Imagination*. Baltimore, MD: Johns Hopkins University Press.

– 2016. *Martyrs Mirror: A Social History*. Baltimore, MD: Johns Hopkins University Press.

Weller, Robert. 1999. *Alternate Civilities: Democracy and Culture in China and Taiwan*. Boulder, CO: Westview Press.

Welty, Emily. 2010. "Faith-Based Peacebuilding and Development: An Analysis of the Mennonite Central Committee in Uganda and Kenya." PhD diss., School of Oriental and African Studies (London).

Whaites, Alan. 1999. "Pursuing Partnership: World Vision and the Ideology of Development – A Case Study." *Development in Practice* 9, no. 4: 410–23.

Wiebe, Katie Funk. 1976. *Day of Disaster*. Scottdale, PA: Herald Press.

Wiebe, Rudy H. 1962. *Peace Shall Destroy Many*. Toronto: McClelland and Stewart.

Wierzbicka, Anna. 1997. *Understanding Cultures through Their Key Words: English, Russian, Polish, German, and Japanese*. New York: Oxford University Press.

Wildan, Muhammad. 2013. "Mapping Radical Islam: A Study of the Proliferation of Radical Islam in Solo, Central Java." In *Contemporary*

Developments in Indonesian Islam: Explaining the "Conservative Turn," ed. Martin van Bruinessen, 190–223. Singapore: Institute of Southeast Asian Studies.

Wilson, Chris. 2005. *Overcoming Violent Conflict: Peace and Development Analysis in Indonesia.* Jakarta: UNDP.

– 2008. *Ethno-Religious Violence in Indonesia: From Soil to God.* Milton Park: Routledge.

Winland, Daphne. 1992. "Native Scholarship: The Enigma of Self-Definition Among Jewish and Mennonite Scholars." *Journal of Historical Sociology* 5, no. 4: 431–61.

– 1993. "The Quest for Mennonite Peoplehood: Ethno-Religious Identity and the Dilemma of Definitions." *Canadian Review of Sociology and Anthropology* 30, no. 1: 110–38.

Wolf, Eric R. 1956. "Aspects of Group Relations in a Complex Society: Mexico." *American Anthropologist* 58, no. 6: 1065–78.

Woodward, Mark. 1989. *Islam in Java: Normative Piety and Mysticism in the Sultanate of Yogyakarta.* Tucson: University of Arizona Press.

Yoder, Janet. 1989. "Ten Thousand Villages." *Global Anabaptist Mennonite Encyclopedia Online.* https://gameo.org/index.php?title=Ten_Thousand_Villages.

Yoder, John Howard. 1972. *The Politics of Jesus: Vicit Agnus Noster.* Grand Rapids, MI: Eerdmans.

– 2003. *The Jewish-Christian Schism Revisited*, ed. Michael G. Cartwright and Peter Ochs. Grand Rapids, MI: Eerdmans.

Yoder, Jeff T.M. 2008. "Final Report for the MCC Indonesia Tsunami Response December 2004 – June 2008." Mennonite Central Committee Indonesia. MCC Archives (Akron, PA).

Yoder, Lawrence M. 1989. "Tunggul Wulung (Tunggulwulung), Ibrahim (d. 1885)." *Global Anabaptist Mennonite Encyclopedia Online.* https://gameo.org/index.php?title=Tunggul_Wulung_(Tunggulwulung),_Ibrahim_(d._1885).

– 1990. "Gereja Injili di Tanah Jawa (GITJ)." *Global Anabaptist Mennonite Encyclopedia Online.* https://gameo.org/index.php?title=Gereja_Injili_di_Tanah_Jawa_(GITJ).

– 2006. *The Muria Story: A History of the Chinese Mennonite Churches of Indonesia.* Kitchener, ON: Pandora Press.

– 2017. "The Villages of Tunggul Wulung and Pieter Jansz: Vision and Reality in the Javanese Countryside." *Journal of Mennonite Studies* 35: 149–72.

Yoder, Lori. n.d. "Penny Power." Mennonite Central Committee, Akron, PA. http://pennypower.org/resources/pennysong/PennyPower_Yoder.pdf. Viewed April 2011.

Yoder, Richard A., Calvin W. Redekop, and Vernon E. Jantzi, eds. 2004. *Development to a Different Drummer: Anabaptist/Mennonite Experiences and Perspectives*. Intercourse, PA: Good Books.

Yoder, Shirlee Kohler. 1998. *Savoring the Times: Stories on MCC Indonesia's 50th Anniversary 1998*. Semarang, IDSA: Mennonite Central Committee Indonesia.

Yoder, Wanda L. 2010. *Together We Can ... Our Seven-Month Journey with the MCC Mobile Meat Canner, 2008-2009*. Morgantown, PA: Masthof Press.

Zerwas, Katherine R. 2010. "No Strict Scrutiny – The Court's Deferential Position on Material Support to Terrorism in *Holder v. Humanitarian Law Project*." *William Mitchell Law Review* 37, no. 5: article 28.

Zharkevich, Ina. 2010. "The Changing Face of the "War on Terror": New Developments in Counter-Terrorism Legislation and Its Impact on Civil Society." Oxford: INTRAC. https://www.intrac.org/wpcms/wp-content/uploads/2016/09/Briefing-Paper-26-The-changing-face-of-the-war-on-terror.pdf.

Zulkarnain, Iskandar. 2019. *Jejak Sang Duta: Biografi Pdt. Soehadiweko Djojodihardjo*. Semarang: C.V. Sarana Gracia.

Zwissler, Laurel. 2017. "Markets of the Heart: Weighing Economic and Ethical Values at Ten Thousand Villages." *Research in Economic Anthropology. Anthropological Considerations of Production, Exchange, Vending and Tourism* 37: 115–35.

Index